INTEGRATION AND SELF-HEALING

INTEGRATION AND SELF-HEALING

Affect — Trauma —Alexithymia

Henry Krystal, M.D.

With a contribution from

John H. Krystal, M.D.

Library of Congress Cataloging-in-Publication Data

Krystal, Henry, 1925—

   Integration and self-healing.

   Includes bibliographical references and index.
   1. Alexithymia. 2. Traumatic neuroses. 3. Emotions.
   I. Krystal, John H. (John Harrison) II. Title
   [DNLM: 1. Emotions. 2. Mental Disorders—etiology.
   3. Psychoanalytic Theory. WM 460 K94i]

RC540.K78   1987   150.19'5   87-1279

ISBN 0-88163-180-9

First paperback edition   1993

Printed in the United States of America
10 9 8 7 6 5 4 3 2 1

To my teacher, John M. Dorsey, M.D., gratefully.

If only we arrange our life according to that principle which counsels us that we must hold to the difficult, then that which now seems to us the most alien will become what we most trust and find most faithful.

—Rainer Maria Rilke, age 20

Contents

ACKNOWLEDGMENTS

In my attempts to understand and work with the challenges and mysteries of alexithymia, I have been most fortunate to have the help of many people. First of all, my Professor of Psychiatry, John M. Dorsey, who taught me many things that I tucked away for a long time deep in my mind. Two decades after my graduation, when confounded by my work, I went back to review his writings and was lucky to find an incredibly rich legacy—which contained many answers to my quest. I have a faithful helper and supporter in Carolyn R. Tourkow and other friends, who, like her, have encouraged me. Much of my work was gone over in study groups with my dear colleagues, Channing T. Lipson, T. A. Petty, Max Warren, and the late and sorely missed Herbert A. Raskin. Special appreciation goes to Myron S. Magen, D.O., Dean of the College of Osteopathic Medicine, Michigan State University, for his giving me the opportunity to do original work. I have had encouragement and support from Donald H. Williams, M.D., Professor and Chairman of the Department of Psychiatry at Michigan State University, and members of our faculty. Among my colleagues, I am most indebted to Sharon Wittenberg. I have received many helpful comments from William H. Rickles, John Mack, and Edward Khantzian. I found the work of Joseph M. Jones and June Hadley very exciting and inspiring and have admired and borrowed from them and the work of Joyce McDougall and Graeme Taylor. The patient care and indulgence of Dorothy Eckert, Ph.D., Ester Fiksman, and, most of all, Lucretia Shinozaki made this book possible. To them I will be forever grateful for their support and highly gifted and devoted hard work. I am forever in debt for the love given me by my special friends as a gift outright.

I gratefully acknowledge with thanks permission to reprint or extract from the following:

The genetic development of affect and affect regression. *The Annual of Psychoanalysis.* Copyright 1974 International Universities Press.

Affect tolerance. *The Annual of Psychoanalysis.* Copyright 1975 International Universities Press.

Self representation and the capacity for self-care. *The Annual of Psychoanalysis.* Copyright 1978 International Press.

Aspects of affect theory. *The Bulletin of the Menninger Clinic.* Copyright 1977 The Menninger Foundation.

Trauma and affect. *The Psychoanalytic Study of the Child.* Copyright 1978 Yale University Press.

The hedonic elements of affectivity. *The Annual of Psychoanalysis.* Copyright 1981 International Universities Press.

Integration and self-healing in posttraumatic states. *Journal of Geriatric Psychiatry.* Copyright 1981 International Universities Press.

Activating aspects of emotions. *Psychoanalysis and Contemporary Thought.* Copyright 1982 International Universities Press.

Alexithymia and the effectiveness of psychoanalytic treatment. *International Journal of Psychoanalytic Psychotherapy.* Copyright 1982 Jason Aronson.

Adolescence and the tendencies to develop substance dependence. *Psychoanalytic Inquiry.* Copyright 1982 The Analytic Press.

Trauma and the stimulus barrier. *Psychoanalytic Inquiry.* Copyright 1985 The Analytic Press.

Special thanks go to Ms. Cynthia Ozick and to Theron Raines, of Raines and Raines, literary representatives, for permission to use "The Shawl," a short story of penetrating brilliance.

Finally, I thank Mary C. Dorsey, representing the John M. Dorsey Estate, and the Center for Health Education of Wayne State University, publishers of the works of John Dorsey, for permission to quote from his works.

Preface

Alexithymia is the single most common cause of poor outcome or outright failure of psychoanalysis and psychoanalytic psychotherapy. The reason that this glaring problem has escaped recognition for so long is part of the mystique and paradox of emotions. Affects are familiar to everyone. They are part of our experiences, so ordinary and common that they are equated with being human. But affects also are, in their physiological form, the responsiveness we share with the entire animal kingdom. Yet their very universality and constant presence with us throughout life make them as unidentifiable as the prose in our speech.

Another example of the same phenomenon is that most doctors are accustomed to their patients' complaining of palpitations, shortness of breath, sore and stiff muscles, and other physical components of emotions. After the physical examination, the doctors frequently observe that the symptoms are due to anxiety, but even then the patients fail to recognize that they have been experiencing this feeling. The doctors accept this state of affairs as most natural and proceed to prescribe benzodiazepines (over 100 million prescriptions per year in this country alone) and never wonder why it is that the patients fail to recognize that emotion which is so conspicuous in their mien, posture, gesture, and words.

The first part of this book is devoted to those mysterious and much studied experiences: emotions. The second part of the book concerns psychic trauma. Certain aspects of these two subjects have to be established in order to give us a broad enough view to approach the third subject: alexithymia.

The exploration of emotions starts with chapter 1, in which we look at the clinical practicalities of dealing with emotions and their regression. Before I get into the clinical studies, however, I describe and define my use of terms pertaining to emotions. I use the terms *emotion* and *affect* as synonymous, and I reserve the word *feeling* for the subjective experience of an emotion one recognizes as part of one's own self. Among the affect components and aspects that I single out are the cognitive, hedonic, "expressive," and activating ones. I do not assume the cognitive aspect always to be present, but in clinical situations it is useful to look for the meaning implied in the affect as well as the "story behind it."

The second chapter is devoted to the exploration of the experience of "having" an emotion. How one interprets and reacts to having an affect becomes an important part of one's ability to bear it. Responsiveness to the experience of emotionality includes the customary ways of keeping the affects within a tolerable range. Consequently, the degree of affect tolerance will be seen to determine whether emotions can be kept within the range of intensity that permits obtaining the maximum information from them. Only such successful information processing permits one to consider the repertoire of possible responses to the situation at hand and to choose one on the basis of one's best judgment.

In reviewing the misconceptions about affect, I found that a major source of confusion is Freud's choice of anxiety as the model affect. In chapter 7, I propose, instead, love as the model affect and discuss the implications of this model, which includes the concept of emotions as one's self-contained signals. A major contribution of this volume is in the presentation of the genetic point of view of affects. It is certainly amazing that we psychoanalysts have traced the epigenesis of every element of the mind and personality but, until 1955, failed to apply the same kind of thinking to affects. Catching up on the processes and manifestations of the genetic development of affects takes up two chapters, one of them devoted to the exploration of the special maturational events of adolescence. The point is made that the affective developments of adolescence permit the consolidation of self-representations.

The second part of the book is devoted to the exploration of psychic trauma. In preparation for the study of our protection against traumatization, as well as the consequences of its occurring, psychic reality is researched in chapter 8. The assertion that psychic reality is the only knowable reality has wide-reaching consequences for the review of psychic operations, for example, repression. What is not consciously recognized as part of the self-representation is found to be functionally repressed, even if it retains the quality of consciousness. Other revisions are of the very definitions of the term trauma. It is necessary to distinguish infantile trauma from adult-type trauma in order to provide models corresponding to observations of the process of traumatization and, particularly, the aftereffects of trauma. These are issues dealt with in chapter 9, "Trauma and Affect."

In the two chapters that follow, we reexplore some aftereffects of traumatization and the observations on the healing process. The unconscious connections of some of the aftereffects of trauma, particularly disavowal of parts of one's own past, force a confrontation with the task of affective grieving necessary for integration. In chapter 11, to highlight their role in trauma prevention, these posttraumatic affects are reviewed in pursuit of the psychic operation involved in creating one's psychic reality. The same processes and defenses, including perception, cognition, fantasy, and affect signaling, are consequently reexamined for posttraumatic effects.

The idea of a passive stimulus barrier is replaced by the multitude of functions involved in information processing. In the posttraumatic modifications, these functions may be more defensively oriented but do not necessarily serve better in their multiple other applications. The dynamics of perception, memory, and recall are found to be intimate parts of one's personality. Since there is in the traumatic process a trancelike submission to inevitable danger, a blocking of affect, and constriction of cognition, such patterns may remain or recur in posttraumatic states.

This brings us to the third part of the book: alexithymia. Now all our previous topics fall together. Alexithymia may be a major posttraumatic sequel, and it represents an affect regression and/or arrest in the genetic development of affect. But in order to determine whether a patient may benefit from preparatory psychotherapy, we need to know whether we are dealing with a regression or an arrest. If alexithymia is accompanied by anhedonia, then this coincidence is a good indication of the traumatic origin of both. However, if we do not get clues, it is important to make a diagnostic determination early; trying analytic psychotherapy with such patients not only is futile, but may be dangerous. I enlisted the help of John Krystal, who reviews the available means of testing the presence, severity, and extent of alexithymic characteristics, and offers a new instrument of his own design.

Doing psychoanalytic psychotherapy with alexithymic patients inspires such humility in therapists that we are not apt to consider ourselves above accepting help from any quarter if it will enable us to work effectively with these patients. In psychoanalytic psychotherapy with alexithymic and anhedonic patients, one also finds various degrees of inhibition of self-regulatory, self-caring, and even self-preserving functions. These are highlighted in chapter 10.

To enable us to perceive the enormity and depth of these problems, I have to wander far afield looking for up-to-date conceptual tools with which to restudy these operations. The enormous explosion of knowledge about the physiology of hedonic regulation that disproves our previous assumptions requires that we psychoanalysts revise our theories and come up with a psychological explanation of the function of hedonic regulation of an individual in the light of the new knowledge. Further, with the enormous progress made in cognitive psychology and in the dynamics of perception and cognition, we have to revise our views to accommodate all these new discoveries. Similarly, since fascinating new knowledge is available about infantile psychological development and the role of attachment in psychological genesis, we have to update our views of early mother-child interactions.

Most of all, however, to approach alexithymia we have to learn how to recognize and deal with early memory traces and the early transferences. Since these early memories are affective only—devoid of any verbal, cognitive, or symbolic component—we must face the novel and exciting challenges they pose. To be able to work with alexithymic, psychosomatic, addictive, or posttraumatic patients, one has to deal with early maternal transferences. These transferences are *conflictual*. The conflicts are over the freedom and ability to exercise certain affective and vital functions. In several places in this book, we come upon evidence of a universal phenomenon: these functions are experienced as reserved for mother. Related are observations I find amazing: 1) that we usually fail to acknowledge that we are functioning in a condition exactly corresponding to an hysterical paralysis of our major vital and affective organs and 2) that commonly in "normal" individuals the self-representation contains major distortions so that important parts of oneself are attributed to the maternal object representation.

In chapter 10, dealing with patients who have severe inhibitions in exercising self-caring and self-soothing functions, I find that they experience any self-solacing to be absolutely forbidden for them. That privilege is reserved for the "divine" maternal transference objects. Violation of this taboo is, in their most profound belief, punishable by a fate worse than death—by eternal Hell. The psychotherapeutic exploration of these intrapsychic blocks is the major theme of Part III of this book, particularly of chapter 15. In a number of instances, in dealing with the inhibitions in regard to self-caring and self-soothing, I found myself using the expression that the patients experienced the idea of exercising their self-caring capacities to be a *Promethean* sin. I found that the inhibition of self-caring was the keystone of the entire structure of alexithymia. It occurred to me that the myth of Prometheus may in some way reflect this most basic of all human conflicts. Following up this hunch, I found that there is such a wealth of allusion in this story that I would like to offer it now in brief review as an introduction to the themes of humankind's struggle for its integrity.

The myth of Prometheus is related to various folk conceptions of the origin of mankind, the world, and the gods. It thus parallels the child's early conceptions of the parents, particularly in regard to their identity, their differences, and their relative power. Prometheus is a character parallel to the Archangel Michael. Some of their common attributes are that they are the creators of man, and they share the power of prophesy and announcing world-changing events. Prometheus stood in a special relationship to his mother, Earth. Hence he has an intimate relationship with cosmogony as well as the myths about the way the gods themselves came to their "final" position and form.

The idea that the male god was not the *creator* of the world was common to gnostic theology and to the stories about Prometheus and the Archangel

Michael. Both in the Aeschylus version and in the Pelasgian and Canaanitic creation myths, the son of the Earth acts on behalf of a female divinity to create man out of dust or mud.

In the biblical account of creation, there are discernible traces of the myth of Gilgamesh, who created man on orders of the Babylonian goddess Ururu. Babylonian history demonstrates the gradual removal of the power of the Mother-God and the shift to male domination of heaven and earth. There are interesting traces of this change even in the Bible, where in the account of creation the noun used for "Spirit of the Lord" which hovers over the earth is of the feminine gender. Eve, like Pandora, brings mischief on mankind, acting not naively but as the vulnerable dupe of a vengeful male God (Graves, 1959, pp. 3–5). The major parallel, however, is that the victorious male god (Zeus) decides to destroy the human race exactly as Jahwe does and by the same means: the flood. Zeus, not satisfied with the flood, decides to destroy mankind and to turn it back to dust. He is irritated that mankind has acquired too much power, and he is disturbed by the human's searching and questioning spirit. He plans to destroy mankind and perhaps later to create a new and better "race" more to his liking. When Prometheus saves mankind from the flood, Zeus curses mankind with a lowly fate devoid of the secret of fire. Prometheus not only brings fire to mankind, but on behalf of mother Earth he bestows parental blessings on man. In other words, he provides all the elements of civilization.

In Aechylus' version of the Promethean myth, the gift of fire was symbolic of man's acquiring the ability to take care of himself. Fire was "the teacher of each craft . . ." (p. 315). Prometheus was a seer—a Titan who, under the tutelage of his mother, Earth, represented the mother's love for the child. When chained to the rock, he reviewed what he had done for mankind and declared that his prime gift to the human race was: "I caused mortals to cease foreseeing doom." When asked how he did this amazing feat, he responded simply: "I placed in them blind hopes" (Aeschylus, p. 320). This is a profound insight into the indispensability of effective denial of our mortality and maintaining hope, for the maintenance of normal function, as we shall see in our work with trauma (chapter 9). It also conveys the *permission* for mankind to attend to its well-being by psychological means. In other words, Aeschylus's Prometheus *wanted* to communicate to mankind the permission for self-caring and solace. This issue is at the heart of this volume.

The blessings that Prometheus gave mankind and that illustrate this point are indeed many (if he says so himself):

. . . there were many troubles among men, how I found them witless and gave them the use of their wits and made them masters of their minds. . . . Men at first had eyes but saw no purpose; they had ears but did not hear. Like the shapes of dreams they dragged through their long lives and handled all things in bewilderment and confusion. They did not know of building houses with bricks to face the sun; they did not know how to work with wood. They lived like swarming ants in holes in the ground, in sunless caves of the earth. For them there was no secure token by which to tell winter nor the flowering of spring nor the summer with its crops: all their doings were indeed without intelligent calculation until I showed them the rising of the stars, and the settings, hard to observe. And further I discovered to them the numbering, preeminent among subtle devises, and the combining of letters as a means of remembering all things, and the Muses' mother, skilled in craft. It was I who first yoked beasts for them in the yokes and made of those beasts the slaves of trace chain and pack saddle that they might be man's substitutes in the hardest tasks; and I harnessed to the carriage, so that they loved the rein, horses, the crowning pride of the rich man's luxury. It was I and none other who discovered ships, and the sail-driven wagons that the sea buffets [p. 327–328].

But finally he comes to the key issue, what he himself considers his most glorious blessing, which has the most direct relation to our concerns:

Hear the rest, and you will marvel even more at the crafts and resources I contrived. Greatest was this: in former times if a man fell sick he had no defense against the sickness, neither healing food nor drink, nor unguent, but through the lack of drugs men wasted away, until I showed them the blending of mild simples wherewith they drive out all manner of diseases. It was I who arranged all kind of seercraft, and I first adjudged what things come verily from dreams, and to men I gave meaning to the ominous cries, hard to interpret [p. 328].

In the myth of Prometheus there is the dramatization of the mysterious conflict and doubt whether it is permissible for mankind to exercise all of its self-caring, self-regulatory powers. Aeschylus, speaking through his Titanic rebel, is trying to remove the already obvious inhibitions in self-caring, self-soothing, and self-solacing functions.

Prometheus, who at the behest of the feminine spirit of God, and his mother, Earth, created man out of dust, dramatizes the struggle over the most basic conflict of every human: whether it is all right to enjoy fully and consciously one's power for life and love; whether it is permissible to claim one's soul as one's own and carry out all one's life with conscious self-recognition. Against this right stands the dark power of the victorious tyrant, the male god Zeus. We have to assume that in this context Zeus represents the death forces contained in the newborn himself, which are deflected through projection by introducing "father." Arvanitakis (1985) has postulated that "father" was introduced, first as a joint creation in the potential space between mother and her infant. This triangulation, which protects against annihilation-disintegration fears, forms the basis of symbolic thought which will permit a transformation of archaic anxieties. It is argued that the foreclosure of this process to evolve adequately may eventuate in disturbances of symbolization and a predisposition to psychotic states [p. 438].

(Note the connection with the cognitive difficulties in alexithymia, chapters 9, 13 and 15).

The human newborn is confronted with death, from which he can be saved only by his mother's loving care. Mother, and all who act on her behalf, save the child from the forces of death within the child. We can see in the Prometheus myth the model of the work we need to do for those who, like Prometheus, have become chained to the rack of their aggression and suffer constant torture and cannot solace themselves.

The puzzle is how to bring the message of love to those who are afraid of it, who think of it as prohibited. This question inspired Shelley (1925), who responded with his lyrical drama "Prometheus Unbound," in which the Titan is liberated by Hercules after Demogorgon conquers Zeus and commits him to deepest Hades. Prometheus joyfully embraces his wife, Asia, and tells her that they will live the rest of their lives in love. He kisses mother Earth, and love infuses all.

Prometheus sends a Spirit to announce to the entire world that love is victorious. Later, a Spirit of Earth comes to the cave where Asia and Prometheus live and tells them that a transformation had come upon mankind. Anger, pride, insincerity, and all the other bad feelings are gone, thrones are empty, every man is his own king, free from guilt and pain. Love rules the world.

The many mysteries of the promethean transference start from the question of whether it is all right for mankind to exist and exercise all those talents which Aeschylus listed in his Prometheus portrait. The hidden question uncovered in this volume is whether one may exercise all the possible self-regulatory and self-caring functions.

In this book I speak of people who have particularly great difficulties in the basic spheres of affect and exercising their imagination. It is surprising to find that even though such intrapsychic blocks are of an infantile origin, they cannot be approached as we are accustomed to approach the later neurotic conflicts. There is a long way between Shelley's romantic solution of the liberating proclamation of love to all mankind and the practicalities of the therapeutic situation. Quite literally, this whole book is addressed to bridging that gap.

Henry Krystal, M.D.

INTEGRATION AND SELF-HEALING

Part One
Emotions

1
Clinical Aspects of Affect

In this chapter we consider the nature of affect development and affect regression and their implications for the theory of psychoanalytic therapy. By way of introduction, it may be valuable to explain the use of the terms for affects in this book now, although their utility and relative merit will be taken up at a later time.

I find it useful to think of emotions in terms of certain components. The *cognitive* element of affects is of clinical importance. It is useful for both patients and therapists to pay attention to the *meaning* of the affect, that is, the message contained in the affect experience itself as distinguished from the "story behind it." The meaning of an affect frequently needs identification for clinical purposes because it clarifies some aspects of the problem at hand that the patient may not have consciously registered. Thus, both anxiety and fear signal the perception of impending danger. Their meaning is, *Something bad is about to happen*. But the story behind them is different. Fear refers to the possibility of external, veridical danger, whereas anxiety refers to some danger deriving from within oneself. Exploring the latter gives only limited results because part of the story is not conscious, and experience shows that patients readily rationalize the fears in terms of global dangers. By way of illustration in depression, the "meaning" of the affect is that something bad has happened already and the fault or responsibility is attributed to oneself. Seligman has arrived at a similar definition of depression based on the attribution of the state of helplessness to oneself and an expectation of future helplessness as well (Miller and Seligman, 1982, p. 151).

"The story behind" the depression may contain a nucleus of a loss, but that is frequently buried by various self-blaming and complaining responses, beneath which may be the ambivalent relationship to the object. The unconscious aggression is one of the determinants of unfinished, unresolved mourning.

To illustrate again, in anger the idea of the affect is that something bad has happened, and responsibility is attributed to an external factor. This constellation accounts for the angry person's feeling justified and even righteous about the anger and therefore tending to promote it. The story behind the anger is that the perpetrator is experienced as bad, and the angry person feels entitled to hate and punish him/her.[1]

In Figure 1, I distinguish current sources of an affect from memories of the past. Approaching the "syntax" of emotions analytically is a major aspect of adaptive information processing. Knowing what measure of affect is derived from the current situation is helpful in moderating one's responses and choosing, on the basis of one's best judgment, the most appropriate response. Probably the key operation in affect handling is the ability to recognize instantly the extent to which the intensity of the affect experience is appropriate to the current event and when the associative linking of this event with a similar one or one involving similar "objects" from one's past has rendered it much greater than it needs to be. The accuracy of this evaluation, however, refers to the reaction to having the emotions; in other words, affect tolerance or affect handling. Affect tolerance, in turn, will determine the selection of the appropriate responses to the situation (the left column of Figure 1).

Note item No. 2 in the right-hand column, the "expressive" element of affects. This term refers to the physiological component of the affects, for the most part, an activation of the parts of the body innervated by the autonomic nervous system. The term "expressive" is retained here in preparation for a later discussion on the psychoanalytic conceptions of the expressive function of affect.

The hedonic (3) element of affects refers to their being endowed with a quality of pleasure, or suffering, which lends them the motivating role. Along with that, the hedonic element of affects supplies an important coloring or blending of the affect experience. For instance, anxiety attended by a pleasurable, hopeful expectation of winning at the races is experienced differently from anxiety in posttraumatic states, in which the profound pessimism and expectation of the return of the trauma rules out a pleasurable or "racy" experience. Thus, the blending of affects (discussed in chapter 6) contributes to the meaning and the message of the affect, as well as to the state of psychic reality that will be established. These three components of affect—the cognitive, physiological, and hedonic—represent the totality of the informational or signal contents of an affect. But only if these three components of affect occur simultaneously, free of blocks that cause isolation or dissociation (or other "defenses" against affects)—and only if one is capable of adequate "reflective self-awareness" (Rapaport, 1951b; Schafer,

---

1. By naming the cognitive component at this point, I do not imply that *every* affect must have a cognitive element. These classical conceptions of Freud have been discussed in detail by Jones (1981). I do agree with Jones that affects may represent a nonsymbolic information processing system and that some affective memories are devoid of verbal, symbolic, or cognitive elements.

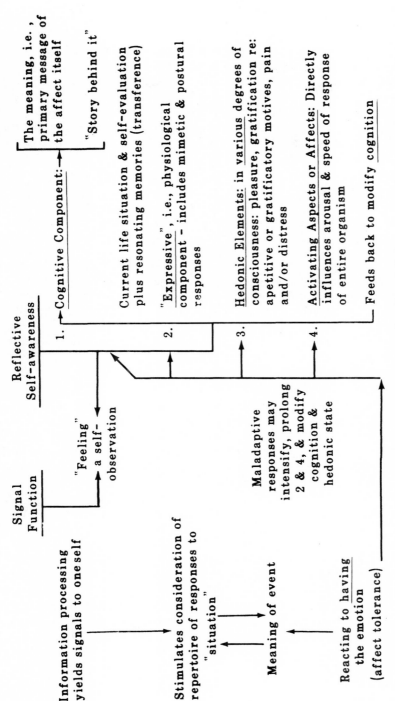

FIG. 1. Information processing view of affects

1968a) or has the capacity for sensitive self-observation—can one make the observation that one is experiencing a "feeling." In my thirty years as a teacher of physicians, I found through direct inquiry that fewer than half the ordinary run of patients in a doctor's office are able to engage in the process of self-observation. Being able to determine and consciously recognize that one is experiencing a feeling makes it more likely that one will be able to utilize the emotion as a signal. It is sometimes an early, but key, psychotherapeutic challenge for patients to discover that they are the persons who are having feelings rather than that these scary and powerful bodily reactions have taken them over.

In addition to these three components, which are purely signal and autonomic information, there is a fourth aspect to emotions that goes beyond mere signaling. This is the activating aspect of emotion. In essence, affects influence the state of arousal and most bodily functions—such familiar phenomena as "psychomotor retardation." This aspect of affect is, in fact, the heart of psychobiology. That is, when the activating aspect of affect is fully acknowledged, the essential unity of the individual becomes clear.

Figure 1 notes that the state of activation influences—"feeds back"—and modifies the cognitive style, which, in turn, influences the nature of the evaluation of the perception or impulse, which, in its turn, modifies the affective state. But the activating aspect of emotions represents the rate at which the entire organism functions. Thus, the effect of emotions goes beyond the autonomic system activation (see Figure 1, No. 3) to the whole psychobiological activity of an individual. Another feedback loop was mentioned earlier, that affect tolerance represents a store of memory and response patterns to *having* an emotion. This subject is so crucial to my conception of the clinical problems of dealing with affective disturbances that chapter 2 is devoted to it. At this point, the comment pertains to the diagram in that the left side—that affect tolerance, or the reaction to the affect—may influence and thus modify the right side. For instance, when people become involved in certain vicious circles of maladaptive responses to *having* the affect, their attention is taken up with the affect instead of with the message that the affect communicated originally. If that problem can be avoided and one has been able to get the information from the affect, then one may consider the repertoire of *responses* to the stimulus, situation, or whatever mental element is at hand, and select a response.

This scheme is designed to facilitate the observation of the function of affects as signals and the related factors that may interfere with that function. It represents the hypothetical state in the adult who has adult-type affects that are best suited for signal functions. Such affects are minimal in the intensity of "expressive" components and modulated according to the intensity of the experience. For the most part they are cognitive. That is, they are idealike and work well in dealing with oneself and the world.

But, beginning with my paper in 1962, I realized that this was not always the case, that there was a great deal of variation in the way people experienced their emotions. Once the genetic point of view of affects dawned on me, I became aware of a variety of clinical problems related to the variation in affect *form*.

In this chapter, I review the kind of clinical problems that can be understood as manifestations of a regression in the affect form. All we need to assume is that such regression is possible. In considering affects, we find that there is a special communication on a nonverbal plane, which is, of course, the primary mode of communication between mother and infant. As a result of this universal experience, we clinicians, and other people as well, tend to assume that our perception of other peoples' feelings are correct and that, given a situation we "know," we can imagine what another person's affective reactions are. Such assumptions have enough validity to make them an important part of human interactions, and they are an essential aspect of empathy.

Our ability to perceive and imagine the nature of another person's affective experience, however, is subject to significant errors and distortions. We expect the affects of another person to be like our own, and, in adults, we expect them to be mature affect reactions. To the extent, however, that affect regression is a reality, such an assumption is not warranted. As clinicians, we have learned that patients' reflective awareness of their affects is unreliable. We have become accustomed to look for the physiological aspects of affects, such as moist palms, dry mouth, rapid pulse or respiration, even in patients who profess to be "fine." But even if we do observe such physiological signs, we tend to attribute to them the mature type of affects, for example, anxiety, when they may represent one of its regressed forms. The possibility presents itself that the reason for our *failure to recognize affect regression lies in our repression of the memories of our own infantile affects.* This amnesia is evident in our failure to recognize pain as an affect component or its equivalent.

It is important, therefore, to study affect regression and our recognition of it. It is not unusual to find that some types of psychiatric emergencies (including those occurring in psychoanalytic practice) consist of "affect storms," affect experiences that envelop the patient in a panic with the dread that the affect is about to overwhelm and destroy him. Even in the absence of such overwhelmingly threatening situations, many patients present themselves to the physician because they "cannot stand" some feelings, such as depression or anxiety. Doctors are inclined to respond by agreeing that the patient had "too much feeling" and by trying to diminish that unbearable "excess of affects" by drugs, psychotherapy, or a variety of other techniques.

For the most part, psychoneurotic patients are able to verbalize the nature of their affects and to discover with a reasonable effort the nature of the fantasies behind them. However, as analyses have become more prolonged and the explorations have extended to preoedipal phases of development and at times even preverbal ones, we find that even in "healthy-neurotic" patients there may be (or perhaps there inevitably exists) a core of disturbing affects that cannot be verbalized. The following vignettes from two psychoanalytic patients' work illustrate this point:

Case Illustration

Mrs. A., who could be diagnosed basically as having an hysterical character problem, was especially verbal and had excellent ability for reflective self-awareness and description of her moods and feelings. During the second year of analysis, her husband went away for two weeks, leaving her and her family at home.

Though she was able to verbalize her resentment of her husband's absence, a depressive quality to her function, of which she was not even aware, became apparent. It manifested itself in her reaction to both her art work and her children, whom she started treating as worthless objects (albeit the children only to a very slight extent). When this reaction was brought to her attention, she was able to observe that she felt somewhat "bad," but she was not able to verbalize the nature of her feelings. We were able to utilize clues from her dreams, metaphors, and fantasies in such a way that the analyst had to supply the *words* to the patient, which she then could recognize as descriptive of a *component* of her feelings. These feelings represented a mixture of self-condemnation and hopelessness in which she experienced the husband's absence as a repetition of a rejection and abandonment that she had felt in her childhood. She reacted, as she had then, by assuming the blame, feeling that she must have been bad to deserve it and experiencing herself as thoroughly bad inside.

Her vagina was portrayed as a "rotten hole," her mouth was "dangerous and repulsive"; she used her smoking to illustrate cannibalistic and self-destructive impulses. Also involved in the unverbalized feeling were others that became apparent in somatic symptoms, such as tenseness, "jumpiness," lack of appetite, insomnia, and physical pain. We did in fact wonder for a while if she had the "flu." I concluded that the "common cold" is sometimes a period when just such primitive and preverbal affects are experienced in an especially strong way, as was the case on this day during the husband's absence.

In the presence of such a regression, when memories present themselves in a nonverbal affect-only manner, we have to do a different kind of reconstruction than we are accustomed to doing with regard to the word-traces of the memories derived from a later period. In dealing with memories derived from the period preceding the acquisition of language, we must reconstruct the nature of the affective experience and affective memory and some clues to the nature of the subjective experience. We certainly cannot reconstruct the "traumatic situation" as opposed to the psychic reality of the child. Since the acquisition of language and symbols is a gradual one, subject to lapses and distortion, many infantile memories have to be viewed as nonsymbolic, nonverbalizable affect memories.

Mr. B. had been in analysis for three and a half years, mainly for characterological problems that were, for the most part, phallic-aggressive with some narcissistic aspects and some greed involving a combination of phallic and oral problems. He had been up to then quite capable of verbalizing his affects. When he started treatment, he had asthma, though not as severely as he had had during childhood and adolescence. It disappeared completely after a fairly short time in analysis without our having discovered its affective and cognitive contents.

Occasionally, under circumstances in which one would have expected certain affects to develop, such as anxiety or sadness, he would instead develop stuffiness of the nose and "scratching" in the throat. At times he had a "sighing respiration," which he mistook for a while for asthma.

On this occasion he came to his analytic appointment sneezing, with sighing respiration, and complaining of a subjective feeling of air hunger. He had awakened in this state after the following dream: He was moving to an apartment that was like the apartment to which his parents had moved when he was about 26 months old. It was located above a store. He was furnishing the flat with cheap furniture and very cheap dishes. The patient's associations were mainly to events that had taken place about the time he was two years old, when his parents *suddenly* moved out of his grandparents' home and into an apartment. He pictured the apartment as empty and *dark*. He thought it was possible that there was hardly any furniture. He then recalled (for the first time) that soon after he had moved to this apartment, his younger sibling was born, and he elaborated how he felt "displaced." Three recollections ensued: (a) that he had cried for long hours and pleaded with his parents to let him come back to their bedroom, since he feared the "empty room"; (b) that he developed asthma *at that time;* (c) that he had probably had eczema previously, but at this time it "got so bad that sometimes they had to *tie down [his] hands,* so [he] would stop scratching."

The work with the other parts of the dream brought up associations to things he was acting out in his life, but to which no previous associations were available, relating to disappointment with his mother and shift of affection to his younger sibling, whom in fantasy he babied or wished he had been himself. Other parts of the dream shifted to references to his "discovery" of phallic competitiveness. This trend of thought also involved his "victory" over his father and aggressive strivings in respect to the analyst.

However, while his aggressive strivings had been well verbalized since his childhood, the affects related to his feeling of abandonment, worthlessness, despair, envy, and hopelessness had not been subject to verbalization, but were instead expressed in psychosomatic symptoms and "covered over" by his phallic-aggressive gratifications. Only with the help of a dream producing somatic responses were we able to verbalize these affects and to find some cognitive aspects in them.

Whereas in these two cases, affect regression as manifest by inability to verbalize the affects was limited in scope, in some patients this reaction is very widespread.

The psychosomatic diseases are definable by their being chronic overactivities of an affect-related function and by the absence of verbalization or conscious awareness of the affect. In the following case, the inability to verbalize and tolerate affects was so widespread that it involved virtually every affect:

Dr. C., an alcoholic for a number of years, was now a member of AA and had found that AA "didn't work as far as drugs were concerned." He started supportive psychotherapy, and later the frequency and intensity of the treatment could be increased. He described his many rituals, which took two hours each morning. By the time he woke up, his coffee would be ready. He would drink several cups of coffee while reading the morning paper. He realized that he felt "different" after the first cup and the first page of the paper: he was able to move and even read faster.

At first he felt "very slow" and very tired, "like [he] could not move." He was not aware of mood changes. I often asked him whether he felt depressed, but he always denied it, though he was aware (especially on his vacation) that he did not enjoy anything.

On this occasion, following our previous and preparatory phase of his treatment, he said about the way he felt in the morning, "You can almost say I feel depressed." He then talked about his brother, who was "very slow" and whom he described as an alcoholic and "hypothyroid," though he questioned how his brother could be hypothyroid and still do hard labor. He said that he could imagine how his brother felt, but could not quite put it into words.

This patient also had a great tendency to worry. He worried about everything that was "coming up," any chore or task that was in the future. If he had an evening appointment with me, he "worried" all day about it. He was, however, unable to explain what the worry was; it consisted of a feeling of displeasure or discomfort, vague tension, and it was devoid of cognitive content.

He had changed his job because of his "hands shaking," and at certain times he developed hypoglycemia, which he learned to manage but never recognized as a feeling. His uneasiness could be relieved by alcohol, drugs, and, sometimes, food.

He had limited his work to avoid both the pressures on himself and the physical symptoms, which he did not recognize as affects. In the process, he became victim to a further lowering of his self-respect and a worsening of his problem of boredom.

He could not verbalize these reactions and, even when I did so for him, he could only say that what I said sounded "possible" and "interesting." At times he was aware that his pulse was rapid; especially when trying to fall asleep he would be aware of the tenseness in his muscles and what he called, "a certain feeling like anxiety."

At the same time, his inability to enjoy anything made him unhappy, or, rather, he was "not ever happy." At home he was experiencing "badgering and bullying" by his wife but never felt angry—mostly he "ignored her." He was aware of a subpain discomfort "all over" his body.

One of the things that became apparent was that he had a general fear of affects and that the fear of affects seemed to suggest an equating of affects with trauma. Most of his actions, including the use of medications, were intended to minimize the physiological components of emotion. One of the coincidental findings was a general anhedonia, and his inability to enjoy life often made him act and talk as if he were depressed, though he himself denied being aware of such feelings.

In these cases there is simultaneous deverbalization and resomatization of affect. In fact, I have not been able to find an example of impairment of affect verbalization unaccompanied by some evidence of resomatization of affect. The commonest type of affect regression is the persistence of the somatic (expressive) aspects without verbalization or realization of their precise nature. Verbalization and desomatization may represent two aspects of the same genetic process. In his classical paper on the metapsychology of anxiety, Schur (1955) noted that a patient with dermatosis would ". . . rarely itch during sessions. The explanation seems to be that verbalization is, in the scale of ego responses, counteracting ego regression" (p. 160).

Theoretically, even if affects are neither verbalized nor expressed in their psychosomatic components, we might still become aware of their existence when they are acted out, as by a criminal out of a sense of guilt. While it is undoubtedly true that many people live out their affects in this fashion, there are telltale signs of the underlying problem. For instance, in the case of a woman whose obesity was a depressive substitute, her description of herself and the badness and repulsiveness of her eating habits revealed depressive self-depreciation.

For reasons that will be discussed later, I feel it advantageous to separate *ego* regression in regard to the handling of affects from the regression in the nature of the affects themselves. The distinction, however, is for convenience only, to separate certain types of functions for the purpose of emphasis and clinical utility. Schur (1955) has, in fact, from the beginning differentiated these two aspects of affect expression, and in speaking about patients with dermatoses he referred to the affect regression as "physiological regression."

Broadening this formulation, and using traditional terms, we recognize that affect resomatization involves primary-process cognition, and primitive pregential drives and partial drives, and that the "regressive evaluation" of affects is involved in the ego's reactions not only to anxiety, but to all affects.[2]

Certain inherited factors probably play a role in the course of verbalization and desomatization of affect. Affect expression and symbol and word utilization are, after all, related to maturational patterns and depend on the development of anatomical, physiological, intellectual, and emotional factors. There are variations in the somatic, as well as in the ego apparatus pertaining to affect experience.

AFFECT DEVELOPMENT VS. DEFENSES AGAINST AFFECTS

In early psychoanalytic writings, defenses against affects were not separated from affect development (Freud, 1900). Fenichel (1941) talked of a single process of "affect taming," and Rapaport (1953) generalized about the "alterations in discharge threshold." Rapaport, however, differentiated the "affect alterations" from "affect changes as a result of defensive counter-cathecting" (p. 195). The former represented "more complex and subtle affect discharge-channels . . . created with general maturation, ascending hierarchy, and psychic structure formation," whereas the latter are clearly identified with ego defenses. Glover (1935) described how obsessional systems are used to change affect from "attacks" to a controlled discharge. He pointed out that complicated rituals "provide an ever more complicated meshwork of conceptual systems through which affect may pass in a finely divided state" (p. 274).

Fenichel (1941) was also aware of defenses against affects. In fact, he pointed out that "the conception of 'defense' was originally introduced by Freud as 'defense against affects.' " Fenichel stressed that it is not easy to differentiate defenses against affects from defenses against painful perceptions or "attitudes directed towards without and within" (p. 217).

He also discussed the importance of *delay* in affect experience and pointed out that such delay may permit the displacement, or an alteration, of the

---

2. This point was also made by Schafer (1964).

"expression." He weighted the defenses against affect that are intimately linked with object relations, such as "projection" of affects. Some people experience their emotions as if they were occurring in their objects, or as occurring in them but "caused" and controlled by their objects.

When we talk about defenses against affects, we usually mean those which result in a *lasting interference with affectivity.* The most common of these are various types of isolation. Engel (1963) has listed the following vicissitudes of affects: 1) ideational contents may be stripped; 2) the drive component may be kept from consciousness; 3) the signal component may be silent or conscious, intensely felt, or felt and denied; 4) the "object" may be disguised, displaced, omitted, or replaced by the self; 5) only defensive response to the affect may become conscious; and 6) there may be awareness of physiological changes only, and only part of the psychological responses may be developed (affect components).

Related to defenses against affects are certain uses of affects. Fenichel (1941) talked about "synthetic employment of affects," when affects are used for "sexual defense," or for secondary gain, such as "a pride in one's affectivity." He also referred to "histrionics" as a "reaction formation to the intense unconscious feelings" (p. 226). Seton (1965), however, found that a wide range of defenses against affects may result in histrionics. An important motivation in one of his patients was to have histrionic affect outbursts in order to "indicate to himself some control of his emotions"; at other times, the "histrionic" affects were brought on to avoid a "feeling of deadness or paralysis." I assume that this deadness or paralysis was already a late outcome of antiaffective blocking.

Siegman (1954) made similar observations about the defensive nature of histrionic affects. Both Siegman and Seton have emphasized the use of such affect in controlling other people. I am inclined to put it a little differently, as I will discuss in greater detail later. When one's affect expressions prove to be very effective in controlling the primary love-objects, the motivation to "tame them" is overruled by the advantages of maintaining them in as "explosive" form as possible. This vested interest interferes with their normal maturation.

Case Illustration

Mr. D., a patient with a history of drug dependence, related that he woke up in the middle of the night after a dream he could not recall and could not go back to sleep because of some feeling that kept him awake. Despite encouragement, he could not identify the feeling or put it into words. He ventured that perhaps some anxiety and anger, as well as depression, might be involved. He did recall the dream, however, and in analyzing the dream, the following themes were identified:
    (1) rivalry with his boss and ambition to defeat him;

(2) resentment of his boss for keeping him in an inferior position, and plans to leave;

(3) the expectation that the boss would take his leaving as an attack against himself and become enraged and violent;

(4) the patient's plan to see a lawyer to prepare a counterattack;

(5) his feeling hopeless (and "sort of depressed") because he had been through these plans and ideas many times and had never been able to do something about it;

(6) a fantasy request that the analyst should intervene in his behalf; this could help to resolve the "trap." This wish led to an association to a fragment of a film being made about which he had read the previous night. The film was based on the work of Sechehaye and the book *Autobiography of a Schizophrenic Girl*. What impressed him was the description of a scene in which the analyst gave the girl a bath. He felt that he needed this; if I took care of him in a physical way as if he were a baby, and he could have *normal feelings,* he would not be afraid of his anger and would not feel hopeless;

(7) angry reproaches that I did not act or give him active help, guidance, and encouragement as his "first analyst had," and that like the first analyst I would fail to do the "great and overwhelming job" he required, and he would continue to feel damaged and worthless.

In the process of his associations, he was able to recognize that, contained in what had started as a typically vague "bad feeling," which kept him from going back to sleep (and which he would usually block by drinking at night), were ideas and fantasies that might well have provoked intense feelings of anger, anxiety, and depression and yearnings for love and help. While he did experience a variety of somatic reactions, which kept him awake, he lacked the conscious experience of the various affects. The feelings he experienced were vague and hitherto seldom associated to their cognitive contents.

On this occasion, the cognitive aspects were attained only as associations to the dream (which represented, though unsuccessfully, an attempt to ward off the affects by a fantasy solution). It was only in trying to understand how the dream was involved in averting affect development that some affects were identified and their cognitive and somatic aspects brought together, for example, his waking up with palpitations, sweating, and with much muscular tension, corresponding to anxiety. Simultaneously, however, other affects were present in their regressed form, undifferentiated, resomatized, poorly verbalized, and not identified by the patient as specific feelings with particular meanings.

Mr. D. manifests the two pathognomonic signs of affect regression. First, his affects are expressed in a somatic way, with very limited verbalization; the cognitive aspects of the dream are recovered only from clues in the dream. Second, the affects are dedifferentiated, vague, "incomplete"; their nature is blurred, which characteristically distinguishes them from "mixed" affects, as in ambivalence.

In the following case, we can observe that when feelings present themselves in the regressed form, the patient tends to fear them and attempts to block them by the use of drugs. The tendency to drug addiction is bolstered in this case by the need to ward off feelings of passivity and helplessness by becoming a "work-addict." Secondarily, the patient's physical tiredness, being undistinguishable from the subjective perception of his affects, contributed to the pressures toward dependence.

Dr. E. was a drug-dependent physician whose difficulties in handling his affects were described in an earlier publication (Krystal and Raskin, 1970, pp. 35, 36, 92). On this occasion he related that on his "extra" job, which represented six hours of hard work after his regular office hours, he noticed that as the time wore on, he had a number of "spells" of heart pounding, sweating, and hand tremor. After leaving this "extra" work, he returned to his office, where he immediately, and before seeing his wife, who was coming to see him, drank a cup of vodka from a bottle that he always kept secreted in his desk.

I asked him what he wanted the vodka to do for him. His first thought was that he wanted to be sure he was in control of himself; otherwise his wife might attack his masculinity—attack him angrily. He also took alcohol frequently before seeing patients, to "fortify" himself. At the same time, he also had fears that if his wife or patients detected alcohol on his breath, or noticed an impairment in his functioning resulting from drinking, they would "doubt (him) and desert (him)." I questioned the source of his fears, since he had never had any difficulties with patients, even during a period of severe drug abuse in the past.

Through the associations of the hour we found evidence of feelings of shame about dependency yearnings and helplessness. He visualized himself revealing his weakness and passivity as he "stood there" sweating and shaking. Besides feelings of anxiety and shame, he also experienced resentment for "having to work on such a beautiful day."

I pointed out to my patient that although some of his feelings were clear and verbalized, others were mixed and blended indistinguishably with tiredness, and that, at the time he took the alcohol, the feelings were experienced by him at the somatic level and unverbalized. To the extent that his tiredness and anxiety made him experience passive yearnings, he was reacting to them with shame and the expectation of disappointment and attack by the woman. Taking the drug (alcohol) gratified the passive yearnings and anesthetized the tiredness and anxiety but started the vicious cycle of his guilt and expectation of punishment. In the past, this kind of affective experience set up a vicious cycle, which resulted in his having to take a drink of vodka more and more often (and at one time an injection of a drug) until he was doing it before seeing every patient.

At this point, the patient recalled that on Father's Day he had received a telephone call from his daughter. During the telephone conversation he suddenly became tearful and started sobbing and had trouble "getting out words." He was ashamed that his son and a friend had observed his uncontrollable emotional outburst. He was surprised that they "thought it was great." He expected to be ridiculed. In recalling this episode, he reexperienced the emotional response he had had to the telephone conversation and realized that what he had cried about was directly related to his fear that he would end up as "rejected, unloved, and helpless." He was then able to deal with some of the feelings which had been involved in the episode, bringing together their cognitive and expressive aspects.

Again, the patient's work demonstrates how affect separation, verbalization, and desomatization make possible the experiencing of feelings in tolerable intensities and are used to provide insight into his own yearnings and relation to his love-object representations.

Experiencing emotions as if they were provided by the object and were to be discharged externally is a defense (often effective in helping to tolerate affects) that combines elements of repression and projection. It has been referred to as *"externalization"* (Fenichel, 1941; Schafer, 1972). It permits one to experience some emotions by claiming ownership (self-sameness) of them. Schafer (1964) has made the point that even such personal feelings as

self-loathing or pride are experienced as *emanating from* internalized objects; . . . other affects, such as the apprehensiveness associated with suspiciousness, are *directed at* the internalized objects; and some, such as remorse concerning seductiveness, spitefulness, or withdrawal, are *reactions to* impulses ascribed to the self and directed toward, against, or away from these objects [p. 283].

Although defenses against owning up to the nature of one's affects are necessary to regulate the intensity of experiences, they do become significant resistances in analysis.

Dr. E. was, as noted earlier, a physician with a problem of drug dependence. In the course of his treatment (at first psychotherapy and later analysis), we discovered that he had a general dread of all affects, including anxiety, aggression, and sexual excitement. He related in this particular hour that his admitting privileges in his hospital had been withdrawn because he was (as usual) very far behind in finishing hospital charts. He resented the hospital librarian's nagging him about the charts, but he had set the situation up so that she and he were placed in that position, as he had done frequently with a number of aggressive women. This observation led me to bring to his attention that, in fact, a similar problem existed in his marriage, in which he *had the need* to have his wife attack him regularly and in this way *justify* his own rage. In fact, he had known about her aggressive rages long before he married her. The sadomasochistic pattern of his marriage served (among other things) to prevent his recognizing and owning up to the rage he experienced, a rage that (as can be surmised) was derived to a major extent from maternal transferences.

Of course, such an observation is only the first step toward the patient's discovery of "the story behind the affect," which, besides its meaning, represents affect verbalization. Levin (1964) has described the process of mastering fear in analysis as verbalization of fantasies and conflicts that are part of a chain of mental events.

Novey (1961) has made three points of practical therapeutic value: (1) that affects cannot be handled as separate from ideation; (2) that affects and related cognitive aspects become part of object (and self) representations; (3) that in working with such object representations in analysis (in the transfer-ence), both verbalization of those affects and re-experiencing of them are necessary. The internal representations of objects are affective-ideational dynamic parts of the personality, which exist in both the conscious and the unconscious sphere. Viewing them as primarily affective states takes nothing away from the ideational verbal view of them but identifies the latter as being primarily a descriptive and potentially therapeutic communicative device. Verbalization is necessarily used, but the goal is not only to elicit a conceptual view but to reaching some accord with the patient and to modifying his affectional state through classification of and separation from the fixation to his archaic object-representations. Similar points have been made by Deutsch (1959) and by Murphy (1958).

The fifty-year delay in discovery of regression in affects in comparison to fantasies was matched by our failure to notice the epigenetic history of affect development. Our gigantic blindspot blocks out the infant's only means of signaling.

As the mother establishes herself as an indispensable object for the infant, influencing her assumes paramount importance. At first, the child's affective responses (affect precursors) are the only mode of communication. Thus develops the important role of affects as *signals for another person*. At first, these affect signals from the infant to the mother are artless and simply reflect the baby's state. The toddler, however, learns to use his emotions purpose-fully as signals for her, and in time he uses them to control her. Each step in the development of affects may become a point of fixation and may deter-mine the nature of later affect problems. Fixation in the very first type of affect reactions (the infant's pattern) produces violent physical affect "attacks." Patients (like Dr. E.) may be driven to blocking their emotions altogether, as in drug dependence.

On the other hand, fixation on the use of affect for communication to others causes people to have an unconsciously vested interest in continuing massive somatic reactions with affects to the point that they regularly become frightened of their own affects and become unable to utilize them as signals (to themselves). I have already alluded to studies of histrionic characters. The following case illustrates a more severe, but related problem.

Mrs. G. has several times been admitted to a psychiatric hospital, where she was diagnosed as having various types of schizophrenia (according to the taste of the particular resident). The staff psychiatrist referring the case to me stressed that there was about this woman something remarkable that he had never seen before. She would "decompensate in a flash," as he put it. What really happened was that in situations that provoked her anger, she would become enraged and terrified that her anger would cause her to destroy herself. In the course of developing other feelings as well, such as anxiety, she would similarly build up her physiological responses to the affect to such a point that the very anxiety would terrify her.

As analysis progressed, it became apparent that throughout her childhood and late adolescence, the patient had communicated with her mother through the so-called expressive aspects of her affects. She experienced her mother as omnipotent and controllable by her emotional distress, and the mother promoted that image. Even when the patient was an adolescent and became, for instance, anxious about dates, the mother would move in, take over, and assure the patient that she would be the most beautiful girl, that the boys would be "crazy about her," and that she would be worshipped by them. The mother, who set herself up as an ideal of beauty, goodness, and competence, had, however, been unable to achieve a successful adjustment in her marriage, in which there were increasing (but ineffective) outbursts of rage, which eventually caused her to destroy herself. While, on one hand, the patient had an unconscious fixation on continuing her somatic affect reactions as a means of controlling the omnipotent parental object, she had, on the other hand, a great fear of affects, especially aggression, lest they overwhelm and destroy her. Her fixation on a helpless infantile mode of experience represented a magical denial of the death of her mother and a means "of keeping her alive." Only after she accomplished a great deal of mourning for her mother could she start to experience her affects as signals to herself, to be attended to by herself.

With this development, the gradual verbalization and desomatization could progress.

This case illustrates the key relation of adolescent developments to the maturation of the affects, which will be discussed later in greater detail. For now let us consider the nature of affects as signals.

SIGNAL AFFECTS

Eissler (1953) has described a patient whose "emotions did not lend themselves at all to the purpose of signals. Whenever she was afraid of a situation, she had to cope with terror. . . . Likewise, she never considered the possibility of moderate emotion occurring in others" (p. 203). This type of difficulty is common, although usually to a lesser degree than in Eissler's patient, and it occurs in people with all types of nosological problems. The patient in the following case illustration at first appeared to present "the other side of the coin"; she was a very rigid, compulsive patient, whose major problem lay in her inability to "let go."

Mrs. H. had previously presented herself for treatment to two other therapists and finally came to me because of overwhelming panic states. We discovered that these were virtually always triggered by her anger, which quickly turned into a rage against her husband or daughter. She would then become very angry with herself for having such feelings and had intense guilt about the feelings. She also had a magical belief in the power of her wishes and feared that her destructive wishes would come true. The more upset she became, the more repressed her self-representation, so that she experienced herself as a helpless victim of her cruel and rejecting husband, with a reintensification of her rage against him. As a result, her affects developed into a vicious circle of spiraling intensity.

The historical basis of this reaction pattern was finally traced to events of her early childhood, when she and her mother were evacuated from London during the blitz and the patient experienced herself as abandoned by her mother and faced nearly overwhelming affects. Thus, aside from the resultant fantasies, she developed a dread of affects, including fear of sexual excitement. She endeavored to live a controlled, emotionless life. But, if she became aware of a feeling, especially anger, she became frightened, and the very development of anxiety meant to her that she was having an "attack" of emotion. Typically, such affect storms become mostly somatic (with minimal ideational representation) and increasingly mixed (or undifferentiated) in terms of the affects involved.

The occurrence of trauma in childhood, particularly of the form that can be presumed to have taken place in Mrs. H.'s case, is especially damaging to the process of affect development, as will be discussed later. We are particularly concerned with affects reaching a form that makes them suitable for use as subliminal signals to oneself. Eissler (1966) similarly assumed that a "sub-liminal anxiety signal is given that automatically induces the activation of mechanisms or actions which serve the purpose of avoiding dangers or of neutralizing their consequences" (p. 21). Whereas signal anxiety has a special place in warding off trauma, all affects function as signals (Fenichel, 1941; Eissler, 1955; Schur, 1969; Krystal and Raskin, 1970). In harmony with the principle of multiple function, it may be said with Schur (Panel, 1968) that the signal function of affects works in a way analogous to "a thought process, in that it can also remain unconscious." In chapter 11 of this volume, I elaborate why the predominant uses of affect are best described as subliminal and automatic.

2
Affect Tolerance

Despite certain theoretical objections related to the artificiality of reification of affects, it is clinically useful to consider the patient's ability to tolerate affects of adequate intensity in an undissociated form. Zetzel's classical papers have established the need to tolerate anxiety (1949) and depression (1965a) for emotional growth. Speaking about envy, Joffe (1969) made the point that "affect tolerance varies considerably from person to person and this variability may have several different causes . . ." (p. 543).

Affect tolerance involves a variety of resources and actions that make possible the conscious experience of emotions. The capacity to handle emotions involves the nature of the self-representation and the way feelings are interpreted. If we take variations in the intensity of emotions for granted and limit our discussion to one's resources in "having" feelings comfortably, there are still great differences among people. It is a matter of clinical commonplace that the patients who present with the request to be free of certain feelings, e.g., depression, in fact need to have the depression. They come to us at the end of a vicious circle of maladaptive handling of their emotion by becoming angry with themselves, or frightened, or desperate about *having* the depression, thus perpetuating it.

By contrast, people who can comfortably experience a feeling generally feel secure that their state is justified by their life experience; that it makes sense; and that, having accomplished its purpose or run its course, it will stop. People who recognize the source and meaning of their intense affects, for example the reaction following a near accident or in bereavement, are much less likely to engage in maladaptive pattern, and the emotion runs its natural, short-lived course. While the difficulty occurs more frequently with painful feelings, some people develop a fear of all emotions, even of being in love or becoming sexually excited. The resources for handling one's affects include diverse object investments and the full use of self-regulatory functions. One of the things that makes possible tolerance of painful affects is the ability to modify them periodically for some short period of gratification or respite.

Just as the evolution of the affects themselves depends heavily on identification with parental love objects, so also the patterns of affect tolerance are similarly derived. The identification is mainly with the benign mother, who allows the child to have its feelings to the intensity it can handle but intercedes before the feelings become overwhelming. When she does intervene, she sometimes depends on the child's distractibility. The child-grown-to-adult tries to imitate this action, but the burden of affects is that the emotions tend to *dominate* consciousness and for their duration exclude the possibility of the opposite consideration, or gratification.

The significance of identification in affect tolerance also lies in the *uses* of affect. The patient with a primitive superego feels that he is *supposed* to perpetuate the depression as a punishment, as a bribe of Providence to avert worse disaster. Conversely, identification with a benign parental superego contains the provision that no matter what the offense, the person always retains the right to live and the right to gratification of basic needs. Zetzel (1970) has pointed out that the formation of a self-representation of a heroic nature forever free of anxiety becomes a liability, cascading anxiety into depression.

To recapture the child's distractibility and hedonism, some people may seek to restore the organic imperfection of the child's brain. Thus, the customs of persons of all ages and places include the use of alcohol and other drugs to numb the emotions temporarily. I have even speculated that without alcohol civilization would have been impossible and that the myth of Adam and Eve eating the forbidden apple actually refers to the discovery of alcohol in naturally fermented, fallen fruit (Krystal, Moore, and Dorsey, 1967). The use of drugs or other means to block emotions becomes a problem only if it gets out of hand or if *all feelings* have to be blocked—a situation that predisposes to drug dependence. But the temporary use of drugs or other means actually expands one's ability to handle the feelings in the long run and therefore represents an asset.

From her six years of experience in the British Emergency Medical Services during World War II, Zetzel (1970) has distilled observations of individual differences in the capacity to bear anxiety. Special characteristics of wartime experience focus attention on this variability. As the soldier responds to realistically appraised danger, it is necessary for him to function in a state of anxiety. He cannot afford to have his anxiety "blocked," for it is vital to his survival that he be kept alert to threats in his life and ready for instant, life-preserving action. He must not, however, become overwhelmed by his anxiety or it will interfere with his effectiveness.

There is, in fact, an optimal level of anxiety for all activities, and, in some, the "fine tuning" that is necessary becomes especially conspicuous. In psychoanalysis, for example, we are committed to evoking affective responses. Once these emotions make their appearance, the patient must handle them. If the patient permits his emotions to build up to uncontrollable, threatening proportions, the analyst is confronted with a potential psychoanalytic emergency that may interrupt the therapeutic work (Peto, 1967). Or, if the patient's fear of his emotions has led him to develop extensive disassociations of affect or widespread affect inhibitions, psychoanalytic interpretation remains a mere cliché and its therapeutic potential is limited.

The attention of the psychoanalyst thus inevitably shifts from the intrapsychic sources of affects and their form to the patient's degree of success in handling or "having" his emotions. The value of the ability to tolerate anxiety impressed Zetzel (1970) early on: ". . . the presence of anxiety symptoms, both in childhood and in adult life, is often of good prognostic significance" (p. 30).

One of the observations that alerted Zetzel to the function of affect tolerance as an independent variable was the discovery that people who successfully handled the reality of long-term danger could be overwhelmed by a relatively minor incident. For instance, a fireman with much experience in the fire-bombing of London became overwhelmed and disabled when startled by a falling cinder. In retrospect, one can see that his previous excellent tolerance for anxiety had contained a certain secure self-representation, which included his ability to deal with danger, fear, and anxiety. The ability to bear anxiety is an essential part of emotional maturation and the maintenance of the adult self-image, which includes the affirmation of oneself as the responsible caregiving party, the one who has the emotional reserves for oneself and any dependents. It is this very image of oneself that also is a prerequisite for the ability to tolerate the anxiety of psychoanalytic exploration and the capacity to bear painful confrontations. Hence we can say with Zetzel (1970, p. 51) that the more an individual is able in an internal, unconsciously produced danger situation to develop and tolerate anxiety, the more one is able in analysis to face and resolve the conflicts that determined it.

This statement is especially pregnant with clinical and theoretical implications when we keep in mind that during the intervening years, Zetzel had, with equal perspicacity, studied the capacity to bear depression. She observed that the ability to tolerate depression was indispensable to "optimal" maturation and an important ingredient in withstanding disappointment, loss, frustration, illness, retirement, and many other "painful though inevitable, experiences." She brought together these separate observations in a statement regarding the effect of early object relations on basic ego functions and the tolerance for affects. Similarly, in the introduction to *The Capacity for Emotional Growth* (1970), wherein she summarized her work, Zetzel extended the prognostic significance previously attributed to anxiety alone: "Patients who cannot tolerate anxiety or depression will seldom prove capable of working through a transference neurosis. Many such patients cannot terminate any form of therapy successfully" (p. 11). Thus, Zetzel's writing contain a capsule history of her development of the concept of affect tolerance. But whereas her work evolved through the study of war neuroses and depressive patients, my investigations on this subject have developed in a different context.

The ability to bear emotions in their totality, without isolating the cognitive from the "expressive" aspects, is acquired relatively late in one's growing up. It is not encompassed in a single ego function but is a composite of the attributes of one's personality in relation to multiple functions and factors. We should speak carefully about the quantitative element of affect, for it is not helpful to make concrete our economic metaphors in this area. It can be said only that the intensity of an affect that can be tolerated by one person at any given time is finite. If one approaches the limits of bearable intensity or duration of affect, one is motivated to initiate some activity that evades or blocks the conscious registration of the emotion.

This process of the self-regulation of the affect experience is usually part of the normal handling of affect, and the multitude of such defenses is in the interest of maintaining normal mental functions. The ready availability of many and varied "resources" heightens ability to tolerate affect.

Zetzel (1970) emphasized that the development of affect tolerance is a lifelong process. Let us return to the observation of some of the events and developments by which some of the ego functions related to affect tolerance come to their maturity. Freud (1917) gave us the classical description of a maneuver that helps to increase tolerance of a painful affect; he pictured the mourner as periodically distracting himself and then returning to the painful work of mourning for a limited period of time. He also implied that current love objects and the denial of loss of the object (with flight into fantasy and temporary denial of the reality) were resources, as it were, that the mourner could use to keep grief within tolerable limits.

Each affect has its own problems and history in a given individual. For example, an emotion that was overwhelming at some earlier time is subsequently experienced as dangerous. When affects threaten to become unbearable or seem about to overwhelm one, it is advantageous to have a number of temporary strategies, devices that ease the distress momentarily and permit a later return to the full, conscious attention to one's own painful living. Among the commonly used self-help devices are transient consciousness modifications, shifting one's attention, self-distraction, eliminatory or cleansing fantasies, compensatory acting out. There are also a variety of self-administered or "object-involving" methods of comforting or "mothering" oneself. Where such modes of behavior are experienced as prohibited and therefore inaccessible, objects, drugs, or placebos may have to be used to circumvent inner barriers (inhibitions) resulting from repression (Krystal and Raskin, 1970). The effectiveness of the various ego functions and resources that may be utilized for affect tolerance are often noticeable by their conversion of an affect from its acute form to an extended one—they become moods (Jacobson, 1957). Thus, anxiety may be converted into worry.

In the permanent blocking of affectivity by relatively longlasting defenses, the emotions are experienced as physiological "attacks" and may break through intermittently. Even recurring periods of depression or anxiety are experienced as "attacks." During such attacks, the affects may not be consciously recognized as such (for example in hyperventilation syndromes). This subjective experience is the cause of the tendency, found in both patients and their doctors, to experience their emotions as if they were illnesses. The patient's attitude toward an emotion may compound his difficulties with it. The fear of an affect may set up a selfperpetuating circular reaction such as "being afraid of being afraid."

This entire process may vary in degree of consciousness and capacity for reflective self-observation: defenses against emotions, such as "affect-lameness," isolation, or drug abuse may become important aspects of character development.

When Freud (1923) made his summarizing statement, "The ego is the actual seat of anxiety" (p. 57), he was presenting us with the conflict model of mental function. In those terms, it was important to stress that in the intersystemic tension, the executive part of the mind is influenced (motivated) by the development of anxiety. Most of those conceptions have been expanded, including in Freud's own (1926) recognition of the signal function of affects. Engel (1962b) adds:

> As the psychic apparatus evolves they come to acquire the qualities of ego function as well. Affects have two essential characteristics: they are felt subjectively and are expressed nonverbally, indicating to oneself and to others one's current state of need. . . . As the mental apparatus develops these processes progressively come under the aegis of the ego. The perceptual processes whereby one knows *how* one feels are functions of the ego, as are the processes whereby one learns *what* one feels [pp. 123–124].

The structural theory, which, after all, is but a means of classifying mental contents according to their relation to conflicts, creates some clumsiness in our consideration of affects. Affects are described by psychoanalysts as both drive derivative and possessing characteristics of ego function. They are both "physiological" and ideational. As Novey (1963) put it: "The very structural models we employ in our consideration of personality and its development expose us to the potential for a peculiar aberration of thinking. For example, we are apt to conceive of the ego as something having a psychic structure which 'experiences' emotions . . . as being of the essence of what we speak of as ego" (p. 295). It is useful to consider the interactions between ego and affect, even if *these considerations represent to some extent an artificial opposition of intrasystematic elements.*

Whatever model of mental function we use, we gain some useful tools but also introduce some images that may become concrete and obscure further exploration. Thus, the attractive metaphors about the ego's "recognition" and "handling" of affects should be taken as an indication for further exploration, rather than as the last word on the subject.

We want to explore the nature of all those responses to *having* an emotion that I denote as potentially representing an advantageous, adaptive manner of affect tolerance. This view is taken because it appears that the nature of one's affective state can be influenced by the reaction to the recognition of its existence. Broadly speaking, *it is an advantage to keep affects at a tolerable intensity, so that one's task of information processing is not interfered with.* In a similar way, when experiencing pain, we are best off if we are not totally overwhelmed by the distress and the fear of it, so that we can direct our attention to exploring the source of the pain.

The development of affect tolerance has its parallel in the ego's recognition of, and reaction to, affects. This process is analogous to the development of the ability to bear pain (Krystal and Raskin, 1970). In the transition of affect experience from "attacks" (as they appear in infancy) and the affect-regression problems known as psychosomatic diseases to the adult form of affect experience, there is also a process of ego development in regard to affect tolerance.

One comes to acquire insight, comfort, and familiarity with affects as states of oneself. One develops a multitude of modes of action, defenses, and patterns for keeping affect within tolerable limits of intensity and duration. Along with the developmental patterns of dealing with pain, the mother plays a vital role in helping the child to "interpret his experiences, as well as to organize them and internalize them, even to the point that tension can be experienced as pleasurable" (Panel, 1968, p. 640). What are involved, then, are evaluation and regulation of affect by what we used to refer to as "the ego." But in our exploration of selfregulatory functions, it is useful to note that these functions are part of the perceived core self, which is experienced as a "self-agency" in which one's volition is recognized (Stern, 1985, p. 71). Those adults who experience affects as attacks suspend self-regulatory and self-monitoring functions, especially early in the episode. The detection and recognition of these unconscious operations becomes an essential part of the psychotherapy with patients suffering pains or "attacks" of intense emotions of any kind. One has to detect the primary and secondary gains in the unconscious motivation for the continuation of these patterns.

AFFECT STORMS AS A PSYCHOANALYTIC EMERGENCY

Affect storms represent a very specific type of psychiatric and psychoanalytic emergency and should be distinguished from the more commonly understood fear that certain impulses and drives, such as self-destructive wishes, will get out of hand and cause destruction.

Fenichel (1941) erroneously treated both dangers as if they were the same: "That which is sometimes described in the literature as the 'fear of the strength of the instincts' really ought to be called 'fear that intense affects may appear and overwhelm rational behavior' " (p. 220). The more familiar fear experienced in connection with intense emotions is that cognitive elements of the affect contain an undesirable *wish* that the subject's fears *will "come true"*—that death wishes for the object, expressed in anger, rage, or hate, may "break through" and harm the object or the self. In sexually motivated wishes, other dangers are feared: the wish fulfillment of incestuous strivings, exposure to rejection, humiliation, or, as in borderline states, the merging of the self-representation with the object representation.

In other words, the most common emergency related to affective states is the panic produced by the fear that one's magical powers will make the wish come true. Conversely, the helpless rage may snowball into another type of disaster. But these are problems concerning the handling of the cognitive element of affectivity.

The dread of being *flooded with affect,* however, is less frequently noted or understood, and the common psychoanalytic and psychiatric emergency it presents has to be handled by a specific interpretation related to the ego's experience of the affect. Correct interpretations in states of crisis that are due to the fear of affects can increase one's recognition and tolerance of the affect. Proper therapeutic management consists in helping the patient to réestablish his feeling of security and self control.

Case Illustration

Mrs. H., a woman in her early thirties, had been in analysis for three years in another town. Her professional position required that she move to a small town in Michigan. This created an intense problem for her, because throughout her analysis she was subject to overwhelming emotional reactions, which occurred both during her analytic hours and at other times. As a result, her analyst had to be available to her for emergency calls at all times. She had had to call him a number of times since coming to Michigan.

Her referral to me was preceded by one such occasion when,

overwhelmed with her emotions and uncontrollably crying, she had called her analyst in her home town, long distance, several times a day. On this occasion, her emotions built up to the point where she panicked, fearing that she was going to lose her mind or be permanently flooded with unbearable feelings. When she reached my office (after driving almost 100 miles), she was heavily sedated, having taken about a dozen different drugs, including tranquilizers, narcotic derivatives, antihistamines, and even some "stimulants." She expected that in talking to me she would be overwhelmed with her "hysterics," and before that happened she wanted to discuss with me the "emergency aspects" of her case: namely, that the night before, because of her panic, she had taken several capsules of a hypnotic drug and had managed to fall asleep for a few hours only to wake up in terror in 4 A.M., tempted to take more drugs. She was afraid that at this rate she was going to overdose herself.

When it became necessary for her to leave her analyst, he gave her a supply of medication. In addition, she was taking a variety of drugs for asthma, eczema, and other psychosomatic symptoms of anxiety. She had a history of colic and a very traumatic childhood. At present, she felt that she had to control her emotions at all costs, even by increasing the use of medication to dangerous proportions, in order to maintain her professional position.

After discussing her mental problems, I pointed out to her that she was using her emotions to control the significant objects in her life, including the remote analyst, and therefore had missed the chance to observe that her emotions were signals to herself that she could utilize and live with. The patient protested that she had not been manipulating her analyst "until it was time to leave," but she did allow that her parents had not cared for her, except during her "attacks," which included, besides those already mentioned, "attacks" of migraine and essential hypertension. I then explained to her the nature of emotions and how, unless she became frightened or angry about having them, they would run their course and could be utilized by her to her advantage.

The patient said, "This is the strangest thing anybody has ever said to me. Nobody has ever talked to me like that!" She left the hour quite composed and never did unleash her "hysterics." In subsequent visits, the work was almost exclusively concerned with her handling of her emotions, before a complete history of her other problems was ever obtained. Later, it was possible to deal with the "psychosomatic diseases" of this patient as affect regression and storm.

The most obvious conclusion to be drawn from that vignette is that therapists (or parents) should not be overly impressed with affective responses of their charges. In dealing with adults, we have to recognize that many have learned to "promote" the greatest possible intensity of the "expressive" element of their emotions. When the therapist is overimpressed with or frightened of the patient's emotions and blocks them, or hospitalizes the patient unnecessarily, the patient not only fails to become able to bear his emotions but compounds his dread of them. The psychiatrist may be of great help, especially to some patients, by assisting them in their handling of affects. The success of the self-help group known as Recovery, Inc., which bases its work on the writings of Abraham Low, a Chicago psychiatrist, derives from the help members give each other in learning to tolerate anxiety. Patients need to get acquainted with their emotions as signals, often unpleasant, but manageable and essentially self-limited.

In this respect, the therapist supplies, belatedly, a function that the patient's parental and familial background has failed to perform. To be able to function in such capacity, however, one must appreciate the nature of the subjective experience of patients whose affect tolerance is impaired. They are persons who were traumatized in childhood, whose affects are allowed to flood them. Among the residues of such experiences is a lifelong dread of affects. In such patients, the genetic development of the affects themselves often has suffered, causing the affects to be mostly somatized, poorly verbalized, and poorly differentiated.

AFFECTS AS A CHALLENGE TO ONE'S INTEGRATED FUNCTIONING

What is the affect experience of "normal" individuals who have not had serious childhood trauma and for whom at times affects may still be burdensome? Schafer (1964) has pointed out that "whether a particular emotion is 'dangerous' or 'painful' or not is jointly determined by existing intrapsychic conditions, the nature of the emotion itself, and the structure-building potential of the interpersonal or social context" (p. 296). A good deal of one's reaction to an affect will depend on the nature of the affective element itself (that is, whether it is a minimal, mostly cognitive signal affect, or whether it is somatic, undifferentiated, and related to primary-process thinking) and on the nature of the ego's familiarity and comfort with it. Affects, however, always represent a challenge and a burden for the executive organization of self-monitoring functions. Eissler (1953) has described how emotions tend to enfold and dominate one's conscious mind, thereby excluding other emotions. At the same time, the predominant affects modify the current self-representation and, as we have seen, sometimes noticeably modify the cognitive and even perceptive operations of an individual.

It is difficult to keep in mind the constant interaction of the various components of individual functions; the traditional mode of considering "affect and their impact upon the ego" is already permeated with artificial reifications. Affects are ways of living and experiencing that cannot be separated from other functional aspects without doing violence to the wholeness of the living being. If we view affects as an experience rather than as an expression, it becomes necessary to reconsider just what it is about the affect that could be possibly threatening or dangerous to the process of self-regulation, and particularly to the maintenance of self-monitoring functions. The accretions of metaphors that have been useful through the years have contributed to our difficulties in dealing with affects. The greatest obstacle to our clinical and therapeutic conceptions has been metaphors that refer to the "discharge" of emotions.

Here we have the situation, referred to earlier in the discussion of the basic concept of affects, where certain metaphors, especially naturally occurring ones and those regarding aggression, tend to confuse our therapeutic goals. Although expression of one's emotions still often implies riddance, the only real help patients can obtain is to increase their tolerance and management of their emotions.

Among those who have advocated dispensing with economic theories, Schafer (1972) has addressed himself directly to the problem of affects. He found that a source of difficulty in the effort to conceptualize affect is the prevalent inclination to think in spatial terms—trying to locate affect "inside" oneself as a quantity that can be discharged to the "outside." Schafer advocated that affect be considered an adjective describing self-experience, or an adverb describing a way of acting, thus eliminating the difficulties resulting from reification and the anal and spatial analogies.

THE DEVELOPMENT OF AFFECT TOLERANCE IN CHILDHOOD

The best known, and most conspicuous, educational efforts by parents to help children acquire affect tolerance take place during the latency period. Yet latency is underestimated as a developmental state, and the importance of the parent's role in promoting the essential maturational task of developing affect tolerance is taken for granted. However, even minimal reflection alerts us to the fact that the task of "upbringing,"—in which parents, teachers, counselors, and even siblings and peers are involved—focuses on the development of skill in handling emotions, in effect, the development of affect tolerance. Many kinds of inducements, such as "I can take it" clubs, are used—rewards as well as punishments. Possibly the most crucial and difficult aspect of mothering consists in permitting the child to bear increasingly intense affective tension, but stepping in and comforting the child before his emotions overwhelm him. Her empathy with the child is her only guide. If the mothering parent fails to prevent the infant's affect from reaching an unbearable intensity that overwhelms him, a state of psychic trauma may develop. Conceptions of the nature of the psychic experience in early childhood psychic trauma miss the point if they do not fully appreciate the nature of infantile affect precursors.

Allowing the child to experience both pleasurable and painful affect to an *intensity that it can bear,* but intervening whenever the child can not handle the intense excitation, can be described as functioning as a temporary or auxiliary "stimulus barrier." Actually it is more accurate to say that competent parents assist their children in practicing affect tolerance, in much the same way as they help their children to regulate their excitements and motoric functions in learning to walk or swim. Basically, the affectively motivated disturbances are not allowed to exceed for too long the child's ability to maintain his equilibrium. When the child does lose control, the parent steps in, offers support, and may even later help the child deny that he ever lost control, using the circumstances as a good excuse. Stern (1983) has pointed out that the way mothers achieve this even with infants is by "alignment with the possible and the probable," which means treating the child "as if he were roughly the person he is about to become" (pp. 20–21).

What methods stand at the mothering parent's disposal? The very presence of a caretaker and the caretaker's response is already reassuring to the anxious child. One may be able to offer oneself as an auxiliary organ demonstrating to the child that one is not oneself perceptibly anxious. In the child's need to accept the parent's evaluation of the world lies the foundation of his suggestibility. The young have no choice but to accept the mother as omnipotent. They will therefore exercise their imagination to support this belief, even when the mother cannot relieve their distress. And, so, where there is pain or painful affect, the child is inclined to allow the mother to distract him or to *compensate* him for the discomfort. If the child is to acquire this soothing function for himself, he must feel he has permission to "take her place" as a source of succor. Such compensations may be real gratifications, such as food, which makes one feel better, or they may be symbolic, as when some act of absolution or riddance is performed to deal with feelings of shame or guilt. As one grows, it is the ready access to such techniques and resources within oneself that makes it possible to take in stride the variety of unpleasant feelings and states that occur in the course of an ordinary day of work or study.

Only when protected from infantile trauma can the child in latency and adolescence gradually build up the ability to bear affects with increasing comfort and security. Raskin and I (1970, pp. 25–29) have emphasized that the educational maternal efforts that help the latency child to tolerate pain better also apply to learning to tolerate painful affects. Anna Freud (1952) made the following observation:

According to the child's interpretation of the event, young children react to pain not only with anxiety but with other affects appropriate to the contents of the unconscious fantasies, i.e., on the one hand with anger, rage, and revenge feelings; on the other hand with masochistic submission, guilt, or depression. . . . Where anxiety derived from fantasy plays a minor role or no part, even severe pain is borne well and forgotten quickly. Pain augmented by anxiety, on the other hand, even if slight in itself, represents a major event in the child's life and is remembered a long time afterward, the memory being frequently accompanied by phobic defenses against its possible return [p. 272].

By teaching the child to control affect, the parent also serves as an example and in fact will often consciously and verbally encourage the child to identify with him/her and to exercise that monitoring function in the future himself. When the child shows that he can take over, the parent expresses approval and rewards the child's use of a mode of dealing with emotions in a manner previously demonstrated by the parent. Many such patterns revolve around going to doctors, dentist, school, and the like, and the good parent will offer emotional support as long as necessary but be ready to leave the child to his/her own resources as soon as possible.

Beyond the direct regulation of the child's homeostatis, in the process of which much learning for the child takes place (Lichtenberg, 1983), there is parental dedication to promoting the child's gradual acquisition of the ability for managing his emotions comfortably.

The parent's interventions in the emotional state of the infant are many and varied. The infant experiences his affects passively, as if they were emanating from the mother. When he has good feelings, he experiences them against the background of his maternal object representations, which (he feels) must signify that it is all right for him to have the good feelings. When he feels distress, he must turn to his mother for an evaluation of the *meaning* of his discomfort.

The child's ability gradually to increase verbalization and desomatization, as well as the various ego functions that produce affect tolerance, depends not only on the kind of help he receives from his parents in this regard, that is, what the parents *do* and *say* about it, but also what the parents *are*. Quite likely, identification with the parents and imitation of their way of dealing with their emotions become the most important determinants of the patterns the child will develop for himself. Permissive or, at the other pole, authoritarian patterns prevail in certain families in their handling of anxiety and in their attitude toward emotions. Either style seems to be workable (within limits) as long as the parents are *consistent* about what they teach and what they do about their own feelings. Because of the dual process of acquisition of affect tolerance (by learning and by identification), children whose parents have difficulty in handling affect also have difficulty in developing advantageous ways of dealing with their own emotions. Katan (1961) has pointed out one instance of such difficulties:

> . . . [in] the type of parents who not only are unable to show their own emotions but also do not permit emotions to show in the child. If such parents speak about their feelings which they are unable to show, or speak about the child's feelings, it is clear that their words are used not to further the expression of emotions but to ward off these emotions. If this is the case, the words are not a bridge, as they ought to be, but are a defense against the emotions. The child may now take over the example set by the parents and also use words defensively [p. 187].[1]

Related to the interactions between mother and infant around affect is a fateful development to self-representation or, as it used to be called, "body ego." For all parts of the body related to affect expression are experienced by the infant as controlled by, and belonging to, the maternal object-representation and not to the self. This is so because the infant seems to experience all affect as emanating from the object. If the mother is unable to convey to the child the feeling that it is all right for him to assume the consciously recognized possession of these autonomically controlled parts of himself, serious difficulties may arise. Finkelstein (1975) reported a case of a patient who experienced his penile erections as being entirely controlled by his female partner. His inability to consciously acknowledge control of his sexual excitement contributed to his premature ejaculations. Raskin and I (1970) have described in detail the ways in which the inaccessibility of affect regulatory functions can be a major factor in the tendency to drug addiction. Kohut (1971) has stated that certain narcissistic persons suffer a serious impairment in their ability to regulate their skin temperature and maintain a feeling of warmth: "They rely on others to provide them not only with emotional but also with physical warmth" (p. 64).

We are just beginning to look for those times and signals when the mother conveys to the child permission to comfort himself, for instance, with a transitional object. Some mothers, apparently feeling jealous, may take the transitional object away from the child (Bush, 1974). One wonders whether this action represents the kind of prohibition of self-soothing that cumulatively would lead to the psychopathology we observe in drug-dependent patients.

The mother who is consistently nurturing supports the feeling of trust and active mastery that permits the tolerance of pleasurable feelings that are

---

1. A. G. Green (personal communication) has expressed concern that a similar self-defeating situation is set up by the analyst who verbally encourages the patient to experience his emotions consciously, while he himself sits like a wooden Indian. For the patient who suffers an impairment of affect tolerance, the analysis must provide an opportunity to gain greater comfort in bearing his emotions. Otherwise, he receives his interpretations on an intellectual level, in a state of isolation of affects, and converts the interpretation to a cliché.

basically *proleptic* (Spitz's, 1963, term referring to the anticipation of gratification). In contrast, people who suffered severe disappointments during infancy cannot tolerate any hopeful expectation of feeding or love. Schmale (1964) has considered this development from the point of view of the infant, who from the age of 12 to 16 months becomes aware of his symbiotic relationship with his mother, becomes aware of the need for help, and with undue deprivation is subject to the feeling of helplessness: "Helplessness, which reflects psychic immobilization, is an expression of the infant's inability actively to pursue gratification along with the awareness of a need to be taken care of by external other-than-self object" (p. 294). I am concerned here, though, not with the traumatic potential of such feelings of helplessness, which no doubt can be real, but with the effect of such experience on the person's comfort with positive "proleptic" feelings in his life. It is my conviction that people such as those mentioned by Atkin (1973), who dare have no feelings except anger, are those whose maternal contacts were consistently disappointing and for whom the expectation of gratification provokes an anticipation of hurt and helplessness. Thus, the quality of nurturing by the mother is crucial to the development of tolerance of proleptic affects.

Similar inferences can be drawn about the maternal reaction at other points in the child's psychosexual and psychosocial development. Here I will follow Schmale's (1964) outline, which highlights certain affects in connection with key developments. In the second year of life, when the child becomes aware of prohibitions, he not only contributes to his evaluations of himself but also learns whether it is permissible for him to expect to be good, to expect to find himself virtuous, or whether he must expect himself to fail and be guilty. Although other skills may be learned at this age, for example, the ability to "handle" objects, there may be an inability to tolerate the expectation of what is required. In connection with the establishment of bodily self-control, the child has occasion to feel either pride or shame, and the mother can be helpful in allowing him to gain a degree of comfort with both these feelings.

In the oedipal stage, there is, along with the awareness of sexual identification, a reintensification of feelings of pride, shame, and envy, among others. A key question is whether the child may entertain hopes for sexual and generative wishes. This is a matter not just of the fate of the Oedipus complex itself, but of the child's feelings about the permissibility of his strivings and the associated feelings of hope. If the child is not helped to feel that his hopes are permissible, he is pushed in the direction of hopelessness (Schmale, 1964).

An illustrative case was the patient whose mother could only accept a preoedipal relationship with him as her extension—an adored phallus. Her inability to tolerate any potent men caused the young boy to experience his phallic strivings as prohibited, resulting in impotence and narcissistic character problems. In analysis, he kept asking me to "fix him up" with one of my patients.

Since affective expression is the infant's only form of communication, the mother promotes a certain kind of reaction in the child by the way she responds to him. Most mothers are able to handle the emotions of the very young child as requests for their services and willingly fulfill the child's needs. However, the infant's distress state assaults her ideal of being a loving mother of a contented, "good" baby; increasingly, as the child progresses, she responds to his emotional outbursts with irritation. In later childhood, "overt emotional expression tends to bring disapproval and punishment rather than succor" (Jones, 1967, p. 163).

This development has three major results: (1) It encourages verbalization and formulation of self-observation in the child, since it becomes necessary for him to formulate his demands in words. (2) Internal responses to affects assume a greater role (Jones, 1967). This process thus favors the establishment of psychosomatic patterns as substitutes for chronic affective states. One can trace here a "bifurcation" of affect development into verbalization on one hand and formation of "psychosomatic" (disease) patterns on the other. (3) In identification with the parents, the child responds with guilt and shame to the self-observation that his affects have manifested themselves in an overt and uncontrollable way. For instance, the little boy who cries in fear suffers further mortification upon observing his own "childish" response and attacks himself for it. Blushing betrays an emotion, and the reflective self-awareness of it evokes even more shame. This secondary reaction adds to the fear of the affect. The child learns to respond to his affect first from the maternal and familial reactions and later from his peers. He is thus introduced to the social norms for his affective behavior.

Social influences on the *reactions to having an emotion* are potent forces in the development of affect tolerance, even pain tolerance (Tursky and Sternback, 1967). The interpretation of bodily states is, according to all available evidence, strongly influenced by the social attitudes toward a given emotion that were acquired in childhood (Schachter, 1967). Although, in the main, early psychoanalytic writings emphasized oppressive attitudes toward sexuality, they inspired such writers as D. H. Lawrence to observe that our society was just as repressive in regard to all affectivity. More recently, it has become clear that the antiemotional attitudes of our culture have created a problem with regard to affective reactions that cannot be ignored by present-day analysts (Sterba, 1960, 1969).

Separation-individuation is a process of growth and development regulated by the intensity of the feelings that can be tolerated during the experimental separation. This process provides an opportunity to develop the affect and increase this tolerance. Similarly, during childhood there are such ongoing operations—trial and practice separations. Leaving the child in nursery school or kindergarten provides a major test of the child's ability to tolerate separation anxiety. For children who can tolerate the anxiety, it is an opportunity to diversify object relations, enrich ability for self-gratification, and hence increase affect tolerance even more. Thus, we can add another diagnostic consideration in the disturbance in handling anxiety in latency and later. We have to question whether indeed the anxiety is overwhelming or intense, say in a case of school phobia, or whether the child's *tolerance of anxiety* is deficient.

The unconscious ways in which parents promote the development of affect tolerance go beyond their serving as objects of identification and permitting such identification. They also have *unconscious expectations* for the child's ability to tolerate certain painful affects and communicate these to the child by what they allow him to handle. Conversely, the parent who steps in every time the child's emotions reach minimum distress may leave the child with a fear of affect, lack of self-confidence, and a reaction that betrays the nature of the parent's motivation—to promote inordinate dependence.

Under certain circumstances parents both consciously and unconsciously impair affect tolerance. This may be part of the parent's idea of gender-appropriate behavior, as it is, for example with parents who shame a boy and teach him that fear and crying are not compatible with masculinity. Conscious and verbal experience of grief or fear add to the difficulty in handling these painful emotions. The old Japanese attitude toward shame was apparently directed toward making shame and humiliation unbearable and unaccept-able. The child depends on the parent to provide him with the early interpretations of pain and emotions. When the child experiences pain, he comes to mother to find out whether he has been hurt and to obtain succor. The mother may respond gently, reassure and comfort the child. Or she may become excessively upset and panicky and thus create a secondary anxiety within the child. She may even attack him for having hurt himself, adding insult to injury (Benedek, 1956).

Parents have particular patterns of response to affect distress. The way the parent responds can lead the child to make certain evaluation of pain and painful emotions, which may result in intense reactions to *having* certain affects. Thus, some people will not go to the doctor because they are afraid of *their reaction* to the visit and to what the doctor will tell them. Most parents make special efforts to help the child to develop affect tolerance, particularly during latency, when affect tolerance involves the ability to tolerate frustration and delay of gratification without "snowballing" the affective reactions to it.

Developing tolerance for painful affects is necessary for changing over from play to work and learning. The child's natural quest for efficacy (Broucek, 1979), and for initiative, mastery, and industry, parallels the child's motivation to raise the intensity of the affects he can bear. Klein (1976) has also stressed that pleasure in functioning and affectance (experiencing oneself as an effective agent of change) are powerful motivators. I believe that they represent a particularly strong motive for the latency child to raise the range of tolerance of emotions so as to be able to proceed with his school and social developmental tasks.

Another essential task of the development of affect tolerance during latency is to prepare the ground for the test of emotional prowess yet to come during adolescence. The development of affect tolerance in adolescence is discussed in the next chapter. For now, however, it may be helpful to remind ourselves once more that the basic reason for maintaining the hedonic and excitatory aspects of affects at a low level of intensity is to keep them useful as signals.

3
Genetic View of Affects

S carcely a hint of affect development or regression could be found in psychoanalytic writings until Schur's 1955 paper on the subject. Schur "discovered" regression in the "expressive" aspects of emotions by working with patients suffering from psychosomatic disturbances. These patients share with drug-dependent and posttraumatic patients the tendency to show affects that are undifferentiated, not verbalized, and hence not suitable to serve as signals to oneself. Through working with such patients, a definite developmental history of affects has been worked out. Brenner (1953) picked up a hint from Freud that in infancy certain responses to such emotions as danger and loss may not as yet be differentiated. Schur (1955), Valenstein (1962), and I (1962, 1970, 1975) felt that affects must have evolved from two common precursors, a state of contentment and a generalized distress response. Novey (1959) studied the role of affects in establishing the formation of object- and self-representations. Schmale (1964) has worked out the genetic development of affects in considerable detail.

Schur was the first to "discover" the genetic aspect of emotion *for psychoanalysis,* but he was anticipated by 25 years by Bridges (1930). And even Bridges used earlier ideas by Watson (1919) and Dashiel (1928). Bridges observed that "visceral" pattern reactions, like any other form of behavior, seem to undergo processes of *"differentiation and coordination* in the course of human development" (p. 515). She further observed that at birth there was a reaction of "general disturbance or *excitement.* . . . It is difficult to tell whether a baby is frightened, angry, or even pleasantly excited. . . . This general excitement, within a short time—perhaps days and perhaps only hours—becomes differentiated into two general types of emotion, . . ." which Bridges defined and described as *"distress"* and *"delight"* (p. 517).

Although the work of Bridges has been recently picked up as a basis for direct observation in children by developmental psychologists (their most important work is Lewis and Michalson, 1983), the psychoanalytic and psychotherapeutic view of affects remained unrevised until Schur understood his psychoanalytic (dermatological) patients to be experiencing a regression in the "expressive" element of their affects. Let us then consider the developmental lines involved in the epigenetic development of emotion.

The affect precursors in the newborn consist basically of a state of contentment and a state of distress (Valenstein, 1962; Krystal, 1962, 1974, 1977; Krystal and Raskin, 1970). Out of these basic reaction patterns evolve all the (adult-type) affects. Out of the patterns of contentment and tranquility develop the affect we experience as pleasurable, or "welfare affects"; and out of the agitated state of discomfort evolve pain and all the painful "emergency" affects. One developmental line of affect is differentiation through a recognizable association of specific affective elements. As the affect components mature and differentiate, it becomes clear that the cognitive aspects of the affect have a "meaning" and a "story." When one is not overly impressed by the physiological aspects of the emotion and is able to pay attention to its cognitive aspects, one observes the self-experience of "feeling," provided one also has the capacity for reflective self-awareness. Attaining this degree of development allows one to "diagnose" one's own emotional response as a subjective state and sets the stage for the optimal utilization of affects as signals to oneself (Krystal, 1981a).

The process of affect differentiation, fundamental to all these developments, is continuous. For instance, the affects of shame, rage, hate, depression, and so on can be further differentiated. There are several kinds of shame experience: dishonor, ridicule, humiliation, mortification, chagrin, embarrassment, and disgust. The more precise the recognition of one's feelings, the greater its utility as a signal to oneself.

The other developmental line of affects is verbalization and desomatization (Schur, 1955; Krystal and Raskin, 1970; Krystal, 1974). In the adult, emotions that have matured through differentiation and desomatization function mostly on the cognitive level, and the expressive element is minimal. Only the occasional affective response is intense enough to call attention to itself. This situation leads to the false impression that emotions are episodic phenomena. In reality, every mental event has its affective coloring.

These affective developments take place in the context of the infant's experience of his mother. The average good-mothering parent takes pleasure in discerning the early differences in vocalization and strives to fulfill the baby's needs quickly and specifically. In this way, she/he "rewards" every increment in differentiation in the child's emotional response patterns. Later, throughout childhood, a major part of upbringing consists of the parents' exhorting the child to recognize his feelings and to put them into words rather than act upon his emotions or vocalize uncontrollably.

Within the child certain developments are vitally involved in the developmental lines of affect. The first smile becomes the prototype of the affective linkage and initiates the object interaction. The ability for bonding and attachment depends on these developments. The first specific emotional response is the social smile. Spitz (1963) noted that the smiling response is at first indiscriminately elicited by any human face; it soon becomes related to initiating, and later anticipating, a need gratification and therefore is reserved as a response to the mother's face. The next milestone in the development of emotions is, in Spitz's (1963) opinion, the "eight months anxiety." This notion is predicated on the development of the perceptive apparatus and the ego apparatus, thus permitting object recognition. In Spitz's observation of the proleptic functions of affect, two aspects of the expressive responses to affects become apparent. One is a function of getting the child set, as it were, to participate in the gratifying activity; the other is an "expression of . . . emotion . . . in a centrifugal direction" (Spitz, 1963, p. 57). These two aspects of the child's affect experience have far-reaching consequences for the evolution of emotions.

In using the term "anxiety," Spitz was following the views of Freud (1900), who felt that anxiety existed since birth. He viewed birth as the "source and prototype of the affect of anxiety" (pp. 400–401). This idea led to a number of unresolvable conflicts in psychoanalytic theory (Freud, 1926, 1933); anxiety as we know it in the adult develops only gradually. It is much preferable to follow the usage of Emde, Gaensbauer, and Harmon (1976), who observed infants directly and reported that "stranger *distress*" was an "expectable developmental event" (p. 121), setting in between seven and nine months. In regard to affective communication, in which the mother's responses to the child's affective states is most notable, Emde (1983) demonstrated by experimental means that 12-month-old infants checked back for affective signals from their mothers. However, as affective behavior is the only means of communication between infant and parent, and since some parents respond poorly to anything but intense emotion in the child, there is a tendency to *use one's emotions to control "significant others."* Such a situation favors the development of histrionic styles and retards the desomatization process. Such constellations tend to distract the subject from the discovery that emotions are, in essence, signals to oneself. If such pitfalls can be avoided, every phase of psychosexual development is an occasion for affect differentiation, verbalization, and desomatization.

The maternal object representation becomes so firmly linked with the memories of early gratification and the attendant intense affect that throughout life persons tend to experience feelings as if they were emanating from the object. Clinically, psychoanalysts find that certain moods may stand for early object representations and that manipulation of one's own feelings may represent the symbolic forcing of the object representation to give gratification, a situation especially well demonstrated by patients who are both drug abusers and addictive gamblers. On the other hand, since the mothering parent responds to the child's needs as manifested in his emotions, the tendency is to use one's affects to control one's love object. Experiencing affects as communication distracts from the discovery of the role of affects as signals to oneself (Krystal, 1975).

Spitz (1963) demonstrated how, in the third quarter of the first year of life, a link is established between a felt emotion and a mode of communication that is going to be progressively less somatic and more verbal and related to finer and finer nuances of meaning and facial expression. Although the manifest motivation is the need to communicate and control the love objects, it initiates the transformation of affects that will make them usable later as signals to oneself.

Thus, the "good enough" object relationship is the indispensable condition for the harmonious maturation of affects. Spitz noted that in infants deprived of adequate object relations the affect precursors remain on a primitive level: "The expression becomes rigid and vacuous" (p. 57). Within a gratifying mother–child relationship, emotions unfold in increasing specificity and variety; there is a burgeoning of nuances to the relationship and a proliferation of facial and gestural expressions; and vocalization becomes increasingly effective as it becomes verbalization. Because there is a mutual relationship between verbalization and desomatization of affects, psychosomatic diseases may be viewed as regressions in affect form to a total somatic form. In psychosomatic diseases, the early situation represents a regression of the cognitive aspects of the affect and a denial of its existence. Instead of the full physiological response, only one part of it appears, sometimes referred to as an "affect equivalent."

In the course of maturation, affects evolve from two affect precursors into specific emotions. There is common agreement that the infant possesses affect precursors out of which emotions develop. All writers in this area separate the precursors of pleasurable affects from those of painful affects. However, some disagreement exists as to whether painful affects all evolve out of one ur-affect or whether precursors of anxiety and depression represent two separate basic reaction patterns. Engel (1962a) is a leading exponent of the latter theory. This view was especially popular with those psychiatrists who used anxiety-stimulating drugs to disrupt psychomotor retardation in depressed patients. I believe that Engel complicates matters by prematurely introducing the issue of object relations at this point, in terms of his conception of the deactivating response as "depression-withdrawal." He conceives of *primal anxiety* and of *primal depression withdrawal* and "relate[s] them to the biological processes of irritability and depression respectively" (Engel, 1963, p. 274), but he explains that "the fight–flight pattern" and "conservation-withdrawal pattern" are more appropriate terms for these biologic systems" (p. 275). However, I will discuss separately the multiple involvements of the activation-deactivation aspects of affects and would rather avoid some of the implications of these terms. Still, the point must be made that three patterns of affect precursors are present from birth. As we account for the various states of the infant, which include REM sleep and NREM sleep, we have from the beginning the states of well being and distress, as well as a cataleptic response.

Cataleptic *immobility* is a normal response in the young of all known species, but it disappears if mothering is disturbed (Moore and Amstey, 1960, 1962, 1963). The same pattern has been reported, in the human infant, but it disappears usually after two months: "In . . . dangerous situations a sudden behavioral change in the infant may occur. . . . the infant lies motionless with non-converging, staring *eyes* and sleep-like respiration" (Papousek and Papousek, 1975, p. 251). In this infantile response there are already elements of submission to total helplessness, but the capacity to be rescued by an external object is preserved. This state contains the cognitive and affective elements of the catatonoid state, hypnotic phenomena, and depressive inhibitory responses (Dorpat, 1977).

Engel's (1962a) view on the oppositional nature of the precursors of anxiety and depression has its roots in our clinical attempts to deal with the psychomotor retardation. I take exception to this view, mainly on the basis of my work with drug-dependent patients whose affect I (1962) found represented a primitive form of the unpleasure affect precursors. It was evident, particularly when these patients were in withdrawal states, that their ur-affects contained both anxiety and depression forerunners. Even the neurophysiological basis of the antagonistic view of depression and anxiety—the sympathetic and parasympathetic nervous systems—has been shown to be nonexistent. It is now known that the innervation pattern of adrenergic-, cholinergic-, and histamine-generating nerve endings is most complex and not at all in accord with the old, simplistic view (Wolf, 1970).

The child's liability to traumatization stems in part from the fact that neither anxiety as such nor the other specific affects have as yet developed, and the primitive response continues. The idea, used by Freud and many later analysts, that anxiety is the prototypical affect and can serve as the model for all other emotions is misleading. It would be of considerable advantage to consider love or love and hate as model affects, a view that is the subject of a chapter in this book.

Affects become specific as their meaning and circumstances become associated with certain situations, reactions, feelings, bodily gestures, facial expressions, and words. Often they become associated with certain objects and ego states and may even take on screen functions.

Differentiation and verbalization progress constantly with development, maturation, and acquisition of experience. The establishment of the discrete self-representation is the fundamental event in affect development (Krystal and Raskin, 1970; Krystal, 1975); it permits the separation of the experience of pain from painful affects and thus represents a prototype of all later affect differentiation.

Spitz's (1959) approaches to the genetic development of affects have been pursued by his students (Emde et al., 1976) in direct observation of infants. These investigators have reported:

> By the second half of the first year, affect expressions have become a varied and effective means of communication. Although mothers often respond to affect signals automatically and without awareness, they are seldom puzzled by their message or meaning. In the expanding infant world, emotional expression remains a primary means whereby the preverbal infant conveys his wants [p. 135].

THE DEVELOPMENTAL LINES OF AFFECT

There are two developmental lines of affect: affect differentiation and affect verbalization with concomitant desomatization. Out of the state of distress evolve all the affects we experience as distressful (Rado, 1969, called these "emergency affects") and out of the state of well-being evolve all the emotions that we experience as pleasurable (Rado's welfare affects).

In tracing the patterns of affect differentiation, we could postulate that the infant's states of gratification and stimulation evolve into the affects that indicate a sense of intactness, success, and gratification, such as contentment, confidence and joy, pride, and hope, as well as affects accompanying gratifications, such as love, tenderness, affection, and sexual excitement. Other arousals and affects could be postulated with activities other than sex, for example, stimulation about and during eating and satiety. The patterns of differentiation are represented schematically in Figure 2.

In tracing the emotions derived from the unpleasure ur-affects, we list anxiety, shame, guilt, disgust, sadness, helplessness and hopelessness, anger or rage. With regard to what exists before affect differentiation, we can only postulate a state that has been quite aptly described by Ramzy and Wallerstein (1958):

> The neonate has internal tensions (homeostatic disequilibria) which are "perceived" (referring to a precursor of perception) not as mental status, but as diffuse tensions on an *undifferentiated biopsychological level*. It is only later in development that such a tension state, as for example, hunger, can be separately viewed both on the psychological level (the feeling of hunger) and on the physiological level (concomitant discernible somatic processes) [p. 175].

It is essential to keep in mind the difference between the vague and mixed nature of affects in this early state and the adult type of affect experience, because we see patients with affect regression to various points along this developmental road. One of the problems with handling and understanding

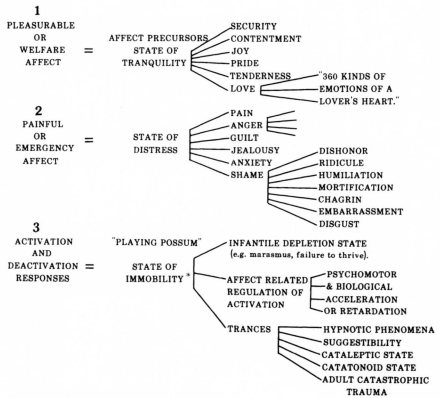

*In infants it disappears at 2 months of age.

FIG. 2   Affect differentiation

affect regression is that the affects present themselves in an undifferentiated way.

In addition to the affective responses that gain conscious recognition and are knowable to subjects as states of their own function, as well as motives, there is a similar acquisition of familiarity with certain bodily needs. Thus, by registering them proprioceptively in the same manner as we monitor the somatic changes attending affects, we provide a mechanism by which thirst, hunger, heat, or cold may function as motivators throughout the animal kingdom and in man. There is an early recognition of such conditions in the child that can be named; previously they were signaled visually or mimetically to the caretaking parent. This does not mean that all affects and physiological disturbances, such as pain, have symbolic components, but many are attributed cognitive or symbolic "markers" along the way. Still, these physiologically derived responses, although they have the same motivating attributes as affects, are subjectively distinguished by their more recognizable bodily reference. However, like affects, they are subjectively recognizable as inner states and in this form have a certain similarity to feelings. This understanding reconciles the use of the term "feeling" with that of Pribram (1970) and J. M. Jones (1981, 1984). However, differences remain as these authors would call these physiologically based experiences "feelings," as opposed to affects, to denote the different nature of these somatic reactions. I think that "feelings" are an important component of the affect processing in which recognition of the subjectiveness of the experience is dominant. However, these "states," derived from somatic needs, also become "feelings" and thus have a parallel effect on information, motivation, and self-regulation.

Let us return to the epigenesis of affects. Every significant event, whether developmental, maturational, or incidental, creates an affective state, thereby simultaneously posing both a challenge to oneself and an opportunity for one emotion to be highlighted and raised to a new level of verbalization, desomatization, and differentiation. Several nodal points in early childhood should be emphasized. If the simplest model of weaning is used, avoiding the span of possible individual experiences, at least one observation can be made: weaning must provoke, in addition to feelings of anger and helplessness, the first occasion of loss, loss of the breast. Freud (1933) pointed out that because the child is psychologically insatiable, this loss is never truly overcome. The failure to give up this attachment is manifest in myriad indications of longing for reunion with the ideal mother and in the struggle against feelings of helplessness and envy. These constellations continue to generate affects that become important influences in character patterns and in motivation for later sexual interests.

A period follows in which a number of developments take place almost simultaneously: mobility, language, toilet training, and separation-individuation. The development of language and symbolization is the fundamental event in the development of affect symbolization. With vocalization it may be the most important protection against traumatization during toilet training and separation-individuation. Mahler (1966) pointed out that if the child does not have the "emotional readiness to function separately from the mother" (p. 154) when other developments propel him to separation, he may be confronted with threatening affective responses. According to Mahler, the child who is unable to verbalize his emotions develops "organismic distress"—a reaction that may become chronic and may interfere with the child's ability "to utilize the mother as external organizer or auxiliary ego" (p. 154). Mahler seems to be describing the danger of psychic traumatization during the process of separation-individuation. Separation-individuation, as well as the development of affect tolerance in general, is carried out under the protection of the mother, who steps in and rescues the child whenever the infantile affects threaten to overwhelm him. The mother's failure to do so would lead to the child's being flooded with somatic and undifferentiated affects—a state representing the essence of infantile psychic trauma.

The danger of this kind of occurrence exists at all the nodal points of affect development. Each stage represents an opportunity for affect maturation through dealing with an intense and therefore potentially overwhelming emotional reaction. Separation-individuation is one of those times of great danger as well as opportunity. By the time a toddler is eighteen months old, he has achieved

> a certain degree of *object constancy* . . . i.e., mental representations of the mother become intrapsychically available. . . . The memory traces of the love object enable the child to remain away from the mother for some length of time and still function with emotional poise, provided he is in a fairly familiar environment. Presumably this is so because inner representations of the mother are available to him [Mahler, 1966, p. 156].

Mahler explains that, on one hand, the toddler may be confronted with "organismic panic" and that the basic mood of this phase of development is sadness and depression; on the other hand, however, some aspects of the "discovery of the world" are elating. She talks, in fact, about the "double trauma" of toilet training and the discovery of differences between the sexes as a "contributing factor in the genesis of the propensity to depressive moods." Thus, separation-individuation presents a number of points at which the affects may become too threatening and may result in a temporary or long lasting regression. On the other hand, giving up the need-satisfying symbiotic object and establishing of object constancy (an easily recallable mental representation of the mother) represent a major step in affect development because they imply autonomy and progress toward using emotions as signals to oneself. Increased motility and muscular skills permit the channeling of some aspects of affect expression from physiologic responses into motoric ones. This development progresses to the point where, some psychologists postulate, emotions develop only when one cannot "do something" about a situation. With each psychosexual stage, there is an elaboration of the wealth of fantasy solutions, which mollify the urgency of impulses. As verbal skills develop as part of the fantasy elaboration, the precision and effectiveness of words demonstrate language to be the preferred way of handling affects. Thus, each psychosexual stage, each psychosexual crisis, each increment in significant relations, concepts, and modalities promotes the verbalization and desomatization of affects, and their mastery.

Although Mahler hypothesized that the loss of the symbiotic object is worked through, I am not sure whether or not she felt that this working through is accomplished by grieving, which I cannot imagine possible at this point in development. I feel that *effective* grieving is possible only in adolescence, after the development of affects and affect tolerance, which takes place during the latency period. Mahler pointed out, "This loss—the necessity for a more or less gradual relinquishing of claims upon the need-satisfying, symbiotic object—implies the gradual giving up of the more or less delusional fantasy of symbiotic omnipotence" (p. 157). In the adult who experiences a loss but who is unable to mourn is found the making of depression. The child, on the other hand, experiences the manic defenses, the exhilarating aspects of development, feelings of conquering the world, the freedom to regress temporarily, as well as constitutional and developmental forces, and out of all of these reactions

. . . a basic mood is established during the separation-individuation process. . . . This characteristic "baseline" of the child's emotional responsiveness seems to derive from the preponderance and perpetuation of one or the other general emotional colorings . . . characteristic of one or the other of the subphases of the separation-individuation process . . . [Mahler, 1966, p. 156].

Still to be considered are the other developments taking place at this time, for example toilet training, with the well-known range of feelings from generosity to defiance and hate. When Schmale (1964) looked at this period of development in terms of his affect pairs, he saw a sense of goodness and guilt evolving in connection with the child's dealing with prohibitions, as well as a differentiation of pride and shame as the child develops an awareness of self-control.

There is a recognition that gratification is conditional and dependent in part on whether the external object permits the activity or punishes the child for having engaged in the activity. The affective quality resulting from the gaining of gratification from a self-initiated object-activity which also has the approval and acceptance of the external object is referred to as a feeling of being virtuous or feeling good [p. 298].

When the external object reacts to an activity with anger, "awareness that the danger from the outside was provoked . . . [by one's own action] leads to an affective reaction called guilt" (p. 298). It is, therefore, not surprising that the first affective disturbances at this age are in the form of infantile phobias (Schnurmann, 1949; Wulff, 1951). The occurrence of phobias in the preoedipal child is a sign of the young child's history of anxiety, with its special problems, for example, separation anxiety.

The cognitive aspects of the affective reactions of the child in the phallic and oedipal stages of libidinal development have been discussed in great detail by many authors. Feelings of envy, competitiveness, and anxiety are prominent at this time: however, to try to catalogue all the affects involved in this turbulent period would be futile. Schmale (1964) emphasized the impact of competitive oedipal strivings on the establishment of another baseline of feelings—feelings of hope and hopefulness in the fulfillment of the longed-for sexual role—which contributes to the later regulation of self-respect. He pointed out, "The intensity of the feeling of hopelessness will depend on the degree of guilt and shame experienced in the previous stages of development" (p. 300) and on the resources for partial fulfillment, displacement, and capacity for sublimation. He does not minimize the richness of such factors as the ability to tolerate narcissistic mortification; and although he does not discuss the development of affect tolerance, he does introduce some related problems that also burden this frustration and that need to be tolerated, notably, apathy and boredom.

A further development illustrates the continued interdependence of affect development and object relations: the oedipal triangle offers a solution to the problem of ambivalence—since the aggression can be channeled toward the rival, the relationship with the object can thereby be relatively free of aggression. Most species suspend aggression toward the opposite sex for extremely short periods during mating (Ruwet, 1972). Hence, the phylogenetic association of aggression and sexuality makes anxiety in a love encounter unavoidable—a point made by Schur (1955) that is most useful in understanding neurotic anxiety.

Although latency does not bring up any new conflicts, affects, or constellation of object relations, it is the necessary period for practicing verbalization, desomatization, and affects in the interest of developing affect tolerance. I shall single out those aspects of affect development—the elaboration of cognitive resources, verbalization, and desomatization of affect as well as the increasing utilization of affects as signals—that occur during later childhood and latency.

By the time the child is two, a number of affects can be identified, including those evolving from the distress pattern: fear, anger, and distress, and, in the hedonically positive group, delight, joy, and affection (Bridges, 1930). Tracing the further differentiation and integration of affect in the preschool child, Bridges found that fear evolved further into anxiety and shame. Anger evolved into distinct responses of disappointment, jealousy, and envy; and disgust was also observable. Joy was elaborated by the additional experiencing of hope and elation, and affection was becoming specialized into various kinds of love.

To Bridges, the processes of differentiation and integration were supplementary, accounting for some continuation of affective patterns: for example, she saw jealousy as a "modified form of anger and fear resulting from failure to receive accustomed or expected attention" (p. 519).

Consistent with the idea of the differentiation of affects from the two patterns (well-being and distress) is the work of Thomas and Chess (1984). They found *temperament* to be an innate characteristic. They defined "quality of mood" as "the amount of pleasant joy and friendly behavior as contrasted with unpleasant, crying, or unfriendly behavior" (p. 3). I feel that the relative intensity of the rage responses have an important hereditary component and represents a major challenge since birth. It determines the tendency to catastrophic reaction (e.g., colic) in many infants.

AFFECT VERBALIZATION AND DESOMATIZATION IN LATER CHILDHOOD AND LATENCY

Verbalization of affect lags behind other linguistic skills because, as has been pointed out, affects must attain a considerable degree of differentiation before they are specific enough to be verbalized. The vague and mixed emotions of early childhood continue to "develop, mix, combine, differentiate, coalesce" (Seton, 1965, p. 235) into their potential richness throughout childhood and latency as the richness and precision of language continue to develop. Verbalization not only increases the ego's control over drives and emotions but also "increases . . . the possibility of distinguishing between wishes and fantasies on the one hand, and reality on the other" (Katan, 1961, p. 188). Katan's direct observation of nursery school children impressed her with the noticeable relationship between children's acquisition of vocabulary suitable for the expression of their feelings and the diminution of physical, uncontrollable, and random affect expressions. However, for those children who were acquiring facility in verbalization, Katan found that when the parents' instructions were contrary to how they handled their own emotions, the children's facility in affect handling did not improve.

Katan suggested that children develop affective expression styles through a variety of learning processes, but mostly through identification. She pointed out, however, that learning and identification sometimes work at cross-purposes, and, frequently confusing and contradictory messages are given the child. Very young children are attended to when they show signs of painful affect states, but older ones are discouraged, shamed, even punished for displaying their feelings. Some mothers experience the child's affective expression as an attack upon themselves. As the expression of affects becomes stifled, the child may discover that illness offers an acceptable alternative—a push in the direction of psychosomatic disorders. Asthma may be a ready substitute for crying; the headache and vomiting attack, an acceptable way of dealing with rage. How patterns of affect responses are channeled in the family may be influenced by unconscious fantasies transmitted by parents to children. For example, as feminists emphatically point out, little girls are expected to dissolve into tears, whereas little boys are shamed into giving up "crybaby" emotionality; the expression of affection is similarly stifled in the pursuit of tight-lipped masculinity.

Attitudes toward anxiety within families can be conceptualized as authoritarian or permissive. In authoritarian families, which seem to be more prevalent among blue-collar workers, the male child is shamed when showing fear, and very little comforting is extended to him. This kind of upbringing favors counterphobic defenses, the development of rigid defenses against anxiety, and of heroic or martyr attitudes, which are harder but more brittle (Tompkins, 1965). A permissive attitude toward anxiety encourages the child to recognize his fears and to verbalize them. This attitude favors the development of affect tolerance and introspection and, in a way, encourage the recognition of neurotic conflicts as opposed to characterological modification and acting out.

The effects of family attitudes, social class, and ethnic and cultural influence on the final patterns of affect use, meaning, and *differentiation* are impressive. As far back as 1973, Leff demonstrated that the nature of one's experience is determined by the availability of words to describe it. He used the illustration of lack of differentiation of certain colors: Pacific Island languages fail to distinguish between blue and green; in Navaho one word stands for brown and grey; and Shona people do not distinguish between red and purple—and these peoples do not experience differentiation in those colors.

"In a number of African languages a single word stands for both being angry and being sad" (Leff, 1973, p. 301). In an international study in which the Present Status Examination was administered as part of the International Study of Schizophrenia to various national groups, it was found that the words "depression," "anxiety," and "tension" were particularly difficult to translate into Chinese or Yoruba. "The Yoruba words used in PSE for 'depression' or 'anxiety' were translated literally as 'the heart goes weak' and 'the heart is not at rest.' It is evident that they refer to the somatic accompaniment rather than the anatomical experiences themselves" (p. 304). Leff's review of a multitude of studies involving international research on the relationship of ethnic and linguistic patterns suggests that the culture in the developed lands leads to a greater differentiation of the emotions.

Other studies revealed ethnic differences in the degree of somatization (or desomatization) of affect. Thus, in Bangkok, 84% of orientals manifested depression somatically, whereas 66% of occidentals had similar depressive equivalents (Foulks, 1979, p. 24; Ionescu-Tongyonk, 1978). And for us, products of western civilization, it is shocking to find that some peoples are able to experience and name emotions we are unable to discern. The Utku Eskimo, for instance, has a great richness of affect terms, including a number of words with shades or nuances all of which have to be translated as "reason." Foulks (1979) reported: ". . . Utku distinguishes at least three different aspects of feeling within what westerners would term affection: 1) the desire to be with a loved person; 2) demonstrativeness; the desire to kiss, touch or express tenderness verbally and, 3) protectiveness, the desire to take care of the physical and emotional being of another" (p. 25).

The affective states of *amae,* which means to depend on and presume another's benevolence, and *kodavari,* a particular disturbance over being unaccepted by others, are essential to the structure of interpersonal relations in Japan (Takeo-Doi, 1962). Takeo-Doi related that he could not imagine that there were no words (or awareness of such feelings) in English or German, when it was so obvious in Japan "that even puppies do it" (Foulks, 1979, p. 25). This brings us back to the importance of the process of socialization, particularly in the young child.

Latency is a period during which the child's blossoming intellectual capacities present him with an elaboration of the nature of his object relations and, with this, a progressive increase in the complexity of his fantasies, the cognitive aspects of affects, and the accompanying desomatization and verbalization. Parents are forever admonishing the latency child, "Speak, don't scream." They are forever demanding, "Do not demonstrate your feelings—contain yourself," "Behave yourself." These demands to "tame" and verbalize emotions are accompanied by rewards and punishments.

In considering the process of "expansion of the affect array," Pine (1979) found certain

> sets of events operative in the transformation or creation of affects: (1) the affect states; (2) the acquisition of new learning that becomes a permanent part of mental life having a 'thing' or 'entity' character (such as conscience, object constancy) and from which new affects flow; (3) control/delay/inhibition processes exerting an influence on current affects (the experiential accompaniments to the bodily events) and become models for later, more purely psychological experiences as well [p. 81].

It may be worthwhile to consider why the genetic view of emotions has not been more widely utilized and accepted. The idea of affect differentiation was offered to developmental psychologists by Bridges in 1930 and even before that by Stratton (1928), and the psychoanalytic observations on the development and regression in affect expression have been accumulating since Schur's contribution in 1955. Obviously, the affective responses of the newborn are not the same as those of adults, and there are differences between adults. Even Izard and Buechler (1980), who disagree with this view and feel that the fundamental emotions are "innately programmed," have to admit that "there are no emotions in the first weeks of life, unless one considers 'excitement' or general distress as an emotion" (p. 173).

Nevertheless, these authors observe that distinct affects do not emerge until some specific time in the child's life (Izard, 1978; Izard and Buechler, 1979; Lewis and Michalson, 1983). The major difficulty lies in the compelling need to assume that everyone's emotions are the same and thus that a named emotion always refers to the exact duplicate of our own experience. This is a particularly urgent need of parents with their children: "Because one often uses the same language to name emotions in two and twenty-two year olds, it is easy to believe that their emotional experiences are the same. American mothers also assume, incorrectly I believe, that three-month-olds can experience the emotions of interest, anger, joy, or fear that are attributed to adults" (Kagan, 1984, p. 172). These mothers, just like the students of emotions who determined the presence of affect from facial expression (e.g., Izard, 1971), pick up but one dimension of a multidimensional phenomenon. Kagan pointed out that to be able to experience depression or sadness "requires retrieval of schemata from the past." In other words, the child has to be able not only to recall the missing object and the original affective value but also to experience his present reaction. Likewise, adult pain can be experienced only when there is sufficient maturation to permit the establishment of a body image. Nonetheless, just having an emotion does not prove that the subject is aware of having it and is able to name or use it as a signal or as information to himself. As noted in chapter 1, the ability to experience simultaneously the cognitive, "expressive," and hedonic quality of affects and the ability for reflective self-observation are necessary before one can observe that one is having a *feeling*. If self-awareness takes place, then one can read the message contained in the affect, with its current and historical derivatives.

But if we say that emotions take time to mature and that at first they are not suitable as signals, then we pose a question covered in the next chapter, namely, how does a baby form the most important attachments of its life? It is this urgency to believe that the child can experience *love* that makes it so counterintuitive to accept the genetic history of emotions.

If we acknowledge that cognition plays a double role in affect—eliciting, evaluating, and attributing meaning (Mandler, 1975, 1980) as well as involving a separate, nonsymbolic, evaluative, nonverbal plane—then we must be alert to the epigenetic history of affect. This need is made more urgent by the discovery that affect memory is separate and independent from cognitive memory and that the two kinds of memory run a parallel course throughout life (Stern, 1983). Thus whatever the variety of affective experience and the kind of consciousness throughout life, there is a nonsymbolically and nonlinguistically based imprinting of personal emotional values onto the various components of object, self-, and world representations.

Most important for me, however, is experience with posttraumatic patients who showed affect regression. The same was later demonstrated even in patients in medical intensive care rooms or on kidney perfusion (Freyberger, 1977). The recognition of the genetic development of affect underlines a new formulation of psychotherapeutic goals in regard to emotions. Once we renounce the idea that we can help anyone to be *rid* of emotions, we are glad to find that we can be helpful in other ways—helping patients to name and identify their emotions and to obtain the maximum information from them.

DIRECT INFANT OBSERVATION

Freud was interested in the genetic development of emotions and wished that he could do direct infant observations. He was apologetic that he was not able to do so because he was working with adult patients for long hours. He was especially interested in the question of the age at which a baby could first be observed showing evidence of *disgust*. He explained in a letter to his friend Wilhelm Fliess (2 August 1897, in Bonaparte, Freud, and Kris, 1954, p. 192) that he had asked the members of his family to watch out for these phenomena and that he was disappointed: "The womenfolk do not back me in my investigations."

The need to study infant and child behavior arises also from many nonanalytic quarters. Piaget was an intermediate researcher inspired by his psychoanalytic experience and determined to create an observationally based psychology. Many psychologists interested in general development provided the panoramic background of the unfolding of the child's individuality against which the epigenesis of affect could be understood (Gessel and Thompson, 1934).

Eventually, Spitz (1963) reclaimed for psychoanalysis the territory of exploring the burgeoning infantile affective and social skills. He was particularly keen about the spurts in development brought on by such "organizers" (he borrowed the term from embryology) as the social smile, stranger anxiety, and, later, language and locomotion.

Gedo and Goldberg (1973), trying to devise models of the mind useful in psychoanalytic treatment, conceived the idea that the earliest problems concerned containing excitement. In their models, the child is subject to being overwhelmed traumatically until cognitive self- and object-representations are developed.

There has been such a plethora of infant observational studies of the early child-caregiver interaction as to thwart any attempt at surveying its scope. To pick just a few examples illustrative of the belated attention to the affective side of these transactions, I will begin with the important work at the NIMH, studies of children at risk. Greenspan (1981) concluded from direct infant observation that establishment of homeostasis, at first through the skillful interventions of the mothering parent and gradually over a period of time by the infant, was the most crucial achievement in the first three months of life. Homeostasis—that is, the regulation of the degree of excitation through the calming response—is acquired only gradually by the infant. At first, it seems to be necessary for the mothering parent to determine, at fairly frequent intervals, whether the baby requires stimulation or soothing and what action, motion, or sounds will be soothing or exciting for this particular child. In doing so, the parent has to counteract the irritants from outside as well as from within the baby. The caretaker also has to moderate the impact of the infant's perception of and reaction to himself or herself. It is a joint effort by the baby and mothering parent, as it were, to maintain the desirable intensity of the physiological aspects of affect precursors. Hyperexcited or apathetic infants are at a disadvantage in the development of their affective responses. Greenspan (1981) considers the establishment of homeostasis to be essential for the next great achievement, namely, the attachment to the primal object (representation). Crucial in this development is the

> range, depth, and phase-appropriateness of the feelings expressed and experienced by the dyad. The adaptive infant experiences deep rich pleasure in attachment with his caregiver. We see a wide range of affects and often a building of low-level excitement to extreme pleasure and joy, followed by relaxation. On anticipating breast feeding, for example, the infant may smile with extreme delight. The attachment pattern, without becoming disorganized, [referring to events of age 2–7 months] . . . also accommodates negative affects, such as protest, early forms of rage, and assertiveness. To carry the above example a little further, if on occasion the mother prematurely stops breast feeding, the infant's desire for more sucking, physical contact and milk will be expressed in easily understood affective facial expressions and body postures rather than disorganized motor responses [p. 55].

A problem in direct observation of infant affective behavior has been the occurrence of early "unexplained" smiling and "unexplained" fussiness (Emde et al., 1976). J. M. Jones (1983) has ingeniously suggested that in the process of physiological maturation there is a kind of "practicing" of certain responses, and he has even included "stranger anxiety" as being significantly determined by the concomitant myelinization of the relevant brain tracts. This observation frees us to train our eyes on purposeful, social smiling and its effect on the organization of mental function of the child and his experience of social relations. At this point, the crying infant gives clear signals, the meaning of which students of infant behavior can agree upon (Ambrose, 1961; Stechler and Carpenter, 1967; Emde et al., 1976). When the baby cries, he requests help for whatever bothers him; when he smiles, the signal means "I like it, keep it up."

Emde and his associates (1976) have identified affective development as marked by the initiation of social smiling at two and a half months, with progressive development of social awareness without distress until the onset of stranger distress, which peaks at seven to nine months. Separation distress was observed to peak at about a year of age, although interview data seemed to more closely approximate both types of uneasiness.

In the view of Emde and his associates there are three "levels of organization" of affects in infancy. First there is only an indication of crying or contentedness, which includes quiescence and sleep. On the second level, the development of the smiling response expands the play and interaction repertoire. Third, with stranger distress there is an expansion of relatedness to the primary love objects and an awareness of strangers. The meaning of stranger distress, as distinguished from separation distress, is felt by Emde to be related to the increasing specificity of the mental attachment between caretaker and infant.

Direct observations of neonate and infant behavior provides evidence of ever earlier capacities of the baby to respond to the mother, by such gestures as opening the mouth and pursing the lips, and that some of these may be interpreted as early "greeting responses" (Lichtenberg, 1983). Lichtenberg points out that Emde's observations may be viewed as implying that "each affect follows a maturational time table. The affect maturation may be inhibited because of further biological maturation (as in the case of REM smile). Alternately, it may develop specificity because of learning" (p. 23). On the other hand, direct infant observation utilizing Izard's (1979) coding of maximally expressive facial movements was supported by clinical diagnosis of depression following abuse and abandonment (Gaensbauer, 1982). Moreover, fear of strangers (particularly men), brief demonstrations of joy/pleasure (attended by activation) and interest/curiosity, as well as anger, were noted at three to four months of age. The significance of this study is that the child's disposition was influenced by the caretakers' paying attention to his/her affective states and responses. Although one may take exception to the author's conclusion that this study suggests the existence of "primary" emotions (p. 63), it is remarkable that we are moved to give official recognition to observations going back to time immemorial that infants and even animals register their states by affective responses, albeit primitive ones.

Since Darwin (1872) minutely described infant smiling, frowning, sulking, and disgust, there has only been a question of *when* and *how* these responses develop and how they are related to the adult form of affects. Spitz (1963) suggested that before we can see clearly recognizable affective responses, we are dealing with prototypical models that are affect precursors.

Having mentioned Darwin, we may reflect on the influence of his grandfather, Erasmus, a physician who studied the affective responses of sheep and who greatly impressed young Charles with the universality of emotions in the animal kingdom. Let us consider for a moment the phylogenesis of affect.

PHYLOGENETIC VIEW OF AFFECTS

In the phylogenetic view of affects, the evolutionary precursors of human affect are the forerunners of language—vocalization and the communication that precedes cognition. Since the affectlike responses in primitive animals refer to physiological responses in situations of life-preserving and species-preserving significance, any self-observation characteristics referred to as "feelings" or any cognitive aspect cannot be attributed to animals. Nonetheless, many responses are communicated among members of the animal kingdom. Certain birds, for instance, possess inherited calls for "danger from above" that are distinct from "danger from below" (Shiovitz, 1973, personal communication). Moreover, the call for danger from above is supersonic and cannot be used by predators such as owls to locate the bird. In most species, readiness to attack (anger?) is manifested by certain gestures, including facial ones, and may be assuaged by a response of submission. Gorillas, for example, signify submission by shaking the head (Ruwet, 1972). They seem inherently to possess certain precognitive, but nevertheless meaningful, aspects of emotional responses. Note Van Lawick-Goodall's (1973) description of the "language" of chimpanzees that dwell in a free, natural habitat:

> The chimpanzee has a wide range of calls. Each call is fairly reliably associated with some specific emotion—a scream usually signifies fear, a bark aggression, and so on. This means that the chimpanzee is able to communicate reasonably specific information about his feelings and his environment through the use of calls alone [p. 10].

Reports by biologists will no doubt continue to accumulate and to demonstrate a great variety of calls and mimetic and postural signals related to affect states. Vervet monkeys have three separate calls signifying the significant dangers from predators in their lives and their location (Seyforth, Cheng, and Mailer, 1980, cited in Dennett, 1983). Adults "call primarily to leopards, martial eagles, and pythons, but infants give leopard alarms to various mammals, eagle alarms to various birds, and snake alarms to various snakelike objects" (p. 344). An observation that launched Dennett on an exploration of the monkey's intentional system was one monkey's use of the predator danger signal to terminate a potentially dangerous social encounter between two vervet troops.

Communication of affective states through gesture, posture, and vocalization is achieved by the use of the "reptilian" part of the brain, that is, the basal ganglia and related structures (MacLean, 1985). MacLean observed affective function in primitive reptiles; for example, a scarlet lizard defeated by a younger male would, having lost his dominant position, turn a muddy brown color and soon die.

MacLean made an even more striking point on the basis of long-term studies on the remains of mammallike reptiles considered to have been the precursors of the mammals. MacLean concluded:

audiovisual communication [had to be] a valuable adjunct to the olfaction and vision for maintaining maternal-offspring contact. For sucklings, any prolonged separation from the mother is calamitous . . . the so-called separation or isolation call may represent the oldest and most basic mammal vocalization, serving originally to maintain maternal offspring contact [p. 411].

The emphasis here is on the connection between the evolutionary importance of affect vocalization in mammals and the derived importance of specialization of the vocal signals in obtaining effective responses. Vocalizing is one of the earliest behavioral demonstrations of intrapsychic attachment. Further, it becomes related to the image of the missing mother and hence is also the anlage of visualization and symbolic representation, which we will consider in the context of what goes wrong in alexithymia.

Observational, physiological, and pharmacological studies reveal that certain affective responses are identical throughout the animal kingdom. Kandel's (1984) research on the intracellular mechanisms of the sea snail (Aplysia Californica) demonstrates cellular reactions involved in anxietylike response, but also in learning-habituation and sensitization.

Clearly, the process of putting emotions into gestures, sounds, and finally words is a basic one. Language can be viewed as an outgrowth or a manifestation of emotions. Human intellectual development can be viewed as an enormous elaboration of a function that was first and most urgently related to the signaling of affective states.

The process of affective and language development in the human being is so complex that, although we see signs of emotions in the first weeks of life, the unfolding is slow and complex (Demos, 1974; Basch, 1976). The slowness of the development of human affects makes it dependent on learning and related to the intrapsychic process of attachment to the caretaking object and to attachment behavior. As Bowlby (1969, 1977) and many of his followers (e.g., Ainsworth, Blehar, Walters, and Wall, 1978; Parkes and Stevenson-Hinde, 1982) have pointed out, crying, calling, and reaching are the major infantile manifestations of attachment, serving to preserve contact with the mothering parent. For this reason, I want to review once more the relationship of affect development to the all-important process off self- and object-representation formation.

AFFECTS AND SELF- AND OBJECT-REPRESENTATIONS

As noted, a number of psychoanalysts, (e.g., Schur, 1955; Novey, 1961; Krystal, 1962; Engel, 1962a; Krystal and Raskin, 1970) have postulated a primary type of affect in the newborn and in infancy. Their assumption is that "primary, undifferentiated affects" indicate only satiety or need, pleasure or unpleasure, connected to the environment and within the organism (Engel, 1963). Prior to the establishment of self representation and object representation as consciously separated entities (at least for the first three months), pain can not be differentiated from the painful affects or sensations from feelings (Schafer, 1964).

The modification of affects in terms of the developmental lines of verbalization and desomatization, as well as affect differentiation, *takes place in the context of the evolving self- and object-representations*. The good-mothering parent takes pride in discerning the earliest differentiation in the affect-related vocalizations of the infant, "rewards" the baby by responding instantly. The gratification of the infant's need with dispatch, along with the parent's pleasure in the child's demonstrating a repertoire of vocal, mimetic, and postural communications corresponding to affective states, promotes the specialization of vocalization and eventually, verbalization. Thus, as Basch (1976) pointed out, affect "is in fact an onto- and phylogenetic early form of communication" and as such is basic for cognition and, by exercising a guiding function or later cognitive development, provides the motive power for both maturation and pathologic development" (p. 776). Izard (1982) gives us his timetable for signals to the mothering parent: the infant can signal surprise and anger by three to four months, and fear by six months of age. Dahl (1982) added that by ten months the baby is able to express all eight emotions and four boundary states that Dahl had put together in an "affect palette." He felt that *love* is not one of them, as it is too complex and so it is learned quite late. Kernberg (1982a) stressed that the early affective "communicative functions" will have a "profound influence on the development of subtle and deepening interactions between the infant and mother" (p. 201).

From these considerations we get a picture of affects as signals to the caretaker and gradually to oneself about the way things are going. More correctly, these early affective responses become the core of the early self and of object representations. To appreciate fully the implications of this observation, we have to renounce Freud's (1900, p. 566) early view (still commonly held by analysts) that affects are always "attached" to ideas or symbolic representations of memory traces or perceptions. There is increasing evidence supporting J. M. Jones's (1984) view that affect can provide a prelogical, nonlogical, nonsymbolic, noncognitive (analogue-computerlike) evaluation and registration in the mind.

Such purely affective registrations and memories, the only ones available in infancy, continue to be a major mode of information processing and object and self-representation throughout life (Hadley, 1983; Stern, 1983). Thus, early object experiences have to be understood in purely affective terms. In this context we might once more review Schmale's (1964) seminal work on the genetic development of affect. Schmale felt that a sense of unity with the mother is a precursor of bliss, whereas recognition of the impossibility of controlling the mother at all times is a forerunner of helplessness. Schmale related helplessness to the recognition of the limits of oneself, that is, to the establishment of self- and object-representations of some constancy. He thought, however, that Jones's (1929) concept of aphanisis, as well as such reactions as Engel's (1962a) "depression-withdrawal," were also evolved at this developmental stage and were closely related to helplessness.

The differentiation of object and self, however, involves additional challenges and opportunities as the various roles and self-representations develop. The development of speech in the second year of life is an "organizer of the psyche" (Spitz, 1959, cited in Schmale, 1964, p. 38) and is of special interest to the development of affect because of the possibility of verbalization and progressive desomatization. Also during the second year of life, with the development of mobility and initiative, the child discovers that "self-initiated" activities can produce gratification and thus generate a feeling of being virtuous and feeling good. When the child's activity meets with disapproval and punishment, the child experiences guilt. Guilt, then, is defined as an affective reaction stemming from the awareness that danger from the outside has been produced by the way in which the object was related to (Schmale, 1964).

Toddlers in the midst of conflicts over autonomy and self-control, discover that success brings pride and failure brings shame. At the same time, the young child discovers the power of improving skills as well as producing pleasurable and gratifying self-experiences.

We must expect that every self- and object-perception, every selfor object-experience, as well as the recognition of separateness, provides an affective memory trace. At the same time, these developments involve affect matura-tion. The interactions and responses are experienced in resonance with increasingly specific affect forms and more consistently recognizable affect signals of a mimetic, postural, and vocal nature on the part of the baby and caregiver.

Lichtenberg (1983) has rendered us a service of inestimable importance by searching the writings of neonatologists and others who observe and interpret infant behavior. It is evident from this report that the classical psychoanalytic models of the process of intrapsychic genesis is too schematic. The formation of self- and object-representation is more complex than has been thought. Instead of a symbiotic infant, seldom emerging from a state of primary narcissism, we now find the baby actively involved in the regulation of his states and rhythms and capable of recognizing his parents from the start. Stimulus seeking, gaze fixation, and mutually established rhythms of attention and inattention are established early. Using subtle cues, such as eye contact, pupil size, and concomitants of alertness and consciousness, the researcher begins to distinguish individual and gender-related characteristics in the child's first half year of life. Lichtenberg believes that the neonate is more highly differentiated than has previously been thought and that the complexity of the process ("the steps") in development of perceptive-cognitive functions necessary to form an intrapsychic representation have been underestimated; therefore, the toddler can show a remarkable degree of *"behavioral"* activity. We need not assume that a constant, reliable object representation has been formed (p. 57), nor is there necessarily any degree of reflective self-awareness.

Lichtenberg considers the implications of Emde's (1981) and Stechler and Kaplan's (1980) work, which indicates that there is an affective monitoring between child and both parents. Beyond mere affect communication, there is an attempt to *influence* the affective state of the partner in baby–mother, and later toddler–parent, interaction. From birth, infants "respond" to parental emotions and affective responses just as they do to colors (Stern, 1983). However, our observations of such phenomena do not tell us how these experiences register intrapsychically and what memory traces they leave. In particular, Lichtenberg (1983) challenges himself (and coincidentally psycho-analysis as a whole) to confront these new data derived from direct infant observations with inquiries about self-awareness and the possibility of recog-nition of a self-experience in these crucial affective interactions.

Building on McKinnon's (1979) conceptionns of auditory-sequential se-mantic forms, Lichtenberg observes that the rules regulating human relations (characterized by separateness, objectivity discreteness, social form, and ritual) depend on the monitoring of one's own emotions and mental activity as well as those of the person one relates to. To this I would add that one monitors one's *experiences* (one's own psychic representations) of the other person, as well as the psychic reality of one's own affective and other responses.

The ability of children to begin to construct a psychic representation of themselves and their objects is based, as we are told by a survey of numerous infant researchers (Stern, 1983), on the development of "intersubjectivity." It is assumed that

> sometime between the seventh and the ninth month . . . [the child makes] a momentous discovery, namely, that he or she can share with another a state of mind such as intention. In other words, the infant develops a "theory of interfaceable minds." This has several implications: that the infant has the ability to impute, unawares, an internal mental state to another; that he or she has some apperception, at the moment of a particular internal mental state; and that the interfacing, in the sense of sharing or reciprocally manifesting these two states is not only possible, but a goal to be sought [pp. 18–19].

I have pointed out repeatedly the maturation of affective states along certain developmental lines, and that this process, although largely "preprogrammed," is essentially affected by the subjective experiences of the infant. With each psychosexual state, there is an elaboration of a wealth of fantasy solutions, which modify the urgency of impulses. As verbal skills develop as part of the fantasy elaboration, the precision and effectiveness of words show language to be the preferable way of handling affects. Each psychosexual state, each psychosexual crisis, each increment in significant relations, concepts, and modalities promotes the verbalization and desomatization of affects and their mastery.

With each increment in the child's ability to communicate and receive communications, parents renew their attempts to promote affect verbalization, desomatization, and differentiation. The child's blossoming intellectual capacities present him with an elaboration of the nature of object relations and, with this, a progressive increase in the complexity of fantasies, the cognitive aspect of affects, and accompanying desomatization and verbalization.

By considering the newer findings from direct observation of parent-infant interaction, we can go beyond our earlier statements that an attentive and responsive parent directly rewards affect differentiation, verbalization, and desomatization. Matters are infinitely more complicated. Some differentiation of the basic affect can be demonstrated even in the four-month-old baby. The mother actually paces the developmental process by treating the child as "the person he is about to become." Stern (1983) has commented that this parenting attitude involves an "alignment with the possible and the probable"

(p. 20). The mothering parent, in speech, gesture, and behavior, presents patterns that are a few months ahead of the child's development. The effective mother stays just the right distance ahead in, say, the use of language, to facilitate the child's utilization of her pattern, switching from the actual state of the infant's performance to the potential that the child may fill. Thus, there is an interaction between the mother's expectation and the child's potential that promotes maximum development of the child's potential.

4
Adolescence and Affect Development

AFFECT DEVELOPMENT DURING ADOLESCENCE

The richness and variety of growth and development during adolescence defy even a cursory survey of the challenges and opportunities for affect maturation. Therefore, I shall discuss only one aspect of affect development during adolescence—adolescence as a time when the ability to grieve can develop. Giving up both the infantile attachment to the parents and the attachment to childhood self-representations, as exclusive of adult self-representations, represents the largest single task of adolescence. This accomplishment not only permits the adolescent to choose new love objects rather than resorting to displacement of incestuous yearnings, but also represents a point of maturation in affects (Katan, 1951; Zetzel, 1965; Wolfenstein, 1966).

Acquiring the ability to grieve effectively has profound effects on a number of functions. The ability to grieve is the prerequisite and limiting factor in a person's ability to give up various aspects of infantile omnipotence as elaborated in a variety of fantasies. Grieving enables one to accept loss and to diminish grandiose views of oneself; it becomes the guardian of reality testing, which would have to be sacrificed if painful self-awareness could not be accepted. An inverse relationship exists between the ability to mourn and the potential for becoming stuck in depressive reactions based on the discrepancy between the ego ideal and ideal self, on one hand, and one's self-perception, on the other. There is also the potential to deal, both in adolescence and afterward, with such losses as the loss of the breast and of the symbiotic relationship with the omnipotently experienced object. As mentioned earlier, I believe that these losses are neither mourned nor resolved in childhood, but either remain as "affective debits" to be dealt with later or persist as lifelong yearnings to regain the ideal mother and recapture the imaginary childhood paradise.

63

In order for the adolescent to be able to engage in the work of mourning, however, the developments in affect that I have reviewed must have taken place. If the affects are not adequately verbalized, desomatized, and differentiated, they become too threatening and overwhelm organized functions; they are so close to the infantile affects that they pose the danger of the return of childhood psychic trauma.

The occurrence of massive psychic traumatization in infancy or toddler age hinders the development of affects and makes the expectation of the return of the traumatic state a constant danger. Under such circumstances, affects are experienced as signs of the impending return of the trauma and therefore are dreaded. To the extent that emotions remain undifferentiated and mostly physical they are not utilizable in a specific sense, as when one clearly recognizes sorrow in response to loss. The vague, mixed, somatic affective responses call attention only to themselves rather than to their meaning, so the response tends to be the desire to block them, for instance, with drugs. Thus, developments in the nature of the affects and of affect tolerance during childhood, latency, and early puberty are specific factors in making effective the work of mourning in adolescence and later.

A number of studies on the acquisition of language skills, in particular adolescents' consciously recognizing, identifying, and describing their feelings, have reported certain individual, hereditary, and even gender-related differences in the rate of verbalization of affects, as well as their localization in parts of the self. For example, Lewis, Wolman, and King (1971) found that school children, ages five to thirteen, exhibited an increasing independence from external clues for the recognition and verbalization of emotions. They observed:

> When girls internalize their emotions they tend to be more visceral and less cerebral in the body sites they associate with certain feelings. . . . In general, the older children of both sexes show more of a tendency to describe emotions as ideas or thoughts than as bodily sensations [p. 1496].

Both Lewis et al. and their discussant Gottschalk (1971) observed that boys were increasingly concerned with both castration and separation anxiety, while girls who were nearing adolescence were prone to internalization of and concern with shame.

Affective development does not take place in the "bosom of the family" exclusively; the child has opportunities to augment home experiences by contact with peers, teachers, and other social forces, for example, television and movies. Especially during adolescence these social influences come into play with regard to affect expression. Lazarus, Averill, and Orton (1970) summarized the ways in which societies shape emotional experience and perception:

. . . (1) the perception or appraisal of emotional stimuli . . . (2) outward expression of emotion . . . *even for those gestures, e.g., crying and laughing, which are generally considered to be biologically determined* . . . (3) shaping of social relationships and systems of judgement which emotional concepts presuppose . . . (4) conventional forms of behavior, e.g., mourning rites, courting and marriage rituals, and institutionalized aggression as in athletics and warfare . . . [pp. 215–16].

Ethnic differences have been demonstrated in responses to pain (Tursky and Sternbach, 1967), which seems to underline Schacter's (1967) contention that social context influences how one interprets one's bodily state in light of the emotion being experienced.

Affect tolerance develops along a line parallel to the development in the nature of affect. Essentially, affect tolerance relates to the handling of affects—developing ease and comfort, as well as reflective self-awareness, in relation to affects. Together, the development of the nature of affect and the development of affect tolerance make possible the attenuation of affects, turning them into moods and making them suitable for use as affect signals. Regression, where the emotions again become undifferentiated, deverbalized, and resomatized, may occur in some or all of the functions that are involved in affect tolerance or in the nature of the emotions themselves.

THE DEVELOPMENT OF AFFECT TOLERANCE IN ADOLESCENCE

The acquisition of the patterns of handling affects by learning and identification that plays such a significant part in the child's emotional growth always raises the question: Under what circumstances can the child exercise the role that the parents have been taking during his childhood? This question is an extension of the crucial point mentioned earlier that one needs, in addition to learning ways to comfort and control oneself, to *feel* that it is permissible to take over all parental functions. That this task is rarely accomplished completely is demonstrated by the common need for religion, inspiration, magic, superstition, and drugs, all of which have one common ingredient: they are all ways of overcoming the inner repressive barriers by which essential self-caring functions have become inaccessible as a result of being reserved for the object representation.

The fundamental operations related to this freedom to use one's own resources take place during the separation of the self-representation from the object-representation in early childhood; they are, however, subject to repeated revisions. Such revisions occur most frequently and conspicuously during adolescence, when the youngster must practice assuming an adult role and must learn to function with increasing self-sufficiency. Each such opportunity, whether minor or major, such as going away to school, presents a challenge and tests the degree to which a young person has been able to assume the exercise of functions hitherto reserved for parents. Pleasurable affects must be kept within manageable bonds, a process that may be conceptualized as the adequate function of paternally derived aspects of the superego. The youngster also needs the freedom to assume self-comforting attitudes in dealing with painful affects and related states (e.g., tiredness and boredom). The failure to take over these functions creates a serious handicap, which manifests itself clinically in a variety of syndromes.

Case Illustration

> Mrs. J. presented herself as a person with a variety of difficulties, many of which were related to her narcissistic personality organization. She was practically crippled by her impairment in affect tolerance. As a child, she had handled her emotions in an isolated manner, with somatic "attacks," which took the form of severe migraine headaches accompanied by days of vomiting. As a student, she could bear neither the tension required for concentrated study nor the anxiety of examinations, and so she failed in high school. Eventually she tried to study nursing but discovered that she could not stand the "bad smells" of sick people; she quit, rather than force herself to acquire a tolerance for unpleasant smells or tasks. She then tried to become a teacher, but, when confronted with children who were difficult, she decided that she could not bear the stress and gave that up too. She married, essentially expecting to function as a naughty child and hoping that her husband would be an ever-forgiving, indulgent mother, who would be impervious to her rages. Her inability to tolerate bad smells and her fear of dirt, combined with her feeling that she could not bear the self-discipline and deprivation involved in work, made it most difficult for her to function as a homemaker. Her idea of work was derived from certain clichés about enjoying one's work. It became necessary in the therapy to ask her such simple questions as: "If work was all fun, why would they pay one to do it?"

Her resulting inability to function adequately intensified her problem of envy. All of these problems made it most unlikely that she could either work in the analysis or be able to tolerate the affect necessary to progress in it. For instance, she had a severe phobia[1] of snakes. However, her attitude was that the way to handle this phobia was for the whole world to conspire to protect her from any exposure to snakes—not only live ones, but even pictures of

---

1. It is to be noted that this was a fear of her *disgust* of snakes, not a phobia in the hysterical sense.

them—for the mere representation of a snake filled her with dread, disgust, and horror. The idea of becoming a mother filled her with so many types of fears that she rejected the possibility categorically. Thus, early in her analysis, dealing with affect tolerance became, of necessity, the major interest and activity.

Despite the popularity of the view that a defect in affect tolerance can be explained by a failure of introjection or "transmuted internalization" (Kohut, 1971, p. 49), I must reiterate that we are speaking of a block in the development or exercise of an inborn potential. Some of Mrs. J.'s problems were indeed handled in terms of narcissistic (mirroring or grandiose) transferences. However, it was also necessary to interpret her feeling so that she did feel free to assume these "forbidden" roles. She wanted me to follow her script by playing the role of the permission-granting mother. She needed, instead, to accomplish the major task of adolescence that had not been accomplished at the appropriate time: mourning for her infantile attachment to her parents and to her childhood self-representation and renouncing the infantile models of the world.

If adolescence is to be successful, the youngster must be able to bear such mourning, a process that enables one to begin to tolerate depression, a task that is, however, completed later. Inability to bear mourning makes it impossible to change self-representations from ideal to realistic ones and establishes a tendency to use denial and projection. Petty and I found, in working with patients who had lost an organ, function, or attribute of themselves, that if they could not go through the process of grieving for the loss, they became enmeshed in denial or some form of self-compensatory compulstion (Krystal and Petty, 1961). The development in adolescence of the ability to mourn is but one of the milestones in building affect tolerance, albeit a monumental one. Wolfenstein (1966) has likened adolescence to

> a trial mourning, in which there is a gradual decathexis of the first love objects, accompanied by sad and painful feelings, with reality testing of memories confirming the irrevocability of the childhood past. It is only after this initiation into mourning has been undergone that the individual becomes able to perform the work of mourning in response to later losses [p. 122].

The adolescent renunciation of childhood privileges and views of oneself makes possible the advancement of conscious self-integration, self-possession, and *self-awareness of one's affects as signals to oneself*. This development is neither easy nor satisfactorily accomplished by most of people. Such an extension of "owning one's soul" is often acquired only in an analysis. It is the key step in the development of adult affect and affect tolerance. Zetzel (1965a) refers to this very process: "However slight its overt expression may be, the experience of depression is a prerequisite for optimal maturation.

Depressive affect comparable to contained anxiety occurs in response to loss, disappointment, frustration, illness, retirement, and other painful, though inevitable, experiences" (p. 87). This developmental approach to both anxiety and depression highlights the effect of early object relations on basic ego functions and the tolerance of affect.

In addition to learning to bear grief, the adolescent is confronted with challenges and opportunities to practice tolerating a variety of other affective states. Doing work and experiencing nongratification also require that one tolerate some boredom, or even discomfort and pain, and that one give oneself credit for accomplishments, small and large, and thus exercise a role previously filled by an appreciative parent. This ability is a "cushion" in facing failure or simply lack of recognition and is intimately related to the ability to tolerate anxiety and shame. The counterphobic and exhibitionistic tendencies of the adolescent are resources that permit temporary relief but should become less necessary with time.

Another temporary device is the adolescent's narcissistic invulnerability. Optimally, as one progresses into young adulthood and maturity, one reaches the point where one can tolerate depression. But only some people in their maturity or old age are able to renounce enough of their need to deny their own death to be able to mourn the loss of parts and eventually all of themselves. Erikson (1959) makes this point in terms of the psychosocial crisis of "integrity vs. despair," in which one develops the ability to face not being. Schafer has (1973) discussed some of the struggles of the adolescent in relation to re-experiencing affects related to separation-individuation. He points out that adolescents are especially prone to experience their feelings as "substances," often fecal ones, which "accordingly may be withheld or expelled and gotten rid of or destroyed; or they may fill one up and either explode or leak (or spill) out. Or perhaps they are oral substances (milk, poison, vomitus) or psychosexual things (urine, semen, babies)" (p. 46).

These primary-process mediated conceptions of affect are ubiquitous, making it necessary for the analyst working with adolescents (and adults in therapy) to proceed in the way that sex education is handled in child analysis. The discovery of unconscious fantasies about affect is often the key to understanding some adolescent activities, whether drug taking, counterphobic exploits, or sexual promiscuity. The adolescent's attitude toward emotions, along with the manner in which they are handled, may be the single greatest hindrance to the completion of his developmental tasks.

I have already alluded to the fact that affect tolerance requires lifelong development. Adolescence is not the last opportunity, or crisis, for the emotions. Young adulthood presents renewed challenges and opportunities to become fully independent, assume a parental role, and so on. Every life crisis presents such opportunities; calamity is opportunity in work clothes. But it may be surprising to consider middle age and even old age as developmental phases as well: we are used to thinking of developmental epochs as preparation for some future time, when life begins in earnest. Nevertheless, every event of one's life, including dying, presents one with a new combination of affects, which one can learn to handle with grace. For, in the last analysis, what is commonly taken as a fear of calamity, disaster, or even death can be seen to be the fear of one's own affects. Affect tolerance is the ability to take our reaction off the signal and put it on to the meaning, the import, of that signal.

THE EFFECT OF TRAUMATIC ANTECEDENTS ON SOME ADOLESCENT PROCESSES

The major challenges of adolescence involve the operation and utilization of affects. Of all the aspects of adolescence, I want to highlight the process of separation-individuation and the establishment of ego identity (Erikson, 1956). The revival of the oedipal constellation necessitates final relinquishment of attachments to the infantile representations of the parents and the infantile views of oneself. In this revival, the object representation formed in the preoedipal phases becomes important to the outcome of the process. It is a psychoanalytic commonplace that the ambivalence toward the lost object makes the process of mourning much more difficult, possibly resulting in depression rather than successful adjustment. Persons who are disposed to drug addiction are known for their inability to deal with losses and for being vulnerable to any loss, real or symbolic (Krystal and Raskin, 1970; Krystal, 1978b).

There are a number of reasons for the difficulties the addictive person has with dealing with loss. As I mentioned earlier, many persons who have a tendency to substance dependence demonstrate through their addictive behavior that they have a great fear of the object, which they also crave (Krystal, 1978b). We can surmise that a great deal of splitting and difficulty in integration follows infantile psychic trauma and that the severe ambivalence makes mourning more difficult. To the extent that the object is experienced as hostile and dangerous, the mourning is likely to be complicated by guilt and become pathological. Ordinarily, we would be concerned here about the development of depression, but, in the presence of impairment of affect tolerance and alexithymia, the choice is between a "psychosomatic" response and the use of drugs. The aftereffects of infantile psychic trauma can be expected to complicate greatly, make more difficult, or even prevent the successful completion of the work of mourning so necessary in adolescence. Thus, in approaching the adolescent, we have to be alert for the kind of object representation and self-representations we found in the adult addicts and interpret these vigorously.

Failing to do so will militate against the crucial operation of adolescence, which consists of giving up attachments to infantile and childhood self- and object-representations. Only through a process analogous to mourning can these attachments be given up. The capacity to carry out effective grieving is the key to the acceptance of a realistic and unified view of oneself and to making peace with one's childhood turmoil and disappointments (Katan, 1961; Wolfenstein, 1966). *Adolescent disillusionment and grieving for the loss of the ideal prototypes are simultaneous and virtually synonymous with this mourning process.* The increment in these affective pressures on the adolescent accounts for many of the characteristic attitudes and behaviors of this stage in life.

POSTTRAUMATIC EFFECTS ON AFFECT TOLERANCE IN ADOLESCENCE

But in adolescence the effects of traumatic experiences become a major problem. Disturbances in affect tolerance, which are conspicuous when they appear in adults, have to be looked for in adolescents, in whom there is an irregular, sometimes rapid development of the ability to bear painful affects and states. In posttraumatic states, the reactions to *having* the emotion tend to be maladaptive. The fear of emotions, the requirement that anxiety be absent if self-respect is to be maintained, the tendency to depression whenever everything is not well—all of these perpetuate vicious circles that prolong and deepen painful affect states. The result is that the lives of many youngsters are regulated by the need to avoid painful emotions.

Impairment in affect tolerance renders the adolescent unable to deal with the increased excitement of burgeoning sexual, social, and work-related activities. But the ability to mourn is based on the capacity to bear grief. One useful definition of depression is that it is a condition in which mourning is initiated but cannot be completed. A major obstacle observable in adolescence is that the slightest exposure to grief is so dreaded that any chance of its continuing has to be prevented. This need provides the motivation to maintain a manic defense against the depressive affects by chemical means if necessary.

A major issue in affect tolerance, then, is how affects are interpreted: whether one has learned that one's emotions are signals to oneself and are self-limited in duration, or whether one experiences them as dangerous attacks. I have already pointed out that in posttraumatic states *affects are experienced as heralds of the return of the infantile trauma state.* This dread is overwhelming and difficult to modify. Usually, those who suffer it have no idea just what they expect to happen. Discovering the verbal elements of untoward reactions to affects is an important early step in dealing with affect intolerance. Again, some of the elements of the reaction to having the emotions must be reconstructed and supplied to these patients.

Since, for the most part, adolescents are not aware either of the history of the psychic trauma or of the meaning of their fears, there is a special challenge in explaining to them how their emotions differ from other people's and how they have been reacting to affects. They do not understand the implications of their fears. They fail to recognize the *meaning* of their affects. Frequently they are not at all aware of the cognitive element of the fears and therefore have no knowledge of the subjective experience of a "feeling." If they recognize that they are frightened, either they say that they fear death or they see danger in everything around them. The therapist's understanding of the cognitive content of the fears, based on the assumption that some infantile disaster took place, aims at reconstructing the intrapsychic experience, not the "external" situation, to which there is frequently no clue. It is helpful, then, for the therapist to understand certain themes that can be assumed to be underlying such an adolescent's dread. The common themes in such situations are: (1) The painful affective states will get worse, reaching some undescribable crescendo of distress. This misery contains both physical and mental agonies, such as might be imagined from simultaneous stimulation of all possible points producing pain and distress. (2) The distress will be so terrible that the adolescent will pass the point of being able to be comforted or receive any relief from outside.. With this destruction of all "receptors" of comfort, there would be a gradual loss of all other functions, such as a sense of time; hence the expectation is that the unspeakable suffering would go on forever and ever. (3) This last step may not be present in all cases, but some patients dread the onset of the catatonoid reaction, experienced as either becoming "dead" or "freezing," that is, developing cataleptic rigidity, losing the capacity for initiative, becoming physically rigid or numb. Fear of *disintegration* of the self in terms of its separate functions may or may not coincide and may represent a different preoccupation. In these cases we are dealing with the fear of dying, of "losing" oneself, of becoming a "zombie," or similar descriptions of the cataleptic process.

The therapist has to understand that the patient's fears are based on something real, namely, the expectation of the return of infantile trauma. The fears are, in fact, the only "memory" of the infantile disaster. Although the person expects that the entire unbearably painful experience of infantile psychic trauma will return, it, of course, will not. The fear that the pain will go on forever represents the "memory" of the loss or the absence of the sense of time in the original traumatic state.

There are inborn mechanisms that protect adults from the return of such unbearable states. These are forms of numbness and include depersonalization, derealization, modification of consciousness, and, ultimately, fainting. These reactions have to be understood as defensive in nature, otherwise they may become additionally alarming. But the most important information to be learned from the investigation of experiences is that such people have been living in dread of the return of the infantile traumatic state—an eventuality that *cannot happen.*

Having established the nature and meaning of the most profound fear, one can watch for the patient's reactions to *having* an emotion and help the patient to discover the maladaptive aspects of it. The maturation of affects as a major aspect of adolescence has been emphasized by Jacobson (1957). Schafer (1973) has written about the ways affects are experienced in adolescence: how they are interpreted to be like substances that can be dealt with in a variety of ways in relation to the significant objects. He has particularly highlighted the experiences and unconscious fantasies of the adolescent in regard to separation-individuation and the formation of self-representations. Writing about the "assumptions" the adolescent makes about emotions, Schafer (p. 46) noted that the youngster is likely to experience mental processes as substances that can be used in the contents of predominant fantasies.

In exploring the problems of impaired affect tolerance, one has to distinguish the problems of the fear of (or other maladaptive reaction to) all affects as opposed to problems in handling specific affects. Particularly difficult may be reactions to feeling shame, which is marked in all adolescents, particularly those who are drug dependent and for whom shame involves the very idea of whether one is worthy to survive (Wurmser, 1981). Another area of affects to look out for is the usually pleasurable, or "proleptic," emotions (Spitz, 1963), which may be experienced as dangerous; this dread may preclude or destroy any potentially good relationship. In fact, despite professional opinion to the contrary, the affect most dreaded is not aggression, but love, particularly in adolescents. This dread may be one of the necessary reasons for us to give some attention to the development of these processes.

For beyond the most obvious aspects of affect tolerance, once we liberate ourselves from the prevailing view that psychic trauma represents a quantitative "overloading of the circuits" and instead recognize that traumatization is related to *meaning,* then we become aware that there is a processing of perception that involves the aggression and affective functions. Each person has a particular style of perception, cognition, recall, and dealing with stressful information, which constitute the adult type of a stimulus barrier (Krystal, 1970). This unique style is consolidated in adolescence, and it may be the product of the very process we are discussing, namely, the adolescent's trial of mourning and the ability to deal with the painful affects related to the second separation-individuation. With it, one achieves a consolidation of one's self-representation (Erikson's, 1959, "ego identity"). Many of the important components of the personality (character style), which are established at this time, are related to the ability to handle affects in a comfortable manner. Thus, to speak of affect tolerance is also to address the establishment of significant personality traits.

Naturally, working with fears based on unconscious fantasies is a slow process, which is further retarded by the distrust and ambivalence the adolescent is bound to experience. One must be prepared for frequent repetition of these explanations and demonstrations.

The Model Affect

CONCEPTIONS OF AFFECTS

I will not attempt here a complete review of the history of the ways in which emotions have been described and conceptualized. Freud's view of emotions, which is the one most familiar to psychoanalysts, simply reflected the physiological and psychiatric attitudes of his age. It was burdened with the mind–body schism and with a mechanistic attitude toward the body processes. Thinking of mental function as a reflex arc produced a consideration of emotions as discharge phenomena.

Rapaport (1953) demonstrated that each phase of the development of psychoanalytic theory left its imprint on theories of affect. Some elements of each phase remain part of current workaday assumptions, although the original theoretical framework has been renounced. I shall isolate some of these residuals and discuss them briefly.

THE DISCHARGE THEORY AND THE TOPOGRAPHIC VIEW OF AFFECTS

Rapaport (1953) demonstrated that each phase of the development of passed on virtually unchanged from Freud's earliest theorizing, when the theory of cathartic hypnosis and psychoanalysis were not yet differentiated. Even in the second period, when unconscious fantasies were the center of interest, affect continued to be viewed as related to drive cathexis. The entire original theory of anxiety represented, after all, a model of converting libido into an affect for the purpose of discharge (Freud, 1898). In Freud's view, then, affects were physiological discharge phenomena, which could become attached, although fairly loosely, to "ideas." The cleavage between affects and ideas and the weakness of the attachment between them were considered to be demonstrated in such defenses against emotions as displacement (Freud, 1926).

One problem resulting from the conceptual splitting of mental processes was the difficulty of dealing with unconscious affects. In "The Interpretation of Dreams," Freud (1900) said that he "presupposes . . . [that affects are] a motor or secretory function" (p. 582)—by implication, therefore, always a conscious phenomenon, although he envisioned that the cognitive aspects of affects could be unconscious. Freud encountered many theoretical difficulties, as in trying to deal with the possibility of an unconscious sense of guilt.

The residue of the topographic theory hampers the free view of emotions and creates problems in two areas: (1) It separates the organic unity of affects from their cognitive aspects; and (2) it portrays consciousness as a yes-or-no phenomenon. Since consciousness represents a continuum, a spectrum, the psychoanalyst's concern is the form, degree, and manner in which emotions become conscious.

The relationship between the experience of affects and the state of consciousness is a complex and mutual one. On one hand, emotions help determine the quality and state of consciousness; on the other hand, modifications of consciousness are sought in order to handle emotions (Krystal and Raskin, 1970). Rapaport's (1951) research on the character of cognition in falling asleep and waking adds even more dimensions to the variations of consciousness. Of special interest are the dreamlike phenomena experienced under the influence of hallucinogenic drugs; these phenomena show that affect experiences also vary with consciousness modification. Some of these experiences are reminiscent of childhood febrile states, in the sense that experiences in various parts of the body are sensations that might be part of emotional experiences, except that these sensations are only physical or represent fragments of the usual affect experience. But the main reason people take drugs "for kicks" is to modify the affect experience, in many ways beyond the traditionally expected manner of splitting ideas from feelings (Krystal and Raskin, 1970).

Clearly, affect memory is older than cognitive and symbol memory and persists as a separate and essential function throughout life (see, e.g., Stern, 1983). It is also true that affect states regulate cognitive and other information-processing operations. I am referring to state-related memories. Since memories are related to the state of consciousness in which they are acquired and may be retrievable only in that state, it follows that affective states function similarly to regulate perception, registration, problem solving, evaluation, and decision making. Hence, depressed individuals cannot bring back to consciousness their "happy" memories (Ianzito et al., 1974; Bowers, 1981; Hirschfield et al., 1983; Silverman, Weingarten, and Post, 1983) and cannot make advantageous decisions or moves. Thus they perpetuate their depressive state. A major obstacle to understanding these interactions was derived from Freud's mistaken idea (1915b, p. 177) that affects must be, by their nature, conscious.

Affects function as constant, but "subliminal," signals in the processing of perception and impulses on the preconscious level. Consequently, we become aware of an emotion only seldom—when, for example, an affect becomes intense enough to force itself into our consciousness. Of course, every mental event, every idea and memory carries its own affective coloring. However, that too is usually so close to the "midline" of the quiescent security state that it is ignored. Again, only an "intense" and "outstanding" emotional reaction gets our attention. Under those circumstances, the "expressive," that is, physiological, aspect of the emotion is so impressive that it tends to be equated with the whole affect experience. This is one reason why Freud (1926) considered affects to be "discharge" phenomena.

In trying to differentiate unconscious affects from latent ones, Pulver (1971) concluded that the very concept of affect is involved. Under the clinical approach, which dominated Freud's work, present-day psychoanalysts view affects as a periodic discharge reaction, varying in intensity from an "attack" to a moderate or even slight, but, limited phenomenon. In attempting a systematic view of emotions, it is useful to consider that there is an *affective component to every mental event*. Emotions thus viewed are a constant manifestation of the analyst's evaluative function. Affect is best viewed as a *quality* of all experience (Schafer, 1972). It follows that the affective dimension of every mental event is the inevitable, albeit often minimal, accompaniment of every cognitive experience. The consciousness, registration, and evaluation of the affective aspects of mental function would, of course, be subject to variation along several gradients. Greenblatt (1963) reflected on the continuity of feelings:

> People have spoken of expression of emotion as though it were a discrete, time-limited act. Now, as a matter of introspection, it is difficult to assume that emotion arises as discrete events; it seems rather that emotional value is attached to almost every moment of time. Certainly in the conscious waking state we find prevailing background mood, tones, or qualities of affective experience at all times; and in dreams, emotional meaning of some significance appears to be attached to every dream event. On this affective background more or less discrete emotional events take place, some rising as modest swells over the background, others appearing in sharper wave forms, and some so large and strong as to dwarf into apparent insignificance the background from which they arise [pp. 199–200].

A novelist (Nietzke, 1972) used the analogy between the weather and mood in its ultimate form by portraying the various emotional states of the protagonist as a condition of "weatherlessness." Clearly, no state of emotionlessness can exist any more than can a condition of "no weather."

The "discharge" metaphor of affect did not, of course, originate with economic theory. On the contrary, it was a way to "scientize"—in the same way as the "humors" of Galen—a subjective experience of relief that had been reflected in folklore, poetry, and philosophy for ages. Perhaps that fact accounts for the ready acceptance of the economic view. It is tempting to think of affects, especially anger, in terms of anal analogies, as a substance to be eliminated. The metaphoric use of the discharge phenomenon is especially apt for certain subjective experiences and wishes, especially those related to riddance. Knapp (1967) commented on the tenacity with which we link aggression with anal metaphors. The fateful coincidence that toddlers develop their reaction formations to both soiling and aggression at the same time seems to determine our lifelong proclivity to experience aggression in excremental terms. Perhaps the achievement of a sense of autonomy and self-control requires that aggression be experienced in these terms. But how is it possible for us to continue this view of aggression as a part of psychoanalytic theory?

This phenomenon has to be understood, too, as deriving from topographic and economic points of view. The economic point of view of metapsychology gives us the "discharge" metaphors in general. The topographic theory defines repression as being equivalent to rendering unconscious. As will be discussed in greater detail later in this chapter, aggressive impulses and affect can be repressed by depriving them of the conscious recognition of selfhood. In other words, whenever one experiences aggression as a vector directed toward an object rather than as a form of pain, it is because the aggression has been repressed.

CONSCIOUS EMOTIONAL CONTINENCE

Many of the metaphors that have become part of psychoanalytic lore involve the idea of elimination as the true meaning of the idea of affect "expression." All of them are related to the continuing use of the model of energy transformation, instead of information processing. Another source of difficulties in psychoanalytic approaches to affect stems from the use of anxiety as the model emotion (Novey, 1959). Novey felt that the choice of anxiety as the model affect had had most unfortunate consequences because anxiety was not a typical affect—"a theory of anxiety is not a theory of affects" (p. 94).

There were good historical reasons for the psychoanalytic preoccupation with anxiety. The editor of the *Standard Edition* (Freud, 1926), adding a list of Freud's papers dealing with anxiety, commented that "the topic of anxiety occurs in a very large number (perhaps in the majority) of Freud's writings" (p. 175). Anxiety is of special interest to the clinician—it is the most common presenting problem, the "danger signal" for all other affects in their signal function and for pain as well. And yet throughout his life, Freud kept insisting that anxiety developed when one's libidinal impulses were thwarted. Freud's wish to be able to translate the function of the mind into the conception of Newtonian physics obscured for a while the ultimate meaning of this insight. When he spoke (1893a) about conversion of the "libidinal cathexis of the instinctual impulses" into anxiety, it is not immediately clear that he was also referring to some affects. In his last published note (August 3, 1938), however, Freud (1938) made this meaning clear: "A sense of guilt also originates from *unsatisfied love* [emphasis mine], like hate. In fact, we have been obliged to derive every conceivable thing from that material: like economically self-sufficient states with their 'ersatz [substitute] products' " (p. 300).

Dorsey built his work on affect on this view: he claimed just as Freud did, that love is "all we got." Hence, he (1971a) prefaced his discussion of emotions: "Whenever *any* affect of mine arouses itself, its arousal merits my full appreciation as being my only momentary way of helping myself. Whatever *I live is deserving of my complete love, for it is that very living with which I preserve my life*" (p. xiii). Love becomes essential to survival because it is necessary in the tolerance of painful affects: "Only by loving when my flow of life seems unlovable can I feel my self-identity enlarging itself. Endurance begets endurance, furthering appetency for endurance, the very staying-power of life" (p. xvii).

Just as white light contains all the colors of the spectrum, so love encompasses all the feelings reflecting our living process. When we get a chance to observe it, as in self-healing or in promoting the expansion of the conscious recognition of our selfness, we are especially prone to equate it with life forces, or the full enjoyment of our identity and unity. Love is the affective state that is favorable to the achievement of the most comprehensive self-representation. This kind of self-representation includes the conscious recognition of the authorship of one's object representations. It is also, incidentally, the affect most conducive to the recognition of the essential nature of affects in general—that they are signals of our life processes.

Because of the pain inherent in the affects of anxiety, anger, sorrow, and the like, it becomes more difficult to see these dysphoric affects as indispensable bits of information necessary to one's conscious self-discipline. Thus, grief not only helps us to observe the "loss" of the object, but forces us to review our previous inability to recognize that very mental representation of the same object as a mental event of our own creation. In recognizing one's wholeness, "my grief helps to confront myself with the evidence that I *am* whatever I am mourning as gone. My appreciation for my wholeness is obscured when my attention is *compelled* by my grieving or fearing that some of me is 'lost,' but gradually my concern for this lost selfness reveals itself as the beginning of acknowledging its presence" (Dorsey, 1971a, p. 90).

In other words, beginning our affect studies with the recognition of the centrality of the concept of psychic reality, that is, that we must create every perception and memory, as well as every self- and object-representation, clarifies Freud's (1917) idea that mourning results in the "introjection of the object." The fact is that every perception, registration, memory, and mental representation is the product and creation of one's mental activities. Thus, if, as Freud suggested, one discovers only *after* the loss of the object that the object representation (plus the information about its loss) is safely ensconced in one's own mind, then the process of mourning is just a matter of correcting one's bookkeeping. With the onset of grieving, we experience the "return of the repressed," the pain of the aggression that was warded off in the original externalization.

If love is the affective experience of life affirmation and the acceptance of all aspects and events of our living, we can readily see that some developments in our lives are, by their painful nature or by their opposition to previously formed ideals, *difficult to love.* Hence love can be seen as the desire to feel one's present living as part of the self-representation, while hate is the desire to separate one's identity from that repulsive perception.

What one cannot accept as part of one's self-representation and life (history) one is forced to reject angrily and keep fighting against the recognition of its self-sameness. One can strengthen oneself by growing able to live (and integrate) *whatever* is difficult to love. In reviewing our mental contents, we encounter many memories, impulses, representations that we cannot accept easily and integrate lovingly. We must maintain our rejection and righteous indignation, and protest ever having had anything to do with them. Moreover, we must maintain vigilance lest they take over the good (idealized and purified) part of our self-representation.

We are using here Dorsey's idea of love as the model affect, and from it follows the view that other affects represent modified love. What we cannot accept lovingly and peaceably we must reject and alienate—but most of all we must denote it as "nonself." Our memories, wishes, representations of self and objects must be consciously (lovingly) accepted, tolerated, and utilized to advantage (adaptively) or handled by repression, isolation, or projection angrily and painfully.

Dorsey (1971a) embraces pain and unhappiness as a means to accomplish one's happiness. Unhappiness is seen as the denial, or lack of consciousness, of one's wholeness and integration.

> The basic importance of unhappiness, including pain, is that it indicates an individual is not making his self consciously happy or pleased in his psychological functioning [p. 110]. . . . My thesis that happiness is the natural expression of the *appreciated wholeness* of human being, that joy of living consists of *sensitive awareness* in the *unity* of human nature, does indicate that any life event serving to obscure the reality of

the integrity of the self be characterized as interference with conscious happiness [p. 129].

Pain and the painful affects can be lived only under protest and demand for relief, for they are signals of protest. However, it is advantageous to be able to utilize such affects as signals, to recognize them as part of one's own living, to heed them and live them lovingly—in other words, to develop to the maximum one's affect tolerance.

How would it be if instead of affect tolerance we strove to develop anesthesia? To do so is very tempting and frequently becomes the predomi- nant mode of living. In my work with Holocaust survivors, and persons in other posttraumatic states, I found the wish to forget and to benumb oneself to be the predominant one. At times survival was possible only at the price of continuation of affective anesthesia. In one case, where a man complained of being unable to work because of a loss of memory, I discovered a secret that he did not share with me: For almost a year he had been taken from place to place by a special S.S. Kommando. Their assignment was to dig up mass graves of whole towns and cover up the evidence by burning everything. On his return visit, I gave my patient advice borrowed from Carl Sandburg: "Sometimes a good forgettery is better than a good memory."

It is certain that every posttraumatic development necessitates the mainte- nance of intrapsychic barriers and numbness of varying degrees, but it seems to be so difficult to maintain conscious awareness of one's painful affects as the creation of one's own mind that we must question its value or necessity. What are the possible advantages of living all of one's pain and painful affects unconsciously? The motivation for self-numbing is that through it one can avoid being overwhelmed with the impact of a response to a perception and cognitive development. The element of the mental events that presents the danger is the affect.

In chapter 9, on trauma and affect, we find that affects can result in emergencies, or they may be part of the development of traumatic states. In the wake of traumatic experiences, or of warding off of trauma by denial, splitting of one's conscious self-recognition—the cognitive and affective blocking characteristic of alexithymia—is the rule. Giving up these defenses is painful and dangerous. We should reconsider carefully the advantages and utility of consciously living all of one's pain and painful affects and giving up the protection of numbing.

I must confess a bias in favor of extending my conscious self-awareness as much as possible. I expect that since every affect does have its life-affirming value, it can be viewed as self-love modified, suffering, or struggling. For this reason alone, one is at a disadvantage in blocking the conscious awareness to any affect. As Dorsey (1971a) put it:

To make my mind anaesthetic for my emotion carries with it all of the kind of hazard that I create when I make my "body ego" anaesthetic for its sensory experience. My emotionality is my standard human equipment. The reality that I am alive carries with it the power of my wish to live. My love of living is my love of my self. Whenever I create experience that I live with difficulty, the difficulty consists of my trouble in living it as lovable selfness [p. 129].

In this view, every emotion represents self-interest (self-love modified) or self-evidence. Owning up to all of our self-representation and object-representation is to recognize the full nature of our identity. Dorsey felt that the most difficult first step to this always difficult revelation lies in the recognition of the fact of emotional self-continence. However, maintaining conscious awareness of one's wholeness is always difficult because it entails assuming responsibility for and complete care of it. We see in self-observations and clinical studies that our lifestyles frequently involve denying possession or control of major parts of ourselves. Conscious recognition of ownership of one's own body is limited. It seems easier to feel guilty over any part of one's life than to assume conscious and positive responsibility for it. It is a mind-boggling paradox that the hardest thing for us to own up to is our own affective and cognitive expression. Equally astonishing is the consideration of the "artificial paradise" of self-numbing.

Dorsey (1971a) had his own way of advocating expansion of one's affect tolerance and affect verbalization and naming: "Substantial relief from my unhappiness (including pain) is secured only from my gradually discovering that it consists entirely of helpfulness of my own nature, that it is truth of my own existence, that I am able to live only by it and through it" (p. 38).

While we realize that self-numbing is necessary and has to be accepted lovingly as an indispensable part of one's self-medication, we might consider what in real life appears less self-evident: that it is beneficial to identify all the components, aspects, meanings, and derivations of one's pain. Living one's affect consciously makes possible the use of its full informational potential.

Just as we need anesthetic in surgery, so also in our growing up we require much self-analgesia in order to bear the excitement that floods us. Extraordinary resources are needed to discover the diagnostic and therapeutic helpfulness of pain and the potential danger to life in obscuring or deadening it. It seems to be so much easier and so much more natural to use a drug or to go on hurting oneself, without feeling the injury.

The problem in discontinuing denial of selfhood and recognizing our painful affects containing the information about the absence of integration and lack of wholesomeness in our living is that it provokes self-judgmental trends. We want to imitate the behavior of the parent who punished us for hurting ourselves. Hence the struggle against the discovery of the meaning of our painful affects is the enormous difficulty in accepting our self-destructiveness lovingly. Another way to put it is that it is very difficult to recognize the modified forms of love. Thus it is hard to see one's rage as love outraged and accept it comfortably.

Case Illustration

A patient, who will be mentioned again in the chapter on the hedonic aspects of affect, experienced a great deal of rage and envy, to which he was addicted, and was finally able to verbalize what happened to him. When he encountered a desirable, strong, "ideal" man, he had wishes for the man to love him and thereby make him happy, whole, and perfect. His first affect was love and yearning to be loved, but that feeling was momentary and obscured by the next reaction. When no response came from the distant stranger, his feelings would change to envy and rage, in which he wallowed. This was a frequent re-enactment of the story of his life; for, having to repress his love early in childhood, he barely managed to survive by promoting the "other side" of his love potential.

Painful emotions and physical pain are a "call" for special attention to some aspect of oneself. The problem is with the tendency of a painful affect to drown out, as it were, all other affects by its sheer intensity, making it temporarily impossible to experience the other feelings, the "opposite" feeling and view of oneself. Such temporary exclusions are from the conscious sphere only: "Although a stronger emotion may seem to be able to exclude the presence of a weaker one, such prohibition really serves as preservative and emphasis in the repressed emotion" (Dorsey, 1971a, p. xvii). In addition, we may become "hypnotized" with a disturbed part of ourselves, in effect becoming "all sore thumb." Hence Dorsey (1971a) stresses: *"My consciously disowned unconscious hatred functions continuously"* (p. 107). Since it is not possible to eliminate or destroy an emotion or an affectively charged idea, there is just a question of whether one can live it fully consciously, or whether one has had to alienate part of himself and continue to live with it in its alienated form. Affect is commonly dissociated, so that the cognitive aspects are separated from the expressive aspects of the affect, and sometimes displaced. We have already denoted all permanent affect modifications as "defenses against affects." In harmonious development with the desirable degree of affect differentiation, verbalization, and desomatization, and with the development of desirable skills of affect tolerance, one is in a position to see one's emotions as information for oneself.

If affects have not matured in this fashion and consist mostly of physiological, mimetic, and motoric responses, then they will have an "imperious" quality, dominating and sometimes disorganizing the conscious sphere of mental function. From this vantage point we can expand the definition of affect maturation and affect tolerance: We need to cultivate the ability to bear the intense excitement of affects with sufficient composure to preserve awareness of our wholeness at the same time. "What cannot be cured must be endured" is deeply passionate wisdom. Enduring hardship with a good-natured acceptance of one's wholeness is a self-healing attitude. Its wisdom is revealed in the fact that though the pain must be lived in the present, the memories from the distant past retain their sting because they cannot be accepted as having been justified by their causes. We need to accept ourselves retroactively with forgiveness and kindness. To make peace with oneself, to accept one's past, one can choose whether or not to own up consciously to authorship of all self- and object-representations that exist in one's life (mind). The choice of self-integration represents the exercise of self-love; denial of acceptance inhibits the love potential.

Hence Dorsey (1971a) proclaims, "Conscious self-love is required for biologically adequate self-esteem. . . . Love is the power of power. . . . Real relief from depression, as from every unhappiness or pain, occurs only as I discover its seeming 'unloveableness' itself, is a modification of love" (p. 88).

As therapists and as patients, we have to face the challenge of loving what is very difficult to love. We are called on to approach attributes that were disliked and rejected by ourselves and the significant objects in our past. We are called on to help people love themselves although they feel unloved and conclude they are unlovable. Strong love is needed for one to love what is at first experienced as repulsive. Wurmser (1981), who in his scholarly exploration of shame uncovered depths of humiliation of such severity and quality that sometimes only psychosis or death could measure its intensity, also ended up talking about love. He concluded:

> I see it as the true testament and dedication of this inquiry into shame that word is being lent to this ideal of love. It is in many a sense that true "transcendence" so many philosophers have been searching for— "Eros, the great healer" of the Symposium. In it union and separateness are fulfilled and overcome in a higher reconciliation [p. 309].

Naturally, we have to start by gradually and slowly practicing loving the unlovable in our own selves and patiently developing the courage to deal with what was "difficult to be courageous about." We can expect intense passions to be encountered in ourselves and in our patients. How shall we build up "strong" forgiveness to face the "unforgivable" wrong? Are we ready to encounter "strong" hatred where it developed because it includes intense opposition?

Dorsey (1971a) explained:

The intensity of each of my unhappy emotions may be understood as subsuming its corresponding ("opposite") happy emotion. My hatred is strong exactly to the extent that it includes whatever is *difficultly* hated. *Strong* hatred is not required whenever it is "easy" to hate. Only when I can live with hatred that which I formerly lived merely with love (extending all my adoration) can I ever realize what strong hatred is. My fear is strong exactly to the extent that it includes whatever is difficultly feared. Only when I must live with fear that which I formerly lived courageously can I even realize what strong fear is. *Strong* fear is not required whenever it is "easy" to fear, and so on [p. 89].

The idea of the wholeness of oneself, and the self-contained nature of one's emotions, starts with the definition or basic conceptions of love itself. Aggression is the attempt to purify our love idealistically—to achieve the perfect love free of hate that may lead to a diminution of our conscious self-awareness. The most helpful attitude is to recognize hate as a complement to or attribute of love. This view has been put forth by Dorsey (1971a) repeatedly: "Insight that love 'and' hate are basically one, not two, provides the emotional orientation needed for my appreciating my intact oneness, my only firm foundation for my feeling of reality or of sanity" (p. 145). As Dorsey defines it, the difference is not between love and hate, or love and another affective attitude, but rather it is in the degree of consciousness of one's love. It is really not startling news for a psychoanalytically knowledgeable person that hate conceals unconscious love. But the ability to live an experience with conscious acceptance of it, that is, conscious love of it, means merely that one is able to by fully conscious of the self-experience.

We are coming full circle to the question of why love is the best model affect. Freud (1906) said that psychoanalytic treatment was an effort to free inhibited love. Dorsey (1971a) pursues some of those original metaphors by insisting that all emotions are love inhibited or modified:

In inhibited functioning of any kind, self-love does not disappear to be supplanted by a self loveless emotion. Rather *every* emotion is made of nothing but love. All pathology is merely physiology struggling under stressful ordeal. Anger, or grief, or jealousy, of whatever painful emotion, is merely inhibited love struggling under stressful ordeal. Hate is hurt (hindered) love, deviltry is hurt (hindered) divinity, doubt is hurt (hindered) belief, fear is hurt (hindered) safety, guilt is hurt (hindered) innocence [p. xxxvii].

Elsewhere in this book I discuss the nature of the perceptive, cognitive, and other functions involved in the formation of the mental representations of oneself, of objects, and of the world. What I talk about is generally related to self-representations and object-representations.

But in the discussions of this aspect of affect, that is, its nature as a self-contained self-evaluation and integration system, I am alert to the additional view that affects also represent the concordance of our self-evaluation with attitudes that we experience toward the environment but that, in essence, are extended self-manifestations. That is the point in saying "All love is self-love."

As we have already observed, affects are unique in that we experience them as if they were object-directed and even object-generated (Brierley, 1945; Schafer, 1964), but when carefully inspected, they prove to be our own evaluational and physiological responses. It is the study of affects, particularly their self-contained character, that forces us to acknowledge (reluctantly) the essentially solipsistic nature of our experience. In the context of this recognition, we can understand why all love, being self-love, includes everything we behold and cannot be separated from any other emotion without illusory self-splitting.

Dorsey (1971a) found that consciously experienced and acknowledged self-love is the feeling of happiness that one can strive for. It represents the ideal of renouncing intrapsychic attempts to alienate parts of one's life by experiencing them as nonself and by attempting to modify the love for them. Both parts of the attempt of self-alienation are, in fact, impossible. Repression, in the topographic point of view of psychoanalysis, represents a cognitive incongruity. It assumes an impossible attempt to repudiate one's own mental material by organs of the mind behaving as if they were not of the mind. Hence the repudiation of one's mentation takes the guise of being nonexistent, nonmental, or nonself. In other words, one attempts to deny selfness to part of oneself. As for affects: "The hindrance of a positive emotion brings out its negative (unconscious) aspect so that only *its* 'opposite' excitement of unhappiness, or pain is felt. Inhibited love takes on its negative aspect of hate, inhibited innocence or responsibility, takes on its negative aspect of guilt, and so on" (p. 110).

That the lack of conscious recognition of repressed ideas and inhibited affects is signaled by anxiety or other alarming forms of pain has its historic derivation in our common developmental hazards. Fenichel (1941), explaining these misfortunes, stated that originally "every outburst of affect was . . . a trauma . . . later the ego learns to defend itself against affects and master them . . . danger is always anticipated trauma, in the last analysis every fear is actually a fear of a traumatic state" (p. 219). Hence, in traumatic living we keep finding again and again that the most disabling consequences are the loss of integration and the loss of personal identity. One tries to help oneself posttraumatically by creating a manageable state for regaining one's wholeness by all available means. The path to self-healing and self-reintegration is very painful. Dorsey (1971a) reflects upon the inconvenience of posttraumatic dissociated living, in which one's life is not one's own.

One of the consequences of this ubiquitous defensive operation is that affects and their related cognitive aspects are experienced as part of externality (Novey, 1959). It is this characteristic of the object representation that makes it necessary to work with transferences in the psychoanalytic process. Through the work in the psychoanalytic situation, where the analyst avoids interference with the patient's need to deal with the nature of his object representations and the affects involved in them, one may reclaim ownership of one's soul. In the development of the transference and transference neurosis, the patient is able to re-experience, and perhaps this time discover the true nature of, his own object representations and find that they are his own creations, endowed by their creator with his own unclaimed, unconscious affective memories. One might say that this, the most crucial aspect of the work of psychoanalysis, represents an opportunity for mastery, acceptance, and integration of one's affective life, which has hitherto been handled as if it belonged to the objects. This is the heart and soul of the psychoanalytic process. Everything else an analyst does is preparation for this achievement or an interference in the patient's task.

In dealing with adults, we find a multitude of infantile and archaic defensive operations that have long been a liability. The attraction of living one's "external" love objects is that it keeps one busy trying to manipulate them and obtain from them what they can never give. Disowning one's feelings by attributing their psychogenesis to an external source is patently (adorable and necessary) inaccurate bookkeeping.

Our ability to enjoy our love is promoted by the discovery of the self-centered nature of all emotionality. We should inquire why it is so difficult, well nigh impossible, to be consciously aware of one's self-contained integrity—particularly in regard to affective responses. Dorsey explains it in a manner very similar to that formulated by Fenichel. In regard to affect, it is clear that one starts life without being able consciously to acknowledge oneself as an integrated being, owning one's own emotions. From the beginning, the ability to develop intense physiological components of emotion far exceeds the ability to register them, and this is a long way from being able to recognize them as self-experiences. We are nowhere ready to recognize the unity and wholeness of our selves.

The best evidence (e.g., Gedo and Goldberg, 1973; Lichtenberg, 1983; Stern, 1985) indicates that it takes the concerted efforts of both parents and all the resources of the child to prevent the infant from being overwhelmed by his affective responses and to enable the child to establish a secure homeostasis by the age of three months. Hence, it is life-saving to be able to start one's conscious identity formation gradually and to begin by attributing selfness only to the pleasurable experiences. The illusion of externalization of affects, along with the emphasis on communication and control of the various kinds of object representations, becomes necessary and imposes itself with a hypnotic power. That by fits and starts, we discover our identity and unity at all is, in fact, an amazing development, a difficult one to trace.

In another book published in the same year, Dorsey (1971b) showed that the development of language is, from the beginning, put in the service of supporting these illusionary repressions. Our common modes of linguistic usage are supporting externalization and discouraging the development of an integrated self-representation. The last territory in this world to be explored is one's own self.

In Dorsey's view (1971a, p. 74), we live without the conscious recognition of the self-experience in transference living. As is discussed in chapter 11, since depriving our own mental activity of self-recognition is a form of repression, transference living is also protected by various "resistances" to self-discovery.

In this view, then, the lack of conscious recognition of the scope of one's selfhood and the self-continence of one's affects can be considered to be a means of preventing infantile traumatization. It might be said that beyond the parental protection one must receive in infancy, it is necessary to develop these linguistic and externalizing defenses in order to prevent oneself from being flooded and disorganized early in life. We have found in our work with adult victims of catastrophic trauma that its sequelae were also splitting of self-representations, repression, and externalization.

The most profound statement of the ideal goal in posttraumatic living turns out to be the most basic truth: that the healing process involves self-reintegration. Recovery involves restoration of the ability consciously to claim one's whole self (world). The most essential part of posttraumatic healing, which is most difficult to do, is to be able to recognize consciously the self-continence of one's emotions.

Emotional self-continence represents the fact that one's feelings are always one's own. The temptation to deny this reality stems from the impulse to denounce something that exists—it should *not be*, because it hurts too much. In the attempt to rid oneself of painful aspects of oneself, there is also an unsuccessful attempt to negate part of oneself. Although it is impossible to destroy, eliminate, rid oneself of any part of self, it is possible to rob oneself of the conscious recognition of selfhood. Hence repression involves an impoverishment of the self-representation of access to, control of, or self-recognition of part of oneself.

The psychoanalytic process is virtually the only learnable method we have for recovering of repressed memories, for reconstructing disconnected memory traces, and for discovering the nature of transference. The importance of consciously recognizing affective wholeness and emotional continence has not been recognized until now. That is why Dorsey's explication of the *conscious awareness* of emotional self-continence has immense clinical usefulness. In order to become consciously aware, one has to acknowledge the impulse to rid oneself of everything painful and unpleasant. One has to accept lovingly the need to protest that it "should not be that way." Acceptance of all the rage and loving protest permit the consideration of their complement: "Whatever is, is justified by its causes" and is not knowable in its absolute. The only thing knowable is one's own psychic reality, and therefore one can repress only part of oneself. For this reason, all seeming division, separation, dissociation, fragmentation, plurality—no matter how realistically it is experienced as existing in external reality—represents repression, (as Dorsey might put it), "the illusional consequence of withheld conscious loving."

6
The Hedonic Element
in Affectivity

The hedonic quality of affects is, prevailing impressions to the contrary, not an inherent, inseparable part of the emotions. A study of conditions in which there are changes in the subjective quality of emotions, such as anhedonia, or the so-called libidinization of affects, indicates that the qualities of pleasure and distress are separate and are only epigenetically linked with the rest of the complex experience that constitutes emotions. A metaphoric view of the anatomic and physiological apparatus illustrates this conception and further suggests that in infancy, before affects have matured enough to be utilizable as signals, the direct experience of pleasure and distress provides the qualitative signal. This response becomes an essential factor in self- and object-representation formation.

The assumption commonly is made that some emotions are intrinsically and invariably pleasurable and others are equally constantly unpleasant or painful. I question this assumption, particularly because it does not square with certain clinical syndromes in which the hedonic quality of affects changes. I propose that the adult experience of affects is a blend of self-perception of responses from several sources. Among the elements of the emotion are the perceptions of pleasure or distress, which derive from a phylogenetically and ontogenetically ancient somatic and mental apparatus. The experiences of pleasure or distress become quite closely related to certain emotions, but their separate derivation makes possible later shifts in quality of pleasure in affects. The understanding of these shifts is necessary in order to deal with anhedonia, as well as such phenomena as "libidinization" of anxiety and other affects. Rather than thinking of emotions as unitary phenomena, it is helpful to consider their identifiable elements.

What we have learned so far about the epigenesis of affect suggests that they are useful as signals only after lengthy maturation. But such assumptions have a serious theoretical problem concealed in them. If we postulate that the utilizability of affects as signals depends on their having undergone a process of differentiation and verbalization-desomatization, we would expect that affect regression would be accompanied by serious impairment in virtually all "information processing" functions—certainly in those which have been demonstrated to involve signal affects. *Moreover, the expectation that the maturation of affects would have to precede the development of such basic functions as perception seems to conflict with the basic assumptions of object relations and self- and with object-representation in early life.*

We have, of course, no way of knowing how perceptions are processed in the infant, how they are registered, or when they start leaving lasting memories. But it is puzzling that there are some adults whose affects have undergone imperfect development or regression and consequently have difficulties in using their emotions as signals to themselves. These people show a disturbance in object relations, a lack of empathy with the significant objects in their lives, and even a tendency to treat themselves as robots. If that is so, then we can assume that in the young child, in whom the affects have not yet reached maturity, the perception and registration of object representations has to be different from those in the best functioning adults. And yet, in psychoanalytic theory, we have assumed that people keep forming object-representations of some kind from the beginning—even before the full recognition of the separateness of the self-representation from the object-representation. Moreover, it was always assumed that emotions were involved in these object-representations. For instance, Kernberg (1976) stated:

> My formulations imply that cathexes are, first of all, affective cathexes, that is, the quantitative element of economic factor involved in the intensity of primitive affect dispositions, which are activated in the context of primitive units of internalized object relations and constitute the organizers of such primitive units [p. 113]. . . . Cathexes are first of all affect cathexis [p. 114].

Kernberg (1982b) elaborates:

> Affects, operating as the earliest motivational system are therefore intimately linked with the fixation by memory of an internalized object relation. I would suggest that affects are the primary motivational system in the sense that they are at the center of each of the infinite number of gratifying and frustrating concrete events the infant experiences with his environment. Affects link a series of undifferentiated self-object representations so that gradually a complex world of internalized object relations, some pleasurably tinged, others unpleasurably tinged is constructed [p. 907].

With the renewal of interest in the process of attachment (Bowlby, 1969) and the studies on attachment behavior (Ainsworth et al., 1978; Parkes and Stevenson-Hinde, 1982), the schedule of attachment has been moved back to as early as two to seven months of age (Greenspan, 1981). We must wonder: In these early stages of development, what could be the effect of the affect signals on the capacity to register them?

Bowlby (1969) assumed "affects and emotions" to be available from the start as appraising processes. Bowlby (1977) later made explicit his view that in all the attachment steps, including its earliest precursors, the affects of security, fear, anxiety, and anger were indispensable tools of the whole process. Biologically oriented students of depression find that the most reliable way to produce an animal model of it is to separate the young from their mother (J.H. Krystal, 1984). If the mother is not quickly restored, and the child survives, serious impairment of all affective development and of all ego functions will ensue. But let us ask now: How can it be that primal self- and object-representations develop at an early age, before any affect signal can have evolved through desomatization and differentiation? And how do these object relations develop at all if there is no affect *signal* available in a form suitable for the development of a "loving memory?" We have postulated an interdependence in these processes without providing for one of them to mature enough to be available for the other. What is the way out of this quandary? Have we arrived at another *non liquet*?

A possible solution offers itself in the consideration of the distress or psychic pain signal as separately derived from the rest of the affect experience. Before we can explore it, however, we must critically examine our conceptions of the emotions to see if such a possibility is feasible.

The need to reconsider psychoanalytic conceptions of affect arises from other difficulties as well. One of these problems derives from the "discharge" theory of affect, which represents an uncritical incorporation of the common idea that the affects are sporadic, occasional occurrences (Krystal, 1978b). Current views of affect are much more in harmony with Cannon's (1915) idea that every perception and every mental event is accompanied by an "emotional quota." He acknowledged that the affective component was not always conscious, and he tried to account for this lack by a theory that affects were primarily thalamically registered and became conscious only if cortical inhibition was abolished. In the long view of theories and conceptions of affects, the discharge formulation is by no means the only, or even the predominant, one. In fact, it is amazing how many interpretations and theories of affects have been advanced. In the multiplicity of hypotheses about the nature of emotions, I have found one that describes them as having "three dimensions," which I hope to demonstrate as having disparate psychological bases. Wundt (1920) suggested that the three dimensions of feeling were: (1) pleasantness (unpleasantness), (2) tension (relaxation), and (3) excitement (quiescence). The question is whether these elements in the subjective experience of affects are indeed intrinsic, inseparable parts of a given affect.

Offhand, one is inclined to assert that certain emotions are always pleasant, others distressing, and that each emotion has a characteristic level of arousal. But, on reflection, one finds that, even in the normal person, emotions vary considerably in degree of pleasure or unpleasure. Even anxiety may be quite pleasurable and in fact is a regular source of "thrills." Anxiety and variety (in the sense of divergence between a perception and the accustomed expectation) are the most effective "arousers" (Pribram, 1968).

THE TERMS: SEXUALIZATION, EROTIZATION AND LIBIDINIZATION

Although there appears to be agreement that various affects can be experienced and "utilized" in a gratifying way, there is much confusion in terminology. The three terms mentioned have been used interchangeably and in several frames of reference, creating an additional confusion.

Sexualization generally refers to the involvement of cognitive mental material, primarily fantasies with unconscious sexual meaning. For instance, sexualization of thinking in obsessive-compulsive neurosis permits a certain degree of self-gratification; but at the same time, because it brings this ordinarily conflict-free activity into the conflictual sphere, it may result in inhibition of thinking (Fenichel, 1945, p. 299). Hartmann (1955) equates sublimation with neutralization (desexualization and deaggressivation) and therefore considers sexualization a form of regression. He states that sexualized ego functions are subject to regressive tendencies. Whereas sexualization usually refers to a function, or the nature of the transference, another use of the term relates to the use of an organ other than the naturally erotogenic ones for sexual gratification. Fenichel (1945) also spoke of "sexualization of non-sexual relationships" and discussed at length the possibility of inhibition of virtually every function that has become sexualized. He also referred to "sexualization of anxiety" (p. 483), limiting this phrase, however, to masochistic distortions in which fear or pain becomes a source of sexual excitement, a condition for genital sexual gratification.

The term *erotization* illustrates the problem, because it is sometimes used interchangeably with sexualization (as in "erotization of the transference") and was used in this sense by Freud (1926, p. 89), and sometimes as equivalent to "libidinization" (LaForgue, 1930). The fundamental question, then, appears to be: "Is there a meaning to libidinization that connotes something different from sexualization?"

Fenichel, who used both terms extensively, seems to have thought so. In his essay on "The Defense Against Anxiety Particularly by Libidinization" (1939), he deals with a defense not against *anxiety* but against the *traumatogenic potentials* of it. But he is talking about "a defense against anxiety by developing libidinal pleasure in it" (p. 307). Note the expression "libidinal pleasure." By using this expression, rather than just saying that people derive *pleasure*, he was glancing over and covering up a problem in this area.

The problem is that in the libidinization of anxiety, or other affects, there is no sexual excitement as there is for the perversions, nor is there necessarily a conscious quality of pleasure in it. This observation leaves us in a quandary. We postulate a gratification in anxiety, and then we must add that this may happen without the conscious recognition of pleasure in the experience. This phenomenon seems to be perfectly well described and explained by the economic theory: one would say that because of conflict, the conscious experience of pleasure is blocked, along with the repression of the "forbidden" fantasy or impulse. But this very defensive operation permits the anxiety (or other affect) to take over the discharge of instinctual energy, which was what was needed in the first place. This model has been used countless times since Freud (1926) described anxiety as a miniature hysteria; it is what Fenichel (1939) referred to as libidinal pleasure rather than pleasure. The more precise expression would be libidinal "gratification," since the conscious recognition of pleasure varies. It is precisely because this term lends itself to covering up the problem by "sweeping it under the carpet" of the economic theory clichés that we must abandon its use. Instead of talking about libidinization, which always carries the risk of confounding us with thoughts of cathexes, let us simply consider shifts in the quality of pleasure related to an affect. We have many clinical observations to ponder. Observations abound about the extraordinary capacity for gratification that specific affects have for some people. Equally common are observations of people for whom the emotions that are usually pleasurable lose that quality or become distressful.

How can we account for these shifts in the gratification potential of affects without alluding to the economic point of view of metapsychology? We know from clinical observations that the conscious awareness of pleasure in an affect may vary greatly and may be virtually totally unconscious, even where this affect has become the only gratification available to the person. How do we theoretically explain the psychic reality of those who bitterly complain of an affect experience or ego state they are driven to produce in themselves with the compulsiveness of an addict? Our language fails us here. The defenses that prompt the repression of conscious recognition of gratification in unpleasure and pain, the difficulties we have in admitting that certain assumptive gratifications are "not fun," also result in a general impoverishment of our language in this area. I will simply refer to the shifts in the quality of pleasure or distress attending the affective experiences. We must free our terminology regarding observational data from hypothetical valences. And in regard to these hedonic shifts, I am referring again to the *theoretically feasible situation in which there is a shift in the capacity for gratification, without the involvement of stimulation or an erotogenic zone.* There are still some unanswered questions. Does a shift in the capacity for gratification involve a change in the *quality of pleasure?* Can gratification or pleasure take place unconsciously? Since the consideration of these questions may involve a revision of the entire concept of what an affect is, let us consider some clinical observations in this area.

CLINICAL ASPECTS OF THE RELATION OF AFFECT TO THE QUALITY OF PLEASURE

In regard to the well-known examples of anxiety experienced as pleasurable, as in an amusement park and in sports activities, we hasten to comment that the pleasure relates to the *mastery* of fear. When anxiety is associated with helplessness, it may be experienced as distressful, but in association with other feelings—for example, optimistic expectation—it is usually downright pleasurable. The following illustrates a "discovery" that became the precursor of what we usually call "libidinization of anxiety." Again, I must renounce this terminology and state only that, indeed, in this person there was evidence of considerable pleasure and gratification in experiencing anxiety in situations that did not involve helplessness:

Case Illustration

A man of European background recalled in analysis that as a child (age six to twelve), living on the fifth floor of an apartment house, he had had a curious pastime. He would sit at the window, facing the inner court, in which there were usually a variety of activities. He found that he could lean out of the window far enough to become frightened of falling out. He would either stay in this position or pull back just a bit, and then lean out again, producing within himself "bursts" of anxiety. This activity was not of a compulsive sort, but it did have a distinctly masturbatory quality, albeit a self-gratification devoid of any genital masturbatory stimulation. He simply learned to provoke his anxiety in a playful fashion; but only now, thirty years later, did he realize that he had done this for fun.

In considering that clinical vignette, our thoughts drift almost automatically to the gratification involved in the *idea* of falling, which has such attraction. We are all familiar with the kind of cognitive material that no doubt contributed to the fantasy gratification in this experience. However, the widely prevalent (among psychoanalysts) idea that thoughts, fantasies, or other cognitive acts are gratifying is mistaken. *An idea can be pleasurable only if it mobilizes a reaction at an erotogenic zone or a direct stimulation of hedonic centers of the brain, or produces a pleasurable affect.* Thus, in the foregoing case, if a fantasy had also been involved, it would have resulted in some affective response. Also, if this person had learned to think of, recall, or fantasize his leaning-out-of-window experience and be able to obtain the same response, it would not have been the *idea*, but the affective state, that was perceptibly pleasurable. A major clinical fact hinges on this consideration: that regardless of the fantasies involved, patients come to their doctors because they cannot tolerate the resultant affective states, specifically the expressive, physiological components of the affects and their distressful quality. With medication, the patients no longer mind their conflictual or previously anxiety-producing cognition.

Let us, then, return to my patient who as a child made the remarkable discovery that he could produce anxiety within himself and could keep it within bounds of comfort and thereby devise a most remarkable and reliable means of self-gratification. It is a kind of "masturbation" that does not involve the stimulation of any of the usual erotogenic zones, for the locus of pleasure for him was somewhere deep in front of the lumbar and thoracic wall, where he experienced a tingling of the greatest pleasure he was capable of, similar to what he later experienced after an especially intense and gratifying orgasm or at certain moments of dozing off. In respect to the capacity for gratification in an affect, every part of the body is an erotogenic zone. Thus, we have to distinguish pleasure in the *mastery* of an affect from the potential pleasure in *having* it.

Even in counterphobic behavior, with its compulsive nature, there is frequently a quality of pleasure (Fenichel, 1939). In contrast to the phobics, counterphobic persons have a deep-seated conviction of their capacity to master the danger, and even the uncomfortable "expressive" aspects of affect. I would say that when one discovers early a significant conscious pleasure in anxiety, one creates within oneself a motivation for a counterphobic attitude, which may carry the day if at a future time one is forced to choose between attempting mastery or withdrawal and avoidance. In later life the patient just described showed a tendency to counterphobic and active mastery, as opposed to avoidance and passivity. However, even in those persons who do develop phobic and avoidance patterns, in the advanced states of their analysis one finds a "core" of enjoyment and a high valuing of anxiety. Katan (1951) showed a clinging to the experience of anxiety in a case of an agoraphobic:

> It was amazing with what stubbornness my patient defended her agoraphobia . . . she clung to her anxiety desperately, and as the interconnections began to become clear to her, her anxiety concerned the loss of her anxiety. Whenever she was walking or standing, she had to make sure that she could still command her anxiety, she might stop because . . . this is what produced anxiety, then she would say to herself: "It'll come up, it'll come right away, immediately." If it did not turn up immediately or not intensively enough, she would predict the

onset for the next street corner and would not give in until she again experienced the longed-for sensation. In her analysis, there occurred actual grotesque scenes; in moments of great excitement, she would wring her hands, and either scream or implore me with tears, "Please let me keep my anxiety, don't take it away" [p. 48].

The patient is pleading for the return of her precious anxiety, as a drug addict would for heroin. In fact, most addicts do crave the production of an emotion, mood, or consciousness modification at the same time as they block another affect precursor (Krystal and Raskin, 1970). Hoppe (1962) observed that survivors of Nazi persecution behave as if they had a "hate addiction." Lifton (1963) has called a related phenomenon in the Hibakusha "survivor hubris."[1] But, as every psychoanalyst knows, ordinary childhood traumatization may produce similar disturbances, which commonly manifest themselves in patients as gaining pleasure and gratification from anxiety, which is also predominantly painful. Other affects can be "libidinized" in the same fashion.

Valenstein's (1973) study "On Attachment to Painful Feelings" contains a careful description of this process. His paper emphasizes the relation of attachment to pain as a function of early object relations—a most useful view, which is confirmed in some of my cases but which represents another aspect of the problem. Valenstein, too, finds difficulty in the linguistics of gratification in painful affects. He speaks of "fixation to pain" (p. 373). He says: "For the most part this is psychic pain, although such patients do not emotionally neglect the possibility of *fulfilling themselves* with physically occasioned pain, should it present itself" (p. 365; italics mine). He refers to the painful "Erlebniss" as "paradoxically fulfilling even though not pleasurably or harmoniously satisfying" (p. 390).

The effective manipulation of the hedonic aspect of emotions may be accomplished by "mixing" emotions or dealing with the aspect of helplessness or hopelessness in a situation of danger. Thus, to inspire hope or to deny the hopelessness of a situation will shift the anxiety toward the more optimistic and pleasurable side of the spectrum.

Affect modification need not always be motivated by pain avoidance and pleasure seeking. Like the poets, we sometimes choose to renounce excessive boisterousness or manic defenses against sadness and depression in order to attain a more profound, emphatic, or wise view. Goethe stated this point explicitly:

> Zart Gedicht, wie Regenbogen,
> wird nur auf dunklen Grund gezogen;
> darum behagt dem Dichtergenie
> das Element der Melancholie.

---

1. Hoppe, Molnar, and Newell (1965) have also pointed out that problems of love or hate "addiction" are common in delinquent male adolescents. In the therapy of these youngsters, the addiction problems have to be approached as a specific issue.

A tender poem, like a rainbow
shows only against a darkened ground;
therefore the element of melancholy
suits the spirit of the poet.

[Goethe, 1815, p. 73; translation mine]

Poetic expression becomes relevant when we turn our attention to the prevalence of fondness for sadness in everyday life. Benjamin Rush professed that poets "view the human mind in all its operations, whether natural or morbid, with a microscopic eye; and hence many things arrest their attention, which escape the notice of physicians" (quoted by Edel, 1975, p. 1006). At the same time, poets and artists demonstrate that the pleasure of synthesis, functioning, performance, intellectual mastery, and playing may effectively balance the distressful aspect of the "emergency affects"—thus making them bearable (Klein, 1976). The playing of children lends the same kind of comfort and is also endowed with beauty, order, harmony, and poise (Huizinga, 1950).

Thus, once alerted to changes in the quality of pleasure in affectivity, one discovers them to be a common occurrence. In many patients the manifestations of pleasure or gratification in painful feelings, or the anhedonia affecting their experience of pleasurable affects, are side issues, often overlooked. There are patients who have "successfully" completed analyses only to discover later in life, when they are no longer able to distract themselves with their work, that their capacity for joy and pleasure and their capacity to feel the pleasure quality in affects is absent or severely diminished. Frequently such people develop a serious depression at this point in reaction to the inability to experience gratification, in contrast to those patients who develop their anhedonia as a symptom of depression.

Conversely, some persons freely use their imagination and their capacity to "look for the silver lining" when life is depressing. These are people with a good hedonic capacity. This function has been identified as a character trait by Meehl, Likken, Schafield, and Pellegen (1971) who, using a term coined by Cattell (1935), have called it "surgency." These observations are easier to accept than the opposite—where the patients become attached to the maximization of a painful affect.

Case Illustrations

Although virtually any affect can become the focus of modification of hedonic regulations, in some cases there may be a major shift in the pleasure and gratification role of a particular affect, most commonly, anxiety. Thus, Valenstein (1973) speaks of patients "deeply attached to pain." I have had two patients who shared an attachment to and gratification from anger, and two who (surprisingly) did the same with envy. Although the problems and difficulties involved varied, these four patients had one thing in common: at one point in the analysis we discovered that the particular affect (anger and envy respectively) was their secret way of getting their "kicks" out of life, other ways being blocked by inhibitions. The two patients with the "envy addiction" presented themselves with disparate problems—one with a tendency to depression and the other with overt homosexuality to which he continued to respond with distress. However, when the latter's behavior was observed, we found that what he really was interested in was not homosexual gratification but rather approaching men, being refused, and then spending a lot of time nagging and feeling deprived.

The following is a vignette from the analysis of one of those patients who has enjoyed and treasured his anger:

On the occasion of his son's obtaining a driver's license, he went into a tirade against his own father, who had never taught him to drive; he had had to do it on his own, at a later age, while other boys, taught by their father, got their license at 16. After the patient raged on for well over a half of the hour about how terrible his father had been, I brought his attention to his repeated need for this kind of outburst, which was especially inappropriate since he knew that his father had been schizophrenic and since the father had now been dead for a number of years. This was part of his distortion, designed to maintain the image of his father as *bad* (unwilling to teach his son), in order to continue his own rage.

The patient became very angry with me, as if I had taken his father's place in a battle against him, and he went on giving argument after argument as to why his father should have taught him to drive. Suddenly, he realized that he was *defending his anger*, and, in questioning himself about it, he discovered that his anger was precious to him and that he did not wish to give it up. He maintained a number of relations in his present life, which he used to "feed" his anger, and was subject to *fits of rage, many of them when he was alone*, in which he yelled, screamed, raged on, and bit his fingers. His sessions regularly consisted in yelling at the top of his voice, until he reached a certain point of relaxation, after which he acted and felt sleepy.

This patient's use of rage took up much work, as he frequently warded off other feelings, such as guilt or shame, by substituting anger. An identification with his anger, as indicated earlier, was also involved. Feeling *stronger* when angry thus also warded off feelings of dependence and helplessness. There was, in addition, a coupling of the rage with a feeling of deprivation, which he used to justify an entitlement that, in turn, was the foundation of his life style. After these and other uses of and secondary gains in his rages were worked through, we ended up with the "purely gratificatory" use of anger. The pattern involved a number of issues over which he would become enraged constantly—for instance, lights being left on. On one occasion he came into his appointment with me and picked up a paper clip from the carpet. He then went on a harangue about people at his office who constantly dropped used staples on the floor and how he raged and screamed about it. When confronted with the fact that his 19 years' experience of running the office had shown that staples will be found on the floor occasionally, he refused to accept it. Instead, he insisted that whenever he saw a staple he *should* rage on—still justifying to himself that he was doing it in order to get people to stop dropping staples, even though this method had not worked in all these years. The outcome of this and a multitude of similar situations was that he was in a state of rage much of the time. The failure to accept the realities of the situation had many determinants, but his need to use anger for gratification was one of them.

Related to the hedonic aspects of affects are the vicissitudes of two sensations on the borderline of pleasure and pain—itching and tickling. In a presidential address to the American Medical Association, Section on Dermatology, Ayres (1964) discussed the "fine art of scratching" and reported that "scratching of normal skin will be felt as painful but . . . scratching of equal intensity in an area of itchy skin produces erotic pleasure, hence the presence of a particular excitatory state has the effect of transforming an ordinary painful stimulus, scratching, into a source of erotic pleasure" (p. 1005).

I am indebted to Dr. William Niederland for a vignette of a case involving tickling. His patient was tickled as a child by his older brother. The experience, which started each time as a very pleasant and exciting one, would regularly go on to such length and intensity that it became unbearably painful, and the patient feared that the brother would kill him by continuing the now terrifying stimulation. Niederland commented that the German word *Totlachen* referred to the general fear of mirth reaching similarly unbearable intensity, with sadomasochistic excitement getting out of control.

These observations on itching and tickling illustrate just how radically pleasure may shift to distress in a given experience. Similarly, in some situations, the affect remains the same but the quality of pleasure is shifted. This action may be mediated by a blending of affects or other affect modification, for example, mirth turning to sadness. The very idea of humor's turning pain into pleasure is a related operation. But for our purposes it is important to emphasize the "pure" modifications or shifts in the hedonic quality of affects. These changes need not be permanent. Once alerted to the possibility of shifts in the quality of pleasure in affectivity, one finds considerable individual variation. Each affective experience, each feeling is a blend of elements, among which the hedonic quality is an independent variable. Since we are not used to such an idea in psychoanalysis, we may borrow a model from neurophysiology and neuroanatomy that suggests a separate derivation of the pain and pleasure experience and its intimate association with the general emotional apparatus.

THE PLEASURE AND DISTRESS CENTERS: ANATOMY
AS A METAPHOR FOR PSYCHIC FUNCTION

Hitherto conceptualization of psychic pleasure has been modeled on the idea
of discharge in male ejaculation, confused with the idea of orgasm[2] and the
idea of foreplay. Several researchers have opened a new view of pleasure by
demonstrating that there are pleasure and distress centers of the brain
(Delgado, Roberts, and Miller, 1954; Olds and Milner, 1954; Olds and Olds
1963). The centers for pleasure and distress are closely associated with the
limbic system, which governs the emotions (MacLean, 1949), but are separate and distinct from it. The pleasure centers have their own extensive
"pathways of reward," which extend to the frontal cortex, the hypothalmus,
the pontine tegmentum, and the medulla. The medial forebrain bundle is a
"pleasure relay station" for the other brain pathways (Routtenberg, 1978, p.
160). There is also an area in the cerebellum, connected with both the
pleasure and distress centers, which functions in such a way that stimulation
of it blocks the distress and pain areas and simultaneously stimulates the
pleasure centers. Heath (1977) has demonstrated that a variety of otherwise
untreatable disorders can be treated by implanting a brain pacer in this
cerebellar site. The importance of such a single action, which simultaneously
assuages bad feelings and promotes good ones, is that it provides the model
for which we are searching. Certainly we must find a way to explain the shifts
in the hedonic quality of affects in a *single operation*. The new physiological
and pharmacological studies give us the answer in the form of hormones that
have an endogenous, opiate-like effect. The endorphins and enkephalines
simultaneously relieve pain while granting a sensation of pleasure as well as
counteracting the "arousing" effect of emotions and pain and hence fulfill our
requirements (Goldstein, 1976; Guillemin, 1977).[3]

Heath's studies on the pleasure and distress centers and their relation to
emotional function and mental illness were inspired by the views of his
teacher, Sandor Rado, who was convinced that "the pleasure economy" was
essential to regulating behavior and object relations (Heath, 1974). Rado
(1964, 1969) felt that hedonic regulations were the major factor in emotional
and mental illness. The discovery of the group of brain hormones involved in
hedonic regulation is an exciting confirmation of these views.

While anatomically and neurophysiologically there are two distinct cen-

---

2. In this regard there has always been some fuzzy thinking, since the ejaculation itself has been
confused with the emotional "discharge."

3. There is also a peptide that is not blocked by opiate antagonists: Neurotensin. Snyder (1980)
has reviewed the mind-boggling multiplicity of polypeptide neurotransmitters, which link the
hedonic regulation with a multitude of visceral, affective, and vital functions and create a
complex interaction between the affective and hedonic states and the homeostatic functions of
the organism.

ters—one registering pleasurable sensations and the other distress—for the psychic reality of an adult, the experience is more of a spectrum endowing each mental event with a quality of relative pleasure or distress. Although the genetic history of this development is as yet little known, an *attenuation* of the intensity of the pleasure (and distress) experience seems to take place, so that the psychological effect in the adult is to make the impact less intense.

Upon the demonstration of the existence of pleasure and distress centers, as well as a whole system of neurotransmitters involved in the regulation of pleasure and distress, we must provide a psychological framework for their function. We must create theories and proceed with studies of the psychological consequences of the development and function of these biological regulators of the hedonic aspect of mental function, particularly the hedonic aspect of affects, and their consequences to the nature and function of the mind. But the application of anatomy and physiology to this work is strictly *metaphoric*. Anatomy and physiology illustrate my clinical impression that the derivation of the hedonic quality of affects may be separate from that of other aspects and attributes of emotion. Raskin and I (Krystal and Raskin, 1970) have discussed the clinical implications of the view that the experience of pain is not a simple perception, but rather a complex experience. The demonstration of the pleasure and distress centers as being discrete from and connected to the limbic system suggests that, similarly, the affect experience should be considered to be a composite.

In addition to the cognitive aspect of an affect (its meaning), there is the "expressive" part. This part of affect is subjectively closely associated with the experience of pleasure or distress, as if either were an inherent part of the emotion. However, both anatomical and clinical observations suggest that the quality of pleasure of affect is quite separately derived and is only associatively linked with a particular affect. The association and the result produced are the same as when one perceives one's mother's face and experiences joy. The joy is not identical with the perception. Nor is the pleasure or distress in the emotion identical with the emotion.

Observations of changes in the experience of the pleasure of anxiety and other affects and the addictive uses of some affects by my patients suggest that the shifting of the hedonic quality of affects is fairly common. This shift can be achieved voluntarily as well, by imagining an appropriate scene and other techniques. We may now return to some of the questions posed earlier. It seems that gratification may take place unconsciously, because pleasure, like guilt and other affective experiences, can occur but not be consciously registered. The possibility of either pleasure or pain occurring without conscious registration is best demonstrated by an experiment in hypnotic analgesia in which the subject denied experiencing any pain while his automatic writing was filled with exclamatives and requests to stop the torture (Hilgard, 1974).

These unconscious gratifications or distresses are clinically noticeable in their actions as motivators—as in the problems of an unconscious sense of guilt or what I referred to earlier as "affect addictions." What we have reviewed also suggests that the perception and conscious registration of the hedonic quality of affects may be shifted, suppressed, or magnified defensively. It may also be modified by association with other affects, as illustrated in poetic "ennobling" of existential despair. Most of all, the very intensity of the pleasure of distress experience can be modified, as seen by these clinical illustrations of changes in the hedonic quality of affects. It is necessary to distinguish the variation in conscious *registration* of gratification (or distress) from the variation in the gratification (or distress) experience itself.

In fact, we can now accept as a premise, based on the work of research hypnotists, primarily Hilgard (1974) and Knox, Morgan, and Hilgard (1974), that we must separate the concept of pleasure from that of gratification, and suffering from pain, as these are capable of separate variations. Moreover, that all four qualities, as well as a multitude of combinational experiences (such as the combined pleasure, pain, gratification and distress in itching) may register in various degrees of consciousness and various degrees of self-sight.[4]

Moreover, as D. Klein (1987) points out, we have to distinguish appetitive motivation and activities from consummatory ones. This view doubles the number of combinations of hedonic regulatory possibilities. We now have to account for, (and we can utilize for the understanding of our clinical observations) the role of pleasure or gratification, pain (distress) or suffering in both appetitive and consummatory principles, and in the broad scope of conscious registration. For it is clear that the quality of conscious registration of affect, and especially its hedonic quality, cannot be accurately assessed through the "conscious or unconscious" duality, but rather must be seen in a spectrum of experiences.

Although I have emphasized the hedonic shifts in affects, probably the most common experience is that the patient's hedonic capacity is low—or secondarily lowered (Meehl, 1975). Of course, these conditions are familiar to us in the form of various anhedonic states, particularly depression. However, not even for depression can we safely assume an anhedonia proportional to the severity of depression. Fawcett and his associates (1983), following up a hunch by D. Klein (1974), have demonstrated by clinical studies that only *some* depressed patients are significantly anhedonic. Still, at least some depressive affective states can significantly alter hedonic regulation. There are also situations when sexual excitement becomes distressful, or when any other proleptic (gratification-expecting) affect is experienced as uncomfortable or painful. Studies in severe posttraumatic states suggest that the most

---

4. The expression "self-sight" was coined by Lawrence P. Tourkow, M.D., in 1953 to denote that only those experiences which are consciously recognized to be a part of one's self-representation are free from repression and therefore utilizable in one's self-interest.

common aftereffect lies in the diminution in the capacity for pleasure and joy, a state of anhedonia that may represent a permanent alteration of these functions (Krystal, 1978b).

IMPLICATIONS OF HEDONIC SHIFTS
FOR PSYCHOANALYTIC TECHNIQUE

In regard to the counterphobic attitude, Fenichel (1945) observed: "The counterphobic individual can engage pleasurably in the activity which he originally feared, if during the procedure he demonstrates to an object with whom he is unconsciously identified that he is protecting or pardoning it" (p. 169). Fenichel was talking about a kind of manipulation that secondarily produces a shift in the pleasure modality of an affect. By finding protection symbolically, the individual diminishes the perception of helplessness in a situation of (subjectively perceived) danger. But the "true" counterphobic continues to have anxiety while carrying out the dreaded act—only he learns to enjoy the anxiety.

How does this happen? A few possibilities come to mind. If the counterphobic activity leads to later pride and self-confidence, a "foreplay" element could be in effect. As Jacobson (1953) put it: "The expectation of future gratification appears to induce pleasurable components which we are entitled to call signal affects too, though of a pleasurable variety" (p. 64). While that view may explain the "pleasurization" of anxiety in certain sexual activities, as in "forbidden games," it could hardly be the whole answer for counterphobics because for them the mastery never takes place, and the individual merely denies this potential insight.

It is helpful to return to the consideration of masochism at this point. In masochistic perversion, pain becomes *sexualized*. It becomes part of the necessary conditions permitting genital sexual gratification, and so it assumes a role similar to a fetish—in the sense that it affects the subjects in a way parallel to perceiving sexual characteristics. Just as an average man might find any aspect of a woman's body "exciting" because it signals potential sexual gratification, so in the perversion, the pain or the actual or symbolic manifestations of sadism in the potential partner takes the place of the usual erotic stimulus. But dependence on stimulation of the genitals for achieving sexual gratification remains.

Not so in moral masochism. If moral masochism exists at all, usually painful affects such as shame, despair, or guilt now become pleasurable or a source of gratification. There is, of course, also a hidden "gain" for the masochist, who by making himself a victim avoids the self-confrontation with his guilt over sadism; but this is a negative quality. The moral masochist avoids greater pain, but the question is, from where does he derive his gratification? The motivation in this shift was originally defensive in nature, and in our analytic work we have to identify these defenses and the underlying infantile unconscious fantasies. When the patient can work with these, he may find that he can dispense with the defenses. But, in addition, we must take into account the "natural history" of this kind of disturbance, namely, that the patient has learned to take pleasure in a previously painful affect related to a masochistically exhibitionistic activity of displaying himself in a castrated condition. *This development has to be dealt with directly* by interpreting the shifts and pointing out their consequences.

Once the therapist conceives of the possibility that gratification may not be derived from pleasure, but rather from pain, and that *all* hedonic experiences may register unconsciously or in a repressed form, a whole world opens up for further exploration or intervention. Thus it may be found that some obsessive-compulsives derive gratification from their self-attacks and depressive mood production (wallowing in sadness). When one elucidates these mechanisms, one finds a virtual addiction to such forms of self-gratification.

The clinical relevance of that observation lies in the fact that if an ordinarily painful affect becomes gratifying, the patient gains a secret, and frequently *not consciously recognized*, source of gratification. No matter how accurate all the other interpretations are, he is not about to give up this secret, most valued possession. Thus the "pleasurization" of an affect constitutes a motivation for resistance that prevents any changes in his emotional makeup and function. This resistance has to be interpreted, and the patient's gratification in and valuing of his "bad" feelings have to be confronted as a major analytic task. The *interpretation and working through of affect goes beyond the work with neuroses, for it often addresses itself to perverbal development.* Only by working through these attachments can the associations of affects with the experience of pleasure be shifted. In this respect, our work consists of a double task. On one hand, the patient has to give up pleasure in an affect or activity hitherto enjoyed. On the other hand, he has to dare to try to explore the affect or activity that he has heretofore experienced as prohibited to him, and gradually learn that *he may do it* (or have it) and that he may *enjoy it.* He then may be able to link it associatively with enjoyment and, as a final step, consciously admit to himself that he enjoys it. As analysts we pay attention to the psychic reality of a patient who is given a chance to discover for himself the defensive values of his past behavior and accomplish an active mastery of his change, having resolved the related conflicts. Here is the clinical utility of viewing all affects as modifications of love as we did in the previous chapter.

Case Illustrations

The patient mentioned in the previous chapter had shown homosexuality with an underlying problem of libidinization of envy, as well as a narcissistic personality disturbance and several other types of difficulties. As he progressed in his analysis, he discovered that his lack of interest in women was defensive in nature and secondary to his giving up his masculine ambitions because of castration anxiety. While until now he kept protesting that he had nothing to offer a woman (because he had only one testicle), he finally dared to approach a woman other than a prostitute and had a successful sexual experience. Subsequently we discovered that his homosexual activities were designed to provide a kind of gratification that was a "secret" from himself. His "kicks" were derived from evoking intense envy in himself and demonstrating that "perfect" individuals rejected him and considered him worthless. There would be produced a "bouquet" of disphoric affects involving helplessness, shame, and self-pity but also a white-washing of his guilt (since he was a victim, and therefore innocent, rather than hateful, vengeful, greedy, etc.). He was addicted to this consciously painful, but vaguely recognizable, gratifying experience.

Once this secret gratification was exposed and explored in terms of its historical, epigenetic derivations, and the multitude of fantasies involved, we found that an enormous creativity was involved in that the development of these behavior patterns made his survival possible. Through exploration of the defenses, conflicts, and impulses involved, the question finally arose whether he would be prepared to give up his secret self-gratification. Here we came to the part of the problem that makes me refer to these problems as "addictions." In substance dependence, drug use represents an attempt at problem solving and self-soothing or self-stimulation and, although it miscarries, the patient is still loathe to give up the only thing that he or she has found dependably helpful. Similarly, this patient demonstrated extraordinary stubborness and defiance by maintaining that the patterns developed were "him" and that he was resigned to live his life as a miserable wretch retaining his secret gratification.

There were, in this case, two separate processes mentioned before: (1) what is commonly thought of as a "perversion"—in which the locus of sexual excitement was shifted from the genitals to the mouth, with masturbation as a "secret" source of gratification, "officially" disavowed; (2) experiencing gratification from the emotions of envy, shame, attachment to painful feelings, and the negative therapeutic reaction. And this—the shift from pleasure to pain as a source of gratification—is the *real* perversion of the hedonic regulation system.

I was, in fact, the third therapist in this case; an analyst and a psychiatrist had worked with this patient for many years. However, it was not possible to deal with the perversion without first enabling the patient to restore the usual associations of joy with his accomplishments and with his successes and renouncing, very gradually, his gratification in affects usually considered distressing.

Once we can separate in our minds the pleasure attribute of an affect, we can observe shifts in the usual pattern and then turn to the use of the usual psychoanalytic technique to uncover their genetic background. They will be found to be defensive and will sometimes yield to psychoanalytic therapy. This is the clinical advantage of the conception of affect as a composite.

PLEASURE AND DISTRESS SIGNALS IN THE INFANT

Last, we return to the question of hedonic functions in the infant that provide the signals necessary to the formation of self- and object-representations. As I stated earlier, our genetic studies on affect tell us that the young do not have signal affects available to them because these are attained only by maturation. Yes, as far as we can determine, the early object- and self-perceptions are dominated by their pleasurable or distressful quality. We must therefore postulate two types of hedonic signals. The "adult type" is indeed derived from the maturation of our affects and becomes available in our "affective memory circuits" as signals. The affective aspect of every mental event provides a qualitative dimension to the experience. Part of this affective experience is a "flavor," as it were, of *pleasure or distress* or a mixture of these. As adults, we experience ourselves most of the time in the midline of this continuum, and at such times we do not register the conscious awareness of an emotion. Most of our operations are carried out with such minimal quantities of affect responses that we are hardly aware of them. However, the hedonic quality, which has through epigenesis become intimately associated with every affect, determines the subjective nature of every self- and object-representation.

In the infant, however, in the absence of signal affects, the direct experience of pleasure and distress, the "naked" activation of the pleasure and aversive centers provides that signal function. This is one of the reasons why in early life the hedonic quality of the perception of the object carries enormous weight. Thus we are dealing with a pure *pleasure and distress signal*, something that is not observable in the adult because of the intimate association of this response with the other aspects of affects.

Hadley (1985) has demonstrated that, indeed, such functions can be envisioned in the consideration of the theories of the amygdala as an amplification-registration system, working in an integrated fashion with the hypocampal error-eliminating system.

Moreover, Hadley showed that the human infant was "preprogramed" to register and become sensitized to the mother's voice in the third trimester of pregnancy and that operation of the hypothalmus, together with the amygdala provide a "reinforce and register" system, that is connected to the pleasure and distress centers. Therefore, the apparatus has been identified that can provide a pleasurable experience when the infant recognizes the mother's voice. Similarly, when the infant registers the perception of a face—particularly if that face becomes familiar and expected, pleasure is experienced. Hadley's work seems to confirm my anticipation that a hedonic evaluation of early object perception must be available before affects have developed to a point where they are available as signals.

Stern (1983) has surveyed a number of direct infant observations further demonstrating that gratification (reward system) operates from the time of birth and that learning theory can explain preferences for the mothering parent as registered through various senses.

The early registrations of pleasure and distress are coded through the phylogenetic makeup of the newborn. The responses relate mostly to the vital functions of the infant: nutrition and elimination and (in mammals) a need for an intimate physical relationship with the mother. This primitive self-reward and self-punishment system takes the place of the signal affect in the infant. It functions in the same way as signal affects, as we understand them, in adults, but it is devoid of the complex background of memories and modifications. George Klein (1976) worked out the functions of the "vital pleasures" without resorting to the economic point of view. He noted that the enjoyment of the sensual experience of infancy was probably "an important primary source of affiliation and attachment" (p. 222). He also reiterated Harlow's (1958) contribution relating "contact comfort" to the pleasures of sensual arousal.

Associative modifications *modify* the intensity of the pleasure and stress experience, which by comparison with those of adults, are quite intense, if not violent, in the infant. The implications of this postulate, of course, require further exploration and consideration.

7
Activating Aspects
of Emotions

The excitatory aspect of emotions is intimately associated with the cognitive elements of the same affect experience and, at the same time, represents the entire organismic participation in the event. Thus, it is impossible to explore the energizing aspects of emotions and still maintain the mind-body split. Hence, this journey of exploration may prove a bit trying to those who are faint-hearted about switching "frames of reference." The activating quality of emotions is both physical and mental. Studying it gives us a chance to reconcile and harmonize the psychological and physiological points of view. If we do not venture into the interface between these views, we remain unprepared to deal with challenges such as the one posed by the experiments of Frankenhauser (1967) and later of Goldstein, Fink, and Meeter (1972), who demonstrated that the injection of a placebo was either arousing or depressing, depending on whether the subjects had been told that they had been injected with a stimulant or depressant.

The risk of confusion resulting from our approaching both the psychological and physiological view of human kind is balanced by the realization that only thus can we heal the Cartesian split that Freud was (reluctantly) forced to follow. Dorsey (1971a) has stressed this point:

> It is my stated purpose to account for human feelings in most specific terms of maintaining and exercising the intact and inviolable *wholeness* of individual human nature. The lifeful meaning of human organic wholeness is a mental creation that may or may not be fully acknowledged, responsibly appreciated, duly honored and heeded [p. 4].

The vital function of affectivity demonstrates and maintains the oneness and integrity of one's living. The present view is trained on precisely that aspect of emotions which enlivens one's being.

OBSERVATIONS ON THE ACTIVATING EFFECT
OF EMOTION

Darwin (1872) was keenly aware of the role of emotions as "a stimulant" that "excites to action"; he noted, moreover, that fear could also become "the most depressing of emotions" and induce "utter, helpless prostration" (p. 31). This observation was continued by Sherrington (1906), who stated: "Emotion 'moves' us, hence the word itself. If developed in intensity, it impels toward vigorous movement" (p. 265). Cannon (1915), following Sherrington's research, concluded that the degree of energy mobilization in the organism was very high during periods of excited emotions.

Inspired by those eminent physiologists, a number of psychologists reclaimed the field of regulation of the levels of energy and excitation by affective states. These researchers, who sometimes called themselves "dynamic psychologists," have elaborated an "activation theory of emotion" (Lindsey, 1951; Malmo, 1959). They explained the continuum of the states of mobilization of an organism and its correlation with emotional states. They appreciated that, whatever measure of arousal was tried or newly invented, the organism was subject to activation or inhibition regulated by the cognitive and affective forces. They stressed that the relationship was not to be oversimplified, in that the degree of "inner" emotional arousal was not necessarily correlated with the extent of measurable overt responses (Duffy, 1957). This discrepancy, however, to which I will return, was to be a fruitful area of exploration of characterological differences and various inhibitory forces (Duffy, 1972).

Duffy, a pioneer and most productive member of this group of researchers, early defined the scope of her work in exploring the "degree of excitation" as the extent to which the organism as a whole was activated or aroused (1934, p. 194). The degree of activation was measured by the relative speed, force, and intensity of all activities. The explorations and measurements involved a very wide range of markers, from skin conductance to heart and respiration rate, muscle tension, performance tests, and the like. Some of the studies pursued the area of autonomic functions and balance (e.g., Wenger, 1947), but others soon progressed to the generalization of the level of energy mobilization and utilization, thus measuring such indexes as the metabolic rate (Duffy, 1951).

The major contributors to these studies held a global view. They were looking for the intensity of the "total reaction" and felt that they were dealing with the basic characteristic of the organism. They proposed that the property of emotional arousal, reactivity, or "degree of excitation" (Duffy, 1934, p. 194) or tension of the individual as a whole should be the fundamental orienting principle in psychology. Duffy argued that the very words "emotional," "excited," or "keyed up" showed that in everyday social intercourse we evaluated each other according to the level of affectively controlled activation. She was equally aware of the emotional blocking of these energizing functions as the other aspect of a fundamental process. Duffy was a particularly careful student, who distinguished activation and excitability from vitality. She suggested that "these two characteristics are more likely to be negatively related than positively related. The tendency to be frequently and intensely aroused leads, no doubt, to fatigue, and to a consequent reduction in vitality" (Duffy, 1957, p. 266).

The paradigm of activation, then, would postulate a basic state of minimal energy or tonicity characteristic of the individual over a relatively long period. This was sometimes referred to as the "postural substrate" or "the general organic background (neuroglandular-muscular)" (Freeman, 1933, p. 326). Hadley (1985) striving to integrate the activating affects with the evaluative aspects of emotion by defining affects as "those activities of the limbic system of the brain beginning with comparator functions in the hippocampus and amygdala and leading to several possible resulting processes, namely, 1) autonomic activation, 2) somatic expression (bodily and facial), 3) general arousal, 4) experiencing a hedonic tone, and 5) subjective awareness" (p. 532).

The basic "at rest" state had some stability and resistance to modification that involved ideas of homeostasis, thresholds of responsiveness, and perhaps even analogs to a stimulus barrier. Despite this impedance, the affective responses regularly produce additional excitation or energy mobilization and utilization. These cycles of response run their own course and vary mainly in the "extent to which an organism as a whole is mainly motivated or aroused" (Duffy, 1941, p. 192). The nature of the characteristic responses and their pattern can be measured; Freeman (1948) proposed standardization of the multiple observation into an "arousal index," a "discharge index," and a "recovery quotient" (p. 100). The composite of these measures would give a picture of the threshold of excitability and the gradient and peak of responsiveness, and in general would mark the excitatory and homeostatic response to emotional excitement. It would give a profile of a personality in terms of its cycles of arousal, which are consistent in a given individual (Duffy, 1957). Wilder (1957), studying the "law of initial value" (LIV), observed that when the initial excitatory state was high, subjects sometimes attained a paradoxical reaction of decrease, rather than increase, of responses to stimulation (p. 74).

However, the measures of intensity and time do not tell the whole story. For, as Duffy (1941) pointed out, "every cycle of response shows the characteristic of direction toward a goal" (p. 195). She further observed: "Response can be appropriate only if it represents adequate discrimination of those relationships which are relevant to his purpose" (p. 188). Thus, for an appreciation of the totality of an episode of emotional response, the pattern of activation has to be considered in the context of the cognitive elements of the effect, including the object- and self-representations, the goals and motivations involved, the hedonic nature of the operation, some organic and characterological variables, and, finally, the person's reaction to what he perceives is happening to him. In order to deal with a phenomenon of such global dimensions, one must view it one aspect at a time.

THE AROUSAL SPECTRUM: ONE OR MORE DIMENSIONS?

The many students of the activation patterns saw them as one spectrum of activities. Typical is Duffy's (1957) summary that "arousal occurs as a *continuum*, from a low point during deep sleep to a high point during extreme effort or great excitement, with no distinguishable break for such conditions as sleep or 'emotion'" (p. 267). This conclusion stems from these researchers' exclusive focus on the "energetics" of behavior. They were striving to explore the ultimate power regulation of an organism and in so doing overlooked a distinction that is relevant in the context of a psychological perspective. Fischer (1971) carried the single-spectrum idea to its extreme when he attempted to "map" a perception-hallucination continuum to organize all mental experience according to the levels of energy or ergotropic arousal. The same scale involved variations in EEG and in consciousness. The central experience was the "I" state or normal routines of perception and relaxation. On the hypo-arousal side were states of tranquillity, meditation to zazen and Yoga samadhi. On the hyperarousal side were, in increasing order: sensitivity, creativity, anxiety, acute schizophrenic states, and, finally, mystical rapture.

Functionally, there are at least two spectra of arousal: one involving the level of wakefulness and the other, of activity. The two frequently coincide but are capable of changing independently of one another. One of the major characteristics of sleep is relative inactivity. On the basis of a simple scale using muscle tension and other activity indexes, Duffy and the other psychologists who were studying arousal assumed that the waking state was a higher energy state.

It is important to separate the two axes of activation before considering certain psychological phenomena that were not studied previously from this point of view. Thus, for instance, in depression there is often a general diminution of activity, but the amount of sleep may be reduced. There is also the broad area of cataleptic phenomena, which is a major consideration of this chapter, in which the state of awakeness or somnolence varies independently of immobility. Both sleep and the degree of activation of the general state of one's body are very complex phenomena and subject to many influences, such as drugs, hormones, the states of exertion, maturation—in other words, a multiplicity of hereditary and environmental factors (Duffy,

1957). Wakefulness and sleep do represent a polarity, but the restorative activity of sleep is not simply proportional to the degree of mobilization. Neither is the degree of wakefulness proportional to the state of excitation of the autonomically controlled organs. The relationship between depth and efficacy of sleep is also not a simple one. Rickles (1972, p. 116) has pointed out that the unitary-activation hypothesis does not seem to hold up in general. There is evidence of separateness of EEG, autonomic, and muscular arousal (Lacey, 1967). There is also the likelihood of yet another triple arrangement involving a system for control of arousal, a second one for the control of activation (defined as "tonic physiological readiness to respond"), and a third that coordinates arousal and activation (Pribram and McGuinness, 1975, p. 116).

There is also renewed interest in the psychomotor regulation of affective swings and disturbances (Greden and Carroll, 1981). Moreover, the explorations go beyond the conventional "psychomotor" conception to the control of all vital and integrity-preserving functions. The exploration and understanding of affect is virtually synonymous with the idea of psychobiology.

ACTIVATION AND PERFORMANCE

The activation resulting from emotions has certain regulative effects on sustaining and terminating of activity. But there is an optimum level of excitation for performance. The curve has been described as an "inverted U," where additional increases in arousal after reaching the optimal reaction range result in a deterioration in performance (Freeman, 1949). This has been described as the psychiatric Plimsoll mark "determining how much residual load the system can carry without sacrificing homeostatic resiliency" (p. 117).

With excessive emotional arousal, the behavior and cognition of the subject become *disorganized*:

> The angry or fearful individual often fumbles in his movements and is confused in his thinking. His speech is frequently incoherent. The depressed individual, too, may manifest incoordination in speech, thought, and movement. However, disorganization of response is a function . . . not of a unique state or condition called emotion, but a function, though not an invariable one, of any behavior which occurs at very high or very low energy levels [Duffy, 1941, p. 288]

Disorganization is especially likely to take place when high arousal is accompanied by conflict and partial (but not complete) inhibitions. Hence the tendency to relatively easy disorganization can be correlated to the degree of neuroticism. (Duffy, 1957).

This observation has some implications for our understanding of impairment of function resulting from affective intensity. First, there are two kinds of disturbances: one based on exceedingly high intensity of affects, say, anxiety; and the other based on moderate intensity of arousal but poor tolerance and easily disorganized function. Second, in therapy with the latter group, we should direct our efforts to increasing affect tolerance rather than trying to diminish emotions.

Interference with performance is not wholly undesirable. In moderate intensity, as when we stumble for words in expressing our sympathy with bereaved friends, the imperfection of our speech is uniquely effective in communicating that we share their pain. Similarly, in psychotherapeutic and psychoanalytic work, the affective state of the therapist, as evidenced in his speech pattern, conveys important messages to the patient. Conversely, the patient's affective state can be judged by the pattern of his or her speech. Mellor (1981) has devised a method of diagnosing depression by timing the patient as he counts to twenty. Both the total counting time and the pause time between numbers are significant.

The intensity of physiological responses in itself seems to be a very consistent, if not inborn, characteristic. In fact, persons have consistent profiles and speeds of recovery to a characteristic baseline level (Freeman, 1948; Duffy, 1957). Duffy (1949) even proposed that since the pattern was very consistent "not only with respect to energy mobilization, but also in the intensity of . . . response to particular persons, objects and situations" (p. 182), the response pattern could be used as the basis for personality classification. This kind of observation is part of our everyday habit of characterizing people as "tense," "excitable," "high-strung," "phlegmatic," or "easygoing" (Duffy, 1949, p. 182).

The tendency to center personality on the intensity and "profile" of physiological reactions kept reverberating in behaviorists' writings (Darrow and Heath, 1932): "The recovery reaction quotient, a measure which is reduced in size by factors enhancing reaction and retarding recovery appears to be one of the better indications of the absence of the 'neurotic' tendencies (p. 242). Murray (1937) also thought that the study of personality was incomplete without the dimension of the "visceral manifestations of regnant process" (p. 163). Roessler, (1972) highlighted the relationship of personality variables to physiological responsivity and performance. The importance of these reactions in respect to optimum performance was emphasized again when it was found that the Mercury astronauts showed very low physiological responses to emotional stress (Korchin and Ruff, 1964; Ruff and Korchin, 1967). The research on the astronauts highlighted the "chick or egg priority" conundrum in regard to the interaction between personality type and the intensity of physiological responses. For, while there appears to have been a spectacularly low physiological and endocrinological reactivity to stress in the astronauts, they were equally spectacular in being unflappable. They had such self-confidence and trust in the favorable outcome of all their undertakings that they are quoted as saying: "Whenever I think of something that may go wrong, I think of a plan to take care of it" (Ruff and Korchin, 1967, p. 306). Also relevant is that the astronauts uniformly had a history of lifelong successes. "They seem not to have been pushed beyond their capabilities or to have been scarred by traumatic failures, but rather moved step-wise to increased levels of competence in the important areas of their life" (Haggard, 1967, p. 322). This seems to be the recipe for producing unanxious, flexible, and generally effective people.

Conversely, certain demoralizing experiences, such as becoming over-whelmed and disorganized in a situation of danger, seem to have lasting harmful effects. This is particularly true of the type of overwhelmed behavior that I have called the "catastrophic traumatic state" (Krystal, 1978a).

ACTIVATION AND THE CATALEPTIC RESPONSE

Just as emotionality or activation has at first a positive effect on *performance*, but after reaching a peak there is a drop in its effectiveness with further energizing, so there is also a difference between cognitive arousal and physical activation. Darwin (1872) made this observation one of his three cardinal principles of expression: "the principle of antithesis" (p. 28). He explained: "Pain, if severe, soon induces extreme depression or prostration but it is first a stimulant and excites to action, as when we whip a horse . . . Fear again is the most depressing of all emotions, and it soon induces utter helpless prostration . . . ." (p. 31). Similarly, the continuum of retardation to excitement in affective disturbances has puzzled investigators since Abraham (1911), who ventured, "whereas the melancholiac exhibits a state of general inhibition, in the manic patient even normal inhibitions of the instincts are partly or wholly abolished" (p. 150).

This issue has confounded many researchers in the field, including Duffy (1957), who dealt with it by trying to separate "excitability" from "vitality." She felt that these two characteristics were "more likely negatively than positively related" and that "arousal leads no doubt to fatigue and to a consequent reduction in vitality" (p. 267). I (1978a) have proposed that there are, in fact, two separate emotional response patterns to danger. The activating response pattern is the affective response and signal of *avoidable* danger. It mobilizes the physiological response preparatory to fight or flight. The affective response to *unavoidable* danger is a pattern of surrender, which Stern (1951a) called the "catatonoid reaction."

The switch from anxiety to the catatonoid response is the subjective evaluation of the impending danger as one that cannot be avoided or modified. With the perception of fatal helplessness in the face of destructive danger, one surrenders to it. This pattern is well established throughout the animal kindgom, and the literature about it (too voluminous to be reviewed here) has been compiled by Seligman (1975). In regard to the psychological and psychoanalytic aspects of the surrender pattern, much work was done by Stern (1951b, 1953, 1968a, b). Meerloo (1959) understood "catalepsy" as a "passive reaction to approaching danger" (p. 385). Freud (1926) had a clear recognition of the impact of helplessness—which he saw as capable of initiating the traumatic state (p. 166). Further, Freud recognized that given an emotional predisposition, an inhibition of responses could take place in the presence of trivial danger.

Later in this volume I describe in detail the process of the adult catastrophic trauma state, which may progress to psychogenic death. At this point, I want to stress that progessive physical paralysis may progress to a cataleptic state. This aspect of the reaction, best known in the animal kingdom (Seligman, 1975), is now known to overtake a significant number of the victims of disasters (Tyhurst, 1951; Allerton, 1964). People likewise "freeze" in airplane and other accidents. The airline industry is concerned and has done research into what they call "behavioral inaction" (Johnson, 1970, 1971, 1972). *Flightlog,* the publication of the Association of Flight Attendants, periodically carries articles about "frozen" panic states (see Editorial, 1974, 1975; Altman and Johnson, 1976).

There is also a progressive blocking of the ability to adjust, take defensive action, or in effect act on one's own behalf—based on a blocking of memory and the cognitive apparatus necessary for problem solving and decision making. Caplan (1981) has carefully registered all the progressive losses of mental function occurring in situations of uncontrolled stress. He listed as components of the loss of capacity for problem solving and accurate evaluation of oneself and the environment, the deterioration of conation, perception, information processing, judgment, memory, recall, association, scanning, symbolization, abstraction, and integration.

CATALEPSY, CATATONOID REACTIONS, AND HYPNOSIS

The immobility of many animals when confronted with a sudden threat has been amply documented and reviewed carefully by Ratner (1967) and Seligman (1975), who noted: "This catatonic response has been called animal hypnosis, tonic immobility, death feint, playing possum, catalepsy and mesmerism" (p. 171). But is this truly an hypnotic phenomenon? What is hypnosis? If we see the same reaction in hypnosis and in the adult cata-strophic trauma state, what can we learn about both states in comparing and confronting them?

Meerloo (1959), who studied cataleptic reactions in humans and knew that they sometimes lead to psychogenic death, also saw the animal reaction as both hypnotic and potentially lethal. He stated:

> The death reflex or emotional stupor is especially manifest in lower animals; it is known in biology as "animal hypnosis" . . . Everyone has heard about the pigeon fascinated by the snake; some birds even become paralyzed by the glare of a photographic lens. The ancient *experimentum mirable*—hypnotizing and paralyzing a chicken—is also well known. The fowl is brought to a state of catalepsy when it is suddenly laid on its back. It even happens that an animal in such a state of catalepsy is unable to arouse itself to normal activity and dies of starvation [p. 386].

Catalepsy is referred to in German as *Totstell-reflex* or "death-posturereflex." However, it is misleading to think of this response as a reflex, which brings to mind an automatic response like a knee jerk. We are dealing with a complex pattern of surrender, necessary and prevalent in the entire animal kingdom and carrying its own means of *merciful, painless death*. When the wild dogs of the Serengeti Plain of Tanzania hunt for zebra (a prey nine times larger than they), the lead dog grabs the zebra by the fleshy upper lip whereupon "the victim would cease its thrashings and stand quietly as the rest of the pack dispatched it" (Malcolm, 1980, p. 64).

This universal experience of surrender, so clearly reproducible in animals, has been observed in precisely the same terms in people in extreme settings. Milechnin's (1962) dispassionate reports about trance developing in starving Soviet prisoners illustrate the "primal depression" element of the reaction in its tragic poignancy. When some of the starving prisoners were given food, the ones for whom there was none would go into a trance, sometimes developing a fainting response with either rigidity or flaccidity. Milechnin called this reaction the "Pavlovian syndrome," because Pavlov had reported that starved dogs (during the famine of 1919–1920) would "whenever they did not receive food immediately after a 'conditioned' signal, fall immediately into a hypnotic state" (p. 162). Howarth (1954) also reported on the sequence of starvation leading to cataleptic states in people. But starvation does not seem to be the essential element. Rather, it is the hopelessness of the situation, such as was observed among the victims of Nazi persecutions (Frankenthal, 1969).

Cataleptic *immobility* is a normal response in the young of all known species, but it disappears if the mothering is disturbed (Moore and Amstey, 1960, 1962, 1963). In the human infant, the same pattern has been reported but normally disappears after two months: "[In] dangerous situations a sudden behavioral change in the infant may occur . . . the infant lies motionless with non-converging, staring eyes and sleep-like respiration" (Papousek and Papousek, 1975, p. 251). In the infantile response there are already elements of submission to total helplessness, but the capacity for being rescued by an external object is preserved. This state contains the cognitive and affective elements of the catatonoid state, hypnotic phenomena, and depressive inhibitory responses (Schmale, 1964; Dorpat, 1977).

The similarity between hypnotic trance states and cataleptic responses to extreme danger is frequently obscured by the terrible distress associated with the latter. Moreover, there seems to be such a contrast between the two states because the hypnotized subject submits to his hypnotist in a state of enthrallment of love. But neither pain nor enthrallment is a truly reliable indicator of cataleptic response. For in the state of surrender and catatonoid reaction, all pain is stilled and a soothing numbness ensues. As for the relationship of the victim to his aggressor, there also are hidden elements of archaic love and adoration, which in fact surface in the survivor and account for certain difficulties (Krystal, 1981b).

Erickson and Rossi (1981) reported that Charcot knew back in 1881 that cataleptic states could be induced by startling, frightening developments or by the hypnotist's efforts, but that regardless of the circumstances, the subject could be described as "fascinated" (p. 26), a description still valid in submission and automatic obedience. As already mentioned, many of the reports of cataleptic states and psychogenic death have the tone of a hypnotic element. Note, for instance, this report: "R.J.W. Burrell, a South African M.D., has witnessed six middle aged Bantu men who have been cursed to their face. Each was told 'you will die at sunset.' Each did. Autopsy failed to show cause of death" (Seligman, 1975, p. 250; see also Mathis, 1964; Hyland, 1978). The pattern is as follows: "A message arrives announcing doom in the form of a curse or prophesy. The victim believes it, and believes he is helpless to do anything about it. He reacts with passivity, depression and submission. Death follows in a period of hours or days" (Seligman, 1975, p. 177). Similarly, the cataleptic states of extreme kinds of hypnotic phenomena, such as trances, can be identified. Note Meerloo's (1959) description: "Many feats of endurance on Indian fakirs are due to their self-induced state of archaic catalepsy. They bring about this autohypnotic catalepsy by staring at the navel. In such a regressive state, the body is able to bear hunger for weeks at a time" (p. 387).

My point about the commonality of the psychic reality in catastrophic psychic trauma and hypnosis is that in overwhelming life situations, particularly in man-made or natural disasters, the subjective reaction is one of submission, wherein the situation (or fate, Providence, God, all representing transferences of primary object relations) is experienced as a *command*.

Whether reality dictates it—or the order comes from hypnotist, magician, shaman, or doctor—if the verdict is a dire one, one submits to it by going into a catatonic reaction. It is exactly so when the order is given by an oppressor, conqueror, or any human or animal predator. Dr. Mengele of Auschwitz was sometimes called the "*angel* of death" by his victims. Many other mythic and poetic figures, such as the *Erlenkoenig* or "Father Time," are poetic representations of this sentence.

Once the reaction of surrender is triggered, a cataleptic response ensues. This is the relevance of the observations of "animal hypnosis" as a universal surrender pattern. It shows that the excitatory (and inhibitory) aspect of emotions, or as Knapp (1981) calls it, the "activation-deactivation" response (p. 420), represents the matrix for both hypnotic and emergency responses. Among those patterns the extreme response is the ultimate surrender pattern, which may become a "self-destruct reaction."

As for the hedonic aspect of the affects, it can shift separately and independently from the tonic one, and that accounts for why we can have cataleptic responses in a pleasurable state, as in hypnosis, or in states of numbness, as in catastrophic psychic trauma and catatonic stupor (see Figure 1).

Erickson (Erickson and Rossi, 1981) has pointed out that catalepsy occurs constantly in everyday life, in transient and momentary forms. These episodes represent:

> gaps in the subjects' awareness as they wait expectantly for an appropriate response from within themselves or from the outside. At such moments, when they are cataleptically posed in immobile suspension, they are open and receptive to appropriate stimuli. *At such moments an appropriate suggestion can be received and acted upon in a seemingly automatic manner. This momentary gap in awareness is essentially a momentary trance. The heightened receptivity during that moment is essentially what we mean by the term hypnotic* [p. 40].

Frankel (1978) has noted that no observable or measurable changes are uniquely associated with hypnosis and that a trance is best defined by the experience of altered or distorted perceptions and memories as a result of ideas offered in a trusting relationship (p. 665). Thus, the occurrence of trances, dissociative phenomena, or cataleptic responses is a normative event, contributing an essential regulatory and self-controlling mechanism. In fact, the very act of attentional activity or orienting responses has been shown to slow the heart rate (Mandler, 1975). But the interactions of the state of consciousness, suggestibility, and various aspects of arousal are just beginning to be worked out, and they show fascinating permutations (Duffy, 1972). The acceptance or rejection of environmental inputs may be just one indicator of responsiveness and may be accompanied by physiological changes in a

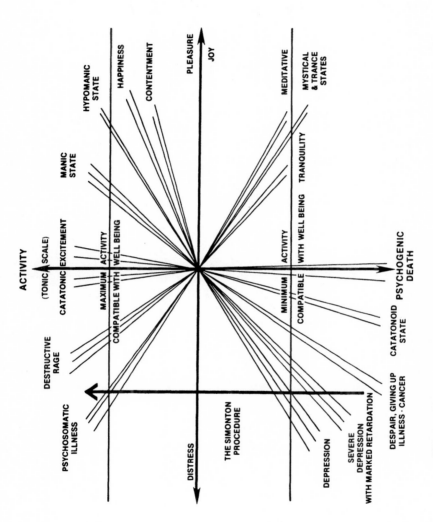

FIG. 1. The correlation between the hedonic and activating aspects of affects.

number of indices (Lacey, 1967). These patterns are an essential aspect of the tonic, excitatory, and inhibitory regulations stemming from the affective coloring associated with every perception, cognition, or act.

The fluctuations in the levels of activation-deactivation may be accompanied by significant increases in suggestibility. The shading in intensity is so subtle, and the ability for self-observation is so limited, that frequently it is impossible to tell whether or not one has reached a trance. Erickson and Rossi (1981) demonstrated that in an ordinary group attending a lecture, a considerable number of students went into trance. As stated already, the components of affective self-regulation are mostly ignored, being of low intensity. However, in special states such as religious or musically induced trances and ecstasy states, or in chronic affective states such as depression, these elements do become very conspicuous (Rouget, 1985).

AFFECTIVE DISTURBANCES AND PSYCHOMOTOR REGULATION

In extreme situations, death may ensue in states of overwhelming helplessness and hopelessness (Richter, 1957; Engel, 1968). Engel's (1971) famous study of newspaper accounts of sudden death cases revealed that both fortunate and disastrous news preceded sudden demise. It appears that the response to either good or bad news can cause sudden death.

This very observation poses the question of the relationship between the hedonic and activating aspects of emotions. Some therapeutic approaches modify either one. For instance, the Simonton procedures, in which cancer patients imagine their defenses defeating the cancer cells, seem to promote an activation, as opposed to passive submission to the disease. This is analogous to the folk remedy for despair by which the subject is made angry. In meditation, presumably both hedonic and vitalizing aspects are influenced. Even a casual consideration of the maneuvers available for such modifications shows that for the most part we are very uneasy about acknowledging this capacity.

While affects and responses seem to occupy a static point in relationship to the coordinates of activation and hedonic quality, the fact is that both of these are capable of separate and independent changes. Thus, a manic state may become very painful; and anger or anxiety, immobilizing, even paralyzing. These independent shifts account for a variety of everyday phenomena and clinical problems.

But it is the chronic depressive who most impresses us with the "power" of emotions to regulate the tempo of one's living. Lifton (1979) has characterized depression as a state of stasis and negation involving "an imbalance between the static and animating" aspects of guilt (p. 192). The "psychomotor retardation" of depression is conspicuous. However, the retardation need not affect the psychomotor sphere primarily, and the clinical diagnosis of depression can be made in only a minority of people whose affective shifts involve mainly their physiological functions. An example of a physiological change resulting from an affective state is pituitary-adrenal disinhibition (Ettigi and Brown, 1977). This phenomenon is the basis of the Dexamethasone suppression test for depression (Carroll et al., 1981) and contributes to the revival of interest in the "retardation" aspect of melancholia. Retrospective studies on cancer patients suggest that despair, hopelessness, and giving up diminish their chances of survival and favor the growth of the tumor (Giovacchini and Muslin, 1965; Achterberg, Simonton, and Simonton-Mathews, 1976; Holden; 1978; Sklar and Anisman, 1979; Bahnson, 1980, 1981).

This is not the place to review the complex factors in cancer defenses or even health regulation. However, it is common knowledge and is regularly acknowledged that depressed children frequently develop illnesses from which they die (Spitz, 1946; Seligman, 1975). Conversely, Flach (1980) put forth the concept of "psychobiologic resilience," according to which creativity and effective dealing with stresses and losses prevent physical illnesses. Vaillant's (1979) retrospective studies showed that the "maturity of defenses was powerfully correlated with somatic illness per se," concluding that "creative management of stress through humor, artistic transmutation or altruism . . . spare the body better than fantasy or paranoia" (p. 733).

The issue related to the matter under study is that the tonic, or activating-deactivating, aspects of emotion regulate many—perhaps all—vital functions. Both short-term and chronic changes in the speed and effectiveness of metabolic and defensive functions are caused by fluctuations in the energizing aspect of one's emotional state. Long-range follow-up studies on Norwegian concentration camp survivors showed earlier mortality and greater morbidity in every category (Eitinger, 1980). I have maintained that the depressive aftereffects of catastrophic psychic trauma and survival of the Holocaust continue to exert a depressive and devitalizing effect until the subject can integrate the experience. Completion of the mourning process and the "healing" of those parts of oneself that had been previously rejected, and therefore continue to generate painful affects, are the key operations in this process. This brings us to the question of the relevance of psychotherapy to the activating aspect of emotions.

DISCUSSION

In studying the affects there is an imperative need to reintegrate the psychological and physiological aspects and the various elements and attributes of the emotional responses. Knapp (1981) proposed that there are "core processes" that involve sensory apperception and hedonic evaluation, central processing (which refers to activation or deactivation of emotional elements), and "expressive mobilization," by which the organism is prepared to deal with the environment (p. 417). This ingenious approach provides a number of useful models and conceptions by which affective functioning can be understood. Freud (1900) illustrated the centrality of affective processes: "A dominating element in a sleeper's mind may be constituted by what we call a 'mood'—or *tendency* to some affect—and this may have a determining influence upon his dreams. A mood of this kind may arise from his experiences or thoughts during the preceding day, or its source may be somatic" (p. 487). In considering the activating property of emotions in some detail, we found some ways by which the state of the organism is influenced by the affective pattern. We also began to appreciate the multiplicity of interactions. The degree of mobilization and excitation regulates and determines the effectiveness and accuracy of all efforts, including cognition. Affects may bring about paralysis or stupefaction and may activate a self-destruct process. We traced some connections between modification of consciousness and self-regulation related to hypnotic states, trances, and cataleptic states.

All these aspects of the "interrelation" of cognitive, affective, and self-regulatory functions have circular effects; the emotional responses, once stimulated, in turn modify the cognitive and physiological processes, thereby substantially modifying the psychic reality, and through it, the self- and world-representation. The various applications and consequences of these processes are the endless variety of combinations in a kaleidoscope of human function. For instance, trances or dissociative states may become paralyzing and deactivating, or they may permit modification of one's own vital and affective functions. Potential insight becomes a useless cliché when devoid of affective mobilization, but emotionality without an epigenetic transformation into predominantly cognitive forms produces only psychosomatic symptoms.

The clinical manifestations of extremes of the activating function of emotions are easily recognizable; at one pole are such phenomena as the hyperexcitement state of psychosomatic "attacks" or affective "storms"; at the deactivation pole are the depressive hypoactivation conditions of diminished vitality and diminished organismic defenses, favoring cancer and other illnesses. But in the moderate sphere of those variations are the fluctuations of everyday life, which present us with a number of relevant observations.

In psychoanalysis, and in fact in all psychotherapy, the effectiveness of one's interpretation or intervention can be determined not by its own merit, but by the patient's state of receptiveness. This in turn may be dominated by the patient's affective state, which through its activating aspect regulates his consciousness and receptivity. Erickson and Rossi (1981) recalled an old observation of Erickson's that putting the subject in a "yes-set" frame of mind made him highly suggestible. That is accomplished by saying something to which he can wholeheartedly agree. What could be a more powerful "yes-set" inducer than an accurate interpretation? Does this mean that some patients go into a very suggestible—perhaps trance—state on the psychoanalytic couch? Could it possibly be otherwise? Only if hypnotizability is just a myth.

A patient in a positive transference in analysis may be experiencing a state of "fascination" (as Charcot used to say) with the therapist. That surely is a very special affective state that modifies a variety of functions and potentials. Hence, the study and understanding of the activating aspect of emotions may permit us to re-animate our conception of the patient's "in vivo" participation in his or her own analysis toward greater self-integration and self-healing.

Just as a painter must render his objects in two dimensions, so the models and conceptions that made possible many useful psychoanalytic contributions have necessitated a "flattening" of our view of the patient and the psychoanalytic process. In particular, the splitting off of "mental" activity necessitated the mechanical representation of the patients. But this convention must be renounced and replaced by the psychophysiological principle:

> Every change in the physiological state is accompanied by an appropriate change in the mental-emotional state, conscious or unconscious, and conversely, every change in the mental-emotional state, conscious and unconscious is accompanied by an appropriate change in the physiological state [Green, Green, and Walters, 1970, p. 5].

Moreover, in considering the relationships among the characteristics of the arousal patterns, we have learned that they have an important influence on the development of characterological traits. These patterns are importantly determined by life experiences, perhaps especially those of early childhood. We have also much experience with catastrophic developments in the activating-deactivating aspects of emotions, which show that once an experience of catatonoid reaction has taken place and lasted for a significant period of time, serious changes in one's affective patterns result. When we consider the problem of modified arousal patterns—the kind that might be measured by indexes of arousal, response, and recovery, there we may be forced to resort to combined psychotherapeutic and *retraining* approaches. Among them, the best known and most available are relaxation procedures.

One dimension necessary to such observations is the relationship between affective arousal (activation-deactivation status) and patient suggestibility. We have not yet been alerted to appreciate fully the whole range of modifications of the affective states in patients. Probably more patients experience transient dissociative experiences or trances while on the couch than we suspect. The induction of those states may have to do with the affectional state of the patients (the "fascination" of love). But in other situations the factors are more closely related to dominance and submission. In the presence of a powerful, self-confident therapist who needs to exert a phallic, narcissistic, or sadistic dominance, many patients will go into a catatonoid reaction or trance. Patients who have significant adult catastrophic trauma in their past will "freeze" and submit. They also do this in everyday life and feel much shame about their inability to assert or defend themselves. Hence, this reaction in therapy may be viewed as a crucial transference reaction—one that permits observations of something that has baffled and confounded the patient.

The development of trances, cataleptic states, and heightened suggestibility in psychotherapeutic sessions may be used for the patients' benefit, to exercise the blocked capacities of regulating their viscera. But, most of all, these are opportunities to deal with transferences to the primal object, that is, infantile conceptions of the mothering parent. However, in order to do so, the therapist must be aware of his effect on the patient, particularly the unwitting or accidental impact of what he is and the way he naturally acts rather than the verbal interventions that he derives from his education and insight. Sometimes, the *way* one talks is more important than what one says.

Our consideration of the "tonic" aspect of affectivity shows that much of everyday activity is done in a *work* frame of mind, which is accompanied by tenseness. With it there is a tendency to seriousness, self-control, and heightened responses as key physiological aspects of the organism. The opposite of this attitude is playing and playfulness. In order to preserve one's well-being, one has to be able to change from the *work* attitude to the *play* attitude and thus provide the setting for relaxation, recreation, and in general a variety of pleasurable and affectionate emotions. This switching or changing of one's affective set becomes very difficult in posttraumatic states; in general in people who are insecure and have a great need to be "in control" and tend to be hyperreactors on a *physiological* level.

People do many things to help regulate the degree of excitation they are experiencing. If they feel excessively energized or overwrought, they can use a variety of relaxing devices—music, drugs, self-distraction, or relaxation procedures. Since excessive arousal often accompanies anxiety or anger, modification may be achieved by influencing the cognitive or physiological aspect of these emotions. Conversely, as with relaxation techniques or drugs, one can address oneself directly to modification of the tonic aspect of emotions. Each of those channels of self-control and self-help can be entered in a variety of ways. For instance, the cognitive aspect of emotions can be modified by psychoanalysis or by a variety of other methods, such as religious practices, rituals, hypnosis and suggestion, or a variety of reframing, reeducational approaches. The approaches to affect modification are many, and that abundance accounts for everyone's having *some* success in dealing with emotional and mental disturbances.

While dealing with states of inhibition or excessively de-energizing affects is a little more difficult and complex, still it is a matter of everyday occurrence. The use of such stimulants as coffee, tea, and tobacco is universal. Some people are quite aware of their constant need to "titrate" themselves to the level of activation that is compatible with their optimum performance. Self-regulation does not always involve drugs but may consist of "working oneself into a lather" by being angry or anxious. The constant search for excitement in gambling, books, movies, and television illustrates the ubiquitousness of this kind of self-regulation. For the most part, we need "external" elements as placebos, so that we can deny our role in self-regulatory activities. So consideration of the energizing aspects of emotions provides both a rationale for and a recognition of the need to reintegrate and self-regulatory activities as part of the psychotherapeutic work. At the same time, it alerts us to the fact that classical (perhaps more accurately, "conventional") psychoanalytic technique may be missing a vital aspect of the patient's and therapist's function. Rather than taking an idealistic view of the purity of technique, we might better direct that idealism to pursuing the goal of the patient's greater self-integration. This involves going beyond the issues related to the phallic identification with the parents to those related to identification with the mothering parent.

Part Two
Trauma

8
Reality

F reud first used the phrase "psychic reality," as distinguished from "external reality," in his "Project" (1895). He did not, however, anticipate at the time what the impact of the exploration of psychic reality would be for his psychological theories. In fact, the history of his "resistance" and struggle against the full recognition of the nature of psychic reality tells of a titanic struggle within himself, which he described later (1914, p. 17). After relating the path of his improbable discovery, he reflected that

> after all, one had no right to despair because one has been deceived in one's expectations; one must revise those expectations. If hysterical subjects trace back their symptoms to traumas that are fictitious, then the new fact which emerges is precisely that they create such scenes in *phantasy*, and this psychical reality requires to be taken into account alongside practical reality [p. 17].

Jones (1953) pinpointed exactly when this "moment of truth" occurred in Freud's life. The struggle within Freud began in the spring of 1897, when Freud's self-analysis enabled him to "discover" psychic reality and at the same time childhood sexuality, the Oedipus complex, and dream interpretation. As Jones put it:

> It was a turning point in his scientific career, and it tested his integrity, courage, and psychological insight to the full. Now he had to prove whether his psychological method on which he founded everything was trustworthy or not. It was at this moment that Freud rose to his full stature [p. 267].

Jones underscored that when Freud discovered the importance of fantasies in self-analysis, "which he had undertaken in the June of that fateful year" he "had to rush to Berlin, if only for twenty-four hours, to commune with his mentor." He related that at the very moment of "discovering" psychic reality, in the very same letter to Fliess in which he joyously announced his discovery, Freud observed that his view of psychic reality focused his attention on the definition of repression. Freud wrote: "I do not know where I am, since I have not achieved a theoretical comprehension of repression." Jones concluded the chapter covering this period in Freud's life by saying: "Eighteen ninety-seven was the acme of Freud's life" (p. 267).

The enormous resistance that Freud experienced and renounced in extending his conscious psychic reality continues to be a problem for every psychoanalyst. What was so difficult for Freud is still difficult for all of us now. In psychoanalysis a great deal of the analyst's attention and conscious effort needs to be devoted to conscious recognition of the nature of his own psychic reality. Attending to the scope of one's conscious reality remains an area deserving of continuing study and reexamination.

In his later writing, Freud returned six times to the consideration of psychic reality directly. Each time, he brought up the distinction between psychic reality directly as opposed to what he referred to as "material," "objective," "factual," or "external" reality. It is my impression that Freud always retained a dualistic view of the etiology of mental illness, namely, that it could be caused by sources from within (instincts, conflict, and intersystemic tensions) or traumatic ones, that is, those derived from external events. Freud's differentiation of the two aspects of reality—as psychic distinguished from "factual"—implied two types of psychogenesis. In 1909, Freud added a sentence to the conclusion of the "Interpretation of Dreams" on this matter. The editors of the "Standard Edition" pointed out that the sentence added in 1909 read: "If we look at unconscious wishes reduced to their most fundamental and truest shape, we shall have to remember, no doubt, that psychical reality too has more than one form of existence." The final version, revised in 1914 and 1919, is: "If we look at unconscious wishes reduced to their most fundamental and truest shape, we shall have to conclude, no doubt, that *psychical* reality is a particular form of existence not to be confused with *material* reality" (Freud, 1900, p. 620n).

Freud's longest exposition of his view of psychic reality is to be found in *Totem and Taboo* (1913). There it appears that he relegates fantasies and impulses to psychic reality but considers *deeds* to be part of factual reality. Talking about a sense of guilt, he indicated that it was derived in neurotics from their "*psychical* realities and never factual ones" (p. 159).

Dorsey's (1953, personal communication) impression of Freud was that Freud was very clear in his mind that the only knowable reality was psychic reality and that consciousness was but fleeting attention given to a given mental event, one of a chain of concatenations, simultaneously excluding everything else. Freud indicated as much by stating that it was the essence of psychoanalysis to understand perceptions as "subjectively conditioned" and "perceptions by means of consciousness" were not to be equated with unconscious mental processes (1915b, p. 171).

By 1943, Dorsey became convinced that the concept of psychic reality was central to all of psychoanalysis. He devoted the remaining 35 years of his life to studying the nature of his own mental function—which included the creation and living of his own reality, consciously. In his exploration of the "meaning of meaning" he found that "a mind is able to experience the meaning of anything in nature only to the extent that it can reproduce that 'anything' with its own psychological constructs" (p. 151). By his work he anticipated the explosion of studies and knowledge in the fields of perceptual and cognitive psychology. He felt that it was everyone's life challenge to achieve the integration of one's own mind. To be able to extend the conscious self-recognition to one's entire mind and to one's soul was the last step in everyone's weaning. Just as his analyst, Freud, had done, Dorsey strove to be able to see his "I" where he could previously conceive of "nonself."

I have placed the concept of psychic reality at the center of this volume. Particularly in the study of trauma and its aftereffects, it is essential to appreciate the nature of the reality of each person. The acknowledgement of self-conscious mentality as central to the interpretation of one's world makes possible the cultivation of self-responsibility. It permits the expansion of narrow (infantile) selfishness to its broadest possible scope wherein one recognizes the subjectivity of one's experience. My view of this process is that each one has to create all his self- and object-representations. Dorsey (1965) went further: "The mind's objects are not representations of the real objects in external reality. Everything is its own self and cannot represent anything else. My mind's reality does not consist of "Images but of its own *reals*" (p. 48). In that case, how should we define reality testing? Dorsey responds:

[It] is not the product of judgement, or of reasoning. It is *the particularly distinctive way I live* (create whatever I create) is all that accounts for the specific nature of the existence I ascribe to it. *My observation of the way in which I am living provides me with my only means of my only measure of reality testing of any kind* [p. 48].

To be able to carry out observations on psychic reality, we also have to go back to Freud's idea of the "I," which Dorsey restates as follows:

In this report the term "self" is a synonym for whole being and means the inviolable oneness of the human individual. The specific purpose of this use of the all inclusive term "self" is to indicate that any of our mental material which is not entirely observed as exclusively our own is not observed truly, the lie constituting the psychopathy of repression [p. 48].

The idea of the "self," or Freud's "I" is indispensable to the original conceptions of psychoanalysis. This point was stressed by Barrett (1984), who observed that the model of the basic "I," from which mental material is split off by repression but to which the repressed must return, is the core of Freud's pioneering work in psychoanalysis.

However, according to Dorsey and Seegers (1959) the idea of "splitting" off parts of one's mind was illusory, since to them oneself and one's mind were synonymous. Selfhood was the process by which one's life was endowed with meaning. For Dorsey (1965, p. 167) the nature of oneself is determined; that is, it is only "a momentary existant" in that one can experience one's wholeness and life only in the present moment. Both past and future were also illusions, since they could be evoked and experienced only in the present.

Thus it appears that Dorsey's definition of the self exceeds the totality of self-representation and self-feelings and yet is the crucial orienting principle. The matter revolves around the key observation that one can only live himself and only now. Everything he lives *is* his own self.

REPRESSION AND RENUNCIATION

Centering our work on the conscious awareness of psychic reality leads us to broaden the concept of repression. What is repressed can either be conscious or be denied to one's selfhood and attributed instead to the nonself. The "repressed" is without insight, taken for granted, ignored completely or partly.

Repression, then, is not necessarily accomplished by rendering a mental element unconscious or blocking its potential for retrieval into consciousness, but rather by alienating it from one's consciously recognized self-representations. Making unconscious ideas conscious does not necessarily lift repression, unless those ideas are also made "self-conscious," that is, as Freud (1933) would say, "they have to become part of the "I." Dorsey (1965) defined repression as the "exclusion of some of my self-experiences from my self-conscious living" (p. 10).

Lifting repression is not accurately described in Freud's original models based on the topographic point of view. Only that which becomes part of the consciously recognized identity and functionally integrated with oneself is truly reclaimed. Material that is conscious, but strongly defended makes up much symptomatology (Arlow and Brenner, 1964). Most of our work is done with characterological problems in which the repressed impulses and conflicts are not exactly unconscious, but the acting out is attributed to fate in the fashion of the ancient theater.

Dorpat (1985) has pointed out that Freud made a mistake when he assumed that "perfect" perception was automatically registered consciously and later repressed and could, therefore, be brought back from repression in the original "perfect" form. Upon perception of painful affects, the "painful object" demands denial and, with it, a constriction of cognition and of substitute, "screen" behavior. Hence, memories and thoughts are subjectively created in a distorted fashion. Although the presence of stress greatly magnifies the kind of distortions that I discuss in the chapter on trauma and affect, every perception is a subjective creation, a compromise formation involving one's own creativity and inventions. One can deal only with the products of one's subjective processing.

The failures of psychoanalytic treatment are for the most part recognizable in the patient's being able to quote interpretations they have heard and memorized, but not being able to make them part of themselves. The interpretations seem to them true enough, but their lives appear to be driven by alien and undesirable mentation they would like to eliminate. Respecting the nature of subjective reality directs all the therapy toward the ultimate goal of reclaiming and reintegrating one's own mind's products, so that they can be lived fully (affectively). In this effort, whatever is within one's purview is accepted lovingly and granted the right to be. Impulses that cannot be fulfilled, wishes that are denied by reality or by their appropriate causes have to be *renounced*. Dorsey (1965) added, "Repression is my imagination's condemnation proceeding, a prohibition which creates an emphasis. My repressed power seems to me to be involuntary. My renunciation is loving appreciation for whatever I live. My renounced power is ever accessible to me as volitional" (p. 3).

Psychoanalytic theory need not entail riddance or subordination and constant controlling of conflictual or disfavored parts of oneself. What we may have unsuccessfully tried to rid ourselves of and what we experience with horror, pain, or other painful affects, must be lovingly reclaimed. Psychoanalysis permits recognition of the selfhood that appears to have been rent apart so that it can be healed. The dangerous, "poisonous," or otherwise disturbing mental material that is so difficult to attend to is discovered to be made of one's own fantasies and notions about the world. Dorsey (1954) found that the mental material most difficult to own up to and most difficult to love was registered consciously but relegated to "otherness." Repression is the illusion of self-negation, in which one has to create the fantasy of both the rejecting and the rejected parts.

Instead of relegating one's mental material to repression by exclusion from the self-representation, if one grants oneself the right to experience every necessary wish, impulse, idea, or emotion, one may be considered to have achieved the highest level of integration. What one chooses not to indulge in may be renounced without resorting to the infantile defenses that impoverish one's inner resources. The difference between repression and renunciation bears repeating. The original externalization of object-representation and self-representation (registration of them as nonself) is necessary to prevent overwhelming the immature psyche with affective precursors. But the price of maintaining these self-alienations is reflected in the way we conceptualize object loss and reactions to it—for instance, Freud's (1917) idea that we introject the object *after we lose it.* Virtually all psychoanalytic discourse uses such models in explaining the process of *giving up* the object. My view is more in harmony with Marris's (1982) derived from years of studying bereavement: " . . . people work through grief by retrieving, consolidating, and transforming the meaning of their relationship to the person they lost, not by abandoning it" (p. 195).

The image and memories of the lost object continue to manifest its existence in our mind. The effect can be likened to the "return of the repressed." The previously externalized object, having lost its physical existence, shows itself always to have been (to us) our own mental product. In this view, the challenge of grieving is not "giving up" the object, but self-integration. The only thing that is to be given up (by renunciation) is the expectation of future gratification and the future use of the object to maintain its (illusional) externality. Whereas repression denies our wishes the right to exist, in renouncing them we lovingly accept their existence and grant ourselves the right to have had them.

If the lost object, or part of our own past, is externalized, then the intrusion of the idea of it into the mind does not necessarily result in the acceptance of what needs to be accepted. Grief is experienced until negation and denial are reestablished. Lifton (1979) aptly summed up this kind of an impasse: "What eats away at everyone in depression is not so much ambivalence toward the dead person, as Freud thought, as it is the terrible duality of simultaneous immersion in deep sadness or irreplaceable loss and the perpetual, ineffectual protest against that loss" (p. 189). The kind of posttraumatic dissociation in self-representation that we are about to look at can best be understood if one defines repression as Dorsey (1965) has: "ignoring and denying part of his human nature in which he cannot see his identity with composure" (p. 255). Dorsey considered it a major discovery that his consciousness and self-consciousness were not one and the same idea. Self-consciousness is the manifestation of one's mental functioning by which one consciously asserts one's individuality.

Thus, the term "identification," as used at present in psychoanalysis, refers to the fantasy of magically regaining unity with one's own object-representation, which has been long externalized. What we really need to achieve, when we center our thinking on Dorsey's insight of reality, is to explain to the patient that he is merely trying to extend his "I" feeling to all his object-representations, whether they are living, deceased, or inanimate. Most of all, however, one has to claim ownership of all of one's self-representations, including its disowned parts. We might call this process "tertiary identification"—discovering that all our object representations are our own creation.

A number of the current usages in psychoanalysis so concretize metaphors that certain insights that are essential in the exploration of affects are obscured. For a clear view of "object relations," we have to start with Dorsey's often repeated statement that perception is not the object, and the registration of the perception is not the perception. But the determination to expand one's conscious self-awareness therapeutically had best start with the acknowledgement of the indispensability of repression, which is originally achieved in the interest of maintaining a *limited*, but integrated, self-representation. And, just as we expect that repressions and externalizations were necessary to prevent the traumatic overwhelming of infantile self-sight, so also in setting out to be of help we must remember that repression can be given up only under extraordinary circumstances.

Similarly, in preparation for the kind of problems that cannot be dealt with, we cannot use the commonly accepted definitions. We have to redefine the term "transference" as any mental registration of the world that is *not* endowed with a conscious recognition of selfhood. Whatever one experiences as "not me" is repressed (Dorsey, 1965, p. 73). And because the traumatic state and posttraumatic sequelae have much in common with trances, it is helpful to consider Dorsey's idea that repressive living is analogous to hypnosis. As Dorsey put it, "Whatever I cannot see *as* myself, I *must* claim can have some influence *over* me, and I over it" (p. 134).

Transference is the very aspect of psychoanalytic work that can be utilized by the analysand to discover that all of his mind is his own. The patients we are about to discuss are the furthest from being ready to explore the nature of their psychic reality. But no psychotherapeutic approach, short of an attempt to heal the illusory splits in their mental representations, can address itself to their "basic fault." Balint (1968) and Little (1981) understood that some patients' problems involve special kinds of transferences other than the oedipal one, notably transferences related to infantile symbiotic fantasies. For alexithymic patients we also have to expand the nature of the psychic reality we are prepared to understand, imagine, and interpret (Little, 1981, p. 75-80).

Dorsey used to say to his students: "What I cannot identify with, I cannot help myself with, but I can only hurt myself with it." To deal with patients whose distortion of self-representation and object-representation results in an unbearable, unmanageable psychic reality, we have to take an extreme stand about the process of self-exploration. The question of how many patients we can get to embark on the exploration of the true nature of their reality is irrelevant to our determining what is there and how it got there. Most of all, if one contemplates accompanying, even leading, a patient through this dark and scary territory, one had best consider the all-aloneness of being one's own everything. For what our patients have in common is a hypnotic type of transference based on what Dorsey called "addiction to illusional otherness" (Dorsey and Seegers, 1959, p. 56).

For patients who have no conscious recognition of the psychological nature of parts of their own bodies, it is crucial to consider that whenever one refers to any part of one's body, or any function, as "nonmental," this is as clearly a sign of repressive living as calling it "nonself" (Dorsey, 1954, p. 97).

Recognition of the nature of psychic reality brings back childhood fears of being alone, of being abandoned and motherless. Solipsism is a code word for the fear of helplessness—certainly fear of the loss of the privileged power of a therapist. But in dealing, for example, with posttraumatic patients who in order to preserve their lives had to extensively split and externalize their minds, and to whom the idea of restoring the unity of one's world representation is terrifying (and dangerous), we have to prove our competence gained by our own acquaintance with facing pain and daring to try for the greatest possible self-integration.

It is particularly in regard to anticipated countertransferences that Dorsey's (1965) elaboration of the nature of our psychic reality becomes significant:

> My psychoanalytic treatment is all and only my persevering effort to discover and renounce my counter-transference as I live my patient discovering and resolving (learning to renounce) his transference. Quite as in my dreaming, my counter-transference enables me to attribute "impersonal" meaning to any of my living for which I cannot currently acknowledge self-responsibility [p. 308].

Some of the problems of countertransference, which are referred to in other chapters (e.g., the oppressor-victim polarization) are self-evidently difficult to handle and require much attention. However, the special need to focus on the nature of psychic reality is in dealing with residues of infantile trauma. The transferences are rarely verbalizable and revolve around conflicts over assuming self-caring functions, which are experienced as reserved for mother. Since the maternal image posesses the power of life and death, as well as of indescribable torture, and is often affected by splitting, idealization and vilification, approaching such transferences is very difficult. Left to the patient's initiative, it may never happen. It may become necessary for the therapist to challenge the entire material and architecture of the patient's psychic reality in order to be able to free up these early building blocks of the infantile world view. But to chance such a profound shakeup the therapist has to have struggled to reclaim his own soul and be able to name everything in his experience as his own, his self, his reality. In other words, he has to have exercised his own mental healing powers by extending his selfhood ("I" feeling) to everything he beholds.

9
Trauma and Affect

Freud's earliest observation about psychic trauma, which remains the cornerstone of our understanding it, goes back to something he learned from Charcot (Freud, 1886), which he confirmed in his own work (1893a; Breuer and Freud, 1893–1895), namely, that some hysterical attacks are the aftereffects of unbearable experiences in the past. The nature of the traumatic *situations* the Freud postulated in 1893 was vague: "a single major fright (such as a railway accident, a fall, etc.) . . . [as well as] other events which are equally well calculated in their nature to operate as traumas (e.g., fright, mortifications, disappointments)" (1893a, p. 152). While the question of sexual seduction provided a temporary distraction, in the renunciation of that theory Freud was able to focus on the fundamental area of psychoanalytic observations: *psychic reality*. The emphasis on the nature of the subjective experiences, as well as on its unconcscious aspects, directed the main interest to the "final common path" in the traumatic *event*—the emotion involved. And so, in the "Studies on Hysteria," Breuer and Freud (1893–1895) give us the following definition:

> In traumatic neuroses the operative cause of illness is not the trifling psychical injury of the effect of fright—the psychical trauma. In an analogous manner, our investigations reveal, for many, if not most, hysterical symptoms, precipitating causes. . . . Any experience which calls up distressing affects—such as those of fright, anxiety, shame or physical pain—may operate as trauma of this kind [p. 5-6].

On the same page (6) the authors recount that "to [their] great surprise" the hysterical symptoms disappeared when the meanings were recovered from repression and brought into consciousness, but that "recollection without affect almost invariably produces no result." Here, then, is one paradigm of psychic trauma: A person is confronted with *overwhelming* affects; in other words, his affective responses produce an unbearable psychic state that threatens to disorganize, perhaps even destroy, all psychic functions. Stra-

137

chey (1961) pointed out that "the notion of the ego being 'overwhelmed' . . . occurs very early in Freud's writings. See, for instance, a mention of it in Part II of his first paper on 'The Neuro-Psychoses of Defence' [1894]. But it plays a prominent part in his discussions of the mechanism of the neuroses in Draft K of January 1, 1896, in the Fliess correspondence" (p. 57). It should be noted, however, that Freud left open the question of what makes an affect unbearable or overwhelming. One's first impression of Freud's words is that *any* intensive and painful affect could be traumatic, but we know that usually this is not the case. This naivete contributes greatly to the confusion, which was multiplied as the concept of psychic trauma was expanded and built upon.

If we set these unanswered questions aside, however, we find in Freud's early writing a complete theory of the relationships among affects, trauma, and hyterical symptoms. When emotions are unbearable, repression takes place; the memory "retains the affect," and so *"hysterical patients suffer from incompletely abreacted psychical traumas"* (Freud, 1893b, p. 37). In this model, then, the *unbearable affects* developed in the traumatic situation; and one of the consequences of the trauma was that in order to terminate the unbearable state, the perceptions and associatively induced ideas were repressed, thus becoming unconscious but retaining their affective charge. Their affective charge was envisioned as "strangulated" because repression prevented its normal working off not just by "abreaction" but also because the cognitive aspects of the repressed "complex" could not be dealt with in "another manner which may be called normal" (Freud, 1939, p. 73).

Alongside that model of psychic trauma, Breuer and Freud (1893–1895) developed another one: that of the dynamics of unacceptable impulses.

> It turns out to be a *sine qua non* for the acquisition of hysteria that an incompatibility should develop between the ego and some idea presumed to it . . . [p. 122].
> The actual traumatic moment, then, is the one at which the incompatibility forces itself upon the ego and at which the latter decides on the repudiation of the incompatible idea. That idea is not annihilated by a repudiation of this kind, but merely repressed into the unconscious [p. 123].

Freud (1926) was able to reconcile these two conceptions of trauma only after he developed the second theory of anxiety. Having clarified the role of anxiety as the signal of (internal) danger motivating defenses, Freud explained that if the defensive actions—notably repression—failed, anxiety would mount and progress to "automatic anxiety." There was an *automatic* development of infantile trauma, the model for which was the affective state at birth.

Thus, for many years, Freud had two separate models of trauma in mind.

One was the "unbearable situation" model, emphasizing the affective states, a view that was reinforced by observations on war neuroses (Freud, 1919, 1939). The other point of view might be called the "dynamics of pathogenesis" model. Although Freud (1926) explained that *in the neuroses the development of the traumatic situation was actually prevented*, still the point was made that such neuroses were traumatic, unlike those allegedly determined by hereditary predisposition. In this view, every mental illness that could be demonstrated to have an understandable epigenetic history could be considered traumatic, and its point of origin was thus, by this definition, a traumatic moment.

Freud's assertion that hysteria had a traumatic origin was part of his struggle against the accepted opinion of his day that the cause of the neuroses was degeneracy. The concept of the *traumatic* origins of hysteria and such ideas as psychic determinism and the influence of the unconscious part of the mind were directly opposed to the then current condemning attitude of the medical and psychiatric establishment and must be appreciated in the light of history. Freud (1937) finally made explicit his view that the causes of mental illness were either "constitutional" or traumatic (p. 224).

Freud maintained both models of psychic trauma throughout his life. He used the "unbearable situation" and the "unacceptable impulses" theories in parallel fashion. Possibly the key to understanding the history of psychoanalysis is that the entire economic view of metapsychology represented an effort to reconcile these two views.

Some of the confusing writing on this subject by other authors resulted from their straddling the two views of psychic trauma. Kris (1956), for instance, talked about "*traumatic effects*" resulting from the "accumulation of frustrating tensions" (p. 73; italics mine), but the traumatic effects are from pathogenesis, not from the unbearable state. Khan (1963), elaborating Kris' concept, made the point that the cumulative trauma "operates and builds up silently throughout childhood right up to adolescence" (p. 301). Why, then, did Khan talk about "cumulative *trauma*" rather than an accretion of pathogenic influences? Some circular thinking seems to have been involved. Clearly, there is a need for a better definition of the concepts of trauma. The entire thrust of Khan's paper was that the mother's function is to provide a temporary stimulus barrier for the child. He discussed the mother's failure to function as an effective stimulus barrier. Freud had defined trauma as a breach in the stimulus barrier.

Khan identified the effects of the mother's failure to protect the child from a variety of adverse circumstances. However, he did not consider what a trauma experience might be. In fact, he indicated that cumulative trauma is entirely silent, goes unnoticed by everyone concerned, and "becomes visible only in retrospect" (p. 296). Khan made clear that he was talking about "pathogenic effects," which he attributed to the failure of the mother to function as a protective shield, a definition he broadened radically to include any development or experience that is not conducive to the child's optimal development. Thus, "breaches in the mother's role as a protective shield" (p. 290) may result in inadequate phase-appropriate frustrations, which can hardly be imagined to produce trauma. Khan used the term trauma to cover a multiplicity of sins, in fact, just about anything except trauma itself. He quoted Anna Freud to support his view of trauma as "subtle harm . . . inflicted on this child, the consquence of [which] . . . will become manifest at some future date" (p. 302). According to this view, childhood trauma consists of all unfavorable influences, anything leading to the development of psychopathology. In fact, Anna Freud (1967) expressed great concern about the confusion and abuse of the term "trauma," which, like other concepts that are used carelessly, would "in the course of time, lead inevitably to a blurring of meaning and finally to abandonment and loss of valuable concept" (p. 235). She reflected on how she would limit her use of the term:

> Like everyone else, I have tended to use the term "trauma" rather loosely up to now, but I shall find it easier to avoid this in the future. Whenever I am tempted to call an event in a child's or adult's life "traumatic," I shall ask myself some further questions. Do I mean that the event was upsetting; that it was significant for altering the course of further development; that it was pathogenic? Or do I really mean traumatic in the strictest sense of the word, i.e., shattering, devastating, causing internal disruption by putting ego functioning and ego mediation out of action [p. 241].

If, like Khan (1963), we accept the definition of trauma to be every unfavorable influence in childhood, or if we assume, as many authors do, that every event and experience in the life of an adult production of psychopathology is also self-evidently trauma, then the usefulness of the term is lost and it may well be discarded. There is, however, a wealth of information indicating that traumatic experiences do occur both in children and in adults. The problem is that we have tried to account for too many kinds of adverse effects by this term and that within the conception itself there is a lack of distinction between two disparate models that became fused by reason of historical circumstances.

The tendency to mix the models of psychic trauma pervades psychoanalytic writing. It reflects Freud's wish and lifelong efforts to create a unified theory that would account for and unite his two models of trauma. This tendency can be observed in Freud's continual shifting of terms from "affects" to "excitation" and finally to "stimuli." If the generalization can be made that stimuli can be overwhelming, then a unified theory of trauma and pathogenesis is secure.

PARTIAL TRAUMA AND EGO STRAIN

In the very same paragraph in which Breuer and Freud (1893–1895) described the traumatic situation as an unbearable state, they introduced the concept of "partial trauma":

> It the case of common hysteria it not infrequently happens that, instead of a single major trauma, we find a number of partial traumas forming a *group* of provoking causes. These have only been able to exercise a traumatic effect by summation and they belong together in so far as they are in part components of a single story of suffering [p. 6].

The question remains. When there is a "summation" of partial traumas, do they culminate in the development of the same unbearable state that was postulated for the acute traumatic event? If so, then partial traumas are simply preliminary events that sensitize the individual and exert their influence in such a way that when their "suffering" is added up, a traumatic situation is produced. Unless an accumulation of some noxious influences can be demonstrated, we can consider Breuer and Freud's language regarding the "summation" of suffering as purely metaphoric.

Each of the partial trauma events predisposes to a later overreaction to a certain psychic constellation. Probably only a minor part can be attributed to the "suffering" engendered, for example, fear of the pain. The major aftereffects will lie in whatever changes have taken place in the available defensive operations and the fantasy explanations of the event. If the first misfortune has resulted in a feeling of guilt, subsequent ones may be experienced as the "doomsday signal" of dreaded punishment, the substance of which refers to infantile psychic trauma. *But none of the separate components of the "partial trauma" chain of events is productive of a trauma—save the last one.* In the end, it is only the psychic trauma that retrospectively makes those (subjective) experiences trauma related.

Murphy (1961) showed that contained in what might be considered an acute traumatic event is frequently a susceptibility resulting from mounting depression and anxiety at the peak of which an otherwise manageable event will become traumatic. Like Murphy, Sandler (1967) started from observations of the mounting vulnerability that results from an "accumulation" of potentially traumatic factors. Although it is possible for the traumatic event to be averted, the person will nevertheless be significantly affected by the state of strain. Sandler demonstrated that significant symptoms, behavior, and developmental modifications can occur in the absence of trauma. He described how, in the process of trauma prevention, serious emotional difficulties may still develop. Some of the effects have been summarized by Solnit and Kris (1967):

Strain trauma not only promotes the development of rigid ego defenses, but such trauma also renders the individual more vulnerable to shock trauma. Thus an acute trauma is magnified because the individual does not have a repertoire of ego defenses necessary for a flexible adaptation to challenges from the environment or from the inner instinctual demands [p. 205].

Keiser (1967) pointed out that because of the complexity of ego functions, the loss or impairment of any capacity must be compensated in ways that greatly magnify a feeling of insecurity and dread of annihilation.

THE PHENOMENOLOGY OF TRAUMA

Since the evidence of trauma is in its phenomenology, we need to keep the following picture in mind; a paralyzed, overwhelmed state, with immobilization, withdrawal, possible depersonalization, and evidence of disorganization. There may be a regression in any or all spheres of mental function and affect expression. This regression is followed by characteristic recuperative attempts through repetition, typical dreams, and eventually long-term neurotic, characterological, psychosomatic, or other syndromes. The so-called traumatic neurosis is *just one of many possible sequelae of traumatization.*

Although the aftereffects of the psychic trauma are many, there is a syndrome of affective disturbances that reflects *direct* sequelae of trauma[1] and is related to the nature of the traumatic state. In these patients we see a lifelong disturbance of affectivity. They have a history of multiple, even severe, traumas. The events were clearly of the "overwhelming state" variety.

The experiences gathered in a 40-year follow-up on survivors of massive psychic traumatization in the German concentration camps showed that while virtually any symptoms or diagnosis may be found, there is in the sequelae a common element consisting of certain chronic disturbances of affectivity. The problem is most commonly referred to as "mixture of depression and anxiety" (Bensheim, 1960; Niederland, 1961; Krystal and Niederland, 1968). These observations led me to explore other affective disturbances in the survivors. As a result of these studies, I came to the conclusion that the "final common path" of traumatization was the development of overwhelming affects, as Freud had originally indicated.

---

1. I am emphasizing the *direct* sequelae of trauma, that is, those related to the trauma experience per se, because I hope that by paying attention to them we may learn about the nature of psychic reality in trauma. The development of, say, a neurosis would be a reaction not to the traumatic experience itself, but to the fantasies to which it becomes attached in terms of an attributed meaning, for example, as a confirmation of the threat of castration, as evidence that dangerous wishes may come true or bring punishment. In the psychiatric and psychoanalytic literature virtually every diagnostic entity has been linked etiologically with trauma.

THE CHALLENGE OF THE AFFECT EXPERIENCE

All descriptions of the phenomenology of trauma include a disturbance in affectivity, but the precise role of affect in the genesis and prevention of trauma is not clear. The appreciation of the role of affect and the models used have varied considerably. Breuer and Freud (1893–1895) were quite straightforward about it: "Any experience which calls up distressing affects— such as those of fright, anxiety, shame or physical pain—may operate as a trauma of this kind" (p. 6). Under what circumstances do affects become a challenge to the ego and become potentially traumatic?

The key word in Freud's conception of trauma was "helplessness." He asserted that "the essence and meaning" of the traumatic situation consists in "the subject's estimation of his own strength . . . and in his *admission* of helplessness in the face of it—physical helplessness if the danger is real and psychical helplessness if the danger is instinctual" (1926, p. 166; my italics). Freud reemphasized this point in the closing sentence of the paragraph, saying in effect that it is the *subjective experience of helplessness (erlebte Situation)* which determines that a situation is traumatic as distinguished from one of danger. The point of helplessness in this context is that it implies "giving up," *surrender.*

The essence of recognized and admitted helplessness is *surrender* to the inevitable peril. With helpless submission to unavoidable danger, the affective state changes from anxiety to cataleptic passivity. Anxiety is the signal of the perception of *preventable* danger. Helplessly surrendering to the peril changes the affective state from the hyperalert and hyperactive response (anxiety) to one of blocking emotions and progressive inhibition. This surrender sequence has been referred to by Zetzel (1949) and described in great detail by Stern (1951a, b, 1968a, b; see also Meerloo, 1948, 1959). These observations are also in harmony with those of Kardiner (1941; Kardiner and Spiegel, 1947).

When the emotions change from anxiety to surrender and the catatonoid reaction described by Stern (1951a), the latter state itself becomes a threat to functioning, integrity, and even survival of the individual. With the catatonoid state, we are dealing with the very moment a person is overwhelmed with a phylogenetically determined surrender pattern, which is also a potential psychological "self-destruct" mechanism. Jones (1929) was, of course, well aware of the lethal potential of such reactions, which he called "aphanisis."

SURRENDER, PSYCHOGENIC DEATH, AND TRAUMA

My experiences with survivors of Nazi persecution indicate that a progression from the excited state to the passive surrender of the catatonoid reaction does take place in the face of unavoidable and overwhelming danger. In this state, even military personnel, such as thousands of Polish officers in Katyn, obeyed orders leading to their mass murder. Many European Jews similarly obeyed orders in an automatonlike fashion, took off their clothes, and together with their children descended into a pit, lay down on top of the last layer of corpses, and waited to be machine-gunned. In this state, a condemned person cooperates with his executioner. In fact, if this process is allowed to continue to its full potential, the executioner becomes superfluous—the victim will die of his own accord (Menninger, 1936; Burrell, 1963). Richter (1959) quoted the coroner of the City of Baltimore: "Every year men die after suicide attempts when the skin has scarcely been scratched or only a few aspirin tablets have been ingested" (p. 311).

In concentration camps, two forms of psychogenic death were observed. A large number of prisoners died soon after arrival (Bettelheim, 1943; Des Pres, 1976). Another form of lethal surrender reaction was called the "mussulman stage." It generally took place after some time in the concentration camp when the prisoners' emotional and physical resources had become exhausted (Niederland, 1961; Krystal, 1968b).

As we have observed, psychogenic death is much more common than one would suspect and has been reported many times since Cannon's (1942) famous paper on "Voodoo death" (Menninger, 1936; Engel, 1971; Seligman, 1975). A few deaths of psychogenic origin have been recorded in the psychoanalytic literature as well (Coolidge, 1969; Knapp, Mushatt, and Nemetz, 1966). While the circumstances varied, the subjective state of all these patients was of "unbearable situations of impasse, of 'no exit' in which [they could not] fight, and from which they [could not] escape" (Saul, 1966, p. 88). The helpless and hopeless surrender, documented in the studies of Engel (1968, 1971) and Meerloo (1948, 1959), can, as noted, progress to psychogenic death; moreover, there is an increasing awareness and documentation of transient catatonoid reactions.

It has been found, for instance, that these surrender patterns are more common than panic in mass disasters (Dill, 1954). Allerton (1964) reported: "Almost all available studies indicate that a stunned and bewildered response is a far more likely group reaction than is panic" (p. 206). Tyhurst (1951) found that in four disasters studied, 10% to 25% of the victims became stunned and immobile. As many as half the passengers in aircraft accidents develop what the airlines call "inaction due to negative panic" and therefore fail to evacuate the burning or sinking craft (Johnson, 1970, p. 3).

As Freud wrote, the nature of the danger is of secondary importance; it matters not whether it is "external" or purely psychogenic. Neither does it matter whether an actual threat of peril exists. Lest anyone misconstrue my considerations as pertaining only to extreme, life-endangering situations, I reiterate Freud's (1926) statement that the *sole* determinant of psychological consequences is a person's subjective evaluation of the danger, and "whether he is wrong in his estimation or not is immaterial for the outcome" (p. 166).

I am stressing the lethal potential of the psychological surrender pattern because it makes us appreciate the magnitude of the forces involved in these reactions. The question is, What happens to people who surrender to what they experience as overwhelming danger but do not die? The survivors of the Nazi persecution, for example, spent long periods of time in a condition of robotization or automatization or, as Lifton (1967) called it, "psychic closing off." Such a state was often preceded by depersonalization, which represented an attempt to deny the reality and to "numb" one's emotional responses. In "closing off," there is a virtually complete suppression of all affect expression and registration. Lifton (1979) has continued his studies of these conditions and elaborated the reactions: "The survivor undergoes a radical but temporary diminution in his sense of actuality in order to avoid losing this sense completely and permanently; he undergoes a reversible form of symbolic death in order to avoid a permanent physical or psychic death" (p. 173). The physical immobilization observable in the catatonoid state is accompanied by a massive blocking of virtually all mental activity— not just affects, but all initiative, judgment, and other activity—to the point that a state of "walking death" may ensue. This may serve as the *model of an adult traumatic state*.

INFANTILE PSYCHIC TRAUMA

If the concept of trauma is to be rescued from the dilution that threatens its usefulness at present, we must assert that trauma refers to an overwhelming, paralyzing psychic state, which implies a loss of ego functions, regression, and obligatory psychopathology (Furst, 1967; Solnit and Kris, 1967). In attempting to clarify whether adult psychic trauma is the same phenomenon as childhood trauma, I must separate the effect from the phenomenology. I have pointed out that *massive* psychic trauma in adults may have sequelae very similar to those of significant (i.e., frequent, severe) childhood traumatization.

In the infantile situation, if the mother is not able to relieve the child's distress, the excitation mounts and extends to ever wider parts of the child's body and mind. The child finally reaches a point of frenzy and becomes inconsolable. It is a difficult and arduous task to calm such an infant, and the child's screaming seriously interferes with the caregiver's ability to maintain composure. Thus, the potential source of succor is frequently endangered as the child reaches a totally wild, uncontrollable and overwhelmed state.

What can be the psychic state of a child overwhelmed with the primitive affect precursors that involve a massive response mobilizing the entire autonomic system as well as the precursors of pain? How can we imagine the child's *timeless* horror? Our clues from experience with adults who suffered severe psychic trauma as children indicate that this kind of experience is the most terrible and indescribable hell known to man. It is literally a fate worse than death, an unspeakable horror that is expected to mount and get worse—to go on and on. Stern (1968a, b), struggling with the perceptions of this state, felt that Freud had intimated that such a state referred to *Todesangst*—not a fear of death, but a *mortal terror*, an unbearably deadly state, which Stern called the *biotraumatic situation*. Earlier Stern (1951a) had used *pavor nocturnus* as a model of childhood psychic trauma. There we can get the feeling of the inconsolable state of a totally overwhelmed child.

The difficulties of imagining the dire cataclysmic nature of the infantile traumatic state are illustrated by our tendency to speak of the child's experience in an adultomorphic way as "anxiety." Freud (1900) stated that birth is the precursor of anxiety and is thus "the source and prototype of the affect of anxiety" (p. 400). He considered birth to be the model for anxiety state (1926, p. 93), "the earliest anxiety of the all—the 'primal anxiety' of birth" (1926, p. 137).

To appreciate the quality of the infantile traumatic state, one must consider not only the immaturity of the psyche in general—its timelessness and objectlessness, and other primitive characteristics—but that the affect precursors cannot be understood by reference to the psychic reality of adult-type affects. *Anxiety as we know it in adults does not exist in the neonate and infant but develops only through a gradual and complex process.*

The infantile gross stress or "alarm" pattern in all animals is basically designed to prevent separation of the young from the mother. Since separation is a matter of life and death, the whole affective apparatus of the young is mobilized, and they become as frantic and noisy as possible. They instantly assume whatever search pattern is permitted by their motor skill development—at its highest development, searching for the mother in widening circles and vocalizing in a way that provokes caring responses. Periodically the young give in to exhaustion and apathy and become still, whimpering in the most piteous way possible. This "freezing" represents another basic response pattern (Stern, 1951a). The young have a safety valve of sorts: They will go to sleep for a while, only to awaken with a start and resume the frantic search. The young in this traumatic state are in a frenzy of "total excitement." The whole organism is in a state of alarm and mobilization.

The emotional responses of the human child represent an activation of affect precursors, or ur-affects, and with it the entire emotional brain and hedonic regulation apparatus. The affect forerunners are general—there is only one pattern for all states of distress and one for well-being and contentment. In other words, there is a mass response involving the child's whole psychological and physical repertoire. The whole organism is in a state of alarm. I have long puzzled over the psychic representation of this state and its psychological residues. I must emphasize once again that it is impossible for an adult to imagine the nightmarish horror of an overwhelmed child. I think that all descriptions of hell try to represent this terrible state and its *timeless-*

ness. The feeling conveyed in the church description of the tortures of hell that go on forever and ever is matched by the reaction of persons in pain. Physical or mental pain can engender a regression to the infantile state wherein the sufferer loses the sense of time.

It is nonetheless valuable to try to imagine the psychic state of an infant who is totally overwhelmed with every sensation (painful and otherwise), who suffers coliclike spasms throughout his body, as well as activation of the entire limbic circuits and all of the higher and lower pain and distress, as well as pleasure, centers. I realize that I have suddenly switched to anatomical referents here, but I must use this tack simply because psychological ones are not available to conceptualize this state of total distress and alarm. In trying to envision how a baby in this condition appears to the onlooker, the examples of the infant in a state of colic or the unconsolable distress in *pavor nocturnus* give us the best idea.

If this infantile emergency pattern goes on for an appreciable period of time, the child's pleasure and pain regulatory centers, including those for vital functions, are modified. If this state continues too long, or is repeated too often, it leads to a failure to thrive, marasmus, hospitalism, anaclitic depression, and eventually death. This pattern has been found in all mammals. It must be noted that the issue is not one of nutrition but of the necessary affective support of mothering. If adequate mothering is not resumed promptly, but enough care is available to make survival possible, anhedonia sets in.

Among the *direct* effects of severe childhood trauma in adults is a lifelong *dread* of the return of the traumatic state and the *expectation* of it. Emotions are frequently experienced as trauma screens; hence, there is a fear of one's emotions and an impairment of affect tolerance. Along with these disturbances there is a general and lifelong *anhedonia*, which becomes interwoven into a variety of masochistic problems.

Lipson (1976, personal communication) has posed a most germane question: How is a traumatic state terminated? In childhood trauma there appears to be a secondary "safety valve" between the traumatic state and its continuation unto death. The wisdom of the ages is that left alone in a state of extreme distress, the child with neither die nor remain in the traumatic state, but will go off to sleep. This is how parents have always been able to get away with letting the child "cry itself to sleep." But the natural resilience of children is greatly exaggerated by the myth-making needs of generations of guilt-ridden people who were driven to "do unto others as was done unto them."

One of the most tragic instances of this long-ignored lesson of history took place between 1784 and 1838. During that time, 146,920 out of a total of 183,955 newborn "foundlings" died at the University of Vienna Children's Hospital (Gracey and DeRemee, 1981). We can speculate that the survivors were also damaged for life. The most devastating changes are possible. The products of orphanages used to be classified commonly as "mentally re-tarded." Clearly, where we see a change in the hedonic self-regulatory system alone, we can consider it the aftereffect of the "primal depression." The hedonic complex is made up of both anatomical and physiological compo-nents, involving a complex multitude of polypeptide neurotransmitters (Sny-der, 1980), and I think that it is especially susceptible to permanent changes in early life but remains vulnerable for life.

AFTEREFFECTS OF INFANTILE PSYCHIC TRAUMA

The aftereffects of infantile traumatization are widespread. There is apt to be a "doomsday orientation," that is, profound pessimism frequently accompa-nied by chronic fears and depressive lifestyle. The expected doomsday signifies the return to the infantile traumatic state. Affect tolerance is likely to be impaired, evidence of an arrest in affect development and anhedonia. However, the anhedonics may miss the deficit of joy and pleasure in their lives and may keep very busy hoping that their reward will come any day— when great happiness and joy will come to them. For example, most people expect that after they retire they will enjoy themselves; perhaps they will "travel a lot." Yet after retirement, some people become aware of the anhedonia, and this discovery may bring on a severe depression. The following is a case illustration of such an "involutional" depression.

Case Illustration

This patient, a man in his late 60's, consulted me because of depression. He was the youngest child of a large family, an unwanted burden to an already exhausted and depressed mother. He somehow obtained enough care from his many siblings to "make it." Although he seemed stunted physically, his intellectual development was precocious. He assumed a "provider" role early on, starting to work at about nine years of age. Eventually he became successful and was known for his good deeds. During his 40's he underwent a lengthy analysis, mainly because of obsessive-compulsive problems and difficulties with sexuality involv-ing a feeling of deprivation and resentment of what he experienced as his wife's "monopolistic" controlling. Despite many opportunities, he was not unfaithful, but he always felt deprived and profoundly un-happy. His analysis, which lasted for many years, produced satisfactory results in regard to the neurosis, and he "absorbed" his unhappiness by redoubling his work and good deeds. In his mid-60's he managed to retire. Although he was able to keep meaningfully busy, the retirement turned out quite badly.

In the year following his retirement, he developed a severe depression that led him to withdraw from most social contacts. He retreated to a brooding self-preoccupation in which he seemed unable to carry out the simplest task because of severe obsessions and self-doubts. Every thought or impulse was blocked by a simultaneous counterthought.

In psychotherapy we gradually reconstructed the onset of his depression following his retirement and its relationship to his sensing his lifelong anhedonia. When he finally became able to deal with this issue consciously, he would go over his life and enumerate his many and varied successes, lamenting, "What did I get out of it all? I never could *enjoy* anything, and I was always preoccupied with the worries and troubles!" He experienced much self-directed rage, but behind it was a feeling of having been cheated since birth—not only by the original deprivation of affection, security, and well-being, but also by becoming permanently unable to experience any degree of pleasure, happiness, or joy.

We found, in retrospect, that he had been motivated all his life by a dread of deprivation and by a search for something that would give him a state of well-being—the "nirvana" of a contented child going blissfully off to sleep. Unfortunately, every one of his successes and every occasion that others might have enjoyed were just additional stresses to him that he grew to resent. He enjoyed none of his achievements and continued to feel tense, insecure, deprived, and increasingly angry and depressed.

He had never quite realized that his capacity for pleasure, joy, and happiness had been nil. He had been driven by his insecurity and the enormous "hypertrophy" of his sense of duty and responsibility. In looking back, we found that awareness of his anhedonia had "flickered" on and off in his mind. He had learned to dismiss it by denying it and promising himself that with one more achievement, his work would be done and he would devote his life to travel and pleasure. In the meantime, however, it was his own well-kept secret that he enjoyed none of the recreational activities in which he participated.

Thus, one major difference between the sequelae of infantile and adult types of trauma is this lack of memories or even the slightest suspicion of it in some people who experienced overwhelming trauma early in life.

INFANTILE TRAUMA AND ADULT TRAUMA

Although many adults fear the return of their infantile trauma, it is not possible for them to have exactly the same kind of experience as they had in childhood. In some psychotic states or in severe delirium tremens, it is possible for adults to come close to the horror and overwhelmed state that we can infer the child suffers. Under prolonged torture and in other externally or internally caused panic states that combine suffering with total helplessness and reach the catatonoid states, the existence of a traumatic state frequently cannot be questioned. Nevertheless, there are significant differences between those states and analogous states of children. Regression in affects is an everyday phenomenon, but in adults the regression is spotty and incomplete. Adults can block emotions and constrict cognition. It is therefore *not possible for an adult to have such a complete regression in the form and nature of affects, and the rest of psychic functioning, as to experience the psychic state of infantile trauma.*

One of the reasons for this difference is the structure of the adult psyche. It contains all the resources for trauma prevention that we used to refer to as the "stimulus barrier." In regard to the trauma *experience*, however, the most important single difference has been pointed out by Petty (1975, personal communication). In the *adult* traumatic state, an "observing ego" is retained. Hence, as self-observing functions develop, traumatic experiences and "near-trauma" states can be used in the development of "trauma signals" (Sandler, 1967), the ultimate emergency response mobilizing alarm, which may serve later for trauma prevention. The trauma signals may mobilize a person's defenses or may be involved in his obtaining help from others (Petty et al., 1974).

Another major difference between the infantile and adult form of psychic trauma is its relationship to affects. For the child, the affects themselves become overwhelming and traumatic because of their primitive nature and the child's primitive state of mind. In the adult, intense affects do not *themselves* constitute trauma, and under certain circumstances they may actually be desired. Even affect storms are distinguished from psychic trauma in that they *threaten* to, but do not in fact, overwhelm one's integrative and executive functions. It is the overwhelming of the ego, the surrender to total helplessness and hopelessness, and the progression to the catatonoid state that make a situation traumatic. The traumatic state can neither be equated with nor understood through the intense affects that may initiate it. This may be what Eissler (1966) was referring to when he said, "Anxiety cannot traumatize the psychic apparatus, any more than the defense mechanism can" (p. 26). That statement holds true only if we are dealing with the mature, adult type of affect.

What, then, is the nature of the psychic reality, the subjective experience in the adult traumatic state? In the psychoanalytic literature there is an amazing paucity of subjective reports of what it is like to live in a state of trauma. What is available is generally in the realm of external, behavioral, and aftereffect-related data. Furst (1967) reviewed and summarized the report by Solnit and Kris, who reconstructed the "psychic content" of trauma as a "feeling of helplessness in the face of overwhelming danger" and described the trauma state as "paralyzing, immobilizing, or rendering to a state of helplessness ranging from numbness to an emotional storm in affects and behavior" (p. 37). This definition includes the disorganization of feelings, thoughts, and behavior, as well as physical symptoms reflecting automatic dysfunction. Although Solnit and Kris reported on a traumatic incident in the life of a 3½-year-old child, their description is a composite that fits the *adult type* of psychic trauma as distinguished from the infantile one.

PSYCHIC TRAUMA AS A PROCESS

In the traumatic state, there is a psychological paralysis that starts with a virtually complete blocking of the ability to feel emotions and pain, as well as other physical sensations, and progresses to inhibition of other mental functions. The subjects themselves are able to observe and describe the blocking of affective responses—a circumstance that has led to such terms as psychic numbing, "psychological closing off" (Lifton, 1967), and "affective anesthesia" (Minkowski, 1946). The paradox in the traumatic state is that the numbing and closing off are experienced as relief from the previously painful affects such as anxiety; at the same time, they are also experienced as the first part of dying, for, along with the affective blocking, there is a blocking of initiative and all life-preserving cognition. The severe constriction, desymbolization, and fragmentation of mental functioning are not as easily observed through reflective self-awareness as is the "psychic numbing." The accounts that are available have been obtained in situations that were not *completely* overwhelming. For instance, Jaspers (1923) found a personal account of a soldier in World War I: "We were reduced to having to 'wait and see,' although we were in immediate danger. Our minds froze, grew numb, empty and dead." His soldier further reports that "feeling is frozen. . . . The threatened man becomes numb, cool, objective—the senses slowly grow enveloped with a merciful stupefaction, become clouded and conceal the worst from him" (p. 367).

The following quotation is taken from the *Chronicles of the Lodz Ghetto* (Dobroszycki, 1984), an official record of events in which "just the facts" were recorded in such a way that they could be inspected by the Nazi "authorities." It speaks for itself in showing both the psychic numbing and the unease of the investigator in trying to make some generalization that would include the Holocaust experience:

> Incidentally, the populace's strange reaction to the recent events is noteworthy. There is not the slightest doubt that this was a profound shock, and yet one must wonder at the indifference shown by those— apart from the ones who were not directly affected and who returned to normal life at once—from whom loved ones had been taken. It would

seem that the events of recent days would have immersed the entire population of the ghetto in mourning for a long time to come, and yet, right after the incidents, even during the resettlement action, the populace was obsessed with everyday concerns—getting bread, rations, and so forth—and often went from immediate personal tragedy right back into daily life. Is this some sort of numbing of nerves, an indifference, or a symptom of an illness that manifests itself in atrophied emotional reactions? After losing those nearest to them, people talk constantly about rations, potatoes, soup, etc.! It is beyond comprehension! Why this lack of warmth towards those they loved? Naturally here and there are some mothers weeping in a corner for a child or children shipped from the ghetto, but, as a whole, the mood of the ghetto does not reflect last week's terrible ordeal. Sad but true! [entry by Zelkowicz, p. 255].

It appears that cognitive constriction rather than "numbing" accounts for the sparcity of reports of the psychic state in trauma. Those we were able to unearth show that at the peak of distress, the descriptions shift from the subject's feelings and experiences to an account of the events, as if described by a third person. Personal accounts of traumatic states may make brief references to the early phase of the process as being painful or frightening. They may mention some numbing or depersonalization, but the stories invariably lapse into a description of the *events*.[2] Spectacular examples of this process are provided by Kosinski (1965). Schlieman gave several accounts of his shipwreck in his "exercise books," yet this extraordinarily verbal man describes his traumatic experience as follows: "I fell, hitting my mouth against the deck and broke all my front teeth. But my terror was such that I didn't feel the pain. I pulled myself up and fastened myself with ropes [to the mast] . . . I expected to die with every new wave" (Niederland,1965, p. 382). In other versions, there are some details of the circumstances, but no description of his feelings, as Schielman always skips from that sentence to loss of consciousness and then the rescue.

The readers or listeners to such accounts, in contrast, mistakenly anticipate that recounting the event will cause an increase in pain, suffering, and distress. They also dread that the description will become unbearable and they will no longer be able to empathize. Actually, audiences presented with a portrayal of great calamities or destruction (for example, in the movie *The Killing Fields*, which depicted the genocide in Cambodia), experience great distress, because they are not able to develop intrapsychic blocking. Artistic accounts of historic disasters are limited to the depiction of minimal vignettes

---

2. I am indebted to Marlene Handler, M.S.L.S., who was most helpful in searching for the psychiatric, autobiographical, and fictional accounts of traumatic states.

alluding minimally to their terrible circumstances; audiences cannot confront realistic, detailed accounts of the events. Survivors usually comment, "The truth was much, much worse!" Freud (1930) touched on some of these points when he wrote:

> No matter how much we may shrink with horror from certain situations—of a galley-slave in antiquity, of a peasant during the Thirty Years' War, of a victim of the Holy Inquisition, of a Jew awaiting a pogrom—it is nevertheless impossible for us to feel our way into such people—to devine the changes which original obtuseness of mind, a gradual stupefying process, the cessation of expectations, and cruder or more refined method of narcotization have produced upon their receptivity to sensations of pleasure and unpleasure. Moreover, in the case of the most extreme possibility of suffering, special mental protective devices are brought into operation [p. 89].

I suppose that the "special protective devices" are derealization, depersonalization, and, perhaps, other states of modified consciousness, all of which may derive from the child's going off to sleep in the traumatic state. This mechanism may also underlie what follows the affect of blockings: a progressive surrender of self-preserving initiatives through the *constriction and progressive blocking of mental functions such as memory, imagination, associations, problem solving, and so on.* A person in this state may become aware of the hopelessness of his situation and think "I am going to die," a brief thought that may be couched in sardonic humor and bitterness. Other thoughts may come to mind—for example, anticipation of unbearable suffering associated with the return of the horror of childhood psychic trauma—and these may break down the functional inhibition of action. A purposeful or random attempt at action may result. These are the spasms of activity amid the catatonoid state. The memory of the unbearable infantile state may mobilize adaptive action at the last moment. Frequently, however, such outbursts of activity are devoid of planning and even of psychic contents and are reflexive in nature and self-destructive in outcome.

As the state of psychic trauma develops, there is an increasing envelopment, with self-surrender to death progressing to a point of both psychological and physiological irreversibility. Many of the aftereffects of psychic trauma result from this immersion in the early stages of psychogenic death. The problems of massive psychic trauma resulting from the confrontation with death and survivorship following events that destroyed entire communities or peoples have been described repeatedly. (This literature was reviewed by Hoppe [1971] and can be followed in the writings of Lifton [1967, 1976, 1979a, b]).

CATASTROPHIC PSYCHIC TRAUMA AND TRANCES

Catastrophic psychic trauma is defined as a *surrender to what is experienced as unavoidable danger of external or internal origin.* It is the psychic reality of this surrender to what one experiences as an unbearable situation with no escape, no exit, that causes one to give up and abandon life-preserving activity.

Evaluation of the situation as one of inevitable danger, and the surrender to it, initiates the traumatic process. The affective response to the signal of avoidable danger is fear, dread, or anxiety. The affective response to the perception of inevitable danger is the catatonoid reaction.

There are, as mentioned before, similarities between traumatic catatonoid reactions and various cataleptic states including "animal hypnosis." Understanding trances has relevancy to the continuation of submissive behavior and other self-limiting states. There is a part of the phenomena in which we can understand trauma as a trance state and as a command. Recent studies, for example, reveal that Vietnam veterans with Posttraumatic Stress Disorder show disproportionately high hypnotic suggestibility and very high imagery scores (Struttman and Bliss, 1985). This state of being in a trance and being able to obey orders is described in perfect detail by Filip Muler, a survivor of the "Sonder Commando" of Auschwitz (Lanzmann, 1985). He tells that after he was herded into the incineration chamber of the crematorium at Auschwitz he was ordered to undress the hundreds of corpses lying in the chamber and then the following happened:

> When we undressed some of them, the order was given to feed the ovens. Suddenly an SS man rushed up and told me: "Get out of here! Go stir the bodies!" What did he mean "Stir the bodies"? I entered the crematorium chamber. There was a Jewish prisoner, Fischel, who later became a squad leader. He looked at me and I watched him poke the fire with a long rod. He told me: "Do as I'm doing, or the SS will kill you." I picked up a steel poker and did as he was doing. I obeyed Fischel's order. At that point I was in shock, as if I'd been hypnotized, ready to do whatever I was told. I was so mindless, so horrified, that I did everything Fischel told me [p. 59].

The catatonoid reaction to danger is of ancient phylogenetic derivation. Miller (1951) states that there are two basic effects of fear:

> One is a tendency to remain motionless, which reaches its extreme form in death-feigning in certain animals and sometimes produces results suggestive of waxy flexibility of catatonics. The other is the pattern of startle, withdrawal, running, and vocalization. Both of these incompatible patterns seem to be activated by fear, and behavior may shift rapidly

from one to another, or when a frightened animal just freezes, then suddenly scurries for shelter [p. 441].

Catatonoid reaction can be induced experimentally in most, if not all animals (Tomkins, 1962), and in many it becomes the end reaction of a chronic anxiety-producing situation from which the animal cannot escape (Liddel, 1967).

The first reaction of young vertebrae animals to danger—to "freeze" and lie still, especially when the mother is away—may be an interesting preamble to the study of the development of affects in human beings. The human infant has lost this fundamental, life-preserving reaction. A tragic example of this loss was observed during the Nazi period. When families were hiding from persecution, the uncontrollable crying of a child frequently jeopardized the whole group. Among the kinds of traumatization that assume a nightmarish quality are those of some survivors who, as infants or little children, were choked almost to death by their mothers to keep them from betraying their presence.

The progression from excited anxiety to passive surrender and catatonoid reaction occurs in the face of unavoidable and life-threatening danger. Thus, the effects of the overwhelming of the defensive and expressive function of anxiety to the point of inhibition, with a surrender to destruction, are traumatic and cause a disturbance in affect handling and tolerance (Greenacre, 1958).

Stern (1953) contended in his early work that the specific danger of automatic anxiety was that it could produce a severe state of stress—of neurogenic shock and death. Later, Stern (1968a, b) wrote of the *meaning* and the physiological aspect of that ultimate in anxiety, which we tend to think of as fear of death but which actually is deadly fear. He postulated that the mental representation of the danger of dying was based on the infantile experience called "biotraumata." In people who suffered severe traumatization in infancy and childhood, the mortal dread is linked with feelings of helplessness, immobility, and suffocation, which are considered to be reasons for the overwhelming nature of automatic anxiety, castration anxiety, fear of dismemberment, and losing one's mind. Perhaps this dread is also what Melanie Klein (1946), linking it with the ideation of "falling to bits," called "psychotic anxiety." *This unbearable feeling is what causes or, more properly, is the first part of the traumatic process.* It initiates a series of unconscious pathogenic reactions that represent the trauma syndrome. The adult's moral dread—with the feeling of impending annihilation, immobilization, suffocation—Stern interpreted as the reexperiencing of the infancy panic and total stress reaction that resulted from the absence of the indispensable mother. Extraordinary traumatization, with the infants experiencing a hostile rejection, morbidly reinforces the commonly occurring biotraumata resulting from normal frustrations and separations (Stern, 1968a, b). Under these circumstances, the reaction to affect becomes permanently excessive.

In addition to residual childhood influences, intense affects are also disruptive to adult functioning. Arnold (1950) makes a salient point: "Intense anxiety interferes with thinking as well as action because of its physiological (sympathetic nervous system) affects. Anger is disruptive because it represents intense parasympathetic stimulation which results in incoordination" (p. 30).

There are remarkable similarities between the psychic state in trauma and the mental state of some suicidal patients (Shneidman, 1976a). This finding should not come as a surprise in view of the possible progression of the psychic trauma state to psychogenic death. Indeed, some suicide attempts and repeated self-mutilations may represent a means of interrupting the traumatic state (Simpson, 1976). When psychic numbing sets in and the person becomes aware of a feeling of "deadness" and some of the accompanying reactions of constriction, depersonalization, and the like—and especially when there is a sentience of the lethal potential of the traumatic state—the suicide attempt or self-mutilation may (paradoxically) be life-saving in that the person asserts mastery, thereby interrupting the state of helplessness and surrender. Some of the sudden outbursts of activity in the catatonoid state represent the same type of last-minute protest. It is the process of psychological *surrender* that is the lethal one.

Another startling similarity between suicidal patients and patients in the traumatic state lies in the severe constriction of mental functions, which includes a blocking of and dissociation from one's past. The inability to describe the mental state in psychic trauma even in retrospect is due to severe inhibition of the mental functions, which reduces self-observation and cognition to a minimum. Shneidman (1976b) has made this point about suicidal patients, stressing that they cannot write a "full and explicative" note (p. 91). He even asserted that if they could do it, they would not have to kill themselves.

THE CATASTROPHIC TRAUMATIC STATE AND ITS AFTEREFFECTS

In situations where the subjective evaluation is that dire danger is *inevitable* and in no way subject to any deflection, the affective state changes from anxiety to the catatonoid reaction and the progression of various blocking responses outlined earlier. I would like now to take each one of those responses, and in reviewing it, consider the nature of the *direct* aftereffects, consisting basically of the continuation of these responses beyond the period of the emergency.

1. Recognition of and submission to unavoidable danger.   This very act, by breaking down the feeling of safety and invulnerability, may have long-lasting consequences for psychic structure. One's security depends on a set of beliefs in one's own powers, augmented by various "external" security resources, whether they are from one's family, from the community, or supernatural ones. This set of beliefs includes a set of illusions that promote the denial of death and of a variety of dangers and the denial of the actual lack of security with which we live. However, the assumption of safety is the basis of all of our behavior patterns, including some of the most important personality traits. This (illusory) sense of security permits normal function. In the wake of the breakdown of the feeling of security, some people cannot return to the previous personality type but assume submissive, slavelike personalities, and their ability for assertive behavior becomes impaired to one degree or another.

Studies of disasters, such as the Buffalo Creek flood, showed that the destruction of the *community* resulted in serious and longlasting handicaps to its members (K. Erikson, 1976), who were unable to function without the usual supports. These ordinarily familiar supports and assumptions of security are, of course, taken for granted. However, their breakdown can be seen as the common element in all misfortunes and disasters. The apathetic, stuporous state of people in these situations, sometimes referred to as the "disaster syndrome" (Wolfenstein, 1977), may be the common sign of the loss and the surrender pattern accompanying it. The continuation of the breakdown of either the feelings of security or of the ability to utilize community supports for one's function seriously interferes with the resumption of normal life patterns.

The idea of people functioning by themselves and warding off whatever problems come their way is spurious (see, for example, Caplan, 1981). In fact, people function within a social setting and derive countless measures of support from its influences, even though they may be intangible. Caplan reported that even in "ordinary" disaster situations there was a deterioration of mental and intellectual functions:

> disorders of attention, scanning, information collection, access to relevant memories that associate significant meaning to perception, judgment, planning, the capacity to implement plans, and the capacity to implement feedback. In other words, the individual's usual orderly process of externally oriented instrumental ego functioning is upset. This happens precisely when it is important for him to be operating at his maximum effectiveness so he can grapple with his problem [p. 415].

This is exactly why in situations of stress, victims become dependent on "external" support. E.H. Erikson (1959) pointed out that most areas of one's function depended on values derived from one's whole social frame of reference. These values are subject to periodic "historical" revision and are essential to the maintenance of one's own sense of identity and integrity.

2. The surrender pattern.   When surrender to a real external enemy has taken place, two patterns may be produced. On the conscious level, there may be problems with shame—either directly experienced or defended against in any of a number of ways. At the same time, there may be an inability to assert oneself, which actually represents a continuation of surren-der behavior. The conscious recognition of the tendency to submit to phallic, sadistic, or narcissistic objects may be strongly warded off and replaced by intense shame, which follows every incident of inability to resist and the need to submit. The problem evident in the anguish and shame related to the inability to act assertively or aggressively may also result, especially in men, in an inability ever to exercise an assertive or dominant role.

3. Catatonoid reaction as a "primal depression."   Niederland stressed in all his writings on the subject, beginning with his 1961 paper on the problem of the survivor (and restated in 1981), that chronic, recurrent depression was part of the picture. In 1968, Niederland wrote that the reactions covered "the whole spectrum from masochistic character changes to psychotic depression" (1968a, p. 313). However, many of these depressions are not diagnosed as such, but manifest themselves in a lifestyle of despair and commonly in physical symptoms of chronic tiredness, weakness, and lack of resistance to all kinds of (not just infections) illnesses. In our work with the survivors of the Holocaust, we focused on the link between these depressive reactions and the problems of guilt, particularly those relevant to issues of survivorship. However, problems of depression are part of the posttraumatic picture and are not limited to the survivors of genocide (Krystal, 1978c). In this context, one is inclined to ponder Stern's (1951b) view that the catatonoid reaction also represents a "primal depression." The point here is that posttraumatic depression may be viewed as the continuation of this aspect of the traumatic state. But that raises the question: Why should these responses be carried on chronically? In contemplating what it means when we say that in the surrender, in the state of total helplessness, pain stops (both physical and emotional) and a feeling of tragic sadness is experienced, a most important insight is at hand. Having *experienced* its own mortality and helplessness, no living creature is quite the same again. The reconstruction of one's feeling of security, or even faith, is never again complete. It is as if the encounter had provided a black background upon which the rest of one's life will be painted. Never again can one diminish the dark hues in one's emotional palette.

Experiencing the full impact of the helplessness and hopelessness of the surrender to unavoidable danger forever changes one's view and experience of one's self and the world. The illusions of childhood are irreparably damaged, "Paradise Lost" as it were. Thus, the depressive attitude in posttraumatic states represents, to an important extent, loss and a reaction to that loss.

4. Affective blocking. This was the earliest aftereffect of traumatization reported by Minkowski (1946). In his early observations of survivors of concentration camps, affective anesthesia was most striking. The same observation was made by many other investigators (Lifton, 1967; Niederland, 1961). Since part of the catastrophic trauma response is the blocking of the conscious registration of pain and painful affects, one can assume that one is dealing with the continuation of numbness. However, there are some important related issues. One is the question of concurrent alexithymia. Were some of the early observers picking up alexithymic characteristics?

5. Continuation of "emergency regimes." In a manner exactly corresponding to the depressive problems, there is a tendency to continue hypervigilance (Niederland, 1961, 1981; Krystal and Niederland, 1968). The superalert state may include such physical anxiety responses as startle patterns, increased muscular tension, and all those components of anxiety sometimes referred to as "sympathetic nervous system overreactivity." Hypervigilance is in contrast to the depressive tendencies that are sometimes referred to as "general asthenia" (see, for example, Bastiaans, 1957). Once the feeling of security has been destroyed, there is an experience of repetition of states of distress. This fear of recurrence is now known to be one of the regular aftereffects of disaster (Wolfenstein, 1977) and of individual stress (Horowitz, 1976; Krupnik and Horowitz, 1981). I found, however, that what survivors usually refer to in terms of the fearful expectation of the return of the traumatic *situation* (such as, "I am afraid the Nazis are coming back" or "I think we will have a great depression next year") is, in fact, the expectation of the return of the traumatic *state* and, in particular, the return of the unbearable affective reaction. Many clinical syndromes of chronic anxiety and panic states need to be understood from this point of view.

Chronic anxiety states may manifest themselves entirely in physical symptoms (particularly in the presence of alexithymia) or in a cognitive set of chronic worry, insecurity, and the like. Thus, a survivor of the Nazi persecution might comment when being shown a home of a new acquaintance: "Oh, this would make a very good hiding place!" (E. Tanay, 1970, personal communication).

As already mentioned, the physical symptoms of anxiety may be difficult to modify by techniques that explore the cognitive elements of the affects, that is, psychotherapy or hypnotic "uncovering" techniques. One has to address oneself directly to modifying the hyperactivity states by various relaxation and retraining techniques. Repetitive anxiety and persecutory dreams are part of this problem, as may be certain waking confusional states (Niederland, 1961, 1981). Here is one of the few places where we can see a difference in the effects on victims and on perpetrators.

6. Alexithymia.   Observations about the very high frequency of psychosomatic diseases in survivors of Nazi persecution abound (Bastiaans, 1957; Niederland, 1961; Krystal and Niederland, 1968). Similarly there are many well-documented studies on the exceedingly high incidence of psychosomatic diseases in veterans, particularly after World War II. Some of these studies have been reviewed elsewhere (see Cohen and Cooper, 1954; Brill and Beebe, 1955; Archibald and Tudenham, 1965). Some observations suggested that the high incidence of psychosomatic diseases in posttraumatic states was related to the nature of the trauma. One was my finding (1971) that whereas the overall incidence of psychosomatic disease was 30%, among survivors who were under 20 years of age during the persecutions that rate rose to 70%. The adolescent's higher rate of psychosomatic diseases seemed to me to have something to do with an epigenetic development or pattern of emotions and possibility of regression.

7. Continuation of cognitive constriction.   Constriction of all of cognitive functions, including memory, judgment, problem solving, discrimination, and perception, which was previously described as part of the traumatic situation, may continue to a varying and unpredictable degree. Why the constriction persists is not clear. There certainly is a lack of motivation to re-expand one's mental function; there is an identification with death, and among survivors of a group disaster, identification with the dead (Niederland, 1961; Lifton, 1976, personal communication. There is also the possibility of lasting organic changes (Weiss et al., 1975). At any rate, posttraumatic psychic constriction is a widely occurring state, although it varies greatly in its intensity. Lifton (1976) has conceptualized this disturbance as "a form of desensitization; it refers to an incapacity to feel or to confront certain kinds of experience, due to blocking or absence of inner forms or imagery that can connect with such experience" (p. 27). The manifestations of the continued constriction of mental function take the following forms:

(a) A general dullness, obtuseness, and concomitant lowering of occupational, social, and familial status. Some persons manifesting this form of cognitive inhibition attempt to return to their previous occupations or continue their studies but find themselves unable to do so and drift down to the lowest, most menial work. At home, they are not able to function as parents because their anticipation of the possible consequences of their own or their children's actions is limited. They can neither serve as role models nor offer parental guidance. The often withdraw to a very passive role. Their behavior resembles the defeated position some animals take, of a secondary role in the pack, or the lifelong docility of a broken horse. Seligman (1975) has demonstrated that animals subjected to unavoidable pain and that do not die in the surrender reaction (trauma) develop a lifelong helpless reaction; they do not try to avoid future exposure to pain, but lie down and whimper. There is also evidence that organic, at least psychophysiological, changes are involved here. These problems in the parents result in emotional disturbance in the next generation.

(b) Episodic "freezing" or startlelike responses. In contrast to submission to unavoidable danger, which has a depressive or masochistic flavor, this reaction is related to a chronic state of hypervigilance, a tendency to startle, and occasionally panic. The panic, however, is manifested in the worst possible actions in situations of stress or danger. Persons with this type of response tend to be blunderers, displaying the type of behavior caricatured in the movie character of Inspector Clouseau of the "Pink Panther" series. In the blunderer type of behavior, there is a combination of wrong decisions with physical uncoordination, jerkiness, or inappropriate action in which excessive anxiety and physical tenseness ("excessive activation") contribute to the impairment resulting from the cognitive difficulty.

8. Pseudophobia.   It is not certain whether this difficulty has any relationship to cognitive disturbance. But it definitely is related to the creation of traumatic screens. This function has been known for a long time, and Freud (1894) built much on it in connection with childhood memories. The difficulties here resemble phobias, in the sense that there is an irrational fear of a certain object and that the fear may become disabling. However, the structure of the pseudophobia is different, there being no repressed unconcsious wish involved. Rather this response represents a reworking of the fear of the return of the psychic trauma state in a manner similar to the one in which an anxiety neurosis is transformed into a phobia from the "free floating" neurosis. In these states, patients frequently complain that they are afraid of some specific thing, such as uniformed men or the sound of explosions or some other stimuli. These fears reflect fears from the past. Some people may also be afraid of their own dreams, which represent "reruns" of the traumatic past. They may take sleeping pills to suppress dreaming rather than to regulate their sleep. Their chronic, intense anxiety may appear to be multiple phobias, but these people are not able to describe what it is they are afraid of. Ultimately what they fear is the return of the *infantile* trauma state; the object of the original fear is not forgotten. Still other people are especially fearful of certain stimuli or dreams that may bring back feelings of (survivor) guilt (Niederland, 1961) or depression.

The dissociative affects of trauma produce a multitude of traumatic screens, which combined with impaired affect tolerance force the posttraumatic person to ward off an ever increasing number of stimuli. Thus, it is common for a Holocaust survivor to be unable to view on television anything reminiscent of Nazis. This fear and intolerance extends to all uniformed people, any situation of strife, and any anxiety-producing story or situation. Another example of this intolerance is that hospitalization may evoke memories of incarceration, and many concentration camp survivors panic and may end up in psychotic or paranoid psychosis.

The traumatic situation, as contrasted to the traumatic state, is also frightening and presents one with a variety of other affects such as shame, guilt, or triumph. This is one of the reasons why the aftereffects of trauma involve a great need to experience affects—like an enormous magnification of the delayed anxiety of the "near-miss" car accident. Another cause for the repetition of the intensive affects is the need to regain comfort in *having* these affects. "Affect-rebound" and the need for repetitious reliving of the traumatic or even near-traumatic state is, of course, the impressive part of the "traumatic neurosis," which is so inviting to economic metaphors.

Related to these phenomena, particularly the "traumatic screen," are the symptoms of repetitive images, including repetitive dreams. My most helpful observation in this sphere came from the reports of concentration camp survivors, many years after liberation, that when they awoke from a repetitive dream, they were often in pain or coming down with an illness. The dream imagery was selective; for example, they dreamed about arriving in a camp— a point of maximum danger—or about circumstances of transport in some freight car, either open cattle cars or closed cars. Those images referred to specific dangers, as well as to specific ways in which survival was secured. For instance, victims of Nazi persecution who were able to take the initiative and actively secure their survival for a significant period of time were relatively intact psychologically. Their repetitive dreams referred to scenes of the chase. They awakened frightened, but at a point in the dream where the outcome was not certain. Yet, as in the examination dream, having the dream many years after the danger had passed must have had some element of self-reassurance. Nonetheless, the survivors frequently reported feeling anxiety and depression for days after such dreams. Brett and Ostroff (1985) have correctly inferred that students of posttraumtic disorders who emphasize recurrent imagery see the posttraumatic state as influenced by the need to complete cognitive processing that was overwhelmed or disrupted (Horowitz, 1976). Particularly relevant to our considerations are the findings of Laufer, Brett, and Gallops (1984), who suggest that participation in (or even witnessing of) atrocities produced widespread and continuing numbing, whereas combat participation was more commonly follwed by repetitive and intrusive imagery accompanied by the physiological (but not cognitive) elements of the disturbing affects. I might add that although intrusive visual imagery is more often noted, any sensory modality (e.g., smell, sense of tightness) or thought may become part of a traumatic screen.

9. "Dead to the World" reaction.   Murray (1967) was able to synthesize from the work of Herman Melville the characterology of a person whose behavior dramatizes a self-image of being "dead to the world." Murray defined the "dead to the world" reaction as being a cessation of one's affect or part of oneself; the feeling of being almost dead, or a cessation of the orientation of conscious life; or experiencing part of one's external world as being dead. One's social world may be experienced as being dead. There may be the equivalent spiritual death. Murray also pointed out that some people stop at the point of near cessation, being as good as dead; or the identification with death or the dead produces a self-diminution. The previous chapter has provided us with cognitive tools with which to understand Murray's findings.

Survivors of severe psychic trauma—trauma that has progressed well into the catatonoid state—who were in the incipient stages of psychogenic death, especially those who remained in such a condition for a long period of time, sometimes show a residual picture of extreme damage, even devastation. Murray (1967) has described such people with sensitivity and poignancy. I have noticed the dire consequences of fear of "prolectic" (Spitz, 1963) that is, gratification-expecting, affects for the chances of forming satisfactory object relations. But Murray (1967) elaborated the tragic picture resulting from the tendency to "deanimate the animate":

> Here it is as if the person's primal springs of vitality had dried up, as if he were empty or hollow at the very core of his being. There is a striking absence of anything but the most perfunctory and superficial social interactions; output as well as intake is at a minimum. The person is a nonconductor. To him the human species is wholly uninviting and unlovable, a monotonous round of unnecessary duplicates [p. 9].

This extreme state can be seen as a giving up of all hope of satisfactory human contacts, resulting from the destruction of basic trust. Murray summarizes his observation of a patient: "All empathy was dead in him; he was inert as a stone, unmoved by the events or confrontations which moved others" (p. 10). This description fits exactly the effects of severe psychic trauma as outlined earlier. A case in point is The Pawnbroker, a fictionalized portrait of a survivor of Nazi persecutions by Wallant (1962). Camus's character Meursault is another example, what Leites (1953) called "the syndrome of affectlessness." It illustrates that this condition can develop under traumatic circumstances that occur in everyday life. Murray (1967) felt that Herman Melville was the same kind of person and that he portrayed his state in many of his characters, particularly Captain Ahab and Bartleby the Scrivener.

This tragic depletion of life's resources, a picture of life in death, has been referred to in the Holocaust literature by many names, among them a "break in the lifeline" and "loss of personality" (Venzlaff, 1963). Here again we may recall the idea of the traumatic state's being a primal depression, for these states of chronic surrender, self-diminution, and cessation have much to do with the causation and conceptions of suicide (Shneidman, 1976a).

In essence, there is a catastrophic process of mounting pressure manifest in increasing irritability, sleep disturbances, and psychosomatic startle reactions that terminates in an "explosion" or surrender. This picture was described and has been called "combat exhaustion" (Bartemeier et al., 1946). Shneidman (1976a) summarized the observations on successful suicides in a Veterans Administration hospital by naming the following key developments: 1) heightened *inimicality* (self-hate); 2) perturbation (psychologic imbalance); 3) *constriction* of intellectual focus (funneling or narrowing of the mind's contents; 4) the idea of *cessation*: the insight that it is possible to stop consciousness and put an end to suffering. This is the igniting element that explodes the mixture (pp. 621-653). These pithy summaries identify the very same elements we see in the traumatic state in all situations. There is an overwhelming danger, failure to resist it, recognition of one's helplessness, and surrender. Once the surrender starts, the process is no longer voluntarily terminable but may be stopped by the intervention of an "outside" caretaker. However, while there is a progressive paralysis of volition and ability to resist, the sudden urge to make a (violent) exit may break through. Suicidal patients, in order to be able to give themselves up to death, must undergo a constriction of their cognitive functions as revealed in their suicide notes.

This brings us to the question of the aftereffects of the confrontation with death. As already mentioned, Lifton (1963, 1967, 1968) has elaborated these aftereffects—identification with death and the dead. It is virtually impossible to separate the aftereffects of the continuing cognitive constriction from those of the identification with the dead, and this is why the idea of the "dead to the world" identity and behavior has such great poignancy for us. A special, related issue has to do with the confrontation and immersion with death that may result in a variety of fantasies and ideal of identification with death and with the dead. This sometimes results in the survivors seeing themselves as walking dead or "dead to the world."

One may be affected by traumatization by disrupting one's own *symbolization* of life (Lifton, 1979). The confrontation with death may be fashioned into a "death imprint," which overloads the fantasy life with images of "unnatural" death that are really an evocation of sadistic images. Although Lifton feels that this is the essence of the "death anxiety," I see this state as a reactivation of the fear of the return of infantile trauma (as discussed earlier), and the death imagery serves as a screen for the unfathomable infantile trauma state. This idea is particularly in harmony with Lifton's image of "ultimate horror," which is also related to survivor guilt, and other ways by which the whole order and causality of the world is seen as destroyed (for example, the Hibakusha were horrified by the image that the landscape had been destroyed by the atomic bomb). The psychic numbing resulting from the destruction of nature is related to an inability to feel related to normal people of the "world of the living," as it were, and instead identifying with death and the dead (Lifton and Olson, 1976). In this type of imagery, survivor guilt and the expectation of counterfeit nurturance, the loss of ability to establish loving human bonds can all be seen as irreversible consequences of trauma. But confrontation with death *alone* produces a disruption of life symbolization that impairs human relationships and produces a need and yearning for help, but at the same time such suspiciousness and rage that the victims do not behave in ways that evoke favorable responses. Once the victim identity is established firmly, it may support the vicious circles of guilt, rage, and despair that drive posttraumatic persons further into self-numbing and isolation.

A common residue of survivorship of mass destruction is the sense that the meaning of one's life consists entirely of memorializing those who perished. Where lost relatives and others were victim to an external enemy, these reactions become more driven as they were reinforced by the need to deal with residual chronic aggression. Once established, the "monument" or "witness against evil" pattern in survivors' lives becomes a means to "work off" some survivor guilt.

10. The problem of aggression.   Anger, which so often has to be suppressed in the traumatic situation, only goes underground and returns as a permanent challenge to the future adjustment of the subject. Its appearance can be marked as soon as safety is re-established. Sterba (1949), working with adolescent Holocaust survivors, found, for instance, that as soon as they were brought to this country and placed in foster homes, they gave vent to constant complaints and unbridled aggressive behavior. As long as she was able to follow up these patients Sterba (1968) found them struggling with managing their smoldering rage. Anna Freud and Dann (1951) similarly described these children as aggressive and difficult to handle. In his psychotherapeutic work with survivors, Hoppe (1962, 1968, 1969) found them to show either depressive or aggressive problems. His patients, who developed "reactive aggression" and "hate addiction" (1962), were

> protected from unconsciously relating to their torturers as parental figures by a firm ego-ideal, and by shame, pride, and the idea of having a mission. The aggressive survivor permanently externalizes a part of his superego and is fighting against representatives of the externalized negative conscience. The aggression creates new guilt feelings, especially if the survivor's hate addiction turns against his own family members [Hoppe, 1971, p. 179].

The opposition of the depressive versus aggressive survivor takes on an additional dimension in the work of Danieli (1981a), who described the "adaptational styles" of survivor families. She contrasted the depressive families of *victims* (whose victim identity predominated and was shared by the family) with those of *fighters*. The latter were characterized by a need for mastery, and neither depression nor guilt (or shame) could be tolerated. "Unlike victims . . . they encouraged aggression against and defiance of outsiders" (p. 10).[3] The *activity* that differentiates these family styles reemphasizes the difference that total helplessness makes. My clinical experience showed that any type of activity during the traumatic situation tended to minimize the severity of the aftereffects. However, activity in the face of overwhelming stresses exacts its own price. Terr's (1979, 1981a, b) work with the kidnapped children of Chowchilla showed that the children who were heroic in the traumatic situation had, in follow ups, a driven need to repeat the heroic activities, resulting in maladaptive behavior. The activities of the heroic and otherwise actively resistant survivors show a similar drivenness, as Danieli demonstrated.

THE TRANSITION FROM INFANTILE TO ADULT TRAUMATIC PATTERNS

At what age can we expect psychic trauma to take its "adult" form? Freud (1939) studied those traumas whose major effects were neuroses. He concluded: "All these traumas occur in early childhood up to about the fifth year. The periods between the ages of two and four seem to be the most important" (p. 74). As we identify the multiplicity of factors in psychic trauma, we have to allow for individual developmental sequences. The infantile form of trauma continues as long as the affects are undifferentiated, unverbalized, and mostly somatic. The adult form of psychic trauma comes into the foreground with the development of ego functions and the ability to mobilize such defenses as denial, depersonalization, and derealization.

Thus, while we can postulate a gradual development of the capacity to prevent the infantile trauma state, we can say that in the first two years of life that state generally prevails. The infantile form of trauma coincides with preoedipal conflicts and lends them some of their characteristics, for example, the nightmarish intensity of the fears. By the time the fantasies of identification with the parents in regard to the "family romance" are noticeable, the child has identified with the parents' handling of affects and has made much

---

3. Danieli (1981b) also described two other types of families: The "numb families," who eschewed all affects and excitement (relating to the earlier described affective anesthesia), and "those who made it," compensatory hyperachievers.

progress in affect verbalization, desomatization, and differentiation. To the extent that this process has advanced, and to the extent that affect tolerance has started to develop, we can expect a *gradual transition* of trauma from the infantile to the "adult" form.

Since the affective development in a child is subject to rapid regression, the nature of the traumatic incident, its severity, and duration may cause a shift in its form. A child may initially be able to respond with affect blocking and cognitive constriction, but if the traumatic situation continues, there may be a regression with a massive response of primitive affect precursors.

Take for example, the case reported by Solnit and Kris (1967). This was a $3^{1}/_2$-year-old girl who was misbehaving in the car, whining and making noises while she and her mother were driving through a swampy, desolate area. The mother, enraged, stopped the car and yelled, "Get out!", whereupon the child became frightened and promised to behave. At this point, the child "demonstrated evidence of having been traumatized. She immediately allowed herself to be strapped into the front seat of the car and became a good, frozen child. She was dramatically inhibited. Her overwhelming fears of abandonment and castration were from the time of the marshland incident repeatedly played out in thinly disguised ways in the analytic treatment" (p. 209).

I said earlier that the child showed the adult type of trauma response because she was able to respond by blocking her affective responses and, one may assume, recognition. What would have happened if the mother had actually left the child in the desolate area and driven away? The blocking of affects might have continued for a while and become even more severe. It is more likely, however, that the child would immediately have started to call desperately for her mother and pleaded for forgiveness and rescue and perhaps promised to be good from then on. If she had not been rescued right away, her emotional expression would have become more and more violent, and in the process the affects would have become mostly somatic and varied, and overwhelmed her with sheer pain. After a while she might have become exhausted or stuporous or slept for a while, only to wake up startled, to resume her frantic affective pattern until the next point of exhaustion. When the affective patterns assumed the overwhelmed, inconsolable infantile pattern, they would have become like those of an infant, and we would obviously be dealing with the infantile form of psychic trauma. We can also imagine that the sequelae of such an event would be more in line with those outlined in this chapter. The aftereffects described by Solnit and Kris would, of course, not have been cancelled out, but they would have probably been buried under the more severe consequences of the traumatic event per se.

Thus, in evaluating childhood psychic trauma, we have to consider the development of affects and their tolerance vis-à-vis the regressive potential of the event. The other functions related to trauma prevention—the stimulus barrier and the ability to accomplish transition in the form of psychic trauma—are relatively slow. The establishment of executive functions of such reliability and autonomy that the self-observing functions are preserved in the midst of the traumatic state shows what it takes in terms of development to survive a period in that catatonoid state of aphanesis and return to life. These self-monitoring and self-integrating functions must be able to continue in the face of imminent annihilation and despite the loss of virtually all of their usual supports. While in the longer lasting traumatic states it may be possible to recall benign object-representation for fantasied protection, in the acute traumatic state one stands alone, abandoned by all sources of feelings of security. To be able to survive the kind of trials soldiers are exposed to requires an ability to face helplessness and death. The stability of the self-representation must be such that it can be maintained while all executive and self-regulatory functions are surrendered to automatic, even vegetative responses. If the self-observing functions can be preserved under such circumstances, then it becomes possible to develop a utilizable "trauma signal" rather than continuing the usual dread of infantile childhood trauma, a dread so great that it sweeps away all executive functions. Under these circumstances there is a further refinement of one's resources for the adaptive handling of affects as signals, which prevents the affects themselves from becoming the major threat.

Trauma involves the overwhelming of the normal self-preserving functions in the face of inevitable danger. *The recognition of the existence of unavoidable danger and the surrender to it marks the onset of the traumatic state and with it the traumatic process, which if uninterrupted terminates in psychogenic death.* My consideration of psychic trauma indicates that the full-blown adult traumatic state is relatively rare. For the most part, when the causes stem from intrapsychic conflicts, the process is aborted by the utilization of various defenses, which may, however, result in symptoms or symptomatic behavior. This observation gives me the opportunity to reconcile the two theories of trauma in Freud's work, just as Freud himself did in "Inhibition, Symptom, and Anxiety" (1926).

What is frequently referred to as psychic trauma actually refers to nearly traumatic situations that did not progress to a traumatic state, but that in the process of prevention precipitated neurotic or other symptoms. What we observe commonly corresponds to Sandler's (1967) description of "ego strain," but this kind of situation is referred to in the psychoanalytic literature as "trauma," and this usage is not likely to change. For this reason, I feel that it is best to denote the full traumatic process described here as *catastropic trauma.* Its pathological consequences are superimposed on all the various other problems that may develop if the process is stopped along the way (Furst, 1967).

In the prevention of trauma, a hierarchy of signals is utilized, and thus various pathological reactions are spawned. In this ordering, Freud's (1926) explication of the function of signal anxiety represents the first order of signals; Petty's (1975, personal communication) trauma signal provides a second level alarm, specifically related to the danger of "catastrophic trauma." In the foregoing discussions and the exploration of psychoanalytic emergencies (Petty et al., 1974), other signals and defenses utilizable in the prevention of psychogenic death are suggested and need further exploration.

10
Self-Representation and the Capacity for Self-Care

SUBSTANCE ABUSE AND PSYCHOANALYTIC THEORY

Some of the early analysts, especially Abraham (1908, 1924), Simmel (1930, 1948), and Rado (1926, 1933), contributed significant insight into the psychodynamics of alcoholism and drug addiction, and in the process they enriched psychoanalysis. As pessimism shrouded the prospects of individual analytic therapy for these patients, we lost interest in them and thereby lost the opportunity to learn from working with them. Symptomatic of this impoverishment of our studies is the absence of a course on problems of alcohol or other drug dependence from the curricula of all psychoanalytic institutes affiliated with the American Psychoanalytic Association (Handler, 1977). The Board of Professional Standards of the American Psychoanalytic Association (1985) neither requires nor recommends any instruction in the area of addictions.

Yet I have found this to be a rewarding area to study. Impressed with the vagueness and lack of differentiation of affective states, particularly depression and anxiety in withdrawal states, I pursued a study of affective disturbances in alcoholism and drug dependence (Krystal, 1962). I found that there was in drug-dependent persons an affective disturbance consisting of affect dedifferentiation, deverbalization, and resomatization (Krystal and Raskin, 1970). These patients showed a severe disturbance in affective forms and function. Their emotions came in vague, undifferentiated, somatic form; that is, they experienced sensations, not affects. They were not able to put their emotions into words and therefore could not use them as signals to themselves (Krystal, 1974).

Concentration camp survivors also showed an extremely high rate of psychosomatic diseases. While in the general population of survivors the incidence of psychophysiological disturbances was 30%, among the patients who had sufferend persecutions in childhood and adolescence, the incidence reached 60% (Krystal, 1971)!

Observations derived from patients who presented with the problems of substance dependence or psychosomatic illness apply in various ways to a great number of patients. McDougall (1974b) has pointed out that, like it or not, the psychoanalyst "finds himself constantly confronted with psychosomatic behavior of a general kind in all of his analysands, [and] he will also discover that a considerable proportion of his patients, whether he wishes it or not suffer from authentic psychosomatic disorders" (p. 438).

Another area to which the study of drug dependent and alcoholic patients contributes a helpful view of universal interest is in object- and self-representation, especially with regard to the fantasy of "introjection." For the alcoholic and drug-dependent patient, the nature of their transferences and self-representations poses an often insuperable barrier to psychoanalytic psychotherapy. It is precisely because this area is such an obstacle that we must study it. Very likely our technical weakness stems from a failure to recognize and understand something about these problems.

AMBIVALENCE IN OBJECT RELATIONS AND TRANSFERENCE.

Let us consider the difficulties resulting from the ambivalence in object-relations so frequently noted in the treatment of substance-dependent patients. What becomes difficult to weather is the early surfacing of aggressive transference. One view of this difficulty relates to the disturbance in affect tolerance. One is inclined to expect that painful (or "emergency") affects present the greatest challenge to the ego in terms of the management of pain and secondary anxiety. Drug-dependent individuals, however, are among those who have difficulties with the type of emotion that is commonly experienced as pleasurable. Rado (1969) has called all of these "welfare affects," since they usually favor the well-being of an individual. Out of these, Spitz (1959) has singled out the "proleptic" group, that is, the emotions experienced in the process of expecting gratification. However, these emotions are pleasurable only when accompanied by hope and confidence based on previous good experiences. Unfortunately, with these patients, that is not the case. Because of the nature of their transferences, they expect disappointment and rejection, and proleptic affects may represent a "trauma signal" (Krystal, 1975a) for them.

When exposed to a potentially good object, such patients panic and may have to ward off their yearnings for love and acceptance. Such an untoward reaction represents a fear of the positive transference; it has also been observed in psychotherapy with schizophrenic patients (Sechehaye, 1951).

These patterns have been described in great detail by Kernberg (1975) and Boyer (1977) in regard to borderline patients. Of course, borderline patients also frequently manifest dependence on drugs and use them defensively to deal with these types of transferences. Kernberg, especially, has clearly discussed the need to devaluate, even symbolically to destroy the therapist in order to ward off feelings of envy and the resulting rage.

Whether we consider them a manifestation of the transference or a defense against it, there is frequently an early appearance of unconscious, hateful, and destructive impulses toward the analyst. They represent a threat to the establishment of a working alliance. Because of the prevalence of magical thinking, fortified by the wish for magical powers and in harmony with a grandiose self-representation, alcoholic and drug-dependent patients in psychotherapy become terrified of their death wishes toward the therapist. Relatively early in the treatment they are confronted with their extraordinarily intense envy and need to deal with their poorly mastered narcissistic rages. At this point, they flee from the treatment, because they fear that their death wishes will destroy their therapist. Or they turn their aggression against themselves and act it out in an accidental injury, suicide attempt, or relapse of drug abuse (Simmel, 1948). Early development of ambivalent transferences may be one of the major reasons why alcoholics and drug abusers do poorly in private therapy. For this type of drug-dependent patient, individual therapy works better in a clinic situation, where auxilliary therapists are available and may be spontaneously sought out by some patients with addictive problems.

The idea of using a team to manage the substance-dependent patient is not new. One of the successful psychoanalytic treatment centers was Simmel's Schloss Tegel Clinic. Simmel was concerned with the alcoholic's tendency toward self-punishing ideas and suicide attempts after withdrawal. The patient who was being withdrawn from alcohol was permitted to stay in bed, and a special nurse was assigned to look after him, including his diet. This technique was a conscious attempt to provide the patient with passive gratification, to deal with the "drying out" process as a gentle "weaning" and prepare the patient for "regular analysis" (Simmel, 1948).

It has been my observation that when highly ambivalent patients have access to a therapeutic team, they will use it for the "splitting" of their transferences. In this way they experience their angry and destructive wishes toward one member of the team while presenting a loving relationship toward another, preferably the chief therapist (Krystal, 1964). I believe that this development takes place commonly in treatment clinics and groups. However, most of the time the transferences acted out with various clinic employees are lost from the therapeutic process unless a special effort is made to "gather" them. If everyone in the clinic reports to the chief therapist about every contact and communication with the patient, a picture of the nature of the patient's transference can then be put together. It will be found that the patient is not experiencing a simple splitting of the transference into one love and one hate relation; rather, the picture will be quite complex and rapidly changing. At one moment, the chief therapist may be experienced as the idealized mother whose love and admiration the patient yearns for, while another staff member may be experienced as a rejecting, condemning parental image whom the patient dreads and hates; and still another staff member may be experienced as a seductive, intrusive, destructive parental transference object. The patient who feels frustrated by the chief therapist and needs to experience his rage toward him will instantly experience another member of the team as an idealized parent, while experiencing other partial transferences with yet another member of the clinic staff, whether in a therapeutic role or not. Conversely, when the chief therapist is experienced as kind, concerned, and loving, the patient may suffer enormous guilt over his aggressive, envious feelings; this guilt may drive him to act out in a self-destructive fashion. He may avert that need if he can justify his feelings by some grievance over a deprivation or slight from someone else in the clinic.

To demonstrate to the patient the splitting, idealization, and vilification involved in his transference, his projections must be brought together, and all of these transferences must be shown to represent various object representations, which he needs to experience toward the *one* therapist. The patient's vacillations and changes in attitude toward the various staff members can be used to demonstrate his dilemma. Bringing in the ambivalence in the transference is crucial to working with such patients, because a major force in propelling people toward addiction is that they can displace their ambivalence toward the drug. Szasz (1958) emphasized this aspect of drug problems in his paper on the counterphobic attitude in drug dependence.

A special instance of the efficacy of a group of therapists is the situation where the addicted person is sent to the clinic by a court. The probation officer assigned to the patient becomes an object of transference of a very signfiicant type. The fact that this type of patient has a characterological disturbance that entails his "externalizing" (that is, failing to integrate) his superego function and needs others to enforce controls for him is a clear indication that these transferences cannot be left out of the treatment (Margolis, Krystal, and Siegel, 1964). Back in 1931 Glover commented that drug-addicted patients are able to give up the drugs until "the very last drop." This "last drop," however, is virtually impossible to give up, because it contains the symbolic expression of the fantasy of taking in the love object. The "external" object, which is experienced as containing the indispensable life power that the patient wants to, but cannot, "internalize," characterizes the basic dilemma dominating the psychic reality of this type of patient. This tendency applies to his conscience as well, so that he is unable to experience it as being a part of himself but arranges for others to exercise it for him.

In considering the use of Antabuse, we see that the fantasy solution of swallowing the object not only refers to "goodness," or narcissistic supplies, but is a way of introjecting an external source of impulse control in a concrete way. The failure to integrate—to be able to own up to one's own functions and aspects, such as conscience, and attributing them instead to others, such as parents, spouses, or probation officers—makes the drug-dependent person experience the world in a paranoid way. This idea was summed up by Glover (1931), who said that drug addicts are inverted paranoids and that they are both the persecuting and the persecuted ones. Thus, whether there is a probation officer in the picture or Antabuse or similar substances (or procedures) are used by the therapist, the transferences involved in the patient's failure to see the selfsameness of his superego have to be brought into the treatment through interpretation—if the patient is ever to accept himself as a whole person. We should note also that those operations in which a patient needs to "take in" some external factor in order to exercise his own function are a mode of behavior paralleling the use of a placebo.

SELF-REPRESENTATION AND VITAL AND AFFECTIVE FUNCTIONS

These observations address what I consider to be the basic defect and the basic dilemma in the life of the drug-dependent individual, such as the alcoholic. It is that he is unable to acknowledge, claim, and exercise various parts and functions of himself; he experiences these as being part of the object-representation, not of the self-representation. Without being consciously aware of it, he experiences himself as unable to carry out these functions because he feels that they are prohibited to him, being reserved for the parental objects. Even though exercising self-soothing and self-caring functions is especially difficult for addictive and psychosomatic individuals, self-caring, and particularly self-comforting, has to be understood as a major conflict in everyone's life.

Let us consider what prevents the patient from internalizing these functions; indeed, whether the model of taking in such functions from outside is a reflection of the patient's fantasy or whether, in fact, functions are "taken over" from parental and later transference objects. A new source of observations in this area has become available from studies of biofeedback combined with psychotherapy. There is, however, a certain difficulty that can arise in that setting.

Just as the drug-dependent person is unable to exercise certain functions for himself or even admit that he is doing it, so do we all experience those parts of ourselves that are under the control of the autonomic nervous system as being beyond our volition. However, in the last twenty years, there has become available a whole literature demonstrating that through the use of biofeedback devices, control over these areas can be acquired. For the most part, the reports have an exclusively behaviorist orientation, reporting the degree of success in terms of percentages and number of trials. The concern is with the apparatus, rewards, and results. Rickles (1976) is a rare exception: a psychoanalyst who concerns himself with the psychic reality of the patient and the patient's mental representations and transferences to the machine, the therapist, and his patient's problem. His patients are in psychoanalysis or psychoanalytic psychotherapy while undergoing biofeedback training. They also speak for five minutes into a tape recorder after each biofeedback session and relate whatever comes to mind. Perhaps it is because of this unusual setting that one of Rickle's patients "soon left biofeedback therapy . . . because she was frightened by the depressive feelings which emerged when she relaxed" (p. 5).

I have treated a few patients who also had undergone biofeedback treatment. One had severe hypertension. Several others manifested extremely severe anxiety (one patient had a resting pulse of over 110), and others suffered insomnia or severe headaches that had been intractable by all previously tried methods. Although most of the patients complied with the instructions of the psychologist and achieved some desired results in the sessions, they found it difficult to practice at home and to generalize their newly acquired skills to their everyday lives. There were, of course, a number of reasons for this failure, including certain of the more usual transference problems. However, there was one reaction, quite marked in some and mild in others, that I wish to highlight.

All the patients showed evidence of guilt and anxiety over gaining control over vital functions and over parts of themselves that they had assumed to be beyond their control. Some were conscious of this feeling and expressed fear that such a *Promethean* act on their part would be punished severely. Others dreaded that by acquiring such powers they might destroy themselves. Still others showed indications of only unconscious reactions in that vein. The patients felt that these major parts of their bodies were proscribed for the incursion of their volition, and to assume control over these functions was a forbidden act.

That they did "learn" to exercise a particular action under the direct supervision of the psychologist is consistent with such feelings. While under his tutelage, they were able to do it, as long as they disavowed their responsibility for the act. However, they could not accomplish the same results at home consistently; they acted out their denial in various ways, for example, by falling asleep while practicing. Even when they learned to carry out an activity, such as lowering their blood pressure or relaxing their muscles while practicing, they had great difficulty in generalizing this act outside of the practice session. To do so would have signified a conscious recognition that they had taken control of the "automatic" area of their bodies, which they felt they were not supposed to do. These feelings are universal; they are not limited to psychosomatic patients, although they are more problematic to these patients. A case has been reported, for instance, of a psychoanalyst who learned to relax the spasm of the peripheral blood vessels and thus relieve the symptoms of his Raynaud's disease. After about a year of doing it, he became less successful at it and had to return to the laboratory for "further training" (Schwartz, 1973, p. 672). Appelbaum (1977) offered an experiment in teaching people to heal themselves and found that some terminal cancer patients would rather die than try it: "When offered a simple, painless and harmless method which has proven effective in a number of cases, most patients refuse to try it" (p. 516).

Lest we be distracted from our observation that we are dealing with an emotional block to the exercise of our potential functions, let me re-emphasize that we are not dealing with peculiarities of the autonomic nervous system. As I mentioned, for some of the patients who suffered from muscle tension states or tension headaches it was a matter of relaxing their muscles. Thus, the area of the body excluded from the self-representation does not necessarily coincide with that of the visceral or archipalial areas but is determined by individual fantasy. Frequently, however, the inhibition involves all those parts of the body importantly involved in a given individual's *affective responses*. When patients are referred for biofeedback treatment, there is a significant psychosomatic element in the picture. Unlike experimental animals or subjects, they are addressing themselves to symptoms of their affective, if not symbolic, disorder.

BODY IMAGE AND MATERNAL TRANSFERENCE

The patients had guilt and anxiety about learning to control their viscera, or even to relax their muscles, because, in their unconscious scheme of things, organs such as their hearts were under the special care of God (or fate, doctor, hospital, and the like), who guaranteed their survival. This is illustrated in a commonly held theory of sleep, namely, that God causes it by taking away the soul, which He may, by His grace, return to us the next morning. This theory of sleep is a transference of the maternal image, for whom life-giving powers, as well as nursing, are reserved. This theory is universally shared and incorporated into law; it means, in effect, that we do not own our lives and therefore, do not have the right to commit suicide. All basic life-assuring functions are carried out under a franchise, as it were.

This experience has its roots in infancy, and even phylogeny, for certain newborn mammals will not void, but will die, unless licked by the mother on the perineum (Lehman, 1961). Abandoned young mammals die, sometimes even when a maternal substitute becomes available, if a personal attachment (object constancy) has been accomplished and the object is lost (Van Lawick-Goodall, 1973). The human infant is, of course, most vulnerable, and we could say that the newborn will destroy himself unless rescued by the mother. Much of Melanie Klein's theorizing about the early destructive impulses of the child can be understood in this light. Early mothering is experienced as *permission* to live.

When the biofeedback patients were told that they could learn to control their autonomic functions, some experienced fears that taking over such maternal prerogatives would cause them to destroy themselves. Of course, even dying is experienced as being regulated by the mother, who takes back her child (for example, Mother Earth, or the Pietà theme). It is relevant to remind ourselves again that this area is involved in the "expressive" aspect of affects, because the emotions are similarly experienced as emanating from the object, and the ideas of "managing" them and using them as signals is also experienced by many patients as forbidden (Krystal, 1975). Thus the two areas of disturbance—one in the sphere of affects, and the other in the sphere of self and object- and self-representations—have their common denominator in the historical sources under consideration. The connection goes even deeper. These patients often have the following definition of love based on the addictive fantasy: "If you love me, you will take care of me and make me feel good forever." They not only experience their feelings as emanating from the object, who carries the whole responsibility for them, but even further compound this construction: Whenever they feel bad, they conclude that they are unloved and rejected by the love object. They become convinced that either the object is bad and dangerous or they are bad and being punished. Their rage about this "unfairness" appears to turn either against the object or against themselves. These problems, of course, contribute to the problems of early aggressive transferences mentioned earlier. However, since all the patient's bad feelings are the fault and responsibility of the object, it is up to the love object, and not the patient, to make the patient feel better.

Behaviorists have overlooked this problem because it represents, for the most part, unconscious fantasies demonstrable through the analysis of transferences and characterological patterns. According to the behaviorists, one handicap in acquiring conscious volitional control over viscera lies in the lack of proprioception, which is remedied by the biofeedback apparatus (Stoyva, 1970; DiCara, 1972). But, to their credit, the behaviorists have questioned the limits of voluntary control of our selves, as well as the very concept of volition. In a thoughtful review of the problems of volition, Kimble and Perlmuter (1970) pointed out the narrowness and inadequacy of the academic psychology view of volition as being equal to conscious intentionality. They proposed to explore the development, initiation, and control of voluntary acts. Implicit in operant conditioning is the conception that an organism will tend to repeat actions that bring it pleasurable consequences (rewards); this notion suggests a broader concept of motivation that goes beyond consciousness or reason.[1]

The views of the behaviorists, however, lack the psychoanalytic concept of the mind's functioning in a state of conflict. Therefore, they miss the main point of interest to us: *that volition, intention, or motivation may be opposed by motivations and interests in the opposite direction.* That is why they have not observed the difficulties that subjects encounter within themselves in expanding the limits of their acknowledged function, that is to say, in trying to integrate alienated parts of themselves.

Behaviorists exploring voluntary control of internal states have produced a wealth of evidence that the commonly accepted limits of conscious control of automatic function are not due to absolute anatomic limitations. The following is a good review of their position on these issues:

> It is not possible to define in an operational way the meaning of the word "voluntary," but all of us have a *feeling* of voluntary control, at least part of the time, regardless of the psychophysical and metaphysical implications of that feeling. Few people realize, however, that that feeling or intuition of freedom has unusual significance in respect to the autonomic nervous system, the so-called involuntary nervous system, nor do they realize that the "psychophysiological principle" when coupled with volition makes it possible to regulate a number of important involuntary functions, and at least theoretically to regulate in some degree every psychological and physiological function of one's being.
>
> The psychophysiological principle, as we hypothesize it, affirms that "Every change in the physiological state is accompanied by an appropriate change in the mental-emotional state, conscious or unconscious, and conversely, every change in the mental-emotional state, conscious or unconscious, is accompanied by an appropriate change in the physiological state" [Green, Green, and Walters 1970, p. 5].

Now, what are some indications that our inability to control our physiological states is functionally, not automatically, determined? To start with, there are people who naturally can control various viscera. Some people have conscious control over their heartbeat and blood pressure. One man was even observed to be able to bring his heart to a complete stop for a few seconds and to resume normal function at will (Ogden and Shock, 1939; McClure, 1959). Yogis have been watched in the exercise of control of various functions through volition alone (Green, Green, and Walters, 1970). Of course, we all exercise control over viscera, but usually we deny it by

---

1. There is a corresponding effort to review the psychoanalytic conceptions of volition and motivation, notably in the work of G. Klein (1970) and Holt (1976). For a review, see Santostefano (1977).

giving credit to the various devices we use. When, for instance, we select a certain kind of music in order to calm ourselves or otherwise modify our affective state, we tend to minimize our own responsibility, attributing it to "external" implements.

The functions so laboriously acquired, apparently through learning, may be gained instantly through the use of hypnosis (Shor, 1962; Maslach, Marshall, and Zimbardo, 1972). Barber (1970) did a critical review of many reports in this area and concluded that "a wide variety of physiological functions can be influenced directly or indirectly by suggesting to either hypnotic or awake subjects that certain physiological effects are forthcoming" (p. 243). Among these effects were the production of vestibular nystagmus; the production and blocking of pain; the induction and inhibition of labor contractions; modification of vasomotor function in the skin, such as blood vessel dilation or constriction; cardiac acceleration and deceleration; and the modification of a variety of metabolic and gastrointestional functions. Another group of researchers concluded: "These experimental results free us from the shackles of viewing the autonomic nervous system with contempt. They force us to think of the behavior of the internal, visceral organs in the same way that we think of the externally observable behavior of the skeletal musculature" (Miller et al., 1970, p. 358).

Beyond the evidence of the potential for the control of physiological states derived from hypnosis and suggestion, there is the placebo phenomenon to consider (Krystal and Raskin, 1970). The history of medicine is in essence the history of the placebo, effective drugs being a rare and only recent development (Shapiro, 1960). As is well known, patients under the influence of a placebo are capable of exercising a multiplicity of self-functions over which they usually feel no control. This accomplishment goes far beyond pain control (Beecher, 1961), but the effects are not necessarily beneficial. A variety of untoward reactions have been reported—from transient sleepiness, nausea, skin rashes, and diarrhea to uticaria, angioneurotic edema, and others (Wolf and Pinskey, 1942; Beecher, 1956; Roueche, 1960). Why is it, then, that we are ordinarily unable to exercise control over the parts of our bodies controlled by the autonomic nervous system, yet we can do so under the influence of biofeedback training, hypnosis, or placebo?

I must address that question by making the outrageous claim that *the usual state of humans in regard to the autonomically controlled part of the body is precisely analogous to an hysterical paralysis.* Since we have the potential to exercise these functions but are prevented from doing so for psychological reasons, we are dealing with a functional, or conversion-derived, block. This "normal" inhibition of the exercise of volition over the autonomic or affective aspect of ourselves is, like any conversion paralysis, the symbolic representation of a fantasy. This particular fantasy, however, pertains not to our genital or phallic conflicts, but to the vital functions. In the "normal" state, we dramatize the fantasy that control of our lives and feelings does not belong to us, that it is not a part of the self-representation but is governed by mother, doctor, or God and thus is part of the primal object representation.

When one functions under the influence of the doctor's placebo, the behaviorist's biofeedback machine, the hypnotist's suggestion, the shaman's or curandero's magical incantations, one gains access to the functions previously reserved for the object. Because the needed functions are experienced as part of the object-representation, there is in the ritual of reclaiming them an acting out symbolically of the fantasy of devouring or "introjecting" the object. When the symbol of the object is "taken in," whether as in a prescription medicine, alcohol, illicit drug, or even the ritual of Holy Communion, evidence of the ambivalence toward the object may become noticeable. Kaplan and Wieder (1969) have pointed out that "drugs" and "potion" both denote at once medicine or poison. They explained (p. 401) that the prototype of the drug experience is the nursing one. The evidence for this assertion can be found in suppliers being called "mother," on one hand, or "shit" on the other. Kaplan and Wieder reported that chronically ill children relate to their medication as a magic potion.

Ambivalence about ill effects of drugs is not limited to "junkies" but is a universal phenomenon. Better than half of all patients never fill their prescriptions. However, it is not just a matter of the splitting of the object and the taking in of a poisonous object, that is, "witchmother." Especially clear in religious beliefs is that the Host is always good, and it is only the taking it by the *undeserving* which is punishable. It is the transgression of taking in the object for the purpose of acquiring the walled-off, self-soothing, and comforting function that is forbidden and punishable. That is why, if one is still "supposed to" suffer, taking the medicine will make one even more ill (poisoned or cursed) as was noted among the adverse reactions to the placebo. It is for this reason that psychosomatic patients respond differently to biofeedback than do experimental subjects.

Appelbaum (1977) reported that terminal cancer patients who refused to learn to heal themselves showed another phenomenon: When they found evidence that they had the responsibility and the power to modify the course of their illness, they would take a "nose dive" and suddenly die (p. 516).

What we are facing, then, are barriers within the self-representation, in which the most basic, life-maintaining, and affective functions are experienced as outside the self-representation, and as part of the object-representation. The usurping of maternal (God's) privileges is the feared transgression of what is experienced as the "natural" order of things.

Under the influence of a placebo or another conveyance, there is a temporary lifting of internal barriers between the self-representation and the object-representation, thereby permitting access to, and control of, parts of oneself previously "walled-off." What are these intrapsychic schisms made of? They represent repressed parts of oneself, repressed by *depriving them of the conscious recognition of selfhood.* This does not pertain just to parts of one's body, but, even more strongly, to the spheres of functions.

THE BLOCKING OF SELF-CARING FUNCTIONS

Alcoholics and drug addicts are among those people who have severe inhibitions in carrying out a multitude of "mothering" or self-comforting functions. In studying their difficulties, we can observe that we are dealing with an intrapsychic block that prevents them from the consciously exercised use of these functions. They act as if they were forced to repress (alienate) their potential for self-care.

These repressions take place at various times in childhood in connection with the various conflicts centered in the psychosexual development. As analysts, we are familiar with these conflicts and the inhibitions that the neurotic patients show. On the phallic level of development it is common for us to find the very same kind of structure that I have described in regard to the autonomically controlled affective part of the body. Neurotic patients often believe that their genitals are not part of their self-representation, but belong to their parents, for whom their sexual and pleasuring use is reserved.

A boy finds himself frightened of his competitive strivings with his father because of his fantasies and theories of destroying his father and taking his place; that is, unconscious identification fantasies related to his theory of becoming *the* father may repress these wishes and fantasies. Thereafter, he sees himself as a boy, with adult masculine modes of action being reserved for the father. Unless he finds some way to overcome or circumvent these repressions, he may never be able to fulfill his masculine ambitions or exercise his masculinity. This failure may lead to the kind of inhibition in occupational and sexual goals, with a rise to prominence of homosexual strivings, that the early psychoanalytic writers described in their observations of alcoholics (Abraham 1908; Juliusberger, 1913; Hartmann, 1925; Rado, 1926, 1933; Simmel, 1930). The unconscious fantasy of some homosexuals is that through the sexual act they will regain their alienated masculinity through symbolic introjection.

This type of conflict concerning the fulfillment of one's potential as man or woman is well recognized and taught in present-day psychoanalysis. However, even the pregenital conflicts that are studied are approached from the point of view of how they appear to us in work with adult neurotics. They are seen after they have come under the hegemony of phallic-genital strivings and been revised in the preschool ego in concrete-preoperative terms and again in adolescence in more formal abstract terms. As a result of this point of view and the classical psychoanalytic technique, some kinds of observations are easier than others. That is why in reconstructing the events of the toddler age, we psychoanalysts discovered the importance of toilet training and anal eroticism fifty years before we caught on to the vastly more important simultaneous development of separation-individuation.

In the same manner, I am trying to highlight a type of transference and a kind of conflict, other than the oedipal one, concerned with fulfilling one's sexual and occupational potential. Instead of the conflict with the phallically conceived parents, I am stressing the conflict related to the maternal object-representation: the primal object. The conflict here is not over fulfillment of one's gender role, but over survival. The question is whether it is permissible for one to take charge of one's vital and affective functions and visibly and noticeably carry out self-regulatory and self-caring functions. The conflict is generated by the infantile view that it is the prerogative of the mothering parent to lend all the organizing, nurturing and, in fact, *life-maintaining* powers to the child. The mother seems to have the exclusive right to provide loving, comforting, and soothing, as if she had cornered the love market. Consequently, there is a distortion of the self-representation and object-representation, in which all the vital and affective parts are attributed to the sphere of control or influence of the primal object and excluded from the self-representation. This distortion is the structure behind the mental block analogous to an hysterical paralysis; it determines that we cannot exercise volitional control over our viscera. The same fate befalls our muscles when they come under affective control (as in states of chronic muscle tension).

In point of fact, *any* executive function (or "ego function") can be similarly attributed to the parental object-representation and repressed through deprivation of selfhood. Edgcumbe (1983) described the analysis of a patient who was unable to organize her thoughts. When confronted with a maternal transference object such as the analyst, or even her husband, she could not compose her thoughts and had to be asked specific questions. The occurrence of this extraordinary transference permits us to observe that patients who cannot exercise self-caring functions experience these functions are experienced as being part of the object-representation and "walled-off" within it. Some patients have presented themselves to me with the statement that they have "lost their feelings" and requested that I restore them, give them back to them. I have described the resulting deficits in the drug-dependent patients in terms of the impaired ability to comfort and soothe themselves (Krystal and Raskin, 1970). One reason addicts yearn for the "nods," or use drugs to obtain relief from distressing feelings or to gain "good" feelings, is that they are not able to exerise comforting, mothering functions. Consequently, they may not be able to do the kinds of things that ordinary people do to soothe themselves, relax, and go to sleep. In my discussion of the use of the placebo and other devices, I have stressed repeatedly that there are many patients, beyond the group of drug-dependent persons in whom this is so conspicuous, who do not feel free to comfort themselves when they feel bad. Their affect tolerance is impaired because they do not feel free to exercise the kind of comforting, gratifying care that a mother gives to a distressed child. In brief, I have found an inhibition in the ability of substance-dependent patients to literally take care of themselves physically and emotionally (Krystal, 1978b).

Khantzian (1978) has added to these observations, pointing out even wider implications. He showed that drug-dependent persons had "a type of self-disregard associated with impairments of a multitude of functions related to proper *self-care* and *self-regulation*" (p. 192). Khantzian reminds us that many drug-dependent persons do not take care of their nutrition or general medical and dental care and that they fail to exercise even ordinary care and caution to avoid the multiplicity of troubles and tribulations that "befall them." These patients so consistently fail to exercise these welfare functions that we must conclude that they have an inhibition in this essential area. Zinberg (1975) has also commented on drug addicts' severe impairment in self-care. He pointed out that they are not only self-destructive, but also "manage almost never to do well for themselves in the simplest life transactions. They lose laundry slips and money, choose the wrong alternative at each instance, and are invariably being gypped at the very moment they think they are the slyest" (p. 374).

We have already observed that there are similarities between substance-dependent and psychosomatic patients in regard to affective function. It is relevant to note that psychosomatic patients also frequently fail to take care of themselves, especially in regard to the symptoms of their diseases. McDougall (1974b) has noted that the illness progresses silently; even when the symptoms of psychosomatic illness become obvious, they fail to attract the necessary attention, self-care, nor do they come up in the psychoanalytic discourse (p. 458).

THE PLACEBO AS A MEANS OF OVERCOMING INTERNAL BLOCKING

The placebo effect is an important element in the development of drug dependence. This is the aspect of addiction we have called "an extreme form of transference" (Krystal and Raskin, 1970, p. 71). Drug-dependent patients are not free to take care of themselves except under the "order" of transference or under the influence of a placebo. Again, this phenomenon is observable in psychosomatic patients as well. McDougall (1974b) observed that her psychosomatic patients were extremely dependent on their love object for feelings of "being alive" and that they "tend to fall physically ill when abandoned" (p. 451). But their love objects were "highly *interchange-able*": "the central demand being that someone must be there. This someone is cast in the role of a 'security blanket' and thus fulfills the function as a transitional object" (p. 451). McDougall referred to such object relations in psychosomatic patients as "addictive" and related how one of her patients, having lost her mate, "lost everything: her sexuality, her narcissistic self-image, her capacity to sleep and her ability to metabolize her food" (p. 452).

In her discussion of the use of objects by psychosomatic patients to enable them to take care of themselves, McDougall stressed that the patients seemed to try to make the "external object behave like a symbolic one" (p. 455), in order to fill some psychic gap within themselves. I feel, of course, that there is no real deficiency, but that the patients lost the use of or access to their own powers. I interpret such behavior as the patient's dealing with *the fantasy* of deficiency or defect to be repaired by the incorporation of the object. As psychoanalysts, we regularly "take over" the patient's fantasies and make them part of our theories: "It may be said with Kohut . . . , that the defect in the above patient represented a failure to successfully establish the kind of transmuted internalization that would make it possible for her to exercise certain adult functions . . ." (Krystal, 1975a, p. 200).

However, the placebo does not lend the taker the *function,* only the freedom to exercise it. If a drug-dependent, a psychosomatic, or a "normal" person can exercise a function under the influence of the placebo, drug, hypnosis, love or inspiration, then he demonstrates that his freedom to exercise it had been blocked by a fantasy. That is why we can conclude that substance-dependent and psychosomatic patients alike experience their self-caring functions as reserved for the maternal object-representation, as psychologically "walled-off," inaccessible to them.

It is the child's construction that the mother provides all the comfort for him, that all good feelings emanate from her, and that when he provides such sensations for himself he is "taking over" the function. In concentrating on her powers, he loses sight of the fact that no matter what she did, he always "created" all his feelings and sensations, including his perceptions and mental representations of her. Based on this childhood theory of maternal monopoly of love powers, there are corresponding distortions of self-representations.

Here we are observing the late consequences of the belief that self-comforting and self-soothing functions belong to and are reserved for the primal love object. There is evidence that this fantasy is ubiquitous, notably in the universal blocking of the autonomously controlled part's of the body. This inhibition stems from conflicts and transferences related to the primal object representation and is widely prevalent to varying degrees. Are there any settings in which a child might be likely to develop such attitudes?

THE CHILD'S MENTAL REPRESENTATION OF THE MOTHER AND ITS RELATIONSHIP TO THE EXERCISE OF VITAL FUNCTIONS

Tolpin (1971) has explained the necessity to study minutely the processes by which autonomous functions are acquired. She used observations of the transitional object to explore the development of the child's self-soothing functions. We are concerned here with the problems in this process, especially since we are concentrating on two groups of patients who show serious psychopathology in this area. We are particularly interested in infantile experiences that interfere with the child's gradual acquisition of a freedom for self-soothing; in other words, with those situations in which, retrospectively, permission for self-care seems not to have been felt nor even a prohibition against it experienced.

Our first question involves the kind of mother who, for a number of possible reasons, may punish or discourage any self-gratification or autonomy by the child. One thinks, offhand, of the mother whose need for a narcissistic unity with the child is so great that she is jealous of other objects, even a transitional object, and prevents its use. I do not imply that such direct causation is a necessary condition for the child to infer that conscious self-caring is prohibited. A variety of stiuations might conspire to give the same result. For a while there may be mothers who do not favor the child's separating from them (and we will discuss some of these types), what concerns us is the child's *psychic reality*. It is the child's mental representation of the object that will cause him to attribute various fantasies and theories to his construction of the object and himself. Thus the child will fuse his perceptions of his maternal object and his own illness or other distress and come up with a construct of "bad mother" or "bad-self being punished" or a myriad of other fantasies (Brierly, 1945; Beres and Joseph, 1970; Angel, 1973).

We find illustrations in Spitz's (1962) observations that where the mother-child relationship is not satisfactory (for the child, we assume) autoerotism is diminished or disappears altogether. But in discussing the kinds of unsatisfactory mother-child relationships, Spitz clearly approaches the issue from the child's experience; he considers a variety of examples including Harlow's (1958) monkeys. In our analytic work with adults it is clear that we are sharing with the patients a reconstruction of their original fantasies regarding mother and her messages to them.

From her work with adult analysands who only incidentally to their main (neurotic) problems were found also to have psychosomatic ones, as well as from direct observations, especially by Fain (1971), McDougall (1974b) concluded that either severe prohibition of any autoerotic activity or constant availability of the mother (experienced as the sole experience source of comfort) can predispose the child to psychosomatic illness (p. 447).

Fain and Kreisler (1970) observed children who could not fall asleep. One group of infants was unable to sleep unless continually rocked in their mother's arms. These babies, McDougall (1974b), concluded, were unable to exercise for themselves the psychic activity necessary for sleep, but required the mother to be "the guardian of sleep" (p. 446). Fain (1971) theorized that these babies did not have a satisfying mother, but rather a tranquilizing mother: "The latter, because of her own problems, cannot permit her baby to create a primary identification which will enable him to sleep without continual contact with her" (McDougall, 1974b, p. 446). These children could be said to be suffering from both a *psychosomatic* problem and *addictive* problem. We have here the common root to the affective disturbances and inhibition in self-caring that these two groups share.

The child's ability to maintain sleep is the first achievement in exercising the kind of self-caring functions with which we are concerned. In studying sleep disturbances in infants, Fain (1971) described three patterns: Babies who slept while making small sucking movements, babies who slept with their thumb in their mouth, and babies who sucked frenetically and did not sleep. While the first group accomplished the necessary relaxation by dreaming or hallucinatory wish fulfillment, the second group required a concrete representation of the breast. The need for the *concrete* external object substitute may either be due to the absence of an internal symbolic "good object," as McDougall (1974b) suggested, or it may be the necessary prop that, like the placebo, permits the exercise of functions of "loving" reserved for the object and prohibited to the self. In this sense, the placebo, like the fetish, serves to deny something. For the third group of babies, there is a failure to accomplish relaxation regardless of the continuing sucking. Fain (1971) had explained these disturbances as due to the mother's inability to grant the child its autonomy. Conceivably, however, the child's inability to gain comfort derives from some inner disturbance, as has been reported by Chethik (1977) from his studies of borderline children.

Fain (1971) also described the opposite end of the spectrum, where the child engaged in a type of autoeroticism that seemed to eliminate the mother as an object. This extreme, McDougall (1974b) concluded, demonstrated that "instinctual aims" and autoerotic activity run the risk of becoming literally *autonomous,* detached from any *"mental representation of an object"* (p. 447). However, it may be that in cases of merycism, where the baby constantly regurgitates and swallows the contents of the stomach, we may see the precursor of an inability to retain the yearned for supplies that we see in drug-dependent patients and in bullemia. Observations on these psychosomatic disturbances in infants suggested to McDougall (1974b) that their mothers were "addictive." They encouraged the babies to become dependent on them, as an addict needs a drug, "with total dependence on an external object—to deal with situations which should be handled by self-regulatory psychological means" (p. 448). McDougall indicates that there is, in psychosomatic and addictive patients, an absence of good object-representations on a symbolic level, and hence a need for *concrete* supplies.

I (1966a) have reported similar findings not only in psychosomatic and addictive patients, but in posttraumatic ones as well. In the latter group it is evident that we are dealing with a regression, rather than a failure of symbolic object "introjection" in infancy (1968c). Also, if we consider the concommitant inhibition in self-caring functions, we cannot relegate the mental block to pure psychopathology. It is in this connection that we need to recall the universal phenomenon of the "hysterical paralysis" of our autonomically controlled parts. The occurrence of this universal inhibition, and the use of the placebo to get around it, forces us to study these problems in terms of the nature of self- and object-representation. If we also consider the transitional object as a placebo, we have to propose, instead of McDougall's view, that an object-representation is present but that it is "walled-off" in the sense that functions attributed to it are not available to the self ("repressed").

Therein is the source of the oral character's drivenness to use the drug as a pharmacological means to manipulate his affective states. He craves the drugs as a placebo to gain surcease from his feelings of depletion resulting from the repression of self-helping forces and functions. He needs to make them a part of an object-representation in order to restore his wholesome, fuller self-image. We must recognize that the person who is likely to become drug dependent has to use the drug to help him carry out basic survival functions he otherwise cannot perform. People who drink in order to be able to continue to work thereby gain access to their assertive, masculine, and paternal modes of behavior. People who drink for surcease and comfort obtain their goal, in addition to the pharmacological effects, by gaining access to their maternal functions. The longing to regain alienated parts of oneself is the real meaning behind the fantasies of fusion with the good mother so clearly discernible in drug-dependent patients (Chessick, 1960; Savitt, 1963; Krystal and Raskin, 1970).

These yearnings make their appearance in the transference in the analysis of alcoholics and other drug-dependent patients. This phase of the treatment, as well as the phenomenon itself, has been termed "object addiction" (Fenichel, 1945). This transference needs to be interpreted in the analysis for the very same reason that all transferences are interpreted: so that the patient will discover that the characteristics he attributes to the analyst are actually his own mental representations, which he first perceived as being part of his mother and now perceives as belonging to his analyst. The healing principle of psychoanalysis consists of the patients' reclaiming of their own minds, restoring the *conscious recognition* of their own selves.

But, as we know only too well, patients do not feel free to do this. They fight it with all the means at their disposal, as if their lives depended on maintaining the repressions. Drug-dependent patients often have a terrible struggle with this part of treatment. When we try to understand the nature of the psychic reality that makes removal of repression from their maternal object-representations so difficult for them, we are led to the core of their emotional problems represented by their infantile trauma.

It is this kind of resistance against establishing the benign object-representation and taking over their self-caring functions that makes me take exception to the view of McDougall (1974b) and de M'Uzan (1974b), who feel that the symbolic function of object-representations is absent. I will review some findings suggesting that drug-dependent persons have to repress their rage and destructive wishes toward their maternal love object. This repression manifests itself in a rigid walling-off of the maternal love object representation, especially with an idealization of it. The patients had deposited their own life and love powers in the mother as in a safety deposit box. By doing this, they managed (in fantasy) to protect the love object from their magically empowered destruction and to assure that "someone *out there*" loved them and would take care of them (Krystal and Raskin, 1970).

THE ADDICT'S PROBLEMS IN RETAINING A "GOOD INTROJECT"

Probably the most conspicuous indication of the difficulties of the substance-dependent person has been overlooked because it is too obvious. Drug abuse consists not only of taking drugs, but, equally important, of being deprived of drug effect. All addictive drugs are short acting. The longer acting the drug, the greater the likelihood that the user will panic and develop a "bum trip" (Krystal and Raskin, 1970). Formal withdrawal from drugs is an integral part of the process of addiction (Krystal, 1962). Tolerance for the drug increases rapidly because of the drug-dependent persons' need to deprive the drug of its power (Krystal, 1966a); but the moment the drug does lose its force, they panic (Rado, 1933; Krystal, 1959).

What is the meaning of these apparent contradictions? It is that *while drug-dependent persons yearn for union with their maternal love object (representation), they also dread it.* They can't stand it either way. Schizophrenic patients and some borderline persons yearn for union with their love object and once they achieve union (in fantasy), they cling to the love object passionately, giving up conscious registration of all perceptions or ideas that spoil this delusional fusion.

Drug-dependent people are very busy getting the drug but can feel themselves reunited with the idealized love object only rarely and briefly, and only at moments when they are virtually anesthetized. Even then, amazingly, many of them—at the very moment of the climactic action of the drug—indulge in acts of riddance, such as moving bowels, vomiting, cleaning their bodies, cutting their nails, or even house cleaning (Chessick, 1960). It may be said that they are *addicted to the process of taking in and losing the drug rather than to having it.* The seemingly bizarre behavior of the drug addict who plays with the drug by "regurgitating" it back and forth between the syringe and vein suddenly falls into place here. Isn't this another version of the "psychosomatic" child with merycism, who keeps regurgitating and reswallowing the contents of his stomach?

Drug-dependent persons dread fusion with love object representations because of the way they experienced them in the formative period of their lives. Explanations of these difficulties are linked to the problems of aggression or ambivalence toward the love object we noted earlier. The ambivalence toward the therapist in the transference is matched by the ambivalence toward the drug, and that is a transference of the particularly severe ambivalence toward the maternal object-representation. Our substance-dependent patients are just like the ones who get very sick upon ingesting the placebo. They even get sick on hearing an interpretation that is right on target in content, form, and timing.

We have pointed out elsewhere (Krystal and Raskin, 1970) that the "hangover phenomenon" was identical with the untoward reactions to the placebo. We explained that these were caused by inordinate guilt about oral indulgence, related to cannibalistic problems (p. 47). In other words, when the substance-dependent patient tries to regain his alienated functions by swallowing the symbol of the object-representation to whom he attributed these powers, he is confronted with the return of the repressed—the ambivalently loved mother returns as the poisonous and seductive drug.

Another clinical observation well known to every worker in this field supports the accuracy of these constructions: patients are unable to accomplish normally the work of mourning and the feeling of "introjecting" the lost love object. The introjection fantasy is a form of partial union of the self-representation and object-representation at which most people arrive at the end of mourning. It is a clinical commonplace to say that alcoholics and other drug-dependent individuals cannot tolerate object losses (and that includes therapists) without being so threatened with their affects that they have virtually unavoidable relapses to self-destructive drug use.

These views are in harmony with Woollcott's (1981) insight about the problems of separation-individuation as significant components in substance dependence. While I am emphasizing the *nature* of the distortion in self- and object-representations, Woollcott points out that the morbid craving may result from "faulty separation-individuation" and "particularly intense conflict around symbiotic strivings," which he calls "a fusion-individuation conflict" (p. 193). In this view, the drug permits a restoration of the illusion of symbiotic unity or the disavowal of the separateness of the self and object, since under these circumstances one cannot obtain the fulfillment of yearning for total loving care, a permanent state of bliss, and freedom from all suffering. Woollcott rightly points out that "the search for symbiotic merger and idealized reunion with the good object must be viewed as . . . a necessary part of psychoanalytic treatment" of these patients (p. 202). It is not contradictory to reemphasize that behind the "fusion-individuation conflict" lies a distorted self-representation that makes no provision for self-care and self-directed attainment of the fulfillment of one's needs. Hence, as I see it, behind the yearning to be given the love and caring and to fuse with its source, there is an inhibition in the capacity to exercise one's own adaptive potential.

This is a dimension of the problem of ambivalence that makes its appearance in the analysis of drug-dependent patients. In the early stages of therapy, the very availability of an object creates serious challenges to them. There is the fear of aggressive impulses and wishes, as well as the problems stressed by Vaillant (1973) that when these patients idealize their therapists in the transferences, they experience themselves as worthless and bad.

But these are just preliminaries. The greatest difficulties arise in the fact that the effective work in psychoanalytic therapy is "effective grieving," a process analogous to mourning, by which one can give up one's attachment to one's infantile object-representations and the infantile view of oneself.

The difficulties encountered by psychosomatic and addictive (alexithymic) patients in accomplishing mourning will be discussed in chapter 13. Here I want only to elaborate the relationship of aggression (ambivalence) to the nature of the repression of the primal love object. Earlier I said that the rigid "walling-off" of the maternal object-representations took place in the face of extreme aggressive impulses toward it. The evidence for that came from this stage of the psychotherapeutic work with drug-dependent patients. The intensity of the narcissistic rages, the persistence of the aggressive impulses make one wonder if all addiction is, at bottom, a "hate addiction." The problem of aggression and its apparent threat to the safety and integrity of the self-representation and/or object-representation sets the limits to the kinds and numbers of drug-dependent patients who can be carried to completion of analytic work. Along the way, most such patients, when confronted with their aggression, will relapse again and again into self-destructive activities and drug use. Others will be driven to prove, by getting the analyst angry and provoking abuse, that their childhood misfortunes were real. Still others become so terrified of the dangerous, poisonous transference object that they set out on a frantic search for the *ideal mother* in the form of a drink, love, gambling, or the like.

If the therapist is equipped to bear the disappointments, provocations, and failures entailed in working with this kind of patient, and if he has the time and patience to permit the patient to do this work by minute steps, then the most helpful thing to keep in mind is that the patient is confronted with problems of aggression that make him experience the transference as a life-and-death struggle. Care and caution must be exercised that the patient not be overwhelmed by aggressive feelings or guilt. Emergencies in which the patient's life hangs in the balance will occur, for that may be the patient's way of testing the therapist.

When Simmel (1948) reviewed his lifetime experiences with alcoholics, he was very clear about the problems of aggression in the treatment of these patients. He said:

> . . . during a state of abstinence under psychoanalysis in a hospital, substituting the addiction to alcohol or drugs was an overt suicidal addiction or an overt addiction to homicide. During this stage the addict's only compulsion is to kill: himself or others. Usually he does not rationalize this urge; he just wants to die or, at other times he just wants to kill [p. 24].

The aggression observable in the self-destructive lifestyle of the drug-dependent patient is, in the process of psychotherapy, traced to its ultimate sources and meanings. To do this, the patient has to be able to experience with the therapist that which he has never before dared to face—his hatred. Instead of seeing himself as a victim, and by virtue of his "victimhood" claiming *innocence*, now he is confronted with his murderous aggression. To do so, however, he must give up the treasured view of himself as the victim, which, again, has to be mourned. And so it can be said that an unavoidable step in the treatment of a certain type of substance-dependent patient in intensive therapy is that he has to go through a depressive stage. During this phase of the treatment, the dependence on the therapist is extreme, and no substitutes are acceptable. While early in the treatment many patients do best in a clinic with multiple therapists, for the few who will be carried to this type of therapeutic completion, the chief therapist has to be the one who will be available to the very end. Such are some of the difficulties resulting from the nature of the object-representation of the addictive personalities which determine that those among them who are treated successfully by psychoanalytic psychotherapy will continue to be rare, mainly of research interest.

THE TRAUMATIC ORIGIN OF INHIBITIONS IN SELF-CARE

Among the problems shared by substance-dependent and psychosomatic patients is an impairment in their capacity to take care of themselves. This deficit brings them into the realm of those patients who have deficiencies in strategic functions. This point was made by Kohut (1971), who felt that addicts had an impaired development of "the basic capacity of the psyche to maintain, on its own, the narcissistic equilibrium of the personality." He felt that the "traumatic disappointment" suffered in archaic stages of development, caused by the lack of empathy in the mother, would result in a defect in the person's ability for self-care. He believed, therefore, that the drug was a replacement "for a defect in the psychological structure" (p. 46).

Kohut continued that in the transference the analysand expects to "have his analyst perform the functions which the patient's own psyche is incapable to provide" (p. 47). In connection with the consideration of these patients, Kohut went on to discuss the process of *transmuting internalization*. He spelled out the "breaking up of those aspects of the object image that are being internalized" (p. 49) and the depersonalizing of the introjected function, to accomplish an effective internalization that leads to the formation of a psychic structure.

Here we have the basic theory of impairment in function based on deficiency in a psychic structure due to a failure to appropriately introject an aspect of the maternal image, which was the carrier for these functions. The weight of the evidence for both drug-dependent and psychosomatic patients is that this is the *patients' own theory* of their problem. The idea that they suffer from a deficiency disorder and that the analyst must supply them with the loving care of which they were cheated is often and despairingly proclaimed by these patients. If only the deficiency can be supplied to them, they will be happy. In truth, the patient not only wants his deficiency made up to him, but also wants the analyst to roll back the calendar and "fix" everything "bad" that happened to him. Even then he would bear a grudge that things did not work perfectly the first time. We see the caricature of our fuzzy thinking in the rationale of various nonanalytic therapists who do try to supply to their patients the love they missed.

As psychoanalysts, we deal with distortions in self-representation and objects (world): representation. So it is just as well that our patients do not, in truth, suffer from deficiency disorders, nor are they deficient in their emotional or mental equipment or in their soul. We have made observations of substance-dependent, psychosomatic, and "normals" that suggest that "deficiency-resulting-from-a-failure-in-internalization" is not the most helpful model to explain the problems:

1. We have observed that although the patients are ordinarily not able to perform self-smoothing and general self-caring functions, they are able to perform them under the influence of placebo, suggestion, or any situation in which they can disavow their doing it. Moreover, the impairments in function are spotty and fluctuating in scope and intensity, and not total and constant, as they would have to be if there were a true deficiency.

2. While drug addicts crave to "introject the object" and acquire the

function, they have a great deal of difficulty in doing so, often negate the act instantly, and cannot maintain the fantasy of fusions.

3. The frightening and "sickening" effects of introjected objects suggest that the problem of ambivalence toward the object representation is what prevents them from fulfilling the cannibalistically tinged fantasies.

4. In our perusal of reactions to placebo, biofeedback, and other procedures, we found that psychosomatic patients and other people shared the drug addict's beliefs, albeit to a less severe degree. These beliefs were based on the infantile fantasy that one's vital functions are part of the object-representation and that taking them over implies an introjection of the maternal object-representation, which was prohibited.

The ability to exercise self-caring, self-preserving, self-soothing, and self-regulatory functions is subject to conflict and widespread inhibitions. Khantzian and Mack (1983) have continued their exploration of the relationship of the capacity for self-care to the self-preservatory behavior. They have observed that the functions of self-protection and self-care can be seen in action (or inhibition) in young children. Moreover, they have confirmed that self-caring functions depend on a variety of cognitive and affective assessments by which one can monitor oneself and the environment and take appropriate action with an adequately functioning assessment of the interaction.

Stern's (1985) work suggests that a self-agency ("in the sense of authorship of one's own actions and non-authorship of others: having volition and self-generated actions," p. 71) and self-affectivity should be considered the very basis of the core self, which is the nucleus of an organized sense of self.

I have suggested that the child's attribution of soothing and life-giving functions to the maternal object-representation becomes firmly established and reinforced as a defensive operation. The greater the problem of aggression resulting from the infantile trauma, the greater the rigidity of the "walling-off" of the maternal object-representation and the greater the scope of function attributed to it. The placebo is a means of going around these intrapsychic prohibitions.

My conclusion is that these patients do not have a deficit either in the capacity for self-caring functions or in the psychic structures necessary to exercise them. *They have a psychic block, an inhibition of their function of self-soothing, self-caring, and other self-regulatory functions.* They are in the same position in regard to these functions as we all are in regard to the affect-related parts of our bodies. We are able to influence their state but we dare not, unless we have a placebolike device handy that makes it possible for us to deny usurping these "forbidden" powers.

Although the "internalization of maternal functions" idea has serious weaknesses theoretically (besides my difficulties with it, see also Schafer, 1972) still it is one of the most important of human fantasies and as such represents important analytic material. But we must deal with it to understand that this is the fantasy which caused these patients to develop their inhibitions. It may be recalled from early in this chapter that substance-dependent persons are inclined to *"externalize" their functions in general.* I illustrated their difficulties in exercising impulse control. I discussed the use of a team, including a probation officer, or Antabuse to deal with that problem. In this context, Antabuse may be considered a "superego placebo," enabling the patient to exercise these functions, which also (though inconsistently) are alienated. Wurmser (1978) put great emphasis on the tendency of these patients to externalize—he identified it as the most characteristic and important defensive pattern underlying the addictive process. In common psychoanalytic parlance mother's functions are acquired by the child by "introjection." A cannibalistic fantasy.

In regard to the problems of affect maturation and the capacity for self-soothing, including taking care of one's affective parts of the body, a Chomskian (1975) model of development appears more useful than the idea of introjection or identification. Just as the innate capacity for the use of language unfolds in every human being, so do most of these functions. A favorable environment provided by the mother permits the optimal maturation of the child's own capacities. The problem is not truly with *acquiring* patterns of behavior nor with structures from outside, but the freedom to extend the boundaries of one's selfhood and to minimize the areas alienated and intrapsychically turned over to "nonself."

The availability of a good selfobject not only allows the grandiosity of the child to unfold appropriately but also permits the feeling that it is proper for him to take care of himself. In other words, infantile omnipotence permits the fantasy of self-care when the actual capacity for it is nil. In this fashion, because affective expressions are the only form of communication available, the mother's responsiveness and "fine ear" for the evolving nuances of the child's feelings becomes a crucial aspect of the early developmental milieu. If the child's grandiosity includes a long enough period of his fantasies of "providing for himself" the loving and soothing functions, these may become relatively guilt free. However, as we have learned from our observations on the common "hysterical paralysis" in the sphere of the body innervated by the autonomic nervous system, this process is never handled without attributions of many of our vital functions and affective experiences to the maternal objects.

In the experience of "good enough mothering" (Winnicott, 1965) there develops the crucial feeling that it is *permissible* for the child to exercise a certain measure of self-regulation of his affective and hedonic states, as well as exercising for himself the subjective part of self-comforting so that he can relax and sleep. The rather clumsy term, the "subjective" part in comforting functions, is meant to convey that the child has to participate in his comforting and nurturance always, even when it is done by his mother. The principle of psychic reality dictates that he has to create and register his own responses, perceptions, interpretations, and memories.

We can imagine that serious infantile traumatization results in a premature confrontation with the child's helplessness and dependence. The mother is discovered to be the holder of all external supplies, and the child loses sight of his own active participation in his soothing and comforting. A premature disruption of the illusion of omnipotence, or the illusion of symbiosis confronts the child with a dangerous, omnipotent external object—that cannot be satisfactorily controlled. Among the many problems resulting from this disruption is the attempt to extend magic control of the object by splitting, idealization, and masochistic modifications of the self-representations. In this predicament, affective and self-caring functions are relegated to the object representation en masse. The problems of envy and ambivalence prevent the conveted regaining of one's own functions by incorporation.

THE SHAWL

by
Cynthia Ozick

Stella, cold, cold, the coldness of hell. How they walked on the roads together, Rosa with Magda curled up between sore breasts, Magda wound up in the shawl. Sometimes Stella carried Magda. But she was jealous of Magda. A thin girl of fourteen, too small, with thin breasts of her own, Stella wanted to be wrapped in a shawl, hidden away, asleep, rocked by the march, a baby, a round infant in arms. Magda took Rosa's nipple, and Rosa never stopped walking, a walking cradle. There was not enough milk; sometimes Magda sucked air; then she screamed. Stella was ravenous. Her knees were tumors on sticks, her elbows chicken bones.

Rosa did not feel hunger; she felt light, not like someone walking but like someone in a faint, in trance, arrested in a fit, someone who is already a floating angel, alert and seeing everything, but in the air, not there, not touching the road. As if teetering on the tips of her fingernails. She looked into Magda's face through a gap in the shawl: a squirrel in a nest, safe, no one could reach her inside the little house of the shawl's windings. The face, very round, a pocket mirror of a face: but it was not Rosa's bleak complexion, dark like cholera, it was another kind of face altogether, eyes blue as air, smooth feathers of hair nearly as yellow as the Star sewn into Rosa's coat. You could think she was one of *their* babies.

Rosa, floating, dreamed of giving Magda away in one of the villages. She could leave the line for a minute and push Magda into the hands of any woman on the side of the road. But if she moved out of line they might shoot. And even if she fled the line for half a second and pushed the shawl-bundle at a stranger, would the woman take it? She might be surprised, or afraid; she might drop the shawl, and Magda would fall out and strike her head and die. The little round head. Such a good child, she gave up screaming, and sucked now only of the taste of the drying nipple itself. The neat grip of the tiny gums. One mite of a tooth tip sticking up in the bottom gum, how shining, an elfin tombstone of white marble gleaming there. Without complaining, Magda relinquished Rosa's teats, first the left, then the right; both were cracked, not a sniff of milk. The duct-crevice extinct, a dead volcano, blind eye, chill hole, so Magda took the corner of the shawl and milked it instead. She sucked and sucked, flooding the threads with wetness. The shawl's good flavor, milk of linen.

It was a magic shawl, it could nourish an infant for three days and three nights. Magda did not die, she stayed alive, although very quiet. A peculiar smell, of cinnamon and almonds, lifted out of her mouth. She held her eyes open every moment, forgetting how to blink or nap, and Rosa and sometimes Stella studied their blueness. On the road they raised one burden of a leg after another and studied Magda's face. "Aryan," Stella said, in a voice grown as thin as a string; and Rosa throught how Stella gazed at Magda like a young cannibal. And the time that Stella said "Aryan," it sounded to Rosa as if Stella had really said "let us devour her."

But Magda lived to walk. She lived that long, but she did not walk very well, partly because she was only fifteen months old, and partly because the spindles of her legs could not hold up her fat belly. It was fat with air, full and round. Rosa gave almost all her food to Magda, Stella gave nothing; Stella was ravenous, a growing child herself, but not growing much. Stella did not menstruate. Rosa did not menstruate. Rosa was ravenous, but also not; she learned from Magda how to drink the taste of a finger in one's mouth. They were in a place without pity, all pity was annihilated in Rosa, she looked at Stella's bones without pity. She was sure that Stella was waiting for Magda to die so she could put her teeth into the little thighs.

Rosa knew Magda was going to die very soon; she should have been dead already, but she had been buried away deep inside the magic shawl, mistaken there for the shivering mound of Rosa's breasts; Rosa clung to the shawl as if it covered only herself. No one took it away from her. Magda was mute. She never cried. Rosa hid her in the barracks, under the shawl, but she knew that one day someone would inform; or one day someone, not even Stella, would steal Magda to eat her. When Magda began to walk Rosa knew that Magda was going to die very soon, something would happen. She was afraid to fall asleep; she slept with the weight of her thigh on Magda's body; she was afraid she would smother Magda under her thigh. The weight of Rosa was becoming less and less; Rosa and Stella were slowly turning into the air.

Magda was quiet, but her eyes were horribly alive, like blue tigers. She watched. Sometimes she laughed—it seemed a laugh, but how could it be? Magda had never seen anyone laugh. Still, Magda laughed at her shawl when the wind blew its corners, the bad wind with pieces of black in it, that made Stella's and Rosa's eyes tear. Magda's eyes were always clear and tearless. She watched like a tiger. She guarded her shawl. No one could touch it; only Rosa could touch it. Stella was not allowed. The shawl was Magda's own baby, her pet, her little sister. She tangled herself up in it and sucked on one of the corners when she wanted to be very still.

Then Stella took the shawl away and made Magda die.

Afterward Stella said: "I was cold."

And afterward she was always cold, always. The cold went into her heart: Rosa saw that Stella's heart was cold. Magda flopped onward with her little pencil legs scribbling this way and that, in search of the shawl; the pencils faltered at the barracks opening, where the light began. Rosa saw and pursued. But already Magda was in the square outside the barracks, in the jolly light. It was the roll-call arena. Every morning Rosa had to conceal Magda under the shawl against a wall of the barracks and go out and stand in the arena with Stella and hundreds of others, sometimes for hours, and Magda, deserted, was quiet under the shawl, sucking on her corner. Every day Magda was silent, and so she did not die. Rosa saw that today Magda was going to die, and at the same time a fearful joy ran in Rosa's two palms, her fingers were on fire, she was astonished, febrile: Magda, in the sunlight, swaying on her pencil legs, was howling. Ever since the drying up of Rosa's nipples, ever since Magda's last scream on the road, Magda had been devoid of any syllable; Magda was a mute. Rosa believed that something had gone wrong with her vocal cords, with her windpipe, with the cave of her larynx: Magda was defective, without a voice; perhaps she was deaf; there might be something amiss with her intelligence; Magda was dumb. Even the laugh that came when the ash-stippled wind made a clown out of Magda's shawl was only the air-blown showing of her teeth. Even when the lice, head lice and body lice, crazed her so that she became as wild as one of the big rats that plundered the barracks at daybreak looking for carrion, she rubbed and scratched and kicked and bit and rolled without a whimper. But now Magda's mouth was spilling a long viscous rope of clamor.

"Maaaa—-"

It was the first noise Magda had ever sent out from her throat since the drying up of Rosa's nipples.

"Maaaa . . . aaa!"

Again! Magda was wavering in the perilous sunlight of the arena, scribbling on such pitiful little bent shins. Rosa saw. She saw that Magda was grieving for the loss of her shawl, she saw that Magda was going to die. A tide of commands hammered in Rosa's nipples: Fetch, get, bring! But she did not know which to go after first, Magda or the shawl. If she jumped out into the arena to snatch Magda up, the howling would not stop, because Magda would still not have the shawl; but if she ran back into the barracks to find the shawl, and if she found it, and if she came after Magda holding it and shaking it, then she would get Magda back, Magda would put the shawl in her mouth and turn dumb again.

Rosa entered the dark. It was easy to discover the shawl. Stella was heaped under it, asleep in her thin bones. Rosa tore the shawl free and flew—she could fly, she was only air—into the arena. The sunheat murmured of another life, of butterflies in summer. The light was placid, mellow. On the other side of the steel fence, far away, there were green meadows speckled with dandelions and deep-colored violets; beyond them, even farther, innocent tiger lilies, tall, lifting their orange bonnets. In the barracks they spoke of "flowers," of "rain": excrement, thick turd-braids, and the slow stinking maroon waterfall that slunk down from the upper bunks, the stink mixed with a bitter fatty floating smoke that greased Rosa's skin. She stood for an instant at the margin of the arena. Sometimes the electricity inside the fence would seem to hum; even Stella said it was only an imagining, but Rosa heard real sounds in the wire; grainy sad voices. The farther she was from the fence, the more clearly the voices crowded at her. The lamenting voices strummed so convincingly, so passionately, it was impossible to suspect them of being phantoms. The voices told her to hold up the shawl, high; the voices told her to shake it, to whip with it, to unfurl it like a flag. Rosa lifted, shook, whipped, unfurled. Far off, very far, Magda leaned across her air-fed belly, reaching out with the roads of her arms. She was high up, elevated, riding someone's shoulder. But the shoulder that carried Magda was not coming toward Rosa and the shawl, it was drifting away, the speck of Magda was moving more and more into the smoky distance. Above the shoulder a helmet glinted. The light tapped the helmet and sparkled it into a goblet. Below the helmet a black body like a domino and a pair of black boots hurled themselves in the direction of the electrified fence. The electric voices began to chatter wildly. "Maamaa, maaamaaa," they all hummed together. How far Magda was from Rosa now, across the whole square, past a dozen barracks, all the way on the other side! She was no bigger than a moth.

All at once Magda was swimming through the air. The whole of Magda travelled through loftiness. She looked like a butterfly touching a silver vine. And the moment Magda's feathered round head and her pencil legs and balloonish belly and zigzag arms splashed against the fence, the steel voices went mad in their growling, urging Rosa to run and run to the spot where Magda had fallen from her flight against the electrified fence; but of course Rosa did not obey them. She only stood, because if she ran they would shoot, and if she tried to pick up the sticks of Magda's body they would shoot, and if she let the wolf's screech ascending now through the ladder of her skeleton breakout, they would shoot; so she took Magda's shawl and filled her own mouth with it, stuffed it in, and stuffed it in, until she was swallowing up the wolf's screech and tasting the cinnamon and almond depth of Magda's saliva; and Rosa drank Magda's shawl until it dried.

11
Trauma and the Stimulus Barrier

We psychoanalysts are most comfortable dealing with the kind of material we derive from our clinical practice: fantasies, conflicts, resistances, and defenses couched in the familiar terms of classical formulations. Our complacency is disturbed, however, by patients who do not fit into these conceptions. Such difficulties have developed for me in trying to deal with a very large population of survivors of the Nazi Holocaust. Repeatedly, in my early publications, I despaired of be able to understand the phenomena of posttraumatic residues and the process of traumatization in terms of classical conceptions.

Finding that I could not explain all the phenomena observed in survivors, particularly concentration camp inmates, I proceeded to describe the findings, hoping that they would eventually add up to material by which the process of traumatization and recovery could be understood in greater depth and accuracy. I was finally able to formulate a concept of massive traumatization that corresponded to what I had learned from my patients. In these formulations, I tried to understand the common basis of their experience and to account for the occurrence of certain symptoms not previously explainable. Such posttraumatic pictures included alexithymia, inhibitions in the capacity for self-caring, anhedonia, continuation of extreme hypervigilance, depression, and masochistic patterns, as well as characteristic personality patterns.

Later, I was able to extend the study of the dynamics and consequences of traumatization to a consideration of the recovery process. All these years, I have also been working on the ideas contained in the present chapter, trying to understand the resources for trauma prevention in the context of what I had learned. I have read versions of this paper to the Michigan Psychoanalytic Society (in 1969) and to the American Psychoanalytic Association (in 1970). In the intervening years, most of the elements and formulations had to

200

be changed. Two observations have withstood the test of time. The chief one was articulated by Freud in 1926, namely, that it was the *subjective experience of helplessness* (p. 166)—in other words, the personal explanation of a situation—that determined its becoming traumatic. The second point follows the first: if the nature of psychic trauma is that it was determined by the psychic reality of the subject, then it is necessary to understand all the functions involved in shaping one's subjective experience. The need to study the perceptive, cognitive, and affective processes that might be involved in trauma prevention is further reinforced by the discovery that many of the chronic aftereffects of trauma involve these same functions. Moreover, since the classic formulations about trauma, based on the economic point of view, led to untenable conclusions, it seems that both the quantitative concepts of trauma and the passive model of the stimulus barrier would have to be replaced by an operational approach to the functions and defenses that can serve in trauma prevention. It is likely the term *stimulus barrier* is now only of historical value, but its static sound should alert us to the complex and alive multitude of functions and structures that need to be explored from every possible vantage point and by a variety of disciplines. For this reason, we must extend our vision, our conceptions, and even our language beyond the accustomed parameters, even though it may be somewhat uncomfortable to do so.

We move now to a review of the concept of the "stimulus barrier," based on a reconsideration of the nature of psychic trauma. Originally, the stimulus barrier referred to perception and discharge thresholds, epsecially significant in infancy. However, for some time now it has been clear that this definition is inadequate to contain the function of trauma prevention. Rapaport (1951a) pointed out: "It seems that we can conceive of two kinds of such thresholds; inborn ones (Freud's 'stimulus barrier' is of this type) and defensive counter-cathexes (repression is of this type)" (p. 184). Benjamin (1965) has usefully termed the infantile reaction thresholds "passive" stimulus barriers as distinguished from "active" ones. It is the latter—"active" stimulus barrier—that concerns us here. The weight of clinical evidence supports Anna Freud's (1967) view that "the entire defense organization of the ego is endowed with the characteristics of a protective shield and drawn into orbit of potential traumatic onslaught. Any event for which an individual's defense measures are not sufficiently competent becomes a potentially traumatic one" (p. 236). Gediman (1971) has reviewed the concept of the stimulus barrier in a manner originally proposed by Keiser (1967), bringing together the views expressed by a number of writers who felt that the stimulus barrier is best viewed "as a complex ego function measurable along in a dimension of adaptiveness-maladaptiveness" (p. 254). I (Krystal and Raskin, 1970) have also stressed that the clinically relevant view of the stimulus barrier was in terms of the totality of an individual's resources for trauma prevention. Furst (1978) has reconsidered these concepts and concluded that the ego must deal with psychic trauma "with whatever resources are available to it," and "when these prove inadequate, pathological formations are inevitable" (p. 349).

In this chapter I study individual resources to prevent psychic trauma and to deal effectively with psychic contents that might become traumatic. Before I can do so, however, I must take leave of the economic theory of trauma and the associated passive view of the stimulus barrier, for they represent an obstacle to that task. This move is mainly because we need to focus attention on the meaning and affective aspect of a mental event rather than its intensity.

THE ECONOMIC VIEW OF TRAUMA AND THE PASSIVE MODEL OF THE STIMULUS BARRIER

Although Gediman (1971) emphasized the importance of defenses against trauma, she still talked about the causation of the trauma by the intensity of stimuli. I (1978a) have noted that the challenge to the integrity of oneself stems from the *meaning* of the event and the resulting affective responses. Ultimately, we have to recognize that a number of serious errors are derived from our continuing to use Freud's application of Newtonian physics to mental functions. These applications result in misleading constructions of affects and trauma. I shall try to point out how models related to information processing, combined with updated knowledge of the processes of attention, perception, registration, cognition, momentary and long-term memory, and other mental functions give us an immensely richer and more useful view of the challenges we must face.

First, we must distinguish the adult (catastrophic) type of psychic trauma from the infantile type of traumatization (Krystal, 1978a) as we did earlier. In the previous chapters we found that adult *catastrophic trauma* is initiated not by intense affect, but solely when the subject *recognizes* that he is facing inevitable danger and surrenders to it.

According to this conception, psychic trauma results from a certain perception, evaluation, and effective reaction to a given danger of inner or outer origin. This means that the potential for psychic trauma is related to the nature of self-representation, the way a danger is evaluated, and the entire perceptive, cognitive, and affective apparatus whereby such an evaluation can be effected. While it appears clear that every aspect and characteristic of a person may be brought to bear on the outcome of such a challenge, I want to highlight the functions most directly related to trauma prevention. Primary among these seems to be the process of perception.

ASPECTS OF THE STIMULUS BARRIER

Between the traumatizing event and the traumatic psychic state are a number of mental processes. The perception complex is comonly thought to consist of the perception, awareness of the perception, and the eventual reaction to it. However, the situation has more ramifications than these.

There is evidence of a preconscious sampling of perception, with the result that only some selected perceptions become "amplified" and reach consciousness. This sampling activity, which includes the preconscious scanning and suppression of most stimuli, represents the first line of defense against trauma; it is an analog or prototype of primal repression. Experimental evidence amply supports Freud's (1912) contention that "every psychical act begins as an unconscious one, and it may either remain so or go on to developing into consciousness, according as it meets resistance or not" (p. 264). Already this statement refers to the concept of perceptive defenses as opposed to perception thresholds. The thresholds for perception, whether stemming from neurological (i.e., anatomical) or physiological limitations, do screen out a mass of stimuli. However, this barrier is effective not against *intense* stimuli, but against their *multitude,* characterized by low intensity and relevance. In other words, it protects against redundancy of stimuli. Furst (1978) has reviewed the evidence, stemming mostly from work with children, about the differences in newborn infants. Experimental evidence suggests that to an important extent, early experiences determine later reactivity. Under-stimulation of the young organism seems to result in later impairment in the capacity to handle stimulation (Melzack, 1969). For further clues we must turn to the work of experimental psychologists.

STUDIES ON PERCEPTION

In his discussion of Pötzl's work, Fisher (1960) pointed out that observations accumulated by a variety of observers, from Helmholtz, Purkinje, and Urbanschitsch at the turn of the century to modern experimenters, lead to the conclusion that weak stimuli, even if they do not stimulate peripheral nerves, do not necessarily register and that those which register do so outside of awareness. A preliminary, preconscious phase of perception is assumed by most authors, even if they do not imply a defensive "purpose" or function to that phase (Kragh, 1955; Fisher, 1956; Smith and Hendricksson, 1956; Flavel and Draguns, 1957). Others have shown that even the sleeper discriminates between various words, for example, his own and another person's name, and that this could be demonstrated by galvanic skin responses even in deepest sleep (Oswald, Taylor, and Trierman, 1960). Ephron and Carrington (1967) further distinguished between the orientational process and the rudimentary "orienting response." The former consists of a series of elaborate maneuvers that focus attention on the familiar and the reassuring while simultaneously appraising areas of unfamiliarity and potential danger. If the unexpected occurs, it is assimilated with the familiar as rapidly as possible. The Chodorkoffs (1958) have been able to integrate the finding of perceptual defense into a coherent view, which included psychoanalytic and physiologic dimensions.

These pioneering explorations in perception, sometimes referred to as the "New Look," were followed by a broadening and deepening of studies in the area of perceptual vigilance and defense (Erdelyi, 1974), which led to an immense elaboration of the nature and control of attention. Students of *selective attention* made it imperative that it be seen as a multipurpose phenomenon, thus opening the complexities of information processing (Dixon, 1971). In other words, cognitive processing is seen as a multisystem and multistep operation with many feedback mechanisms in which the new perception is processed by confrontation with the associations it evokes and is evaluated, gradually transformed and endowed with meaning, and recorded, but *not* for the most part in the conscious sphere of the mind. Even listing the names of major contributors of these developments would be beyond our limits. Through the work of many people, defensive selectively in encoding was definitely proven, and that meant that "raw storage" was analyzed to semantic depth and "on the basis of positive or negative biases toward specific emotional content, corresponding encoding biases may be instituted which alter the probability of the materials being transferred to short-term storage, the region of consciousness. Analyzed materials not transferred to short-term storage are not consciously apprehended and are permanently lost to memory" (Erdelyi, 1974, p. 20). Norman (1976) has integrated the many contributions (including his own) in the areas of attention, acquisition of information, short-term memory, the organization and maintenance of memory, the styles of representation of knowledge—all of which added up to the beginning of the psychological approaches to information processing. Psychoanalytic applications of information processing were further advanced by Peterfreund (1971) and Bowlby (1980).

In order to accommodate the new knowledge of perceptive activities, it is necessary to keep in mind that a whole representational world has been actively created and is constantly modified by the very confrontation with every new perception and cognition against which the latter is tested (Sandler and Rosenblatt, 1962; Hadley, 1983). The details of the processing of mental events have been followed by the studies of perception referred to as "microgenesis" (Werner, 1956; Giora, 1981) and "perceptgenesis" by Westerlundh and Smith (1983). These studies show that there is a perception *process* in which preparatory phases of perception, which are unconscious and characterized by diffuse, merging, and subjectively colored meanings (Westerlundh and Smith 1983), p. 605) are reworked until the final phase of correct recognition is reached. This last level is conscious and is considered to be in the realm of "intersubjective agreement" (p. 606).

In the process of reworking these meanings, they can be tested and intermediate stages of registration can be recovered that demonstrate that there is an elaboration of meaning by association, wherein various levels of fantasies are "attached" to the new percept. The fantasies and memories stimulated determine the fate of the perception and the evaluation of the import of the novel development or situation. The subject's personality traits (Giora, 1981) and personality developmental history (Westerlundh and Smith, 1983) can be determined by scrutiny of the fantasies and interpretations activated by vague or ambiguous stimuli. Moreover, the associative linking of one's fantasies with percepts introduces into the perceptive defenses the psychoanlyatically familiar "ego defenses." Thus, the Westerlundh and Smith method of testing derived from perceptgenesis is useful in determining the predominant defense mechanism affecting major themes that preoccupy us in working with, say, neurotic patients. For instance, using their Defense Mechanism Test on exposures of pictures of the "father and son theme," they demonstrate various types of perceptions and registrations that reveal the utilization of a specific defense. They also demonstrate some infantile defenses as resulting in specific types of precept formations.

These studies on perception permit us to integrate the contributions of cognitive psychology with our clinical observations. Whereas Freud's (1900, 1914) application of the model of energy processing could be stretched to provide a number of useful metaphors for the neuroses and even for mourning, in order to proceed with our exploration of trauma and the defenses against it, we must add the information-processing view. There is evidence that it models the nature of perception and learning (Bruner, 1973; Wallach, 1976). All the studies mentioned, however, which represent a magnificent elaboration of cognitive psychology, carefully avoid addressing the role of *affects* in perception, registration, memory, and recall.

INFORMATION PROCESSING AND SIGNAL AFFECTS

It is questionable whether perception thresholds are relatively free from the defensive and adaptive operations of the ego, as Rapaport (1951b) thought. But it is certain that the circumstances under which a perception becomes *conscious* are a major, active aspects of the stimulus barrier and bring us into the area of (rudimentary) defensive functions.

Crucial to the concept of a stimulus barrier and the process of traumatization is how these perception elements are "tested" and by what means it is determined whether they will be included or excluded from conscious registrations. I propose that the *process by which preconscious forerunners of perception are "tested" invokes the production of preconscious associations and a minimal (signal) affective response, at the behest of which the exclusion from consciousness is effected*. I am referring to a quasi-cognitive process involving "registrations" of stimuli on a preconscious level and hence subject to imprecision and primary-process transformations (Fisher, 1960). The motivation for such modifications of perception may be defensive in nature, warding off other perceptions, impulses, or affects. However, defensive operations on the level of perception are not always of a negative type. With wishful influences, certain configurations may be noticed with great facility or even hallucinated.

Novey (1958) came to similar conclusions:

> Conscious perception can occur only after a physical sensory experience has been worked over in the preconscious; in this respect sensory stimuli from without are equivalent in kind to stimuli arising from within the organism. A conscious perceptual experience is bound by the principle of secondary revision (elaboration) in the waking state as well as in dreams [p. 77].

Freud anticipated the preconscious modification of perception (although the emphasis on its role in preventing trauma is mine), by a remark made in connection with the secondary revisions of dreams (1915b): "The completion of the dream-process consists in the thought-content . . . becoming . . . a sense-perception; while this is happening it undergoes secondary revision, *to which every perceptual concept is subject*" (p. 229, emphasis added).

Experimental work has indicated that conscious awareness of perception is highly influenced by the *affective charge* of the reaction to the stimulus. The evidence is voluminous (see, for example, Malamud and Lindner, 1931; McCleary and Lazarus, 1949; Ericksen, 1951a, b). Shevrin (1976) has reviewed the evidence from his work, as well as the research of others, in regard to such areas as subliminal perception, the stopped retinal image, binocular rivalry, neurophysiological correlates of consciousness as separate systems, and attentional processes. All of those areas indicated very consistently that "complex perceptual discriminations can occur, various choices and decisions can be made without benefit of consciousness" (p. 224).

There is also evidence that individuals have a "style of perceptual behavior consistent with their characterological patterns" (Carlson, 1957). Some people seem to have a generally lower perception threshold, which carries over from one function to another. In those who are hypersensitive (or hyperreceptive) to minimal stimuli, there is an observable compensation, which appears to be a broad dulling of and increased tolerance to gross stimulation.

The common pattern in perceptual selection is the regulation of it for the purpose of avoiding painful affects. Many studies have indicated the tendency to augment or minimize one's perceptions (e.g., Lacey et al., 1963; Petrie, 1967).

Other observations confirm my contention that there is a correspondence between the ways people handle both pain and affects and their characterological patterns. Among the studies that indicate such correlations are those of Shevrin and Luborsky (1958), Spence and Paul (1959), Fisher (1960), and Klein (1970). Each of these writers used different terms to describe his results, but the results have a common denominator: people either block the utilization of subliminal perceptions or feel free to register consciously a greater proportion of them. Whether subjects are "decreasers" or "increasers" of their scope of conscious perception depends on their ability to tolerate the affective responses evoked by the perception. Those who can tolerate the particular affect involved can allow themselves greater perceptual freedom. Conversely, people who block their perceptions show impaired affect tolerance or disturbed ability to keep signal affects in the range that is comfortable for them (Eissler, 1966). *I think that a tendency to suppress perceptions, to become "insensitive" or dull, derives from a primary disturbance in the affective sphere and is often posttraumatic.* The implication is that the attitude toward one's affects, which results from the nature and extent of infantile, or later massive, traumatic experience, becomes a determinant of perceptual and cognitive styles, which in turn significantly determine the nature of the defenses employed to prevent trauma. A dread of one's affects may, for instance, determine a tendency to use avoidance patterns, including a dread of emotional "involvement" with objects or even of self-exploration.

Klein (1970b) has elaborated in considerable detail the manifestation of character traits in perceptive function and cognitive attitudes. He pointed to a "perceptual character" that is internally consistent in each person. His thesis was: "Ego control takes form in perception through what I have called 'perceptual attitudes'; special ways each person has of coming to grips with reality. They are pervasive and are not applicable only in situations of stress or conflict" (p. 155).

By integrating the work of many writers, Giora (1981) has advanced our understanding of the characterological traits that influence perception and cognition and has indicated that what they have referred to as *Spaltung,* field-independence and scanning or focusing, can be seen as a grouping of processing strategies. He denoted it a Primary Personality Variable (PPV) of scanning and found that it consistently determined a preference to generalize or emphasize the whole in contrast to scrutinizing the details, variants, and conflicts. In generalizing the aspects of PPV scanning, Giora integrated other investigators' characterizations of cognitive styles as analytic versus holistic concept attainment, punctilious versus less hesitant, or reflective versus impulsive approaches to the perceptual and attentional fields. To these he added the category of *tolerance for violations of logic* and *affective incongruity.* Putting all these attributes of perceptive and cognitive functions together, he not only found consistency in one's cognitive and perceptive function, but was able to find correlation between waking cognitive styles and dream styles as well. In waking and sleep, these characteristics permit classification of persons as "wholists" or "partists" and generalization about their way of functioning: "Wholists are slower at eliminating impaired hypotheses . . . and . . . more ready to live with inconsistencies" (p. 341).

Experimenters and researchers have shown a dynamic interaction between forces that incline us to avoid conscious awareness of a perception and those that favor admission of it to consciousness (see, e.g., Schlesinger, 1954). One of the major influences is the "perceptive attitude" (Klein, 1970b), which is as much the product of one's genetic development as are one's other character traits. Hence chapter 8 (Reality), applies here as a reminder that self-products exist and operate only in our minds.

Klein (1970) has collated from his own research and that of other psychoanalytically sophisticated experimental psychologists evidence that perceptions are at first fragmentary and chaotic, being linked to primary process function: "In *perception,* the primary process is characterized by drive-determined selection and earlier development organization, the secondary process by a high efficient coordination between experience and environmental arrangements" (p. 282). Klein emphasized that preconscious registrations are screened, processed, modified, checked, organized, and "censored" before they are allowed to reach consciousness. Klein studied the complex motivations in perception and their effects on the experiential aspect of perception: "It is in biasing the attribution that motives have their major effect upon perceptual experience. Perceptual relevance is relevance to *aim;* attribution creates order in terms of intention. Through attribution, intentions participate in perceptual structure . . ." (p. 78). Thus we are back to the question of the affective signal. If the affective signal generated by the associative processing of a bit of information is a painful one, then the perception, memory, or impulse will be prevented from registering consciously or will be distorted by substitution of fantasies, a process we denote as "ego defense."

One's evaluation of one's *affective signals becomes a "constant variable" influencing the acuity of mental functions, whether perceptive, cognitive, or conative.*[1] Perception as an example of mental function suggests that conscious awareness is reached through periodic "sampling" of registrations

---

1. Helson (1967) and Leeper (1970) have also commented on a peculiar reluctance on the part of students of perception to fully accept the essential role of affects in motivation in regard to perception. The same can be said of the regulation of cognition—in fact, of all mental functions.

from the inner and outer worlds. This, I think, is what Freud (1925) (using the terms topographic and economic theory) reflected on in his hypothesis "cathectic innervations are sent out and withdrawn in rapid period impulses from within into the completely pervious system *Pcpt-Cs*" (p. 231). Related to this function is the often repeated statement that the ego does not "produce" ideas or affects but is the site of them. But the "selectivity" regarding which impulses become conscious and in what fashion this happens is determined by the "valence" of the affective signal. Conceivably, an affect signal that is experienced as "safe," that is, comfortable, for one person will be experienced by another as threatening (Krystal, 1981a). The interrelation of perception, cognition, memory, and *affect* was also explored by Mandler (1975), whose work has pertinence and expands many of the points I have been making.

However, for the full appreciation of the role of affect signals it is necessary to understand that they function for the most part in minimal, subliminal intensities. They do not depend on an a priori cognitive infrastructure (Zajonc, 1980). In fact, affective responses may be seen as the original activation apparatus present throughout the animal kingdom; even in humans they may be precognitive, representing an analog-computer-like reaction (Jones, 1981). Observations of infants suggest that affect processing is primary to cognitive processing; affect memory is a process parallel to cognitive memory in childhood and throughout life. There are increasing indications that "affects can serve as a nonlinguistically based encoding vehicle" (Stern, 1983, p. 17). Our observations about perceptive and cognitive styles, such as PPV Scanning considerations of the "holistic" versus "partist" processing of mental material, seem related when viewed in the light of the generalizations of Hadley (1983): "We must consider . . . that there are at least two distinct modes of information processing; the holistic, spatial, synthetic, nonverbal mode and the sequential, logical, analytic, verbal mode which have been frequently referred to as primary and secondary processes and which have recently been assigned to right and left hemispheres of the brain" (p. 25).

Clinical and neuropsychological work suggests that a dual coding system model is most explanatory of observable functions (Pribram, 1971). From my review of the work on early infantile registration (1981a), I concluded that pure "affect" memory, that is, an affective charge devoid of symbolic representation, is the mode of infantile mental material. Since there are indications that this kind of memory continues parallel to the cognitively and symbolically endowed affects, we had to postulate a dual type of memory.

It appears, however, that there is another kind of dual coding possible. This view stems from studies of perceptions and their relation to memory and recall. Bucci (1985) reviewed models of two-track mental coding: one track, perception dominated; and the other, cognitive, using verbal symbols. She favored a combined model, in which perceptive memories could be committed to memory and recalled individually or combined and "translated" into verbal symbols.

In verbal coding, information can be represented abstractly, and memories can be grouped according to their various common properties and a multiplicity of classifications, which are subject to semantic and linguistic elaboration.

Perceptual memories are subject to such experiential organizing principles as similarity, enactive or functional relationships, or continuity (Bucci, 1985). A number of other distinctions between verbal and perceptually dominated memories will be omitted here, because we would also need to consider the variety of memory styles, such as motor and affective; now we are interested in gaining an impresison of the complexity and variety of cognitive and evaluative processes. It is relevant to our considerations, though, that imagistic representations have an especially strong affective connection. Conversely, by shifting from imaging and other sensory modalities to verbal, abstract representation, one diminishes the affective intensity and permits *judgment* to become relatively more effective.

These accumulating data about the nature of perceptive and cognitive functions permit the integration of the sensorimotor orientation with the later cognitive styles of information processing (Peterfreund, 1971). Although I (1974) have maintained that, to be suitable for signal function, affects had to have undergone a maturation through the developmental lines of differentiation, verbalization, and desomatization, I found problems with this postulate (1981a). The maturational process, it now appears, makes affects suitable for signals in *cognition*. However, the *hedonic quality or signal is operative from birth in regard to object relations, attachment, and analog-computer-like memories.* Hence, affects and affective appraisal function in a separate sphere throughout life and may not even require cognitive or symbolic representation in order to exert an influence. This startling and unwelcome idea only alerts us to the wide divergence in people's ability to utilize their affects as signals. Clearly, these differences constitute an immeasurably powerful factor in the capacity to deal with danger, stress, and trauma prevention, as well as in the management of the traumatic process. The hedonic aspect of affects motivates the other responses, but these hedonic elements are also subject to separate shifts and transformations.

Finally, in addition to the signal function of affects, there is the "activating" element, which *initiates and controls* the motoric and physiological responses and may lead to such extremes as a readiness for fight or flight, the hyperactive type of panic, cataleptic surrender, and even psychogenic death. Thus, there is an apparent paradox of fundamental importance, namely, that although affects are not sporadic phenomena but go on continuously in minimal, signal, subliminal intensity, yet they must be conceived as *amplifying* the perception and interpretation of one's world and self-representations

(Mandler, 1980; Tomkins, 1980). The latest work shows that affects are active from the beginning in forming attachments (Bowlby, 1980; Krystal, 1981a; Hadley, 1985). Even more important, the development and naturation of affects is seen as the key event in infancy (Emde et al., 1976; Greenspan, 1981; Stern, 1983). Maturation of affective responses is the key operation for building those persistent modes and styles of behavior that become the blocks out of which personality and character are later developed (Izard and Beuchler, 1980; Mandler, 1980). In this respect we analysts can fully agree with neurobiologists (Pribram, 1980).

Thus, the perceptive process and the stimulus barrier become related to the problem of affect tolerance and the question of utilizability of affects as signals. Studies on the direct effects of catastrophic psychic trauma show impairment of affect tolerance to be a significant sequel. Sometimes this problem relates to a specific affect. Some affects are not usable as signals because they are experienced as truamatic screens. In the posttraumatic state, there is a dread expectation of the return of the trauma, a "doomsday orientation." A particular affective state may be experienced as the beginning of the inevitable return of the trauma and may trigger a traumatic reaction. This is why looking out for modification or arrest in an effective function is essential to evaluating the integrity of the stimulus barrier.

VICISSITUDES OF PERCEPTUAL DEFENSES

The best known illustration of perceptual defenses is the "inexact perception" that may be employed in denial (Linn, 1953). What struck Fisher (1956) as a paradox and accounts for many vagaries and vicissitudes of perceptual defenses is that the perceptual and memory ego apparatus "function in their primitive and preliminary stages in a primary-process-like manner, and in their more mature, reality-oriented phases in a secondary process manner" (p. 41). As a result, unconscious wishes may modify conscious registration of perceptions or other mental elements. Deutsch (1959) noted that "perceived objects," or object-representations, as we might say now, are related associatively to memories of perception of similar subjects, as well as to other images of the self in varying affective contexts and in relation to both memories and anticipations. The inevitability of the association of memories with perceptions, and vice versa, demands that perceptions evoke certain memories and, conversely, that the nature of one's memory traces significantly influences the transformation of a perception and the form and affective coloration with which it reaches consciousness. This observation is fundamental to the nature of object-representations, insofar as all memories of object perceptions carry an affective charge. We must acknowledge that, contrary to the classical ideas, there is no "perfect" perception or "perfect" memory to be recalled or repressed, but a composite of the current perception with memories and attribution of identity and meaning to the given mental event.

The multiplicity of involvements of the perceptive-association apparatus sometimes interferes with its function as an effective stimulus barrier. Perception may be rejected as dangerous by virtue of associations and transferences, or the protective or repressive function may fail as the result of association or wish fulfillment. Such are, for instance, the circumstances of provoked or induced trauma. Greenacre's (1952) description of the preadolescent girl's wish fulfillment in traumatization is the most obvious example. Murphy (1961) was so impressed with the retrospective finding that an accumulation of anxiety and depression secondary to losses *preceded traumatization* that he postulated that a "natural history" of trauma would become the standard of reconstruction.

The transferences involved in perceptions, especially those related to object-representation, may lead to the attribution of meaning to the perception, and that meaning or interpretation may become traumatic. The so-called silent traumata of an earlier time, then, have a "delayed trauma" relevance in the sense that they were registered in isolated and repressed form but retain a potential for precipitating trauma at a later time—if one can ever bring the picture together and own up to what one had *needed* to experience.

PERCEPTION AND CONSCIOUSNESS

That defenses are aimed primarily at preventing the development of threatening affects leads us to an alternative to the blocking of perception. Modifications of consciousness can allow the conscious registration of perception or impulse without provoking a dangerous response. These operations are seen most commonly in drug use, but also in trances and hypnotic states and *transiently* in all people (Shor, 1960; Deikman, 1963; Ludwig and Levine, 1965a, b); Ludwig, 1966). In states of altered consciousness, drawing inferences from perceptions and from the development of appropriate affects is avoided.

Variations in consciousness can be viewed in terms of several spectra gradients: (a) Orientation to disorientation; (b) Judgment, evaluation, and reflective self-awareness to suspension of critical function and hypersuggestibility; and (c) Wakefulness to sleep or coma. These aspects of consciousness may, but often do not, change to the same degree. We thereby have some distinguishable types of altered states of consciousness. Reactions to a given drug will differ from one user to another and will vary according to the initial state of the user.

Increased somnolence would likely enhance primary-process cognition (dreamlike and wish-controlled), so that defenses are utilizable that are familiar to us from working with dreams. As alertness diminishes, perceptive style and process change with heightened sensitivity to minimal stimuli and a reduction of the experienced intensity of stimuli. There is a regression to a childlike, minimal scanning behavior, less ignoring of "background" pecep-tions, and overevaluation of the close dominant stimulus (Silverman, 1968).

Where it is possible to study the function of the somatic perceptive apparatus, it can be demonstrated to be also involved in this modification. For instance, saccadic eye movements increase, resulting in high redundancy of information sampling and emphasizing the irrelevant (Wallach and Wallach, 1964; Silvermann, 1968). The perceptive style becomes increasingly passive, with an impairment of discrimination of the stimuli for conscious registration. Awareness of the environment becomes rich with irrelevant detail, and background "noise" is experienced with unusual intensity. Abstract categori-zation is impaired, and points of interest are not highlighted (Deikman, 1963). There is, further, an inability to shift or sustain attention to changing external stimulus patterns (Silvermann, 1968). As a result of all these changes, consciousness modifications have a dual effect on the effectiveness of the stimulus barrier. Distractibility can enable one to *avoid the awareness of the "dominant" stimulus if it threatens to evoke intolerable affects.* In full wakeful-ness, attention is focused on one percept at a time, to the exclusion of everything else. In states of disturbed consciousness, peripheral perceptions and ideas do escape the exclusion as Fisher (1960) found in dreams and hypnotic and hypnagogic phenomena. Under the influence of drugs, sub-liminal registration and activation increased. All this confusion and clutter may be used to diminish the potentially traumatic impact of the *main* perception. This defensive operation accounts for the peculiarly disturbed behavior of people in emergency states such as mass disaster.

Krystal and Raskin (1970) reviewed other aspects of altered consciousness that can be used to modify affect. To mention just a few: disturbed time sense, modification of body image, a sense of the ineffable, and hypersuggestibility. The potential danger of hypersuggestibility (as when persons experience trauma as a command) illustrates the risk in using these primitive defenses. Wolfenstein (1977) studied the coping behavior of people in such situations as tornados. She found that the responses most in harmony with the subject's ideal self was blocking of emotions in order to "remain calm" and thus, it was hoped, to be able to respond appropriately to the emergency. She cited a study in which students who had escaped a burning dormitory were asked to evaluate their own and other people's reactions during the fire. "Every student questioned reported that he (or she) acted rationally in getting out of the dormitory, but most of them ventured that the rest of the people did not behave rationally" (p. 108). This evaluation reflects, in addition to the distortion due to the wish to act calmly and remain in control, an aspect of psychic reality in emergency states, that is, that in the context of the necessary modifications of consciousness and modifications of perceptive and affective functions, there is a causality and rationality in each subject's behavior. The referents are differnt, however, from what one might have in "normal" or nonemergent, nonmodified states. But the essential point about the consequences of modification of consciousness is that while it is an inevitable and necessary response to stress (Caplan, 1981), it is also a major aspect of the adult catastrophic trauma state. There are many essential commonalities between the catatonoid reaction and trance states, and the shared characteristics have an impact on the behavior during the traumatic state (e.g., automatic obedience) as well as important bearing on the lasting effects of massive adult traumatization.

PRECEPTIVE-AFFECTIVE FUNCTION
AND TRAUMA PREVENTION

The conception of the (adult) catastrophic trauma process to which I have referred is of helpless surrender to what the individual perceives as inevitable danger. According to this idea, the full-blown traumatic state is seldom reached. When it does emerge it may go on to psychogenic death or may be arrested at the point of the subject's automatization or robotization. Persons who remain for long periods in this state are often left with *specific* and *direct* aftereffects, which represents a typical psychopathological state such as the survivor syndrome (Niederland, 1961). The characteristic picture may include anhedonia, alexithymia, continuation of cognitive blocking, pseudophobia, and typical characterological changes.

According to this view, most of the clinical syndromes that would commonly be considered of traumatic origin (e.g., neuroses) are not aftereffects of psychic trauma but consequences of autoplastic changes in the process of trauma *prevention*. In other words, the defensive process may be successful in warding off the trauma, but if part of it involves a permanent change in one's own function, defenses, or even self-representation, then an "ego-strain" (Sandler, 1967) or a specific psychopathological state will probably ensue.

Because significant psychopathology may result from *trauma prevention,* it is useful to revise and redefine the concept of the "stimulus barrier." This concept has long suffered from an overextended effort to keep alive the economic view of psychic trauma and, in the process, has become virtually meaningless. In the foregoing review I have brought together an admittedly sketchy and incomplete list of the perceptive, cognitive, sensorimotor, affective, and consciousness-regulatory functions that operate unceasingly and silently in trauma prevention. These operations are like the many aspects of immunological and cellular reactions that are quietly involved in the prevention of infection and neoplasia. We become aware of them only when there is a partial failure or when the defensive process itself becomes excessive.

Similarly, patients sometimes present themselves to us because they are discomforted by their own defensive reaction. They may for instance, be disturbed about modifications of consciousness, interferences in concentration, affective blocking, depersonalization or derealization, and a host of other "problems" that are as intrinsic a part of the defensive process as are fever or swelling. On the other hand, a reaction is "defensive" only if we decide, usually in retrospect, that it warded off something worse than the distress or inconvenience it occasioned itself. In other words, in my survey of certain reactions that may be related to trauma prevention, I have pursued a teleogical orientation by claiming that trauma prevention was the "purpose" of a particular capacity or reaction.

Perception is a complex process, with a prescreening of which the availability of affect signals is an essential part. A predominant style of perception may be especially suitable for trauma prevention. The style will consist of a high degree of filtering out of perceptions and failure to register them in the conscious sphere and will probably be accompanied by a similarly constrictive cognitive style and, very likely, a dulling of one's wealth, range, and scope of fantasy. Problems develop when there is a disharmony between one's style of functioning and one's perception of the demands of the current situation. The child "once burned and twice shy" is inconvenienced by the hypertrophy of a defensive reaction. A particularly effective stimulus barrier in people who do not respond emotionally to threatening situations may be the result of affective blocking (or numbness), which makes them "cold," aloof, or unempathic. As Klein (1970) put it, "The price we pay for efficient perception is partial blindness" (p. 218).

The emphasis on perception is necessary because it is the most neglected aspect in the psychoanalytic conception of psychic reality formation. The very same complexity is involved in cognition and every other component of mental function. The demonstration of the complexity and individual differences in all of these processes is intended to alert us that it is one's evaluation of the situation and one's own resources that determines whether a situation will be deemed to be of inevitable danger. Only then, with the surrender to it, is trauma initiated.

POSTTRAUMATIC CHANGES
IN THE STIMULUS BARRIER

The type of perceptive, cognitive, affective, or other function most favorable to trauma prevention in one respect may make a person more vulnerable in other circumstances. The multiplicity of observations and classifications of personality orientations (Klein, 1970) around perceptive attitudes alone is revealing. Petrie's (1967) classifications of reduction and augmentation and Klein's (1970) dimensions of sharpening and leveling (p. 134) illustrate these approaches. When Novey (1958) wrote of the key role of perception in self- and object-representation formation, he pointed out that five of the outstanding comtemporary psychologists of personality had centered their theories on the idea that the interpretation of one's sensory experience determines behavior: Lewin (1938), Murray (1938), Snygg and Cooms (1949), and Allport (1955). "Leveling and sharpening" was seen as "a principle of personality organization . . . explaining consistent individual differences in perception and cognition . . ." (Gardner et al., 1959, p. 22). Other urseful observations pertained to "importing" (Gardner et al., 1959) and even tendenies to "cautious" versus "risk-taking" cognitve styles (Schwartz and Rouse, 1961 p. 105).

If we were to go back to chapter 9 and review the aftereffects of trauma, we would not likely encounter any that would enable one to cope well with traumatic experiences. There is, of course, an element of benefit in improving one's skills in coping with those stressful experiences which do not become overwhelming. Battle-hardened, experienced veterans have many survival skills and handle themselves better than do inexperienced recruits. They possibly are also self-selected by virtue of having those response patterns, which enable them to function well in situations of very high anxiety and high arousal, an ability that, as we found in chapter 7, contains both hereditary and experiential factors. However, once one experiences a traumatic state, one's responses to similar or other dangers are likely to be less adaptive and one's vulnerability greater. Hence, it is essential to define the terms we apply to trauma. I have repeatedly tried to distinguish traumatic experiences from painful, even almost certainly pathogenic, experiences.

Adult catastrophic trauma and infantile psychic trauma can each be defined by its specific course and specific aftereffects. Among their aftereffects are disturbances in affect tolerance, alexithymia, and anhedonia, which can affect future information processing. The role of emotions as signals in the processing and evaluating of perceptions and cognition simply cannot be overstated. In the most severe posttraumatic states, the intensity of a regressed affect is so great that the patients cannot be approached psychotherapeutically, and one has to resort to pharmacological means (Kolb, Burris, and Griffiths, 1984).

These extremes are fairly obvious, as in the chronically guilt-ridden, masochistic life pattern in posttraumatic states. It is harder to link alexithymia, anhedonia, and impairment to affect tolerance with a history of trauma—particularly of the infantile type. If we consider all the possible flow-charts of information processing and keep in mind that affects and hedonic signals are triggers for switching mechanisms and that affects can be modified by traumatic experience, then we can appreciate that posttraumatic changes in cognitive, perceptive, memory, and other functions do take place.

One way to sum up posttraumatic states from the point of view of the stimulus barrier is that it protects the person against the return of the previously experienced (adult-type, catastrophic) psychic trauma by blocking future ability for fantasy elaboration. Similarly, one's capacity for pleasure, joy, and happiness may be sacrificed—resulting in anhedonia. This is the price of simultaneously (but less successfully) blocking off the excessive intensity of pain and distress. An incidental effect of the hypertrophy of these aspects of the stimulus barrier is that the capacity of the person to utilize and benefit from psychoanalysis becomes impaired to a greater or lesser degree.

Another attribute of the group of perceptive and affective reactions that may be considered part of the stimulus barrier is that they represent modes of operation; but, unlike ego defenses, they are not based on wish-fulfillment fantasy. Therefore, in contrast to, say, introjection or identification, which represent fantasies and therefore are subject to analytic work, these operations had to be detected by direct exploration, experimentation, and comparative studies. Even when found, they have a strange, mechanical ring to them. Since psychoanalytic technique in its strictest sense functions through the discovery and renunciation of fantasies, its effectiveness in modifying these perceptive, cognitive, or affective patterns is limited. Thus, identification of the modes of function useful in trauma prevention also exposes a therapeutic challenge.

Despite the advantages of using the term trauma in my definitions, it is not likely to gain universal usage. The DSM III (APA, 1980) description links "characteristic symptoms" with "a psychological traumatic event that is generally outside the range of usual human experience" (p. 236). In this sense, trauma means no more than injury, and the common use of the term is descriptive, consistent with the DSM III orientation.

This usage leads to a specific style of studies and observations of which the following is one of the best examples. Terr (1979) studied a group of children who had been kidnapped in a school bus and kept buried for 27 hours until they managed to escape. The title of one of Terr's papers (1981a) is "Psychic Trauma in Children." Although this point is not stated explicitly, there seems to be an assumption that all the children were "traumatized," or, more precisely, that the studies show the "children's response to trauma" (p. 19). It is assumed that the situation was traumatic, and therefore certain sequelae were observable. Some were the same as adult posttraumatic states: 1) initial signs of traumatic disruption, such as the formation of omens (or magical control); 2) fear of further trauma and related disturbances in cognition; 3) repetitive phenomena involved in traumatic dreams, posttraumatic play, reenactment, and multiple fears (pp. 15–18). The children's posttraumatic states differed from those of adults in the following way: 1) no amnesia,[2] 2) no denial, 3) no true flashbacks, and 4) children playing games reenacting the themes of the trauma (p. 19). Terr's papers on "Posttraumatic Play" (1981b) and "The Posttraumatic Distortions of the Sense of Time" (1984) reveal sequelae particularly relevant to the stimulus barrier idea.

Valuable and pertinent as these studies are, they represent the effects of presumed (adult catastrophic-type) trauma in children and *not what I have defined as infantile trauma*. It is conceivable that under situations of stress, some children might regress to an infantile state, but this apparently did not take place in this group.

The difference between trauma in children and infantile trauma is particularly well illustrated by Terr's work, for all the aftereffects, including the effects on cognition, fantasies, and time sense, correspond to adult posttraumatic states. To the extent that a child suffers fears of the return of the trauma, cognitive disturbances, and time sense distortions, the child will, for the duration of these affects, be more susceptible to further injury. Moreover, to the extent that the child is experiencing the bad event as a punishment and is more motivated to magical thinking and masochistic attempts to control fate, the child would be more vulnerable to interpret another danger situation in a doomsday fashion. In other words, dangerous, painful, and nearly overwhelming experiences, regardless of what we call them, create a vulnerability to experience future events in a dire fashion, diminish the security, and thus make it more likely that the interpretation, the psychic reality, will be experienced as helplessness in the face of unavoidable danger. In this sense, we may recall Freud's (1893–1895) idea of "partial trauma" (p. 6) and Murphy's (1961) idea that trauma has a "natural history," an accumulation of losses, painful experiences, and reactions of rage and guilt—what he described as a cascading of depressive tendencies resulting in a tendency to experience a situation as traumatic. In general, it may be said that injurious, painful, and discouraging experiences promote a pessimistic and helpless interpretation of one's situation.

Less often in posttraumatic modifications, the new type of affective, cognitive, or perceptive patterns may be utilized secondarily by belatedly attributing to them fantasy explanations (Reiser, 1978), which may result in their "hystericalization" or "obsessionalization" (McDougall, 1974b, p. 453). Alternatively, they may be used in the support of characterological behavior patterns. One patient, for instance, who had alexithymia and asthma and was not able to use his affective and proprioceptive signals such as of tiredness, hunger, or anxiety, used his obtrusiveness to support a narcissistic, grandiose

---

2. In view of what we are learning about the relationship of perception and memory and trauma, here, the "no amnesia" claim has to be taken with some skepticism.

view of himself as being devoid of limits to his performance. At times he also used his asthma medication to produce a pharmacogenic hypomanic state. All of these behaviors served to delay the confrontation with a view of himself as helpless and weak that he had had to ward off as unbearable (potentially traumatic) since childhood. Thus, it could be said that in this patient the dominant personality traits represented the maximizing of certain aspects of the stimulus barrier, which helped to ward off what he experienced as the clear and present danger of psychic trauma in childhood. The process of psychoanalysis may be viewed as a chance to confront oneself with self views that might have been traumatic at an earlier time, but that can now be mastered through the gradual, *piecemeal,* and repetitive presentation of them. Through this process, the modifications, rigidities, or hypervigilance distortions, which had developed in the stimulus barrier in the process of past trauma prevention, are discovered, and after replacing them they may be renounced and given up.

Freud's (1926) view of psychic trauma, which I mentioned at the outset, was that it is determined by the *subjective* experienced of helplessness. He underlined this point by stressing that it did not matter whether one's evaluation of the situation was correct or not. The essence in the initiation of the traumatic state was "the subject's estimation of his own strength . . . and his admission of helplessness in the face of [danger] . . ." (p. 166). Freud's emphasis was on the subject's *psychic reality,* which is the only knowable one. I have described a number of functions and factors that determine the nature of one's psychic reality. In this chapter I have been emphasizing that the evaluation of a situation involves the processing of perception by associations, that is to say, inner sources. Another way to say this is that psychic reality results from the interaction of perception from the outer world with those derived from inner sources, including unconscious fantasies (Michels, 1985).

Studies of trauma and its prevention force us to focus on the traumatic state and then explore in all directions how it came about and what might have prevented it. This is why we became involved in questions beyond ego defenses and ventured into an examination of information processing. We found an extreme complexity of factors involving attention, perception, evaluation, various memory functions, and confrontation of current perceptions with the core of accumulated memories. All the functions reviewed—the processes of perception and cognition, on the one hand, and the imapct of affect signals, on the other—result in a particular self-evaluation in the context of all the things requiring consideration. That there are so many different functions, and that there are many spectra of choices and reactions in each step along the way, permits defensive operations and thus constitutes a "stimulus barrier." Another way to put it is that the challenge of affects is not to express them in the sense of riddance implied by the economic view of psychoanalysis, but rather to keep them within manageable intensities in order to be able to use them as signals. Having available adult-type affects permits one to extract the maximum useful information from them. This is the framework on which we need to hang all the other things we know about personality, character, hedonic regulation, and interpersonal relations.

CONCLUSION

Studies and follow-ups on Holocaust survivors were the specific stimulus to reformulations about the traumatic process. Reexamination of the affective and hedonic regulation of perception, cognition, and memory permits us to reinterpret some of the follow-up observations. But memories and their interpretations do not remain static either but are retrospectively changeable. This would be particularly the case with memories that are difficult to master.

We now know that survivors of the Holocaust have to keep reviewing and changing their perspectives and recollections of the stressful era. The dissociative (self-representation splitting) sequelae impel a continuation of a process resembling mourning. When one encounters memories of events that still cannot be accepted lovingly, peacefully, and comfortably, one may be driven to continue to promote the painful affective responses and renew the struggle against objects from the past that now patently reside nowhere but in one's own mind. Unmastered memories represent unhealed wounds, which keep generating painful affects. Memories that cannot be accepted may have to be reinterpreted or modified in a kind of self-detoxification. We can understand, then, the need for some Holocaust survivors and their children to keep creating new interpretations, even mythologies, that make the images of the past more bearable. Survivors and their children may be sharing a mission that has a number of determinants and positive values yet represents a burden and a driveness to deal with the traumatic past.

However, the very attempt to generalize about Holocaust survivors is bound to introduce much error. It is not possible to achieve either a uniform, singular diagnosis or an all-inclusive view of this population, or even of their shared experiences.

One cannot speak of the experiences of Holocaust survivors without acknowledging that they include as wide a span as one would expect of any survivors of a war. Even when we narrow the classification of survivors to exclude all but concentration camp survivors, or limit our observations to the survivors of a specific camp during a specific period, we still come up with a multitude of circumstances and events and an infinite variety of ways of experiencing them.

It is inevitable that the survivor's own life review necessitates a reworking and reediting of the recollection of the Holocaust experiences, as well as his or her own subjective states during those extraordinary events. For this reason, although a considerable effort has been made to encourage and facilitate communications between survivors and their children—with particular emphasis on obtaining oral histories from the survivors—the benefits derive from the affective, rather than semiotic exchanges.

An important sense of life satisfaction comes from being able to communicate to one's children about the meaning of life, about one's people, and about family continuity in the light of extraordinary developments. It is equally important that the children of survivors feel that their parents were able to entrust them with their secrets of their most painfully humiliating, as well as heroic, experiences. The veracity, the absolute truth of these communications is not the issue as much as is the ceremony of passing on the deepest self, and world views, and the accompanying *affective* memories.

Part Three
Alexithymia and Posttraumatic States

Integration and Self-Healing
in Posttraumatic States

I can now report that my own advanced aging is the choicest product of my hygenic development. In my life's sunset it is wonderful to be able to feel sure that I, as everyone else in the world, can concentrate upon calling my soul my own, and my all my soul![Dorsey, 1976, p. 451]

The difficulties of the Holocaust survivors, which Niederland (1961) described over 26 years ago, have continued to be studied (Eitinger and Strøm, 1973; Eitinger, 1980; Chodoff, 1980). These patients continue to suffer from depression, sleep disturbances, repetitive dreams, various chronic pain syndromes, and chronic anxiety (Eitinger, 1980) as well as characterological difficulties.

Eitinger's follow-up of the entire Norwegian population of former concentration camp inmates led him to conclude that they had a greater morbidity, not restricted to any special diagnosis, suffered longer of all illnesses, and died younger than the controls (p. 155). Chodoff's (1980) review of his experiences in treating survivors shows their continuing unhappiness with "ill-advised marriages," and he describes them as living in "withdrawn depression, uninfluenced by any available measures" (p. 208). Among the aftereffects of the Holocaust that he found to make psychotherapy inapplicable to the survivors were the following: the destruction of their "basic trust," their inability to reexperience and describe some of their harmful experiences, the retroactive idealization of their childhood, guilt feelings over surviving (which Chodoff described as "intractable to psychotherapy"), the continuation of regressive disturbances in body image induced by the traumatic experiences, continuing aggression of an intensity that could not be handled in psychotherapy, and the tendency to deal with the aggression by means of a rigid, religiously oriented superego. Danieli (1981b) described severe and complex patterns of troublesome family systems in which the memories of the Holocaust survivors reverberated mostly in the way members of the family experienced and treated each other.

I have had contact with about 1,000 concentration camp survivors out of a population of over 2,000 survivors of the Holocaust whom I examined in connection with their claim that they had been emotionally damaged. Many were later requested by the German restitution authorities to come in for a follow-up or sought consultation because of difficulties in their lives. About a dozen of these patients, who were as old as 78, have been in psychoanalytic psychotherapy with me. My findings basically coincide with those reported by others. These survivors continue to experience problems of chronic depression and anxiety, masochistic life patterns, and psychosomatic disorders. At the time of their retirement, reexamination of their life reactivated some dormant problems and produced intense pain. For instance, persons who had lost a child or mate during the Holocaust tended to show evidence of "survivor guilt," and some assumed a depressive or penitent lifestyle. Other specific acts or wishes that originated during the persecution became, in similar fashion, the focus of a depressive preoccupation.

I want to focus on the relationship of certain posttraumatic constellations to survivors' revision in old age of their evaluation of their life. Old age normally poses a problem of diminishing gratification, and with the serious to severe anhedonia commonly found in this population (Krystal, 1971), we might expect special difficulty. Progressive loss of gratification, support, and distractions limit one's choices to either *integrating* one's life or living in despair. The major task of senescence is identical with that of psychoanalysis or psychoanalytic psychotherapy. In old age, as in psychoanalytic treatment, we come to a point where our past lies unfolded before us, and the question is, what should be done with it? The answer is that it must be accepted, or we will have to keep waging an internal war against the ghosts of our past. The influences in this task are the elements of one's life story, which continue to generate painful affects, the nature of the affective process, and the hedonic level that one has maintained.

Elsewhere in this book, I reviewed the process of psychic traumatization and its aftereffects. I would like to take another look at the process of dealing with stress with special regard to the effect on the ability to grieve.

COPING AND MOURNING

Observations such as those of Rees and Lutkins (1967), showing that bereaved people have a mortality rate seven times higher than controls, have been part of an immense literature documenting the relationship between life events and health consequences. The work of Holmes and Rahe (1967) and others (Gunderson and Rahe, 1974; Rahe, et al., 1964, to mention just a few) has provided more than sufficient evidence that even the normative events and misfortunes of ordinary life result in harmful aftereffects.

Of course, these observations simply provide the link between life events and such effects as illness; they do not demonstrate *how* the events of one's life connect with the effects. In this area, the work on stress responses has also provided a varied literature that space precludes our reviewing here. To put the extreme traumatic state in its proper context, one has to refer first to the way that one deals with ordinary stresses—those which remain within the manageable range—as well as stresses that are the product of extreme conditions.

Earlier I reviewed Caplan's (1981) views of responses to stress. Most impressive to me was that in any disaster situation one could detect evidence of dazing and progressive deterioration of mental and intellectual function:

> The regularly occurring phenomena include disorders of attention, scanning, information collection, access to relevant memories that associate significant meaning to perception, judgement, planning, the capacity to implement plans, and the capacity to implement feedback. In other words, the individual's usual orderly process of externally oriented instrumental ego functioning is upset. This happens precisely when it is important for him to be operating at his maximum effectiveness so he can grapple with his problem [p. 415].

This observation is of the highest relevance to the understanding of the traumatic process. I found that in the catastrophic trauma state, there is a progressive constriction of all of the foregoing mental functions. My discovery of the cognitive constriction in the catastrophic trauma process and its sequelae must now be amended in light of observations by Caplan and his associates at Harvard. We have to consider the implication of the idea that there is a diminution of problem-solving abilities in any serious stress situation. The speed and extensiveness of this deterioration of adaptive function will be determined by a number of factors, such as the availability of group support. However, the key factor is one's subjective evaluation of one's capacity to deal with the situation. This evaluation, however, must include one's capacity to bear the *distress,* that is, one's own affective responses to that situation. Where the person concludes that the situation is both unbearable and unmodifiable, the deterioration is rapid.

Recognition of one's helplessness promotes a diffusion of one's sense of identity and a dependence on others. This observation relates to the kind of dependence on helpers that is reported from a variety of sources. Fairly early in the experience of a disaster, affect tolerance is sorely tested. There is a readjustment and necessity to function under stress conditions, under hyperarousal and intense emotional stresses, and still preserve function. The ability to tolerate affects, which involves the multitude of possibe reactions to having an emotion (Krystal, 1975), is a key factor in determining whether the person will continue to function or will become overwhelmed. The "emergency affects" are characterized by their dysphoric nature and a high degree of arousal. Hyperstimulation at first improves performance, but after a point, deterioration set in. The point at which performance falls is, however, another variable. Persons who have not been overwhelmed before have a lower physiological arousal and a better tolerance of states of high activation, as we saw in chapter 7. Highlighting the activating aspect of emotions and the discoveries of the special centers for the regulation of anxiety through the noradrenergic system suggest that there may be direct effects of a persistence in PTSD of the high state of physiological arousal (van der Kolk et al., 1984). People with a history of psychic trauma show a physiological hyperreactivity, which is part of their hypervigilance and tendency to startle, as well as a tendency for early deterioration of performance; and, because they anticipate the return of the traumatic state, they also have a tendency to panic.

Conversely, familiarity and comfort with a situation assure longer effective performance. For this reason, if the disaster can be anticipated, certain preparations can increase affect tolerance; such is the effect of Army training under battle conditions. Drill repetitions by personnel on ships or airplanes are designed to put them in better control of their emotions in an emergency. By their own improved affect tolerance, they can be of help to others in the group. Later, in handling a disaster and attempting to restore an affective state of control and comfort, one may use denial and isolation, as well as such defenses against affect as displacement, reversal, or blocking of an affect for a short time. Finally, one must consciously recognize the aftereffects of the disaster and those aspects of the disaster that have modified one's life. Ultimately, one has to deal also with the very idea of its having happened. This confrontation has an impact of its own in diminishing the feeling of safety and denial of danger that is necessary for normal function.

Caplan's (1981) model is most useful in giving us a picture of dealing with acutely *present* stress. Horowitz (1976) has provided a model for dealing with the *aftereffects* of the untoward event and with those situations that leave one and one's environment substantially changed. Horowitz has provided the model of the intrapsychic mastery of the stressful event. The event will result first in a shock state and then in an outcry, the outcry being the emergency response, an acute affective response such as weeping, moaning, screaming, or fainting. The conscious registration of knowledge is handled by a partial denial of the implication of the situation. The tranquil state afforded by denial is disturbed by the intrusion of the new perception, which keeps disrupting the denial and results in a renewal of affective activation. The cognitive and affective response goes on for only a short time and is terminated by denial. There is a period of rest. Soon the ideas intrude again into consciousness, repeating the whole cycle, which may be considered the *working through* process and which goes on until the completion of the work of mastery (p. 56). This process may be seen to be a model applicable to the work of mourning. Writers have in the past commented that mourning comes on in waves. Lindemann (1944) reported that in the process of mourning there were "waves lasting from twenty minutes to an hour" of physical distress, along with "preoccupation with the image of the deceased" (p. 142). Freud (1917) similarly described how the mourner periodically distracts himself and then returns to the process of mourning. These "waves," developing from what Horowitz (1976) described as the intrusion of thoughts about the disconcerting situation, are not merely a restatement of the unhappy fact— "my love is no longer here." Rather, each time the idea comes back to mind it involves a working through of related themes having to do with the cognitive mastery of the acceptance of the reality of the stress. Krupnick and Horowitz (1981) have listed these themes as follows:

1) Rage at the Source (of the serious life event), 2) Sadness Over Loss, 3) Discomfort Over (discovered personal) Vulnerability, 4) Discomfort Over (reactive) Aggressive Impulses, 5) Fear of Loss of Control Over Aggressive Impulses, 6) Guilt Over Responsibility (for inviting the event or failing to control it), 7) Fear of Similarity to the Victim, 8) Rage at Those Exempted (from a loss or injury), 9) Fear of Repetition (of the event), and 10) Survivor Guilt [p. 428].

I (Krystal, 1971) have also described many of the same preoccupations in posttraumatic states (pp. 15–22). These observations demonstrate that the *meaning* and *affects* represent the challenge and, at the same time, are involved in mastery and coping.

The process of mourning and both Caplan's and Horowitz's stress-response patterns are also compatible with the model offered by Bowlby (1961, 1981), who described mourning as having four phases:

1) The phase of numbing which lasts a few hours to a few weeks and may be interrupted by outbursts of extremely intense distress or anger. 2) A phase of yearning and searching for the lost figure, lasting some months and sometimes for years. 3) A phase of disorganization and despair. 4) A phase of greater or lesser degree of reorganization [1981, p. 85].

According to Bowlby, the emotions that develop during the phase of disorganization and despair are anger, anxiety, and mixtures of dysphoric affects. The work and process of mourning are useful in considering *all* situations in which one deals with stress or in which one has to accept "bad" developments. People in disaster or stress situations also describe it as a "work of worrying" (Erikson, 1976).

The process of mourning is, in fact, the process of *mastering* the loss. All stress situations involve losses, even if only the (temporary) loss of the illusion of invulnerability that is involved in every misfortune. Hence, the process of mourning really involves the mechanism of intrapsychic mastery. Particularly in regard to Vietnam veterans, the sequelae frequently relate to the inability to accomplish this mastery (Shatan, 1972, 1973).

Koranyi (1977) has studied the psychological and physiological stresses of battlefield situations and found that people pushed beyond endurance suffer "affective chaos and cognitive distortion," as well as "reflection of disarranged physiology." These reactions can be identified by "hypokinetic withdrawal," or else "disorganization with agitation," and "vacant, helpless, poor judgemental behavior" or "frozen state" . . . (p. 15). The process by which one becomes overwhelmed and one's emotional and physical resources are depleted reminds us of the wholeness and unity of each individual. It helps us to counteract the tendency to think in terms of the body–mind split and prepares us to anticipate that in the effects of traumatic experience it is impossible to separate the psychological effects from the physiological ones.

Another approach to the reactions to stressful situations is through the idea of "coping" (Coelho, Hamburg, and Adams, 1974). Lazarus and his associates (Benner, Roskier, and Lazarus, 1980) also attempted to visualize the process of coping or adjustment to stressful situations as one that provided a framework for both ordinary and overwhelming stresses, including those stresses that involve major loss. It bears restating that every catastrophic event contains significant losses, for example, the loss of security and the loss of the ability to maintain denial.

Cognitive appraisal of a catastrophic event proceeds not in a straight line, but more in spiraling circles of denial and painful recognition as one descends to the necessary *depth* of grief and depression. In the process of maintaining the affective state below the overwhelming level, one "doses" oneself gradually with the painful truths.

Thus, the issue of affect tolerance is that under extreme stress situations, the *affect* may become unbearable. The interest of long-range adjustment is best served by maintaining the affect at a point that is not overwhelming; not only because of the danger of disorganization, but also because otherwise one may trigger the catastrophic response of the catatonoid reaction. Lieberman (1977) found that in the assimilation and mastery of the losses and painful self-confrontation in old age, there is also a need to regulate the pace at which adaptations can be made. There, too, considerations of affect tolerance are of crucial importance in managing the process by which the blows of reality can be assimilated and accommodation can be achieved. The point is that *all stressful situations evoke certain coping responses, which are very similar and in their essential functions are identical with mourning*. The objective is to master, ideally integrate, the perception of the new situation, a process that always entails a new view of oneself. In Horowitz's denial-intrusiveness-reworking-mastery sequence, we see essentially the same pattern following stress as we do in bereavement. And, as Horowitz (1976) points out character traits are a major determinant of the course of the mastery or mourning process and, to a large extent, determine the outcome of the stress response patterns.

The impact and consequences of a stressful situation depend on its meaning for the subject and on the multitude of fantasies and defenses it stimulates. When one is dealing with a loss occasioned by natural forces in an expectable order, there are still a number of reactions and ways to experience it, which may complicate the picture. Freud (1917) and even Abraham (1911) were clear that in bereavement it makes a great deal of difference *how* the object was experienced. The ability to experience objects as whole, separate persons, not partial objects, possessions, food, supplies, or selfobjects cannot be taken for granted. Having to comfort oneself even with a self-caused injury to one's sense of perfection is painful and sometimes unacceptable. When one has to accept losses or damages caused by a' victorious sadistic external enemy, depressive reactions may become more driven as they are reinforced by the need to deal with the residual chronic aggression.

The problem of aggression in relation to mourning results from the fact that the anger, which so often has to be suppressed in the traumatic situation, goes underground and returns as a permanent challenge to the future adjustment of the subject. Its appearance can be marked as soon as safety is reestablished. In earlier chapters, I reviewed the work of Sterba (1949, 1968) and Freud and Dann (1951), who have amply demonstrated the incredible upsurge of aggression in youngsters liberated from oppression and restored to a safe environment. Out of his psychotherapeutic work with survivors, Hoppe (1962, 1968, 1969) felt that they showed either depressive or aggressive problems. His patients, who developed "reactive aggression" and "hate addiction" (1962), were

> protected from unconsciously relating to their torturers as parental figures by a firm ego ideal, and by shame, pride and the idea of having a mission. The aggressive survivor permanently externalizes a part of his superego and is fighting against representatives of the externalized negative conscience. The aggression creates new guilt feelings, especially if the survivor's hate addiction turns against his own family members [Hoppe, 1971, p. 179].

The opposition of the depressive versus aggressive survivor takes on an additional dimension in the work of Danieli (1981a), who described the adaptational styles of survivor families. She contrasted the depressive families of "victims" (i.e., where the victim identity was prevalent and shared by the family) with those of "fighters." The latter were characterized by a need for mastery and an intolerance for either depression or guilt (or shame). "Unlike victims . . . they encouraged aggression against and defiance of outsiders" (p.

10). The factor of *activity* in differentiating these family styles reemphasizes the influence of total helplessness. My clinical experience showed that any type of activity during the traumatic situation reduces the severity of the aftereffects. However, activity in the face of overwhelming stress exacts its toll. Terr's (1979, 1981a, b) work with the kidnapped children of Chowchilla showed that the children who were heroic in the traumatic situation, had in follow-ups a driven need to repeat heroic activities, with resultant maladaptive behavior. The activities of the heroic and otherwise actively resistant survivors show a similar drivenness to continue active and heroic behavior and ward off any bereavement, shame, or guilt. The inability to bear these painful affects may spawn a need to create a mythology portraying the cataclysm as a Heroic Era.

What cannot be faced from the past is changed to produce one's own version of history. Thus, people who committed atrocities do not necessarily suffer from guilt or shame, but see themselves as victims of their former victims and likely have predominantly problems of aggression. What potential guilt or shame there might be would likely be handled by denial and renewal of allegiance to the original ideology or order. While the studies on Nazis suggest this (Dimsdale, 1980; R. J. Lifton, personal communication, 1982), they are sparse. However, we are encountering an enormous problem of aggression in Vietnam veterans. In this context Shatan's (1973) work is relevant. He anticipated that the "strangulation" of the grief responses would predominate in future psychopathology of some veterans. He realized that both counterinsurgency training and the type of combat involved were detrimental to the soldiers' capacity to mourn. This brings us back to the question of grieving and self-healing in posttraumatic states.

ALEXITHYMIA, ANHEDONIA, AND INTEGRITY IN OLD AGE

I see clearly that I owe happiness to myself and I am certain that a reliable way to it is through unhappiness. [Dorsey, 1976, p. 456].

One need not belabor the many reasons why aging involves a gradual diminution in the potential for pleasure and gratification. If the process runs its full course, the person is left to enjoy nothing but vegetative functions. As the attrition proceeds, it is easy to observe that people vary in their hedonic potential and that some enter old age with an already diminished hedonic capacity (Meehl, 1975). Among the factors at the opposite poles of this hedonic capacity are the ability to play and problems of masochism and guilt. The population of Holocaust survivors is, of course, high in masochism and low in their potential to play when they are forced to retire. The hedonic potential of every aged person needs to be carefully evaluated, as there is a marked difference among similar populations. Persons with a good hedonic capacity can enjoy practically anything—even if it is just inhaling and exhaling—and have been known for their sunny dispositions since childhood. Hedonic capacity has been identified as a character trait (Meehl et al., 1971) and has been called "surgency," a term coined by Cattell (1935). But regardless of where on this spectrum of capacity for pleasure, joy, and happiness one falls, one cannot avoid the progressive ravages of age to the hedonic span. Particularly severe losses are sustained in the things one *does*—in all spheres of activity—sexual, occupational, avocational, and recreational. These losses force a shift from doing to thinking, from planning to reminiscing, from preoccupation with everyday events and long-range planning to reviewing and rethinking one's life.

Being forced to recall and remember is in itself frightening and stressful to Holocaust survivors, who have spent most of their time "fighting off" their memories. Many go to great lengths to avoid any historical material. When I asked such patients to associate to TAT cards 1, 3, and 5, their responses were usually limited to one or two sentences predicting a dismal future for everyone in the picture. Some patients even volunteered that they were so afraid of "make believe" that they did not want to view or read any fictional stories. One patient who had had some psychotherapy realized that she kept describing TAT cards in terms of her own life. She commented, "The past is always catching up to the present in my mind." The reasons for "running away from one's history" have been described by Klein (1976) as resulting from the "sensitivity to cleavage and dissonance," which "reaches its crest . . . in the twilight years when irreversible finitude is finally to be faced and the effort to bring together past, present, and the shrinking future into a self-justifying meaning is especially poignant and difficult" (p. 231).

Old age, with its losses, imposes the inescapable necessity to face one's past. One then either accepts onself and one's past or continues to reject it angrily. As Erikson (1959) put it, there is "a dialectic struggle in old age between a search for integrity and a sense of despair and disgust—all three, in dynamic balance, essential to a final human strength: Wisdom" (p. 98; also in 1963, 1968a, b). The choice is between integration or despair. But integration means that one has to *acquiesce* to the "accidental coincidence of but one life cycle with but one segment of history" (Erikson, 1959, p. 98). Erikson explains that to achieve integrity, one must achieve acceptance of "one's own and only life cycle and of the people who have become significant to it as something that had to be and that, by necessity permitted no substitutions" (p. 98). This task, as I mentioned earlier, can also be said to represent the goal and essence of all psychoanalytic psychotherapy.

The heart of the work of psychoanalysis can be reviewed in two parts: (1) the expansion of the *consciously* acknowledge self- and object-representations and (2) the acceptance of the inevitability and necessity of every event of one's life as having been *justified by its causes*. It can be said that the challenge in the acceptance of one's old age and in the completion of psychoanalytic work is the same—to accept and embrace what has happened and renounce denial, externalization, and the promotion of one's rage.

In old age the process is compounded; for one must grieve for current and ongoing losses and grieve in advance for one's completion of life while simultaneously attending to the grief resulting from one's unavoidable review of the life spent. On the other hand, in psychotherapy with posttraumatic states, there are also serious complications to mastery through mourning. Acceptance by Holocaust survivors that what happened to them was *justified by its causes* implies an acceptance that Hitler, Nazism, and the bizarre events they experienced were also justified by their causes. Such an acceptance is too closely reminiscent of the *submission* to persecution. The process of making peace with oneself becomes impossible when it brings back the helplessness and shame of the past. Many survivors would experience this self-healing as "granting Hitler a posthumous victory" and they therefore angrily reject it. To them, self-integration appears antithetical to the only justification for their surfival: to be angry witnesses against the outrage of the Holocaust.

Moreover, to give up infantile wishes—including omnipotence, the quest for perfection, and entitlement to ideal parents and to accept the negative aspects of oneself, including these angry and vengeful feelings—requires a capacity for effective grieving. However, to be able to mourn, one has to have available the adult-type affects that are precisely what (by definition) alexithymic patients are lacking. In addition, the "operative thinking" characteristic of alexithymia interferes further with the capacity for symbolization, transference elaboration, and achievement of changes and sublimations. Finally, one must have good affect tolerance to be able to carry out the process of mourning without it snowballing into a maladaptive state of depression. In fact, the chronic depressive state in which these survivors live can be defined by the mourning that needs to be accomplished but is precluded. These patients keep berating, accusing, and deprecating themselves, yet they never lower their high self-expectations. The belated discovery of their anhedonia is the last blow, which causes bitter rejection of their lifelong self-reparative efforts because they have failed to produce the yearned for pleasure and well-being. The feeling of depression results from the failure to produce gratification.

A common finding in working with survivors of the Holocaust was that even when alexithymia and impairment in affect tolerance were relatively absent, there was a limit to how much loss the survivors could absorb through grieving and the degree to which they could achieve integrity and good-natured acceptance of the past. There seems to be an absolute limit to how much an individual is able to give up through grieving. The limitation is twofold: First a person can grieve over only so much *at one time*. For instance, in the Coconut Grove disaster, people who were severely burned and who lost a spouse at the same time were not able to deal with the object loss for quite some time while they were attending to their corporeal losses (Lindemann, 1944). Second, there is an absolute or lifetime limit to what people can absorb in terms of either loss or accepting negative qualities in themselves. There are both qualitative and quantitative limitations on what can be dealt with successfully through mourning. The quantity or quality of losses may be beyond the individual's capacity to integrate, as in the case of the Holocaust, when one's entire people and way of living were destroyed.

This process becomes even more difficult because of the extreme danger of dealing through mourning with the representation of one's opponent (i.e., the perpetrator or the victim of the tragedy). For to recognize the *intrapsychic* existence of an inimical object might threaten the sanity of the survivor. This problem might be described in the language of traditional psychoanalysis as the struggle against the hostile (abhorred) introject. In this context, we need to apply what we learned earlier, in the chapter on reality: that to the extent that the objects are externalized, an attempt to deal with the mental representation of them is a threat to one's defensive structure. Such mourning is complicated by the "return of the repressed." Since the inability to identify consciously with the enemy is derived from the need to protect and assert one's autonomy, the discovery of the intrapsychic existence of the hostile introject threatens the ability to maintain one's integrity.

Among Holocaust survivors, who did not receive any support from their native population, there are many feelings to deal with in regard to this abandonment and the world's tacit compliance with the Nazis' genocidal activities. During the Holocaust, the "final solution" was preceded by years of perfidious abuse and degradation, mass robbery, isolation, and deprivation of the minimal essentials of dignity and even of cleanliness. The survivors of defeat and humiliation have a multitude of unbearably painful emotions to face before the question of mastery or integration of their past can ever be possible.

But even if we were to discount these difficulties, whose enumeration could fill volumes, we still come back to the simple, basic fact that there are limitations to the kinds of losses an individual can deal with through mourning. Loss of a child is an example in which the parents may not be capable of completing the process of mourning, and various forms of denial, idealization, and introject "walling off" may become necessary. An example of a negative quality within a person that cannot be accepted but must be compensated for is found in Conrad's (1900) story of Lord Jim: the protagonist has to sacrifice his life to show that he is not, after all, a coward.

In addition, the survivor of a genocidal Holocaust stands the risk of polarizing the object- and self-representations into victim and perpetrators. Anhedonia and alexithymia propel the survivors to continue to experience themselves as victims, and with this comes the longing to change places with the oppressor. But the identification with the aggressor must remain unconscious, or else it will flood the self-representation with psychotic rage. This unsolvable dilemma was well portrayed by Robert Shaw (1967) in his novel *The Man in the Glass Booth*. The story, which was subsequently made into a play and a movie, involves a spectacularly successful but very unhappy and unstable survivor. His identity remains in question: Is this Goldman, the former prisoner, or his cousin, SS Colonel Dorff of the *Einsatz* (mass-murder) commandos and death camps? The Jewish community in Montreal became sharply divided over staging the play. Two survivors consulted during rehearsals felt that the play was anti-Semitic and seemed to say that "there is no blame, no culpability, and no guilt for the Nazis and their murderous action" (Rudin, 1975). These survivors and Rabbi Rudin, who described the incident (1974), missed the point about the consequences of a lack of self-integration that the play offers. In commenting on the theme of the play, I (1975) pointed out that the failure to own up to our own memories, regardless of how painful they are, leaves us in the state of "hate addiction." About the same time, the Detroit *Jewish News* (November 21, 1980, p. 42) carried an article about a forthcoming talk by a Holocaust survivor to a women's group; its theme was "never forgive and never forget." This also happens to be the motto of some groups of Holocaust survivors.

It is to be expected that the outcome of mourning in posttraumatic states depends on many aspects, especially the intensity of one's aggression. In turn, the choice between integration and hate addiction is most of all determined by one's capacity to mourn effectively. Dealing with the memories of trauma repeatedly evokes such painful affects as shame, guilt, and helplessness. When affect tolerance is poor, all these feelings have to be warded off and replaced by rage. The primary gain in the continuing rage is a narcissistic one: it makes possible the refusal to admit the possibility that events are uncontrollable, the refusal to face one's helplessness. The secondary gains are potentially so varied that we cannot foresee their nature in a particular situation.

Associated with these defense operations are lasting changes in the personality, especially the superego. This point was made by Hoppe (1962). Similar observations were elaborated by Bergmann (1982). These studies include the question of the effect of the posttraumatic superego problems on the family and the next generation.

Paradoxically, although it may be painful and difficult for a person who has endured serious psychic traumatization to achieve intrapsychic integration, this is what the survivor needs most of all. One of the most devastating aftereffects of trauma is the widespread use of repression, denial, and psychic splitting. Much of the psychic representation of the "enemy," "oppressor," "victim," or even of impersonal elements such as "fate" and of clearly personal attributes like one's own emotions, may come to be experienced as outside the self-representation. *Thus the posttraumatic state is characterized by an impoverishment of the areas of the mind to which the "I" feeling of self-sameness is extended and by a hypertrophy of the "not-I" alienated areas.* The symptoms of "pseudophobia," fear of one's dreams and of one's own emotions, are all the result of this posttraumatic depletion of the consciously recognized spheres of selfhood. (See chapter on Trauma and Affects.)

Moral and ethical judgment is often substituted for self-healing. It seems virtuous to "feed" righteous indignation and treasonous to stop the rage. In this respect, it is useful to consider that hate, anger, guilt, and depression are forms of pain. It is a masochistic perversion for survivors to promote the continuation of these pains within themselves. Instead, to the extent possible, we should soothe ourselves and gain peace through self-acceptance.

Lifton (1979) has addressed the issue of posttraumatic integration and focused on the confrontation with death. As he sees it, "Death tests everyone's integrity; the dying person's immediate survivors, and the attending healers contribute to a collective psychic constellation within which issues of continuity, discontinuity, self-completion and disintegration are addressed" (p. 109). The confrontation with "absurd" death—mass destruction—leads Lifton to understand that the survivors' "life review" is derailed by "psychic numbing. desymbolization, deformation" or "decentralization" (p. 69) and an inability to restore a feeling of intimacy because of a suspicion of "counterfeit nurturance." In effect, then, Lifton's observations coincide with the view expressed in this book that the difficulties that become conspicuous in the survivors' old age can be considered a paradigm of many of the major difficulties found in the attempt at posttraumatic self-healing and mastery of intrapsychic injuries. The main point is that since the work of mourning and grieving requires the availability of adult-type affects, alexithymia becomes a specific obstacle but by no means the only one found under these circumstances.

Survivors of the Holocaust age early and have higher than average rates of early death from all causes (Eitinger and Strøm, 1973). This early loss of vitality should not be viewed as separate from the alexithymia or anhedonia. Rado (1969) long stressed the importance of the "pleasure economy." He believed that a "deficiency in welfare emotions (joy, pleasure, happiness, love, affection, etc.) alters every operation of the integrative apparatus. No phase of life, no area of behavior remains unaffected" (p. 24). My observations and the findings of Eitinger (1980) prove the validity of Rado's ideas. Survivors manifest a combination of anhedonia, special guilt, possibly an attachment to pain (Valenstein, 1973), and a fear of joy and happiness. Psychoanalytic work with survivors has been ineffective because, in addition, they fear their emotions—they have a posttraumatic impairment of affect tolerance because they experience their own emotions as heralds of trauma.

Past that, one encounters the problems of alexithymia. The survivors try to block the distress by the use of medication and keep "proposing a physical illness" (Balint, 1964) instead of utilizing their emotions as signals.

But the underlying problems of depression and guilt still require integration through mourning, lowering of narcissistic expectations of oneself, and acceptance of the necessity of what happened. For instance, survivors of the Holocaust still feel shame over the idea that they did not fight back enough. Efforts by certain groups on behalf of the Jewish people to create a mythology about the heroic resistance are intended to relieve the shame. The futility of these efforts illustrates the task and challenge of integration in the life of every aging person. Whatever one is ashamed of has to be lovingly accepted as an unavoidable part of one's life. Every pain aroused in the process of reviewing one's life as an individual or the history of a group merely marks an area that as yet is deprived of the self-healing application of the feeling of identity, self-sameness, or selfhood. One feels anger, guilt, or shame whenever one is unable (refuses) to accept the necessity and unavoidability of what happened. The trouble is that in this process of reviewing one's life, as memories are restored to the self-representation and are owned up to (in other words, in the process of the return of the repressed) the individual experiences pain. In fact, Freud was puzzled by just this pain in mourning. He (1917) said that he could not explain why mourning was so "extraordinarily painful . . . *in terms of economics*" (p. 245, emphasis mine). But in terms of the task carried out during senescence, one can see many reasons why mourning must be so painful.

The successful completion of mourning or the successful integration of one's life enables one to own up to all of one's living as one's own, including the object-representations. This state gives the person a chance to discover that in ordinary living we maintain our object-representations in a type of *repression through externalization.* That is, we maintain our mental representation of them in a "nonself" status. Thus, if we mourn to the point of owning up to the self-sameness of our object-representations, there is a type of *return of the repressed.* The illusion of externality that was maintained toward our object-representations achieved a kind of analgesia, and when self-integration is achieved, this analgesia wears off. The motivation for the externalization lies in dealing with infantile aggression. I believe that infantile trauma and the resulting ambivalence results in a distortion of the self-representation so that vital and affective aspects of oneself are attributed to the object-representation, which is rigidly walled-off—thus rendering one's capabilities for self-care functionally inaccessible.

Because mourning and integration must include affective components—a situation that parallels Freud's (Freud and Breuer, 1893) discovery that recollection did not do anything for hysteria if it was devoid of emotions—affect tolerance is a major issue. That is also the reason why normal, adult-type, mostly cognitive and signal-like affects are necessary for the completion of the process of mourning. Otherwise, in the presence of alexithymia, the undifferentiated, mostly somatic, unverbalized affect responses are so intense, threatening, and painful that one must ward them off by deadening oneself or abort the process by escaping into denial.

It is worthwhile to reemphasize a point made before: While the inability to bear the pain of mourning is likely to interrupt effective grieving and replace it with depression or some form of denial, for example, projection, the presence of good affect tolerance does not guarantee a successful outcome. The necessary changes in self- and object-representations are intrapsychic accomplishments. The affect generated is a kind of side effect like the heat generated by electricity in the wires through which it passes. But accepting the finality and irreversibility of losses, and that some bad things happen randomly and we have no control over them, requires the renunciation of the infantile magical control of fate. If bad things can occur at random and one is helpless, then one's masochistic fantasies can come true. The worst dread is that if one cannot control fate, one cannot prevent the return of infantile psychic trauma—the fate worse than death.

A question debated within child psychiatry is, Can children mourn? Of course children can mourn; even dogs and other animals can mourn. But their grieving does not tell us anything about their ability to accept the loss of the treasured object and the reason for it. The problem is what is commonly referred to as the "fate of the introject," or how the object- and self-representations are influenced by the meanings attributed to the loss. Often, because of the child's feeling of insecurity, the object-representation is retained as a kind of idol, which interferes with future development of self-reliance and self-confidence.

This brings up the question of religious beliefs in aging, especially in posttraumatic states. We find that many people who have experienced severe traumatization are obsessed with questions of a religious nature: Why did it happen to me? Most people can not accept complex or random events because they cannot stand their helplessness in controlling their fate. The question, then, is whether God can still be seen as the omnipotent, omniscient, benevolent power He is supposed to be. To answer this question affirmatively, one usually must conclude that the bad experience is a punishment for some "sins." Thus, it happens that the most common outcome of misfortune is self-condemnation and masochistic trends.

The issues of religiosity become more urgent with aging. The French have a proverb that when the Devil gets old, he becomes pious. Desperate attempts are made by many survivors to restore and maintain their faith in God. However, the problems of aggression and destruction of basic trust that resulted from the events of the Holocaust make true faith and trust in the benevolence of an omnipotent God well nigh impossible. The yearning for the comfort of religion only results in a piling up of rituals. If one succeeds in establishing a fundamentalist religion under these circumstances, then the benevolent God will be also a vengeful God, demanding that one dedicate oneself to a holy war against the Devil and the predominantly evil world. Hence, the similarity of such a solution to a paranoid system becomes transparent. People who are unable to complete the process of mourning and people troubled with their religious ambivalence have another tendency in common—the building of monumental and ecclesiastic edifices. This propensity can be observed in the survivor group. In addition, the survivor has to maintain intrapsychic barriers against ambivalence, doubts, guilt, and rage. The result is widespread constriction of fantasy in both actual imagination and transference reactions.

In following a large number of survivors of the Holocaust who are *not* in psychotherapy, I have been impressed that in old age one is confronted with certain choices and tasks identical to those offered in analytic treatment. As preoccupation with work and gratification of the senses diminishes, the mind's activities turn inward and toward the past. "Your old men shall dream dreams, your young men shall see visions," said the prophet (Joel 3:1). These dreams may be a renewal of childhood fantasizing—we see this in the current efforts to create a mythology among survivors of the Holocaust. The dread of their own affects extends from anxiety to any sense of aliveness. At least the diminution in the tonic aspect of affect produces a retardation. The retardation may affect the pscyhomotor sphere primarily, but more commonly results in an alteration in life-preserving functions, such as immune responses or other health-maintaining processes. A rapidly accumulating body of evidence indicates that despair represents a most important predisposition for illness (see LeShan, 1959; Stoyva and Budzynski, 1974; Bahnson, 1975; Achterberg, Simonton, and Simonton-Matthews, 1976; Holden, 1978).

The survivors do not necessarily recognize consciously or complain of their depression. More commonly, they handle the problem by constriction of interest, by avoiding both pleasure and excitement. Recently I talked with a non-Jewish survivor of Nazi persecution who usually speaks at home in his native tongue. He tried to tell me that a doctor he saw was trying to take away some of his pension—but the parapraxis came out angrily: "he was trying to spoil my suffering!" We are dealing with a state of chronic depression and psychic depletion that is often accompanied by a lifelong avoidance of all excitement.

In conclusion, I must admit that my attempts to engage aging survivors of the Holocaust in psychoanalytic psychotherapy have been for the most part unsuccessful. I have been able to take a variety of supportive measures that make their life more bearable. Among these, improving the management, that is, the acceptance, of their distressing affective states has been most often necessary. But in regard to the survivors' capacity to work through their losses and problems of guilt and shame in order to gain integration in aging, I have always run into limitations in their ability to grieve effectively (Wetmore, 1963). There are also limitations to what they can accept of the world and of themselves and to the childhood or religious beliefs one can renounce. For many people, some views and developments are simply not acceptable because they make the world and life appear not worthwhile. They prefer to give expression to their individuality by saying No! to what is unacceptable—even to their last breath. Thus they exercise their individuality and freedom of choice. This assertiveness is beyond any possible therapeutic zeal on my part. And, of course, people who make such choices choose a life of protest and are fully aware of the suffering they will endure and the martyrdom it involves.

While respecting their need and right to make these choices, I would like to register the humanistic and medical view that the impulse to human sacrifice, even self-sacrifice, should be lovingly and respectfully renounced. We sometimes find that beyond being able to complete mourning and achieve intrapsychic integration, alexithymic persons become early prey to that devastating preoccupation of old age: "Who love me? Who cares if I live?" The problem is particularly difficult for survivors because of their regression in affect—they do not experience love, nor do they have the kind of empathy that would permit them to sense their object's affection for them. One has to feel love to be able to believe in its existence. Most of all, one has to feel love to be able to accept one's own self and one's own past. The ideal for the Holocaust survivor, as for any other aging person, is summed up by Dorsey (1976):

> I must discipline myself to be able to love difficulty in order to achieve every access of my life appreciation. There can be nothing for me to resist (be unwilling to live lovingly) except difficult self-consciousness. . . . Psychoanalytic psychotherapy is the process of working up the accessible self love required to observe "It is I" of whatever before I could observe only "It is not I" [p. 457].

13
Alexithymia

The assumption that other people's emotional responses are like our own is the basis of empathy and as such is basic to all human intercourse. The uncritical acceptance of this assumption, however, has led us to the false expectation that all patients have available to them the affective functions necessary for the utilization of psychotherapy. This chapter examines some variations of affective function, affect forms, and those factors that make emotions available as signals to oneself. We discuss, in particular, a major disturbance in affective and symbolic function—alexithymia. Here we want to reconsider what various workers in the field have come up with in terms of theories or explanations of alexithymic phenomena that would give us some therapeutic openings. At the same time, these explorations pose views of the psychotherapeutic process that are timely to reconsider in the context of the other views presented in this book. But, first, a final brief review of the history and description of this phenomenon.

DESCRIPTION AND DEFINITION

Alexithymia overlaps diagnostic categories. Marty and his colleagues, (Marty and de M'Uzan, 1963; Marty, de M'Uzan, and David, 1963) described the cognitive and affective disturbances uncovered in psychoanalytic studies of psychosomatic patients. Their work was advanced by Sifneos (1967); Nemiah and Sifneos (1970a). At about the same time, and unaware of the work of the others, I found a lack of differentiation of affects in drug withdrawal states (Krystal, 1962) and was describing the same characteristic problems in severe posttraumatic states (Krystal, 1968c, 1971) and in patients with drug dependence (Krystal and Raskin, 1970).

Since that time a number of authors have reported observations on alexithymia. (For a survey, see Braeutigam, 1977.) Generally, there is consensus on the affective and cognitive disturbances found in this condition.

There are, in addition, problems that I find frequently associated: impairment in the capacity for self-care and anhedonia.

THE AFFECTIVE DISTURBANCE

Alexithymic patients' impaired ability to utilize emotions as signals to themselves is based in the *form* that their emotional responses take. Their reactions are basically somatic, consisting of the "expressive," or physiological, aspects of affects, with minimal verbalization. In addition, their emotions are often undifferentiated; they are vague and unspecific, as if they represented an undifferentiated form of common affect precursors, so that separate responses of such feelings as depression and anxiety do not seem to appear. Because of the concomitant diminution in the verbalization of affects, these patients experience somatic, often distressing reactions rather than complete emotions. Only when one experiences the cognitive aspect of an emotion— the meaning of the affect and some indication of the "story behind it"—and simultaneously has the expressive reaction and an adequate capacity for reflective selfawareness, can one observe that one is experiencing a "feeling" and identify it. Alexithymics often cannot tell whether they are sad, tired, hungry, or ill. They are not accustomed to recognizing their feeling states and discovering their reactions to events in their lives. Sometimes they complain of the physiological aspect of affects, but they neither recognize nor can name a specific emotion or even such states as pain, thirst, or hunger. The following case illustration shows that the diminished ability to recognize, name, and use their emotions as guides to self-monitoring results in an overdependence on and overutilization of reasoning:

Case Illustration

Patient A. had been severely addicted to barbiturates but had not used any in several months. On the occasion of this excerpt he was complaining of general distress. His malaise was quite general, and practically every part of his body was in some pain or discomfort. His head hurt, felt full, heavy; and the skin of his scalp felt tight. There was something wrong with his eyes, and at times vision was blurred. His jaw was tight. His mouth was dry, and his tongue seemed slightly swollen or awkward. His chest also felt tight. His skin felt "creepy." His stomach felt bad, perhaps from hunger, but the distress was not relieved by food, although coffee did make him feel a little better. His muscles were taut and stiff, and the joints, not quite sore, were "heavy" and "stiff." He felt somewhat "jumpy," as if he were on the verge of hypoglycemia.

Whenever patients with a history of substance abuse and addictive problems are under stress from physical or emotional sources, they may develop a syndrome resembling their past withdrawal reaction. When this patient was questioned, he realized that this was the case and was very surprised and impressed with this discovery.

When a survey was made of the patient's complaints, and even when it was recognized that the symptoms were very similar to his drug withdrawal pattern, he did not link his state with his life situation. There were, in fact, many things of a profoundly disturbing and distressing nature in his self-evaluation. He had left his wife and children and moved to a rented room. When he considered his situation in life, his isolation, his terrible financial and occupational position, he concluded that he probably felt very lonely and afraid. He had thoughts of resenting that at his age he was all alone, that he had had to give up his house. He thought he should be angry with himself and with his fate, as well as with a number of people. However, neither these nor a variety of other emotions were identified by him. Nor did he recognize in his distress state either anxiety or depression. Instead, he was experiencing the gamut of physical or expressive aspects of these emotions, which in the past he would have prevented by the use of massive doses of barbiturates. He did not have a cold, nor was he hungry because of a lack of food.

This inability for reflective self-awareness (which enables one to identify one's "feeling" as being an appropriate response to one's self-evaluation) is typical of alexithymia. Since such a deficiency makes it virtually impossible for a patient to utilize psychoanalytic psychotherapy, a preparatory phase of treatment is necessary in which the affective problem is attended to. Hence, the work on this and many other occasions proceeded from identifying his physiological responses as parts of an affect, the cognitive part of which was either absent or appeared isolated and which, after bringing the elements together, he could start to "feel." Up to this time he had frequently named emotions when he thought the situation warranted it. For instance, he would say that he felt angry when someone did not fulfill his wishes. Coincidentally, he was also color blind. On one occasion when it was pointed out to him that he neither felt nor believed in the existence of love he said, "I believe you. But it's like you tell me the grass is green—but I only see it as sort of brownish."

Many alexithymics learn to use the common expressions denoting affective responses when they think they should experience them or in situations in which they have observed others reacting emotionally. Therefore, they frequently behave like the color-blind patient who has learned to cover up his deficiency in perception by using a variety of clues from which to infer what he can not discern. However, they are missing a quality in their self-perception that would enliven their self-view and give it conviction and vigor.

Although the patient just described had some inkling that the distress he was experiencing had something to do with his personal well-being, some patients frequently experience such episodes as "illness." Flannery (1978) reported that alexithymic patients suffering from "unexplained physical distress" were "not an uncommon diagnostic and therapeutic problem for the liaison psychiatrist in the general medical setting" (p. 193). Patients suffering from chronic pain syndrome, "pain prone personalities," turn out to have a very high rate of alexithymia as well.

There is some variation from person to person, and sometimes within a given individual, but these patients share a broad area within which emotions are not differentiated and are unverbalized.

> Many psychosomatic patients, although they use words like "sad," "angry" and "nervous" are unable to describe their feelings further, appear to be at a loss for language to convey their experiences of them to others, and frequently when pressed by the interviewer for a response, assert that they "just can't put it into words" [Nemiah, 1975, p. 143].

With some sympathetic attention, the patients finally realize, and may admit to themselves for the first time, that they cannot describe what they feel because what they experience is a vague and generalized response, often involving every system of their bodies (Nemiah, Freyberger, and Sifneos, 1976' Freyberger, 1977). The emotions are not experienced as distinct, separate, specific responses of a varied and identifiable nature. Rather, a common distress pattern develops, so that the patients refer to a state of tension or unease, which they experience generally with a few areas highlighted as the seat of discomfort. They will say, "It's all in one ball" or "in one spot" (Nemiah et al., 1976). These patients commonly experience a general diminution in the ability to "localize affect in their bodies and they appear unaware of any of the common automatic somatic sensations that accompany the experience of a variety of feelings. If there is a somatic component, it is identical with the symptoms of their bodily illness" (p. 431).

This last comment refers to patients with psychosomatic disorders, as does the earlier mentioned tendency to stoicism and diminution in proprioception. As McDougall (1974a) put it, "Many psychosomatic patients continue on their unwavering tight-rope ignoring the body's signs and the mind's distress signals" (p. 458). This tendency to be like "a rock or an island" (p. 453) is possibly related to a trait of alexithymia that may alert the examiner to the rest of the picture. These patients "sit rigidly, move their bodies sparingly, use few gestures when they talk and maintain a nearly expressionless face" (Freyberger, 1977, p. 433). But the alexithymics who are prone to addictive behavior show a virtually hypochondriacal preoccupation with the affect-related distressful sensations in their bodies and a driven need to block them.

Related to this tendency is an overabundance of sensory perceptions in the place of reflective self-awareness, best illustrated by a case vignette of

McDougall's (1974a): "The patient was aware of *sensations* rather than sentiments in her mother's presence. Encouraged to put these into words she was finally able to say: 'I can't bear to *touch* her. As though her body was covered with filth. Almost as though she might poison me' " (p. 456). The importance of this substitution of sensory preoccupation is that it constitutes a predisposition to an *insistence on the concrete* and *externalization*, a major problem in addictive persons (Wurmser, 1978). Because of their affective impairment, these patients also show an impoverishment in their object relations. The degree of detachment in relations to others and their attitudes toward themselves is sometimes so flat that they "feel" psychotic to the interviewer and give the impression that the patient has deadened his object- and self-representations or at least sapped it of all humanity (Marty, de M'Uzan, and David, 1963).

Another characteristic of alexithymic patients is that they are subject to sudden affective responses of considerable intensity. Nemiah et al. (1976) have referred to "brief but violent" outbursts: "Patients will, for instance, suddenly fill up with tears; when questioned, however, they are unaware of feeling sad and cannot explain why they are crying. Or, though they felt no anger in the face of aggravating circumstances, they may exhibit explosive flashes of destructive rage" (p. 432). Although the patients show this intense, affectlike behavior, they may realize that there is a disparity between their feelings and violent behavior. Such patients sometimes resolve to use it "for show" (Krystal, 1979) and at other times experience the outbursts as a "crazy intrusion into the mind" (Nemiah et al., 1976, p. 458). These sudden outbursts, which stop as abruptly as they start, have led some to say that addicts behave as if they had suddenly switched to another personality (Wurmser, 1978).

PENSÉE OPÉRATOIRE: THE COGNITIVE DISTURBANCE

The sudden changes in affective behavior so characteristic of the emotions of alexithymics are present in the cognitive area as well. While the major characteristic of these patients is that they present a dull, mundane, unimaginative, utilitarian, and sequential recitation of concrete "facts" (de M'Uzan, 1974a), occasionally they spring a surprise. De M'Uzan, who is a co-author of the now classic study on Pensée Opératoire (Marty and de M'Uzan, 1963), pondered this phenomenon: "The symbolization, almost always poor, becomes dazzling at times, but remains isolated and incapable of entering into a syntax" (p. 462). Added to the poorness and flatness of the contents of their communication is an *aprosody* that gives their speech an affective flatness.

These patients usually relate the details of their everyday life, and particularly their complaints, in a repetitive fashion. Soon one realizes that they are oriented to "facts" and that there is a striking lack of wish-fulfillment fantasies. Nemiah and Sifneos (1970a, p. 30) made special efforts to question patients about how they felt, but got only descriptions of "external" events or actions. Trying to elicit fantasies drew a stimulus-bound cognitive style, with a virtual absence of any evidence of wish-fulfillment fantasy of either conscious or unconscious variety.

What is deceptive to those unfamiliar with this disturbance is that these patients, who often function very successfully in their work, appear "super-adjusted" to reality and lead one to expect excellent intellectual function. However, getting past the superficial impression of superb functioning, one uncovers a sterility and monotony of ideas and a severe impoverishment of the imagination. The tendency to externalize is reflected in a cognitive style focused on external processes and activities (Nemiah, 1975). At first glance, objects seem to be of interest to these people, especially since they sometimes can "tune in" with great precision on people around them for manipulative or exploitative purposes, but the exploiters cannot describe the affective inter-personal process from which they are benefiting. Moreover, there is no *personal* investment in these objects as unique individuals to whom there is a utilitarian attachment. Instead, the objects are replaceable, albeit necessary. One patient announced one day without a trace of emotion, "I fired Sam." The therapist mistakenly concluded that the patient was referring to an employee, but it turned out that he was talking about his mistress by that nickname, who at other times had seemed so dear to him.

The problem here was different from that seen in the narcissistic or borderline personality, wherein a devalued object is discarded as useless and worthless. In this patient, as in the cases described by McDougall (1974a), the object appeared very highly valued, even cherished. However, just as in McDougall's cases, "their love objects are highly *interchangeable,* the central demand being that someone must be there" (p. 451). When such persons stay with one object, it is because they think it would be too much trouble to find another one, there being no essential difference between objects. De M'Uzan (1974b) has termed this phenomenon "reduplication": "This concerns a perception of other people strongly marked by a sort of global translation of a rough image of one's self, stripped of truly personal traits and indefinitely reproducible according to a stereotyped form" (p. 106).

The absence of the "human" quality contributes to making these patients' thoughts "operative" or thing-oriented. They are often described as "dull, colorless, and boring" (Krystal, 1979, p. 159) even when they are intellectual and clever. Taylor (1984a) has explored in detail why these patients are boring; he noted that their "speech is lacking in nuance, meager in the use of metaphor and devoid of affect" (p. 218). Like Langs' (1978–1979) Type B and Type C patients, these patients make extensive use of projective identification and "create massive defensive barriers by destroying links between (their) internal world" and the therapist-listener (Taylor, 1984a, p. 219). In psychotherapy one finds, as de M'Uzan (1974a) did, "the patient's language is poor, flat and banal, glued to the present and only producing facts stated chronologically" (p. 462).

The associations of these patients are characterized by an almost complete absence of thoughts relating to inner attitudes, feelings, wishes, or drives; and a recounting "in great and often boring detail, of events in their external environment and their own actions in this setting" (Krystal, 1979, p. 158).

Case illustration

Patient B., a middle-aged professional, was an alcoholic and had severe alexithymia and anhedonia. Although very bright and successful both in high school and in college, she discovered that she was not able to write on any but the simplest themes. In a class in creative writing in college, she was "passed on" because the teacher recognized that she had an "organic inability to make up any imaginative story." On a Rorschach, she saw "mainly inkspots—a few looking like vertebrae or a pelvis." When shown TAT cards she gave concrete, descriptive responses and despite repeated efforts had only the simplest fantasy responses. For instance, on Card 1, she said, "This is a boy with a violin. He is supposed to practice, but he doesn't like to." When encouraged to make up a story about the boy, his past and future, she finally said, "Well, he is not going to become a violinist, but he'll find something else to do and will be okay."

Because of her anhedonia, she was questioned about what might give her pleasure. She answered that she might like to take a vacation. Upon another inquiry she added that she would like to go to certain European cities and go to museums. No other fantasies could be obtained. She did recall that as a child she had a favorite fantasy game: she would sit in an overstuffed chair, sometimes draped in some curtains, and imagine that she was a queen. The fantasizing disappeared abruptly and irretrievably during latency years.

Yet, despite this seemingly total inhibition of fantasy, she did enjoy watching television. However, she insisted that when she turned off the set she never continued to think about the story that she had just seen nor to elaborate on it. Once the television was turned off the story "disappeared." She also enjoyed reading spy mysteries.

All of this patient's productions in therapy were factual, relating events and concerns that had taken place since the previous session. No associations to her material were available as formal activity.

Another example of the impairment of these patients' capacity for fantasy and association is their difficulty in utilizing dreams. Most of them seldom dream and then only very simple, "one sentence" dreams. When asked to associate to the dreams, they are unable to do so. When pressed, they finally produce more *details* of the dream, but rarely can learn to associate to them (Krystal, 1979). Fain and David (1963) studied impairment in dreaming and unconscious fantasy formation in alexithymic patients. They showed that there was particularly a failure to create fantasies to deal with infantile and present-day conflicts. Likening the severity of disturbance to that of psychotic patients, they explained that the alexithymics will develop psychosomatic illnesses whereas a schizophrenic will develop a psychosis. The cost to the alexithymic is the surrender of and inability to exercise unconscious and preconscious fantasies or to utilize dreams to expand conscious thoughts and fantasies. This difficulty illustrates what some authors mean when they say that the psychosomatic process is the opposite of the psychoanalytic one (McDougall, 1974a, 1980b; de M'Uzan, 1974a, b). McDougall, (1974a) described these patients as "antineurotic," in the sense of being unable to create neurotic defenses, but also "antipsychotic" in the sense of being "over-adapted" to reality and the difficulties of existence. De M'Uzan (1974b) also summed up: "Operatory thinking has no appreciable relationship with un-conscious fantasies" (p. 106).

The capacity for fantasy-making and symbolization permits creativity and the formation of neuroses. Symbolization of a conflict makes possible dealing with the cognitive aspect of an affect such as anxiety. In the absence of such capabilities, patients have to contend with the "expressive," that is, the physiological aspects of their affective responses, and thus are prone to psychosomatic illnesses. Alternatively, they may try to block these responses by the use of drugs, thus resorting to the pattern underlying the addictions.

The implications of chapter 12, on the relationship of the self-representa-tion and the capacity to take care of oneself, are so immense that they require repetition and extensive consideration. My view is that the self-representation is severely limited and *all vital and affect functions are experienced as part of the object-representation.* Carrying out any "mothering," life-preserving, or soothing activities is reserved for the "external" mother or her substitute and proscribed for the subject. Their self-presentation is one of a child for whom "taking-over" of these maternal functions is forbidden and very dangerous.

Case Illustration

Patient C., whose problems contained certain addictive and psycho-somatic elements, also had moderately severe alexithymia. He opened the session to be summarized here by commenting that after the previous day's session he had felt very relaxed and had slept for a very long time, as if he had "been drugged." He mentioned that this morning he had attended his biofeedback training session, which he had skipped twice before.[1] Some of his feelings about going to the biofeedback training were explored, including some transference resistance related to feelings of rejection and oral deprivation.

During the previous session, comments had been made about the nature of his feelings and experiences, but these failed to deal with his "conflicts" as well as other elements of a perfect interpretation. It became clear that since no interpretation was truly complete, he always did and always would feel deprived. The patient responded by describing that when he feels that the therapist does not respond to him "adequately," then he has *physical* sensations of emptiness and hunger; and when he feels that the therapist has been mistreating him (i.e., rejecting him), then the predominant reaction is tension, particularly in the muscles of his upper extremities. The flexor muscles in his shoulders and arms become tense and sore. This was identified as the physical component that he experienced at times *instead* of becoming aware of anger or fear.

He then observed that when in these states of distress, he was completely helpless. It was not possible for him to help or relieve this distress, except with the use of some external agent such as food or drugs. It was up to the therapist to do something about it; the therapist must first realize his distress and understand and explain to him what is the matter and instantly relieve it.

In the course of explaining to the patient the nature of his effective experience—how he could not even ask for help and how he felt that certain types of physical distress were beyond his province—his feeling that certain types of distress were beyond his province was also reviewed. It was pointed out that one reason he was having difficulties attending the biofeedback training had to do with the information he was now supplying—notably that not only was he unable to sooth or comfort himself, but also such activities were prohibited for him, as was the acquisition of any such skill.

The patient supplied additional information about his feeling of being prohibited from any self-soothing, vital, or affective function. He described a number of rituals designed to ward off his physical distress (involving precursors of anxiety and guilt). The patient had the kind of feeling that is institutionalized in religion—that he was not capable of assuring his own comfort, just as he could not *assure* his salvation. Not only could he not help himself to the Holy Sacrament, but until recently he was not even permitted to touch it with his hand! These proscriptions represent an incorporation within religion of the process of disowning these parts of functions and attributing them to the maternal object-representation.

---

1. This patient had decided to use biofeedback training on the recommendation of a nutritionist-internist, for two separate purposes: (1) to modify his eating pattern, and (2) to learn to utilize a relaxation procedure instead of food or drugs to counteract the anxiety and tension states.

The kind of transference behavior demonstrated in this case was studied most insightfully by McDougall (1978). She pointed out that these patients were blocked from making their needs known, from verbalizing and listening, and from observing their mental processes. McDougall understood that the alexithymic kind of speech is "an *act* rather than a symbolic means of communication of ideas or affect. Rather than seeking to communicate moods, ideas, and free associations, the patient seems to aim at making the analyst *feel* something or stimulating him to *do* something; this 'something' is incapable of being named and the patient himself is totally unaware of this aim" (p. 179). McDougall went on to describe how these patients become increasingly disturbed, somehow needing the analyst to understand and relieve their distress which they thus signal. She further assumed that such "primitive communications" are "sequelae of early psychic trauma which will require specific handling in the analytic situation" and that "this 'screen discourse' impregnated with messages that have never been elaborated verbally, can . . . be captured only by . . . countertransference affect" (p. 180).

McDougall's cases are illustrative of a posttraumatic inhibition, where the patient is permitted only to signal his distress. All the functions of verbalizing, considering what is needed, and putting it into action is reserved for mother—who alone has the right and the power to sooth the infant.

The inhibitions in regard to self-caring were much more conspicuous and easy to understand than the blocking of the cognitive process. Finally, on coming across cases of people who could not *organize* their thoughts (particularly Edgcumbe's, 1983, case who could not even talk to herself in the presence of the analyst), I realized that this was a kind of transference. In other words, in the presence of a maternal object-representation, the patient felt that she was not supposed to organize her thoughts into a logical, coherent, and interesting communication—and, particularly, that she was not permitted to signify her fantasies, wishes, or desires! Alexithymic patients feel that they must not "take over the maternal function" of making sense of their "babbling," and they have to deny that they are doing it. They are using *time,* pretending that *it* organizes their thoughts, while they, like children, merely signal their distress. This is why they relate a lot of trivial material in chronologic fashion. Edgecumbe's patient did not dare to do any "independent" thinking. When she came home in the evening, or came to an analytic hour, she could not tell what she had on her mind or even what had happened that day—unless she was asked questions to which she could respond by telling what happened to her. When her husband was away, she was able to think by pretending she was talking to her dog, relating her tale to him. Finally Edgecumbe made a transference comment that "made a lot of sense" to her patient: that the analyst had become the part of the patient that did the thinking, and therefore the patient felt incomplete when away from her. Edgecumbe reported that "one of the major technical difficulties throughout the analysis has been to find the right balance between verbalizing feelings and ideas in a way that might be meaningful to her, and falling into the trap of seeming to tell her what she ought to be thinking and feeling" (p. 4).

Just as some neurotic patients with inhibitions related to phallic striving are able to exercise certain functions only if the function that is experienced as forbidden is "concealed" under the pretext that someone else is doing it, the same is true of alexithymics in regard to the inhibition of fantasy and creativity. Thus, we can understand the behavior of Patient C. in this chapter, a woman who had a complete block of any conscious daydreaming, who never reported a dream, but who enjoyed "borrowing" fantasies from television and spy stories. In other words, the inability of alexithymics to consciously assume responsibility for organizing and "composing" their thoughts, and therefore having to depend on a chronological or "thing oriented" scheme for their thoughts is a manifestation of an inhibition.

The very same inhibition of all the other self-caring and self-soothing functions that we have discussed also blocks patients from openly claiming the ability to exercise fully the "adult" potential to use and organize images, memories, and ideas and express them in adult language. Fingarette (1969) has referred to this function as "avowal," which he felt included assuming the authority to integrate the personal interpretation of a thought. The achievement of a synthesis of one's own mental material and acceptance of the responsibility for one's self-governance is commonly one of the demonstrations of being the "in-charge" person, the "grown-up"—a role that is too frightening and is experienced as forbidden by many people.

ALEXITHYMIA AND ANHEDONIA

Another observation that derives from work with states following catastrophic trauma is that alexithymia and anhedonia are separate but concomitant effects of massive traumatization. This coincidence makes anhedonia a very useful "marker" for those cases in which the alexithymia is posttraumatic. Since this subject was discussed at length in the chapter on hedonic regulation, it will be mentioned only briefly here. At this point I want to emphasize the inhibition involved: many anhedonic patients feel that they are not supposed to do anything to make themselves feel good, and that prohibition frequently includes all forms of play. In this area they are much worse off than the inhibited hysterics, who may be able to examine their conflictual (genital or phallic) functions as long as they are "only playing" and not trying to become "real" lovers, mates, parents, or "#1" person in their work. With the alexithymic and anhedonic, we frequently run into situations, described by

Wolff (1977b), in which alexithymics also lose their ability to play. That this problem can be expected to present an obstacle in therapy seems self-evident. In this respect, McDougall (1928b) points out that anhedonic-alexithymic patients are much closer to psychotics than to neurotics in that their anxiety involves the question of whether they may be permitted to enjoy life and be separate individuals. The severe distortion in self-representation is part of McDougall's insight into the question that threatens the patients, namely, whether it is permissible for them to *be* and to take care of themselves.

Finding anhedonia in an alexithymic person indicates that the whole problem is of traumatic origin. All traumatic experiences tend to be experienced as commands; what was most terrible about the trauma was that it was destined for the subject, who deserves nothing better particularly since his own wishes and strivings are often experienced as the very transgression that brought on the punishment. Therefore, the prohibition extends to future wishing, and each goal becomes a source of distress. It is curious that posttraumatic alexithymics have such guilt about any pleasure and gratification that they conceal even minimal gratification. The blocking of the capacity to consciously experience pleasure includes the blocking of playfulness and of experiencing and demonstrating pleasurable emotions. The general attitude becomes one of suppressing and minimizing all achievements and maximizing the negatives.

Under these circumstances, when one proposes treatment to the patient, it is wiser to stress the relief from pain and not allude in any way to the possibility of "feeling better"—such patients could not subscribe to a program promoting well-being or happiness.

IS PSYCHOTHERAPY COUNTERINDICATED?

It is no wonder, then, that we have misgivings about entering into a psychotherapeutic undertaking with alexithymic patients. Alexithymia presents a number of problems in uncovering dynamic, psychoanalytic, or "anxiety-producing" psychotherapy. Patients with active psychosomatic disorders may, instead of experiencing strong emotion, develop a serious or even life-endangering exacerbation of their illness. One must be mindful of Sifneos's (1974) admonition that anxiety-provoking psychotherapy should be counterindicated. In addictive patients, an increase in intensity of their diffuse distress may drive them to drink, or to take whatever their usual form of drug abuse involves (Krystal, 1979).

Most of all, these patients simply do not respond to insights derived from psychotherapy (Nemiah, 1972, 1978, Sifneos, 1972–73, 1974) or to any "form of treatment which emphasized verbal expression and requires a capacity for emotional interaction" (Sifneos, 1973, p. 261). The role of emotions in psychotherapy is so central and essential that we did not catch on to these problems sooner because of our adherence to the conventional "wisdom" that everyone can respond emotionally in an adult fashion but may be obstinately defending against it. Dunbar (1946) and Alexander (1943, 1950; Alexander and French, 1948) assumed that psychoanalytic patients would respond to specific interpretations of their conflicts with adult-type affects, even though the problems themselves did not symbolically represent the conflicts. Pollock (1977) has reviewed years of research at the Chicago Psychoanalytic Institute, in the course of which the earlier (Deutsch, 1926) theories were renounced. A landmark study reported in 1962 (Okun, Grinker, and Sabshin) was the first in which the expression of affect and autonomic specificity was actually observed in a psychoanalytic context. It found that the earlier ideas about the "discharge" of specific affects in a manner corresponding to our metaphors about it were incorrect. Marshall (1972) questioned the assumption that the affective responses in psychotherapy could be taken for granted and pointed out that it just did not work out that way very often. And so we have to return to the observation, first made by Sifneos (1974), that alexithymic patients generally do not benefit from psychoanalytic psychotherapy. Sifneos reconsidered his idea that dynamic psychotherapy was contraindicated for such patients (Sifneos, 1975) and elaborated that "anxiety-suppressive techniques, with emphasis on reassurance and support, possibly in conjunction with psychothropic drugs, are best suited for the majority of these types of psychosomatic patients" (p. 69).

Sifneos's idea that psychosomatic-alexithymic patients should not be treated by anxiety-provoking therapy was related to his seeing it as a *state,* (probably organically determined), a view that was supported by others (Nemiah, 1975; Shands, 1976). Since our (Krystal and Raskin, 1970) experiences were primarily with addictive patients, we saw a greater fluctuation in the alexithymic traits and therefore were less inclined to see it as a fixed, organic state. Hence, though we were also aware of the risks involved in therapeutic intervention with alexithymics, we were not inclined to give up psychotherapy without some attempts to discover the nature of the problem.

My (1962) observations of alexithymic characteristics in patients undergoing heroin withdrawal revealed a mixture of physical symtoms of anxiety and depression that the patients were at a loss to name or describe. We (Krystal and Raskin, 1963) wrote:

> Anxiety and depression may have differentiated only secondarily out of a common physiological distress pattern. In many drug addicted patients, there is a regression in ego function regarding affects with a return of somatic anxiety equivalents, painful symptoms, and dedifferentiation of anxiety from depression attended by a decreased capacity of conscious awareness of affect [p. 6].

When I started to find alexithymic characteristics in Holocaust survivors, with a particularly high incidence in youthful concentration camp survivors, it seemed likely that I was observing a regression—one of the common aftereffects particularly of adolescents—though their backgrounds before the persecution were widely varied. Niederland (1961) also noted "a partial or full somatization, ranging from rheumatic or neurologic pains and aches in various body areas (headaches, tremor), to well known psychosomatic entities (peptic ulcers, colitis, respiratory, and cardiovascular syndromes) usually accompanied by hypochondriacal symptoms" (p. 12).

Anna Freud (1967) commented that evidence of psychic trauma in children may be found in "physical responses via the vegetative nervous system taking the place of psychical reactions" (p. 292). The extremely high incidence of psychosomatic symptoms, which I was finding especially in the youthful survivors, suggested to me (1968a) that their affective responses were resomatized (deverbalized). I felt that because of widespread repression there was a need to substitute "physical" symptoms for the "missing" psychological contents of their reactions (p. 26).

Virtually *all* the patients in this group showed anhedonia, which at the time I conceptualized as follows: "A practically universal finding among 'survivors' is their masochistically tinged tendency toward suffering and expiation, and their inability to enjoy anything in their lives. Most of them have no use for the word 'fun' in their vocabulary" (p. 332). In other words, I was not yet able to distinguish the masochistic, depressive blocks of the hedonic regulation from the more profound and mysterious anhedonia proper.

We also reported that 44% of the patients suffered "disturbances of cognition" (p. 330). The incidence of psychosomatic disorders in this group as a whole was 30%, but in the group of patients who were 15–30 years old during the persecution, the incidence of psychosomatic diseases was 55–60% (p. 337). Struck by this difference in the incidence of psychosomatic disease, I (1971) did another study of patients who had been subject to severe persecution in their childhood and early adolescence. In reviewing the findings on 65 survivors born between 1928 and 1940 (thus 5–17 years old during their incarceration), I observed a very high rate of sleep disturbances, chronic (mostly physical) signs of hypervigilance, "depression-anxiety," and, virtually without exception, characterological and psychosomatic problems. In contrast to the plethora of physical and adjustment problems (difficulties at home, at work, and socially), the patients could hardly explain to me anything that bothered them. They were aware of a feeling of foreboding, but they could not explain it. Thirty-three percent told me that they feared that the Nazis were coming back (p. 22–23).

The impressive inability to verbalize affective states, which was most striking in regard to those persistent "depression and anxiety" states, proved to be true of all emotions. Gradually I became aware of the general inability of these survivors to function in symbolic cognitive ways. These patients were, for instance, unable to associate to their dreams but supplied more of the dream instead of associations.

My personal struggle was to find the common elements in posttraumatic patients, predominantly concentration camp survivors, that could explain their difficulties in psychoanalytic psychotherapy. I did find a good deal of variation from one patient to another and sometimes within a given patient. After I identified the pattern, I found that some patients, who were neither Holocaust survivors nor identified (by me) as addictive personalities, also sometimes showed the very same characteristics.

At present it may be useful to separate the consideration of psychotherapy for the alexithymic, "antianalytic," or, as McDougall (1984) now calls them "disaffected," from that of the classical psychosomatic syndromes. The consideration is slightly different because, as Reiser (1978) reported, since these patients may develop serious, even occasionally fatal exacerbations of illness during psychotherapy, treating them with psychoanalytic psychotherapy for the psychosomatic illness is not indicated. However, Reiser would reconsider the patient's psychological and psychosocial point of view and find it necessary to intervent psychotherapeutically for the purpose of analyzing the "neurotic layers of the personality—with particular attention to maintenance of adequate ego defenses, nurturance of supportive aspects of the therapeutic alliance, and avoidance of intense frustration in the transference neurosis . . ." (p. 72).

The question of what to do about alexithymia depends on what we think it is and in regard to this question there is quite a bit of diversity.

THE NEUROPSYCHOLOGICAL VIEW

The early clinical descriptions we can equate with alexithymia go back to Ruesch (1948). He described the character traits of psychosomatic patients with various disorders and called them "infantile personality." MacLean (1949), in his work on the "visceral basis" and what he named "the limbic cortex," anticipated that psychosomatic disturbances would likely have something to do with an inhibition of higher centers and overresponse of the more primitive paleomammalian, or reptilian, level centers. Shands (1948) considered that patients with an inability to describe their feelings would be unsuitable for psychotherapy. Later (1977), he commented that one can know one's own feelings only by "converting them into descriptions: the bizarre limitation is that when one can do so, he cannot *know his own feelings.* That is, to have feelings in the 'introspective' sense requires *having been able* to 'externalize' these feelings in verbal patterns" (p. 29).

Sifneos (1967, 1975) felt that the alexithymic phenomenon had a biological or developmental cause and that it was a matter of inborn predisposition. A more specific formulation followed (Nemiah, Freyberger, and Sifneos, 1976) based on Nemiah's (1975) view of a *neurological* model, suggesting that alexithymia could be best understood in terms of disturbances in basic function. Specifically, they viewed the cause of psychosomatic illness and associated disturbances in affect expression as physiological, involving a deficiency in transmission of messages from the "visceral brain" to the language centers of the cortex. Nemiah indicated that a blockage of paleos-triatal dopaminergic tracts, which would interrupt or diminish the flow of information from the hypothalamus to the cortex, would explain the symptoms of alexithymia.

Nemiah built his work on that of Stevens (1973), who reported that in schizophrenia there is a flooding of the neocortical sensory imputs (memories and affects) from the limbic area. Nemiah (1975) thought alexithymia would be the obverse of schizophrenia—achieved by an excessive blocking of "impulses from the amygdala and other limbic structures via the inominate to the neocortex" (p. 145). Particularly interesting about this idea is that neurophysiologists and neuropharmacologists working on the effects of neuroleptics in schizophrenia also entertain a major theory of anhedonia based on similar constructions. A current version of the hypothesis holds that "all life's pleasures—the pleasures of primary reinforcement and the pleasure of their associated stimuli—lose the ability to arouse the animal . . . may be transmitted through the same tracts and . . . anhedonia may be caused by dopamine depletion" (Wise, 1982, p. 41). If both Nemiah and Wise are right, then a psychophysiological mechanism has been demonstrated in which alexithymia and anhedonia can be caused by a single factor in one location.

The best documented anatomical causes of alexithymia are the "split brain" studies Hoppe and Bogen (1977) have reported on 12 cases of commisurotomized (by division of the corpus callosum, which links the two hemispheres) patients who showed, among other deficits, severe alexithymia. Hoppe (1977) and associates (Ten Houten et al., 1985a) did careful follow-up studies confirming the alexithymia in the divided brains. They demonstrated the role of hemispheral localization of affective function and showed the importance of hemispheric interaction in the production of normal affective responses. These findings indicate that the

left hemisphere is linguistic, analytic, logical, sequential, and constructive, whereas the right hemisphere is specialized in visual-spacial, synthetic, and Gestalt perception. Without the right hemisphere we are not able to sing in a melodic way and we have difficulty in perceiving the whole Gestalt. The right hemisphere senses the forest, so to speak, while the left one cannot see the forest for the trees [Hoppe, 1981, p. 6].

Hoppe's findings are very instructive. A patient with a right hemispherec-
tomy is able to dream, but the dream shows no "dream work"; it is very close
to reality and logical. Commissurotomized patients have dreams, recall them,
and are able to work with them, but "there is a lack of condensation,
displacement or symbolization." Their fantasies are "unimaginative, utilitarian, tied to reality; the symbolization is concretistic, discursive, rigid" (p. 6).

Another neurophysiological explanation related to Hoppe's work was
offered by Buchanan et al. (1980). These authors showed that any, even
subtle, dysfunction of the right (nondominant) hemisphere would greatly
alter affective function and affect verbalization. They emphasized that alexithymia was not a simple "organic symptom," but an interaction of the
neurological changes with personal and environmental forces. There is no
question about the reliability of findings that hemispheric disconnection
results in alexithymia plus memory deficits, declining sexual interest, reduced
initiative, and curtailed imagination. A positive finding is "hypersocial stability," which I think means that such patients are obedient and easy to manage.
They give only concrete responses: "unimaginative, discursive, and rigid" (p.
283).

A most instructive paper by Hoppe (1979) dealt with a patient whose
hands were each artistically under the control of a different brain hemisphere.
Her creations with each hand reflected the cognitive style of that hemisphere,
and she was in a turmoil because of her inability to integrate these styles.
Hoppe called this phenomenon "deranged bisociation." He applied conclusions from the work of Bogen and Bogen (1969), who postulated that in the
first phase of creativity, each hemisphere develops its processes separately.
Then there is a "creative moment" of free communication between the
hemispheres, and imagery and configurations generated in the right sphere
are realized through the left hemisphere. In Hoppe's patient, the predominant
organization of her memories seemed to be primitive, characterized by a
primary-processlike primitive cognition "mainly processed in the right hemisphere. . . . Communication with the conceptual cognition and secondary
process, predominantly processed in the left hemisphere, gave birth to her
paintings, but simultaneously to the recognition of the discordance and the
painful realization of her endocepts" (p. 24). Hoppe explained that the right
hemisphere is not devoid of speech; it plays a role in speech intonation,
gesture, and expressiveness. It controls melodic and chord progression in
music and spatial relations between objects. In general, it is specialized for a
mode of information that is nonlinear, synthetic, structural, simultaneous,
subjective, representational, and internally focused (Hoppe, 1984, p. 2).

It is worth noting that Hoppe is a psychoanalyst who has worked diligently
with patients with organic lesions as well as with the cited case of an entirely
functional disturbance. Hoppe has been combining psychoanalytic views with
biological observations. Since he started with patients with commisurotomies,

he has provided us with a model of alexithymia as a functional separation or disintegration of the two brain lobes, that is, of the two modes of mental functioning. In effect, then, he suggests that alexithymia could be produced by an analog to an hysterical paralysis or blocking of the corpus callosum. The difficulty with this model is that these patients do not respond to hypnosis as neurotics do (Frankel et al., 1977), neither do they respond to any known psychological tests as neurotics do (Von Rad, 1983). In fact, it could be said that the problem with these patients is that they are *not* hysterics. In other words, we are dealing with a different dimension of problems, even though we grant that there is no reason we could not imagine such an analogy in the abstract. The fact is, however, that, unlike neurotic patients, these are very unsensitive, unimaginative, and unsuggestible people—although neither are they operational like the compulsives. McDougall wrote of the profound nature of the alexithymic's conflicts, pointing out that "psychosomatosis in respect to the depth of the problems, is not far from psychosis. The nature of the conflicts is not the kind we see in the neuroses, but a much more infantile one" (1982b, p. 382).

As studies on alexithymia improve and accumulate, we find additional evidence of functional and reactive developments (Freyberger, 1977) and posttraumatic states (Shipko, Alvarez, and Noviello, 1983; Krystal, Giller, Cicchetti, 1986). There is also growing evidence of organic hereditary factors in the background (Heiberg and Heiberg, 1977).

PSYCHOANALYTIC APPROACHES TO ALEXITHYMIA

We are obliged to the group of French psychoanalysts for much more than just describing operative thinking in psychosomatic patients. They have been faithful to one of the best psychoanalytic principles, namely, that exploration and attempts at understanding should proceed parallel to therapy. De M'Uzan (1974a), for instance, while describing the serious obstacles to the "analytical process" represented by operative thinking, asserted, "Some work from which the patient will eventually benefit can, of course, be done, but it remains piecemeal and limited as if set at a distance from the region where the conflicts are principally invested, i.e., the somatic level" (p. 465). The original group of Paris psychosomaticist-psychoanalysts (Marty, de M'Uzan, and David, 1963) tried to explain their observations of operative thinking from the economic point of view of psychoanalysis. They postulated that the key disturbance was an "actual neurosis," that the blocked instinctual drive is discharged directly through the physiological component of affect (the so-called expressive element), and that therefore there is an impoverishment of fantasy elaboration. In other words, psychic energy bypasses the psyche and stimulates the viscera, producing the psychosomatic illness. Since fantasies are not elaborated, the observations generated in psychoanalysis regarding the patient's character are mostly of a negative kind: the missing element. Stephanos (1975), who is psychoanalytically, though not geographically, related to the Paris group, explained that since psychosomatic patients show archaic, automatonlike, and mechanical thinking, analytic therapy should shift "all but inaccessible psychosomatic process into a historical perspective" (p. 178). By this he meant that operative thinking represented a specific deficiency (p. 179), that by virtue of the absence of fantasies, there is an inability to develop attachments and there is a "psychic emptiness," which he likened to Balint's (1968) "basic fault" and Winnicott's (1965) "environmental failure." Stephanos postulated that his patients suffered a "disorder in integration of a body schema and correspondingly 'broken' relations to their physical symptoms: their symptoms remain isolated, unconnected with their body as a whole, and with their psychosocial context" (p. 186). Based on this idea, Stephanos strove to exercise the "optional degree of holding," according to "the individual patient's capacity to tolerate tension, which is a first condition for the onset of the therapeutic regression . . . " (p. 186). He actively promoted what we would consider an idealized dependency (maternal) transference and ensured that the therapist had no intention to be neutral, but on the contrary, was "always there, as a "maternal-father"[2] ready to help him and take care of the patient.

By far the most important, the most imaginative contributor to the understanding of affective disturbances and their meaning is Joyce McDougall. In over 25 years of psychoanalytic practice, she had been especially sensitive to the profound disturbances in her patients that were handled in a self-numbing and self-dehumanizing way. For instance, she has done much work with perversions and, in retrospect, was struck by the realization that in addition to their many "dynamic" problems, her patients lost love from their sexual life. As she summed up (1984), "Sexual perversions are probably the most *alexithymic* form of libidinal expression that exist!" and come to think of it "many analysands whose psychic economy and equilibrium seemed to depend on their sexual inventions, suffered, in addition, from psychosomatic disorders" (p. 82).

In her classic contribution to the psychoanalytic conceptions of alexithymia, McDougall (1974a) elaborated fantasies and reconstructions that made psychoanalytic sense of her colleague's descriptions of operative thinking. McDougall postulated that the problems of the psychosomatic/alexithymic patient went back to early preverbal difficulties. The problems were based on the child's having to use very early forms of relatedness to tune in to mother's unconscious mind—and there the question revolved around whether the mother would permit the loss of magical union. Little Narcissus' tragedy started when he could not see his reflection in his mother's eyes.

---

2. A term and technique suggested by Marty and Parat (1974).

The problems are more global in psychosomatic/alexithymics than in neurotics. The question here is whether the child may be permitted to be a separate individual. Though psychosis is the alternative, the denial of one's identity subtly erodes the connecting link between one's self-representation and the potential love-object representation.

But the original humanization, in which the mother seduces the child to live, is the cornerstone on which "the creative process destined to give each individual his identity" (p. 438) is built. A number of observations are of missing connections and fantasies, yet one can see the elaboration of psychosomatic problems involving creativity, problems that were life-saving under the circumstances they developed. McDougall focused on the difference between alexithymic patients and neurotics: Alexithymics "often show little spontaneous fantasy, whether attached to their somatic affliction or other aspects of their lives, it is an important note for the attuned ear of the analyst. One may become aware as it were of listening to a song in which the words are present but the melody is missing" (p. 444).

In contrast to neurotics, who are able to elaborate fantasies about themselves and their objects and then have to contend with affective responses to the conflict generated by their conflicts, alexithymic-psychosomatic patients manage to split their self-representations and eliminate wide areas of their bodies from their psychic self-representation. As McDougall (1974a) saw it, these patients manage to totally destroy the mental representations of their own parts and parts of their object-representations. The outcome is a robotlike existence, with what appears to be a superadaptation to reality after the world of imagination and feelings has been eliminated. The supernormal robot is the future psychosomatic patient.

Fain (1971) felt that as a result of a disturbance in mothering there is a symbolic gap between the mental representation of oneself and of the maternal object; hence it is impossible for the child to form the matrix of the mental mechanism by which bodily needs can be satisfied through self-activities. As we are used to saying, there is a "block to the establishment of a benign introject." McDougall (1974a) correctly infers that "unusually severe prohibition of every attempt on the baby's part to create autoerotic substitutes for the maternal relationship . . . vitiates the nodal point for the creation of inner object-representations and nascent elements of fantasy life" (p. 447). To repeat a basic formulation, McDougall explains that "there is a breakdown in object relations due to the attempt to make an external object behave like a symbolic one and thus repair a *psychic* gap" (455). She borrows Bion's idea of "attacks on linking" to explain that here, too, we see "an attack on fantasy life and on the capacity to represent affects. The absence of neurotic, perverse and psychotic mechanisms is a danger signal to the soma" (p. 655). Thus McDougall sees the "basic fault" as the lack of identification with a caretaking mother.

In her 1978 paper, McDougall reported an important discovery—the very same one described here in chapter 9— that severe psychic trauma in infancy cannot be related by the patient or reconstructed by the analyst in the "ordinary" way, that is, by the method devised for dealing with the neuroses. Instead, "psychic suffering at this presymbolic stage is indistinguishable from physical suffering" (p. 177). Consequently, the patient is unable to tell us about it directly or symbolically as no memory traces are verbalizable.

Although such patients may present some sexual complaints, that is not where their significant problems lie. Their real difficulty will show itself to be an inability to get over, or even grasp, pain or bereavement over the loss of maternal transference objects. The issues are really related to the integration and feeling of one's own self, including one's physical sensations and limits. " 'Deviant' sexual desires have been given up *without compensation of any kind*. Instead there is destruction of affect and a loss of symbolic representation of sexual desires" (McDougall, 1978, p. 453).

Since McDougall (1974a) saw the cognitive disturbance in the alexithymic as an absence of, or failure to form essential self- and object-representations and functions, she explained it as a lack of symbolic structures with which one could represent one's wishes and affective states. In the absence of symbolic and fantasy construction to process and contain the message, all that is experienced is a sense "being submerged and losing one's identity" (p. 449).

It is a shocking realization for a therapist to discover that some patients are yearning for a fusional communion and neither understand nor accept communication as a symbolic means of making their needs known.

McDougall makes another point of great significance: the orientation requiring that one be understood as a proof of love—the demand to be understood without words—makes every refusal, or every inability to gain wish fulfillment, horrifying. Therefore, these patients are not able to face the painful realities of life. (I stress particularly their *inability to accept the limitations of the power of love*.) But, as well, all negatives become a narcissistic wound that cannot be psychically elaborated—hence there is no motivation to develop affect tolerance. Therefore, these patients are not able to accept the painful realization of the helplessness involved in "otherness, sexual difference, the impossibility of magic fulfillment of wishes, or inevitability of death. . . . Consequently life becomes meaningless and hard. . . . Other people tend to be seen as vehicles for *externalizing* this painful inner drama of living" (McDougall, 1978, p. 197).

The difficulties posed by McDougall's formulations are mainly with the emphasis she places on the absence or total destruction of basic and essential elements of self-representations and object-representations. Her application of Bion's (1959) thoughts results in the view that attacks on linking virtually destroy the feasibility of object relations. With the widespread destruction, elimination, and foreclosure of major parts of object-representation and self-representation, including of one's body image, one feels as if the mental matrix on which any symbols, wishes, or memories can be reconstructed, are gone. Even bone healing requires the preservation or restoration of such a cellular reticulum.

I feel that something *mental* has to have been retained in these patients if we are going to help them mentally. In this respect, McDougall's own case material seems to be at odds with her theoretical formulations. In many of her case vignettes, given an accurate (though very "deep") interpretation, the patients responded with recognition and elaboration of the themes and conflicts suggested. I think that McDougall is well aware of this problem, and that is why she is searching for some term like "repudiation" or "foreclosure" to indicate that which she sometimes calls a "gap." Sometimes she indicates that there has been destruction of mental material without replacement by anything. At times she seems to say that certain mental representation is absent, but at other times she seems to refer to ideas that are somehow more profoundly defended than in the case of repression. They are, perhaps, repressed more deeply than she suggests. McDougall seems to be aware of an implicit paradox as she describes her patients who "intently eliminated all trace of (her) words and their profound affect impact." She comments, "This kind of psychic repudiation or foreclosure is of a quite different order from that of either repression or denial of affectively toned ideas and experiences" (1984, p. 395). Interestingly, she retains these formulations in that paper, but in order to travel lighter she rids herself of some ballast—the term alexithymia. Instead she calls her patients "dis-affected," but they look and sound just as they did before. In fact, McDougall notes that they are also the same ones whom she previously referred to as "antianalysands in analysis" (1972, 1984, p. 387).

Still the problem remains. If the patients did succeed in destroying most areas of their mental representation and affectivity, why are we even trying to treat them psychoanalytically? The answer involves a great complexity and integration of somatic, heuristic, and ceremonial aspects of the self-experience. The problem with McDougall's formulation is that terms like foreclosure, destruction, and destruction of linking imply that we are now dealing solely with a deficit. However, there is evidence, even in the work of McDougall, that assuming fully conscious and acknowledged, openly admitted self-responsibility and self care still is *conflictual,* still is subject to variation in degree, and still involves regression. But I will have to build up a few more points of observation and departure before I can reconsider this dilemma.

ALEXITHYMIA: A REGRESSIVE PHENOMENON

Alexithymia varies in intensity from one case to another and sometimes within the same individual. While there are neither adequate instruments to test large populations nor enough experience to determine the overall incidence, it is clear that not all psychosomatic patients show clinically diagnosed alexithymia. Assuming, as I do, that we are dealing with a regression or a developmental arrest, I do not expect alexithymia to present the same picture in every affected person. Rather, we must look for differences in intensity or extensiveness of involvement of one's functions by blocking. On one hand, there will be fluctuations in the affective and cognitive disturbances; on the other, I think that ultimately we will need to evaluate the degree of inhibition of self-caring and self-regulating functions. Becoming acquainted with patterns of cognitive self-caring and affective inhibition makes it possible to recognize an alexithymic person sometimes at first glance. For instance, a patient who comes in for his first interview may say, "My friend asked me if I was apprehensive about seeing you. Should I be apprehensive?" Granted, this is a typical conversation showing that he is used to asking other people how he should feel, but we cannot decide in advance for him. What does he feel, and how has he felt in the past? What does he know about the experiences, meaning, and uses of apprehension?

The elaboration of the genetic point of view of affects, the nature of affect tolerance, and the studies on psychic trauma have prepared us for a reconsideration of the alexithymia picture. First of all, we have to recall the difference between infantile psychic trauma and the adult catastrophic trauma, and instantly we are prepared to expect that a variety of pictures will be found, depending on whether we will deal with an arrest in development or a regression.

This framework permits an understanding of those findings in which alexithymia is definitely reactive and where a regression is also apparent in other spheres, as has been reported in severe and life-threatening illness (Freyberger, 1977) and posttraumatic states (Krystal, 1968c, 1978a, c; Krystal and Raskin, 1970). This approach also permits an understanding of why alexithymia varies in severity and how the regression from verbalized, desomatized, and differentiated affects toward the resomatized and undifferentiated form represents a predisposition to psychosomatic diseases (Krystal, 1979).

As already mentioned, alexithymia represents a major factor favoring substance dependence and a serious obstacle to the patient's capacity to utilize psychoanalytic psychotherapy. The basic issue is whether the person has achieved enough affect maturation to make his emotions useful as signals to himself. Emotions that are in the primitive form show a predominance of physical responses and are so vague and undifferentiated that they only call attention *to themselves rather than to what they signal.* Hence, like the patient with a bellyache, this patient wants the pain stopped—rather than paying attention to the pain as a sign of danger. The clinical characteristics of alexithymic patients that can alert us to the problem may be grouped into certain categories that will be discussed presently.

AFFECTIVE DISTURBANCE

These patients' emotional responses are physical and often involve a variety of bodily systems. It is striking that when people who have been addicted are under emotional stress, their responses are very similar to those of the withdrawal state. The reason is that in withdrawal from drugs there is also a "rebound" of the mixed, undifferentiated affect precursors on the physical level. Among drug addicted populations one can see the regression particularly clearly. The most common regression is the dedifferentiation of anxiety and depressive responses. Back in 1933, Rado observed that addictive persons suffered of a "tense depression." In withdrawal they have symptoms of depression and anxiety but do not complain of, nor are able to describe, either (Krystal, 1962).

In contrast to these addictive patients, the alexithymics who have psychosomatic diseases seem to be especially insulated from the impact of the affect equivalents. They show a particular stoicism and a lack of awareness of their physiological disturbances. They also frequently show a rigid posture and expressionless face. But, despite their preference to be unmoved and untouched by anything, they do in fact show a great deal of variation. I have already mentioned the diurnal one—many alexithymics become especially aware at the end of the day that they cannot tell whether they are tired, hungry, bored, depressed, or coming down with the flu, and may use any and all remedies at once. However, the observations also go the other way. Psychosomatic patients may have episodic relapses of their psychosomatic illness after stressful life developments. One patient would develop hives and sometimes even angioneurotic edema after disappointments. He also had asthma, which seemed to have been brought on by situations that might have resulted in anxiety. Another patient, who used to have ulcerative colitis, said, "Now that I don't get burning in my gut, how will I be able to tell when I am angry, and, even more importantly, how will I be able to tell when I am in love?"

Alexithymic traits have been described in the past. For instance, Wurmser (1978), in his encyclopedic study of the addictive syndromes, stressed that a narcissistic crisis followed by a flooding by feelings that are "overwhelming, global, archaic, physically felt, [and] cannot be articulated in words" (p. 109) constitutes the point of maximum vulnerability to the vicious circle of drug use and further regression. Wurmser also pointed out that there is a breakdown of affect defense following which only a vague but unbearable tension" (p. 109) may be the only manifestation of the emotional disturbances: "There may be a longing, a frantic search for excitement and relief, a sense of aimless, intolerable restlessness, and a craving (not unlike the one later seen in withdrawal)" (p. 109). After reviewing the various specific defenses against the regressed affects by matching the drug to the prevalent disturbances, and studying some of the ego defenses, in particular externalization, Wurmser talks of *"hyposymbolization,"* which brings us back to the other aspect of alexithymia.

OPERATIVE THINKING

Along with impairment in verbalization of the emotions, the patients show a general diminution of the capacity for wish fulfillment fantasies, on a level of both conscious daydream and preconscious fantasy. In the adult alexithymic, one is often misled by the appearance of superb adjustment to reality. However, in psychotherapy, one is treated to a boring, chronological repetition of the trivial details of everyday life. This characteristic "operative thinking" (Marty and de M'Uzan, 1963) involves a preoccupation with "things" at the expense of object relations. The combination of impairment in the capacity for fantasy and abstract thinking, and the lack of affective clues, deprives the patient of the ability to emphasize and to be emotionally involved with significant objects. This development results in a particularly "dead" and dull transference relationship as well.

Interpreting these expectations to alexithymic patients would find no internal dissonance with such views. In fact, their relations with people around them are of the same utilitarian, exploitative type. Further, the patients tend to treat themselves and everyone around them as machines. One of the major uses of drugs is to establish "perfect" control over their bodies, to which they take an inimical attitude. The objects, as McDougall (1974b) wrote, are experienced as essential, but replaceable. De M'Uzan (1974b) has called this phenomenon "reduplication . . . a perception of other people strongly marked by a sort of global translation of a rough image of oneself, stripped of truly personal traits and indefinitely reproducible according to as stereotyped form" (p. 106). Many of these schemes and ideas were developed in the course of struggling with the transference manifestations of these patients.

OPERATIVE THINKING AND THE PROBLEMS OF TRANSFERENCE

The foregoing discussion of cognitive disturbance in alexithymia pointed out how it affects these patients' object-representations. Naturally, this problem manifests itself in the type of transference these patients form. It is characterized by being modeled on the medical relationship and on its coolness, detachment, distance, and lack of concern (Nemiah and Sifneos, (1970b). De M'Uzan (1974b) warned:

What is striking is the very slight interest that the patient shows in the analyst. The relationship is courteous and correct but libidinally very poor. The organization of this relationship seems to be conventional and personalized to such a small degree that the neurotic mechanism seems to be lacking. A sort of inertia, noticed during the preliminary interview, persists and results in a stagnant situation [p. 462].

This kind of transference behavior sometimes results in countertransference responses of boredom and a feeling of despair and helplessness, which may be warded off by withdrawal, with a possible retreat into sadistic or erotic fantasies (Taylor, 1977). McDougall (1974b) has expressed the concern that as the elusiveness of the patient's psychosomatic mechanism may be experienced by the analyst as a "narcissistic affront to his interpretive powers," the countertransference may "lead many an analyst to a lack of interest in his patient's psychosoma" (p. 444). This astute observation goes a long way to explain our professional reserve toward psychosomatic, addictive, and other alexithymic patients. Inasmuch as these patients' capacity for fantasy is diminished, the psychotherapeutic process is stifled by their need to continue certain types of object-relations. For instance, it can be said that the "doctor" transference is, in fact, a representation of the oral receptive attitude and that behind it lies a variety of fantasies of oral gratification and theories of the illness as a deficiency, and behind that a problem of ambivalence, envy, splitting, and idealization. But, in fact, the problems of transference beyond these accustomed reactions are very profound. McDougall (1978) explained a major part of the contents in her paper on primitive communications in analysis. As I pointed out, the behavior of the patients demonstrated—beyond their ability to verbalize their emotions and use the communicated symbols—the prohibitions against them to do so.

The point is that we are dealing with a different kind of maternal transference, the kind we discussed in the chapter on self-care and self-representation. It has long escaped our attention that dealing with the maternal transference is difficult for a number of reasons. The maternal transference refers to the primary object-representation, that is, the mothering parent. The conflict is whether it is permissible for one to claim authority and control over all of one's self-representation and exercise the care of all of it. The affect precursors in the infant are so threatening that, as we have already noted, the task of establishing homeostasis requires such special maternal talents that the experience may be less than perfect. For these and other reasons, the child may be faced with enormous aggression—strong enough to trigger the whole distress affect-precursor pattern, bringing on the state of infantile psychic trauma, or as Stern (1951a) called it, the "biotrauma" disaster. There need not be an outright failure in the mothering function nor an identifiable disaster such as colic or a major illness, in order for the kind of traumatization that I described in chapter 12 to take place. I am referring to the premature

disruption of the illusion of unity that confronts the child with an uncontrollable external object who has become the possessor and ruler of wide areas of
his or her self-representation. The problems of aggression are complicated by
another well-known problem, namely, that many mothers experience the
infant's crying as an attack on themselves and an accusation of incompe-
tence. The ability of the mothering parents to maintain their poise and not
become hurt, insulted, or defensive is of life-and-death importance to the
infant. Moreover, various transformations of this conflict persist in many
families for a long time. Many people are shaped by the need to meet the
special needs of their narcissistic or borderline mothers and to "twist themselves into a pretzel" in order to fit the mother's fantasy of them (Miller, 1981,
1983, 1984). But in trying to understand the nature of infant–mother
interaction, we are forever getting lost in oversimplification.

Yes, the process of affect development does involve the mothering parent's
responsiveness to the infant's differentiation of vocal, gestural, and postural
signals. But, in addition, we also have to be aware of the parallel process of
the development of the communicative process (Edgcumbe, 1981) and of
certain rituals developing in the interaction of the baby's crying, to which the
mother attributes communication value and concludes that "he is crying
because he is hungry." She initiates a series of actions that the child soon
learns to recognize as preparatory to feeding and thus works out a nonverbal
set of communicative responses and expectations. In other words, a kind of
code is developed that remains active for life and that represents a sensorimotor underpinning to communicative and affective function (Brinich, 1982).

Next, in the context of the foregoing observations, we have to appreciate
that the mother accepts, as affective communication, a smile or gesturelike
movement by the child, even though the child might be incapable of
awareness of his own affective or communicative performance. Gaensbauer
(1982) carefully followed the development of a troubled child and reported
that "facial expressions of direct emotion" were observable at the age of less
than four months (p. 51). Moreover, these affective facial expressions were
consistent with the infant's life conditions and were effective in communicating essential messages to the empathic observers, which led to important
caretaking decisions. Because the affective responses had defensive and
adaptive value, Gaensbauer recognized affects of the infant from four months
on as "serving to organize inner experiences and facilitate adaptation" (p.
51). Not only were these affective expressions functional, but they could be
observed in transference precursors. For example, an infant treated well in a
foster home was able to be reunited comfortably and joyously with the
mother, which would not have been the case had the caretaking been poor.
Still, there is no clue to the psychic reality involved nor of the contribution of
these experiences to lasting affectively charged self- and object-representation
and potential future transferences.

In considering the affective core of the prerepresentational self, Emde

(1983) proposed that if we view the self as a process, then we can identify three biological principles in its organizational progression from early self-processes at 15 months to early self-awareness in the second year: 1) self-regulation, 2) social fittedness, and 3) affective monitoring. The last, which is a rich and complex area, is social in the sense that the infant's affective responses are guiding the parental responses, while, at the same time, the infant uses affective monitoring to guide his own behavior. And this becomes part of the self-caring functions as well as part of the communicative interactions between child and parent.

Since we now know that the affective core of self- and object-representation goes back to the age of four months, we cannot continue to look exclusively for the kinds of transferences that we learned to recognize in neurotic patients. Those memories referred to the affects and fantasies of a preschool child as successfully reviewed and matured in adolescence. To prepare ourselves to deal with the kinds of transference we see in alexithymia, we review what took place in infancy and the toddler stage. Particularly, we have to consider the emotional availability of the mothering parent and the degree of success—the yield, as it were—of the emotional referencing that is so vital in the formation of a consciously registered self-representation.

The chapter on direct observations of infantile development of affect was intended to alert us to the transference consequences of the developments of homeostasis, attachment, separation, individuation, and, most important, how these phases affected the psychic reality of the child and shaped the capacity for expanding one's consciously recognized nature of oneself.

Emde's (1983) study on social referencing showed not only an awareness of oneself, but a relationship of confidence with a caretaker who is invested with trust and certainty that one's safety can be put in the caretaker's hands. Paradoxically, this kind of trust can be found in the transference of alexithymic patients—not in their verbal productions, but in their need to be cared for totally, which produces frequently unnoted trancelike states. As Brinich (1982) and Emde (1983) have reported, many of the most essential communications are not verbal but must be picked up by a glance, a movement, or other nonverbal affective clue.

If we consider why there is a poor fit between a mother and her child—in other words, if we inquire why the alexithymic's mother's responses were not "contingent" with his needs (to use an expression coined by Greenspan and Lieberman, 1980)—we may find that her ability to function optimally is impeded by her own problems. These problems can be derived most relevantly from two sources: inhibition in her ability to fulfill her potential as a mother, or transference or countertransference problems of a neurotic nature. These can be understood to stem from oedipal conflicts. The child may be experienced as the mother's own mother was experienced in her childhood or as an incarnation of the mother's own infantile self-representations.

We can expect that, in addition to these problems derived from later ages, the baby also brings back to the mother early memory traces of her own self. These memory traces are nonverbal and nonsymbolic and are based purely on affect memory. Excellent examples of such developments can be seen in the works of Main (1977; Main and Weston, 1982). In studying children in daycare situations and experimental stranger situations, Main and Weston established that some children showed angry and avoidant behavior upon the reappearance of the mother (angry crying, hitting, batting away toys, open petulance, etc.). The investigators considered these children to be ambivalently and avoidantly attached to their mothers. But when the mothers were examined, they, for the most part, did not show any specific neurotic reactions or personal difficulties with their own children in particular. Instead, they turned out to be women who had a general aversion to physical contact—a general "don't touch me" attitude and sometimes an unverbalizable physical response of withdrawing, pushing away. Their ability to describe or verbalize was limited to a "yeech" response to cuddling or being held. This response is illustrative of a preverbal affective memory in the mother (a transference reaction). Obviously it would interfere with essential mothering functions and result in potentially serious disturbances in the child. For the child, this affective memory may be the only registration of childhood traumatic experience, of which the only residue is likewise pure affect memory. When the child-become-adult presents himself as a patient with attachment problems or affective disturbances, there will likely be no relevant history obtainable from any family member.

That illustration reminds us that in dealing with the transferences in the alexithymic patient, we have to keep in mind that many transferences are based not on cognitive memory, but on affective memory, which may not have *ever* had any symbolic representation. In the true alexithymic patient, when correct interpretations are given and *feelings* are not registered, the affective responses may still be demonstrated on the physical level (Glucksman, 1981, 1983; Mittelman and Wolf, 1943; Okun et al., 1962). But even if the physiological components can be demonstrated, the patient may still be not be able to use their affects as signals. If patients could understand and process the information, it would confront them with an enormous problem. If we could present to them the necessity to integrate and accept what has happened to them, and the need to grieve and thereby accept the limitations of the powers of love, the limitations of their and our powers—they would most likely angrily reject the proposition. They would likely say that it is *too terrible to be true, too painful to accept.* The idea of an analysis, as designed for a neurotic patient, laid out for an alexithymic patient to see in advance would be rejected on the grounds that it was too terrible to go through or even to consider.

As it happens, this conversation seldom takes place, for such alexithymic patients as drug-dependent, psychosomatic, posttraumatic, "antianalysand", or "dis-affected" ones (McDougall 1984) are secure from such bad news, being protected by those fascinating devices whose descriptions and attempts at comprehension fill this and other volumes.

It is therefore necessary to modify our goals and use the transference and the countertransference to help the patients achieve the possible. Sifneos (1967, 1972–73) clearly understood this point from the beginning. He would (with somewhat of a tongue-in-cheek attitude) advise us to leave the psychosomatic patients to the internists, because "real doctors" get along better with them. That is not only because internists do not try to get to their deep secrets, but also because most nonpsychiatric physicians are willing to continue to act the role of the caretaking parent who enfranchises the patient periodically to continue and to improve his or her self-caring function for specified periods of time under the doctor's authority.

Making a change in the affective attitudes of an alexithymic patient is difficult, but it can be done in a therapeutic atmosphere in which the transference is of virtually hypnotic intensity. That is, the patient is in a trancelike state—a transference of unambivalent love in which the illusional unity of infancy is momentarily restored. In other words, the only way patients can overcome the distrust of the therapist and the prohibition of self-caring is if they are in a regression in which they do not perceive the therapist as a separate person. In these special states (which, as we will see, our European colleagues strive to achieve in their hospitalized patients) the intrapsychic barriers that prevent the patients from exercising their capacities for self-caring and even self-healing may be temporarily suspended. Under such circumstances patients may discover a self-view that they never dared to see before and may be able to make this view part of their self-representations, to reclaim it for their conscious self-recognition.

Alteration in consciousness, heightened suggestibility (in other words, a trance, sometimes called "dissociative reactions"), occurs much more commonly in all kinds of psychotherapy, including psychoanalytic psychotherapy, than is suspected by most therapists. This was the point of our discussion of ecstacy and trances in several places in this book, particularly in regard to trauma. Posttraumatically, persons may retain a susceptibility to submission, but their trust may be so greatly damaged that the submission is experienced as hostile and overwhelming and hence very dangerous. At any rate, the major problem with utilizing trances and such transferences, even in the most benign and careful way, is that they reinforce the alexithymic's typical object relationship. The relationship represents idolatry which is the kind of transference that often results from premature disappointment or loss. The resolution of such transferences is difficult (as discussed in the chapter on integration and self-healing) because the process of disenchantment and grieving is difficult for these patients to handle (Warnes, 1983).

When one attempts to treat these patients as neurotics and interprets their transferences as dependency need or defensiveness against it, the patients cannot react as neurotics do because the affective component is not available and the fantasies cannot be elaborated. McDougall has written a number of papers (1980a, 1982b) in which she talked about the "antianalysand" nature of these patients, who all showed alexithymic traits and some of whom also had psychosomatic disorders. The "antianalysands," McDougall felt, sometimes present themselves very convincingly as good analytic candidates, because their "robot-like structure enables [them] to be correctly 'programmed' in advance for this project" (1980a, p. 340)—a caveat for psychoanalytic institutes' admission committees. However, once these patients are into analytic work, they give a boring recital of information with banality approaching that of mental retardation. They are affectless, do not form or show interest in exploring a transference, and are not at all curious about their problems. These patients live in the present, devitalize their past, lack warmth toward people, and get nowhere in analysis. However, when the analyst offers to stop the analysis, they object and continue plugging away.

SUPPRESSION OF FANTASIES SEEN AS A DEFENSE

The foregoing considerations bring us back to the question of cognitive disturbances or operative thinking. Blocking fantasy in creativity has been demonstrated qualitatively and quantitatively (Demers-Desrosiers et al., 1983; see also next chapter). Particularly instructive are the studies utilizing Rorschach tests (Vogt et al., 1983), which found thinking related to operative thinking to be impersonal, not creative, dry, clichélike, and with a predominance of a factual-realistic orientation. They show "weak possibilities for symbolic expression in psychological contest, ability for abstraction existing but not productive, sensorimotor overemphasis" (p. 71, my translation). The causes of the blocking of wish-fulfillment fantasy and, as far as we can tell, the blocking of most unconscious fantasy are difficult to understand.

This reaction is an illustration of the "psychosomatic process," which, as McDougall (1974b) said, is "the antithesis of the psychoanalytic process" (p. 437). Most conspicuous in operative thinking is the lack of certain fantasies and types of object-representations. Whether there is a true deficiency, however, is questionable. For, although the patients do not produce these fantasies spontaneously, they can "share" or "borrow" them or form them when presented with them in things that they read or see. The earlier mentioned alexithymic patient who tried in vain to imagine what she would like to do for fun on a vacation was certainly able to understand what *other people* would do and imagine doing and enjoying. This patient illustrated that there is no *intellectual* deficit. The "missing symbolic structures" represent an impoverishment of self-representation, as well as blocking by inhibition of conscious wish-fulfillment fantasies pertaining to *oneself*.

As already mentioned, McDougall (1974b) was trying to provide a theoretical framework for this void. She assumed that object-representations were formed by experiencing them "externally," even in a persecutory way, and only secondarily could they be experienced as one's own mental products. However, these patients seemed to have given up their early attempts to form object constancy to reliably available memories and recollections. McDougall felt that psychosomatic patients had "simply lost them." But, she explained, "I would suggest that there are deeply buried archaic fantasy elements encapsulated somewhere in the unconscious, but these are unarticulated linguistically and thus have no access to preconscious thought" (p. 449). Thus McDougall saw the primary problem as a disturbance in the nature of object-representations that are greatly impoverished, as well as in the block of the process of symbolic representation and "symbolic structures" (p. 449). She summarized the psychotherapeutic challenge as pertaining to psychosomatic symptoms: "Because of their non-symbolic quality such manifestations are totally silent before their somatic realization and it is therefore necessary to listen to something which is not there, a psychic gap in which a somatic creation might appear instead of a psychological one" (p. 451).

In a later paper, McDougall (1982a) elaborated her views that despite the wall of "pseudo-normality" there was a great similarity between what she called "psychosomatosis and psychosis":

> Deep uncertainty about one's right to exist and one's right to a separate identity leads to a terror of being in close contact with others: fear of implosion or explosion, i.e., losing one's body limits, one's feeling of identity or the control of one's acts. . . . psychic mechanisms employed to keep primitive terror at bay also reveal some similarities [p. 382].

These similarities are basically that alexithymic patients, like schizophrenics, attack meaning and connections within their own minds, and the attacks on "linking" are particularly in regard to "meanings and attachments to objects, so that an inner paralysis and isolation result" (p. 384). McDougall (1982a) and Taylor (1977) felt that splitting (of the self- and object-representations, I assume) and projective identification are used widely by alexithymic patients with the result that the patients are "unaware that they have split off from consciousness large segments of their inner reality and that a whole series of fantasies and feelings are expelled from their psyche so that they will not feel them" (McDougall, 1982a, p. 385).

OPERATIVE THINKING AND COGNITIVE CONSTRICTION

An alternative view presents itself from the study of "catastrophic trauma" (Krystal, 1979). In the traumatic process, there is constriction of cognition in which memory, fantasy, problem solving, and all other functions become gradually blocked. Frequently, cognition remains severely limited, and from a theoretical point of view this constriction can be considered a form of "primal repression." Primal repression is different in nature and does not appear directly "defensive," nor does it respond to the interpretation of defenses. At least in the posttraumatic alexithymia, this process may be a significant reason for the retention of operative thinking. In any event, it is an enormous challenge to promote the patient's developing a greater scope of fantasy. After the inhibition in this sphere is dealt with, we find ourselves in totally alien territory, with no techniques available to cultivate underdeveloped or deficient functions. The same challenge involves the problem of anhedonia and self-caring. Some therapists have found that sometimes in analytic work when the patients develop the self-analyzing function, they also "seem to develop a self-soothing function . . ." (Nash and Cavenar, 1978, p. 119).

Rather late in my studies of posttraumatic states, I (1978c) discovered the occurrence of cognitive constriction and the inhibition of cognition in the traumatic state. In the patients' own accounts of their experiences, they had not consciously registered this occurrence. Later I realized that even in everyday stress reactions, cognitive constriction sets in early and is a major factor in human behavior in disasters. Moreover, a multitude of studies of coping, decision making, and cognition under *stress* (Janis, 1951, 1971, 1982; Janis and Leventhal, 1968; Sigall and Helmreich, 1969; Hamilton 1975) show a cognitive constriction, an impairment in cognitive function, and even an impairment in the ability to resist rumors at the expense of their own fantasy and cognitive exploration. Mandler (1982) reviewed his own and others' observations—all of which added up to the conclusion that stress and intense emotions narrowed attention, impaired judgment, and diminished cognitive exploration (fantasy). All these widespread inhibitions in cognition, memory, judgment, and the like occur in normal populations. We have already found that in posttraumatic states such susceptibility is greatly multiplied and there is a hypervigilance and hyperreactivity to any stimuli that may be experienced as threatening.

We have also learned that childhood traumatization results in a diminution in interest in people and a turning to "things" (Greenspan, 1981) exactly paralleling operative thinking. New evidence indicates that there is cognitive impairment in abused children (Fish-Murray, Koby, and van der Kolk, 1985). Still, I must confess that the idea that in the traumatic state some superordinary, repressionlike phenomenon takes place, stays in my mind. I am particularly sure that the effects of severe infantile psychic trauma are devastating to the chances of later normal developments. The consequences can be demonstrated on both the psychological and the anatomical level.

But even with the model of adult catastrophic states there are many compelling observations in my work with people who were so irreparably devastated that their social and intellectual level was appallingly low. Others showed a severe impoverishment in some areas, particularly imagination and creativity. And, as I will elaborate later, my experiences showed a high correlation between affective regression and impoverishment in cognition and intellectual life.

The same theme keeps recurring through the work of Cohen (1985), who maintains (in a position with which I find much merit) that there are multiple observational bases for

> a usable theory of primal repression . . . the behavioral manifestations of primal repression in the traumatic state is identical to that in traumatic neurosis (in this term they refer mainly to the conceptions of Kardiner, 1941) which is characterized by loss of effective functioning, diffuse aggression, severe anxiety, inability to sleep or dream, and physiological disturbance. . . . If survived, and whether it occurs first during infancy, childhood or adulthood, the traumatic state results in an absence of structure and representable experience in a region of the self. This absence is primal repression. Clinically, the person is unable to represent his needs. Primal repression gives rise to a variety of mentally primitive self-protective operation, all aimed at avoiding stimuli that provoke it [p. 178].

Cohen felt that under favorable circumstances these protodefenses involve denial, splitting, and projective identification and that many narcissistic and schizoid defenses can be found in the character of survivors. I have to agree with Cohen that what appears to both of us to be a modified primal repression leaves "holes"—areas of unelaborated need-representations. Still, under optimal conditions some elaboration can be achieved that involves repression proper, through which terror is internalized "rather than remaining interpersonal, and a sense of mastery through mental manipulation of culpable wishes and fantasies is achieved" (p. 179).

Our considerations of psychic reality remind us that all of these studies of stress and abuse must be understood from the point of view of the person's living and experiencing, lending meaning to his stress and trauma. Once we reconsider this basic premise, we will be ready to consider that the stress may be self-generated or may be the result of one's own conflicts, even self-judgments.

We should not be surprised at Dorpat's (1985) finding that where there is denial in the psychotherapeutic situation there is also a "cognitive arrest" (p. 4). Dorpat's scholarly work will surely arouse a great deal of interest in the very process we are exploring. It is particularly helpful to note that in his "microanalysis of defenses" Dorpat describes the following four phases of denial reactions: (1) preconscious appraisal of danger or trauma, 2) painful affect, 3) cognitive arrest and, 4) screen behavior (p. 4).

It is good to find myself on familiar turf with material that is in such agreement with chapter 9. Dorpat explains that the painful affect triggers a reaction in which the subject turns his or her focal attention from what is disturbing to something else. A cognitive arrest is brought about by unconscious fantasies of destroying or rejecting whatever is considered to be the cause of the psychic pain (or what [he] termed *painful* object).

> Such unconscious fantasies of destroying the painful object arrest the subject's thinking about the painful object at a primary-process level. . . . The unconscious fantasy attacks on the painful object and the consequent arrest of higher-level cognitive processes are followed by screen behavior [p. 4].

In other words, Dorpat uses a model of microprocessing of perception and cognition similar to Horowitz's (1976) model of stress response processing. Alarm is followed by denial, but the intrusive nature of thoughts about the current stress causes them to penetrate and disturb consciousness, bringing on anxiety and depression. This description corresponds to mine in the chapter on trauma and the stimulus barrier, where we consider the microgenesis of perception and cognition to be involved in the construction and reworking of one's psychic reality. This view, in harmony with the contributions of Arieti (1955) and Flavell (1956), helps us to construct the information-processing approach to cognitive and affective function. There are only two points in need of reiteration: 1) Why does denial cause a cognitive arrest? Dorpat (1985) states, "Whatever is denied continues to be unconsciously active and has far reaching effects on the denier's psychic function" (p. 20). 2) There are disturbances of consciousness and attention: "The cognitive arrest suspends the constructive integrating, and regulatory functions of focal attention and consciousness regarding what is denied" (p. 20). I agree with these descriptions phenomenologically, but I have to go back to the chapters on trauma and affect and on trauma and the stimulus barrier to remind myself that what we observed is that once the traumatic process is initiated, there is a blocking of affects followed by the constriction of cognition. But we also found that any significant stress can initiate catatonoid responses and a blocking and constriction of cognition. Thus, it is not just the denial that causes the blocking of cognition; but, rather, that if the processing of information generates the signal of anxiety and helplessness (as opposed to the activating signal of avoidable danger), then the cataleptic, deactivating aspects of affects make themselves evident.

Once we appreciate the microgenetic process by which perception, impulses, and cognition are processed in the preconscious areas of the mind, then we can understand that it is the affective signal of possible trauma that blocks this transformational process. This is my sense of Dorpat's (1985) statement that denial "aborts this process, thereby preventing the explicit consciousness of whatever is denied, and denial blocks the consciousness of both endogenous and external stimuli" (p. 31).

This view also coincides with that of Basch (1974, 1981), from which

Dorpat (1985) draws conclusions that are in the same spirit as the points made in the chapter on psychic reality in this volume:

> Conflict is . . . not only resolved unconsciously but may present itself to self-consciousness for examination, approval and recycling. What we call self, or acknowledge as being "me" is that aspect of our information processing activity that presents itself in the form of discursive symbols—especially, but not exclusively, those of speech. It is the activity of expressing our thought content in verbal symbols that we call *self,* or more properly should call *selfing* [p. 41].

Dorpat carefully reviewed the literature on primal depression and some related concepts, for example, Basch's (1976) idea that the persistence of sensorimotor presymbolic schemata is adequate to explain infantile "primal repression." Dorpat concluded that the idea of primal repression was identical with denial, as he defined it. He argued cogently that the consequences referred to throughout the literature were the same: All students of this area agree that primitive defenses prevent the formation of verbal representations. As a result, there is no memory in a form that can be recalled. If such experiences are reenacted, they tend to highlight the affective and other developmental defects related to the trauma. I think that Dorpat's work helps us to overcome the difficulties we had with McDougall's idea of foreclosure or repudiation.

Since early in therapy with alexithymic patients one comes up against the "defect" or absence of products of elaborated unconscious fantasy, one is stimulated to go in search of it. Thus, helping these patients to attain a normal level of fantasy-making is of great interest from a theoretical point of view, for in the search we may discover the cause and nature of the problem. Among the most intriguing experiments in this direction has been the use of directed fantasy by Brachfeld and Stokvis (1963): patients were shown pictures and encouraged to form fantasies with the active collaboration of the therapist, who led the patients by his questions. Leuner (1969) has elaborated a similar technique in his Guided Affective Imagery. Tentative explorations by the present author with the use of TAT cards have not produced either significant material or any noticeable increase in the patients' fantasy-making. However, this may not be the end of the story on utilization of TAT cards in this area. Thompson (1981) has used some TAT cards to determine what she called "affect maturity." She used only selected cards and asked different questions from the usual—not about the story of the card, but about who was experiencing emotions about what. She did this because in her studies of the concept of affect development she added two elements: 1) She combined the elaboration of Piagetian ideas by Gouin-Decarie (1965), in which ideational and affective elements were integrated with the work of Riviere (1936), Brierley (1937), and Kernberg (1976). Questions were posed regarding the nature of self- and object-representation from the point of view of affect experience. 2) She integrated an important point by Flavell (1963) and offered it in the service of expanding our conception of the affective experience. Flavell had reported that when the affect experience was under the sway of "preoperational" cognition (ages 2 to 8), although some symbolic representation was available, the general experience was predominantly in presymbolic affect memory. Children are "egocentric"; that is, they cannot conceptualize anything outside of their own perspective and they have not developed the capacity for reflective self-awareness. The child "thinks but cannot think about his thinking" (Flavell cited by Thompson, 1981, p. 59).

But the most important idea that Thompson found in the work of Flavell was that preoperational thought was "irreversible"; that is, it cannot be observed, explored, or reversed, and elements of it cannot be taken apart for modification. This observation is crucial to analyzing and modifying the reaction *dictated* by the affect experience. People whose affects have matured and who can observe and modify their affect experience also are able to tolerate affective incongruity—to bear the idea that a good person can do a bad thing and yet remain good, or that the good object of one's love can also evoke in us painful affects. We learn to deal with these incongruities because they and the distress they generate can be tolerated, accepted, and dealt with through a variety of cognitive options, without our insisting on the all-good perfect nature of object- or self-representations. Concurrent with the introduction of this kind of perspective of the affect evaluation of the object-representation, the child can introduce the *time* element into the affective evaluation. In other words, the child can say "I hate you" to the loved person, understanding that the hateful feeling is a temporary, transient, and forgivable reaction.

On the basis of these contributions, Thompson constructed an affect maturity scale based on the nature of the affect experience—whether it is experienced as an event or as a self-experience, which may also reflect one's evaluation of or reaction to the objects. Thompson strove to measure whether affects are basically attributed to one's self-evaluating function or are experienced as caused, provoked, and controlled by the object.

In intermediate stages, the emotions are attributed to the objects, "but not in a fully independent way. Self and other may be enveloped in the same way (by not very well differentiated) emotions with no understanding of the chance that two people may experience the same emotion but for their own individual reasons" (Thompson, 1981, p. 225). Thompson assumed that at the same level of the scale (three) contradictory emotions exist side by side, and the self was now seen as having some choice about whether or not to act. Affective evaluation of one's impulses and actions is possible and sometimes owned up to. (I am picking this out of the middle of the scale to give an idea of the rather extensive classification.) Each level has five to nine characteristics, which involve such factors as the degree of individuation of self- and object-representations, tolerance of contradictory feelings, the understanding of what I call "the story behind" the cognitive element of the affect, affect verbalization, and reflective self-awareness. Work on the evaluation of affect maturity is being continued (Hering, 1987) and some useful scales and instruments may become commonly available.

The work of Lachmann and Stolorow (1980) indicates that better understanding of affective components has direct implications for the process and technique of psychoanalytic psychotherapy, especially in certain cases. As the authors point out, "an affective state can occur not only as a signal evoked by an unconscious conflict, but also as an indicator of developmental advances in the articulation and consolidation of self- and object representations" (p. 228).

My point, however, is not Thompson's work as a testing instrument, but rather her broad point of view, which demonstrates that we cannot talk about denial and cognitive arrest, or primal repression, or repudiation of cognitive elements without realizing the essential unity of the affective and cognitive elements of alexithymia. Certainly, in dealing with posttraumatic cases, we have to be keenly aware of the self-psychological aspects of survival and the aftereffects, as aptly pointed out by Ornstein (1985). We cannot be squeamish about approaching these patients from various points of view; they will not respond to one particular approach nor to the classical psychoanalytic techniques that work for neurotics.

Robert Langs has extensively studied a kind of patient who behaves in therapy just like the alexithymics and like the "antianalysands" described by McDougall (1980b). In addressing himself to the patient's behavior in the "bipersonal field" and focusing on the *unconscious fantasy* (or "type two") *derivatives,* Langs (1978–1979) classified patients into three groups. The adaptive context determines that a particular type of *"bipersonal and communicative field"* is established. In the Type A field, patients are able to utilize symbolic expression, have a tolerance for regression and anxiety, and, one may add, have access to and use of their fantasies and affects. The type B communicative field is characterized by a "discharge orientation" (p. 102); "The patient or the analyst makes extensive use of projective identification designed to rid the psyche of disturbing excretions of inner stimuli, to make use of the other member of the dyad as a container for disruptive projective identifications, and to evoke a proxy response" (p. 105). Thus the patients are inclined to seek pathological need-fulfillment by demanding noninterpretive gratification.

Finally, in the Type C field, which corresponds to the alexithymic, the trend is to "non-communication, for the destruction of meaning, and the absence of derivative expression" (p. 106). So "the field" is described as "static" and "characterized by impenetrable barriers, falsifications, destruction of meaning, and rupture of the link between patient and therapist or analyst" (p. 87). Like others who have commented on the sterility and unproductivity of psychotherapy with alexithymics, Langs described the Type C field as static and distant, devoid of analyzable derivatives—there is little offered by the patient that the (analyst) therapist can "contain and metabolize" (p. 109). Lang's view of the problem alerts us to a most startling and relevant observation: the analyst, not the patient, may be the alexithymic, or anticommunicative, party in the Type C field.

Obviously the noncommunicative attitude of alexithymic patients corresponds to Lang's Type C field. The question is whether patients who show this characteristic maintain the same cognitive style at all times. The patients who have been seen by the present author—not for psychotherapy or psychoanalysis, but for evaluation and 25-year follow-up (a population of over 2000 survivors of the Nazi Holocaust)—have shown a very high incidence of alexithymia on both the first and follow-up interviews. A questionnaire, which was a modification of the Beth Israel instrument (Apfel-Savitz and Sifneos, 1979), was administered prior to the reexamination interview. From these observations it was concluded that alexithymia and operative thinking were constant characteristics of these patients' cognitive and affective function. It was also found (Krystal, 1978a) in surveying the autobiographical writing of posttraumatic individuals, that "fact" orientation—the inability to observe, describe, and utilize one's own feelings and fantasies—is quite conspicuous. *The Painted Bird* (Kosinski, 1965) is probably the best illustration of this phenomenon.

A useful point of view related to these deliberations is offered by Gedo (1979), who feels that patients capable of establishing a working relationship corresponding to Lang's Type A field represent a relatively small group of neurotic individuals. In Gedo's opinion, their conflicts can be best understood through the model of the topographic theory; they are capable of renunciation and creativity and can be treated by means of interpretation as the peremptory type of intervention.

We are still unable to explain just when operative thinking develops, whether it may be an arrest, a regression, or an inhibition in the sense of a blockage of an established and available function. In a study of the artist Giorgio de Chirico, I (1966b) found that during a period when he was creative, albeit suffering from hypochondriasis and intestinal symptoms, he was able to present a spectacularly communicative and symbolic array of paintings. However, after he suffered a regressive episode, his art lost its symbolic and communicative nature. According to Sarnoff (1978), the capacity for symbolization develops during latency. He feels that two steps are involved in the acquisition of this capacity. First, there is the development of the use of symbols and, second, the discrimination of symbols that are suitable for communication on the basis of their universality. In other words, the child acquires knowledge and judgment about which symbols can be expected to be known to his (her) communicants and, therefore, shared. De Chirico, while in Paris for a few years, was able to express the images, symbols, and colors of "Chirico City," which evoked universal empathy and admiration. But when he was drafted by the Italian Army during World War I and after he developed a "nervous breakdown," there was a regression to the autistic, poorly stimulating "mannequin" style, whereby affective communication was lost (Krystal, 1966b). Perhaps the *pénsee opératoire* has some similarities in its motivation.

Some investigators seemed to sense the breakdown in social contacts to be an essential part, and that may have been why they tried to treat those patients in groups. They soon discovered that alexithymic patients did not "understand groups" (Apfel-Savitz, Silverman, and Bennet, 1979, p. 313), and they found it necessary to place neurotic "shills" in the group to promote more symbolic thinking and reflective self-awareness.

This observation brings us back to the question of inhibition in playing and operative thinking. European workers who deal with hospitalized psychosomatic patients, often with very severe affective disturbances, have explored this area. Wolff (1977a) reported applying Winnicott's (1971) recommendation that patients who cannot play need to acquire that ability before they can utilize psychotherapy. Wolff felt that the therapist had to serve as a model for his patients in "communicating more openly than is the rule in classical analysis now." He recommended using the sessions for "creative play in terms of shared fantasies and exploration of feelings, desires and bodily sensations" (p. 62). In applying play techniques, the therapist is extending to these adults behaviors usually used by the child therapist. The same principle applies to the recommendation presented in this book for supplying patients with words for emotions, as well as helping them with the self-observation of their emotions and their responses to *having the affect*—that the therapist belatedly carry out a function that the mothering parent did originally (and that child therapists perform as a matter of everyday practice). Wolff (1977a) also suggested that the therapist directly address the alexithymic patient's physical state and posture "sometimes by touching him or asking him to modify his posture and breathing pattern" to give the patient an opportunity to become aware of his feelings (p. 63).

Since we are concerned with alexithymic patients' blocking of their imagination and creativity, we have to reconsider the point made by Plaut (1979) that the ability to play is equal to the ability to love and the ability to work is a measure and determinant of normality. But it turns out that this subject runs much deeper than appears to the casual glance. Ogden's (1985) sophisticated reexamination of Winnicott's conception of play may have yielded a most valuable clue about the "potential space" relevant to our quest. Ogden has studied the implication of the paradox to the effect that there was a "potential space . . . a hypothetical area that exists (but cannot exist) during the phase of the repudiation of the object as not-me, that is, at the end of being merged with the object" (Winnicott, 1967, p. 109, cited in Ogden, 1985, p. 129). This potential space was, in Winnicot's conception, filled with illusion, play, and symbols.

Ogden pointed out that what was at stake here was "a dialectical process involved in the creation of subjectivity" (p. 131) by which he referred to the "gradient of degrees of self-awareness ranging from intentional self-reflection (a very late achievement) to the most subtle, unobtrusive sense of 'I-ness' by which experience is subtly endowed with the quality that one is thinking his thoughts and feeling one's feelings as opposed to living a state of reflective reactivity" (p. 131).

These considerations are connected to our chapter on the development of one's "I-ness" and the tragedy of Narcissus, who could not see himself reflected in his mother's eyes. Ogden tells us that "I-ness" is made possible by the other partner in the dyad, that the infant discovers himself in what he sees reflected in the mother's eyes. "This constitutes an interpersonal dialectic wherein 'I-ness' and otherness create one another and are preserved by the other. The mother creates the infant, and the infant creates the mother" (p. 131).

Just as implied in previous chapters, for normal development Ogden too sees that at one point mother has to exist only in the form of the invisible holding environment in which the infant's needs are met in a way that is "so unobtrusive that the infant does not experience his needs as needs" (p. 132). To this I have to add: so that the infant can continue his illusion of self-caring, providing for himself, which becomes the basis of a lifelong faith that it is all right to care for oneself.

In relation to symbol formation—and the question of why in alexithymia there is an inhibition of self-caring—and the blocking of wish-fulfillment symbolism, Ogden made a most relevant observation. Symbols are required only when there is desire. At the stage of development being discussed, only need is met; the satisfied need does not generate desire (i.e., wishing) for which symbols are required (p. 132). Ogden described that the inevitable imperfection of fit between mother and infant creates the frustration that results in the first opportunity for awareness of separateness.

However, in the future alexithymic, a tragedy takes place. The frustration is too abrupt, too painful. Along with the deprivation and the sudden discovery of the external object, there is a simultaneous sentience that because the needs are not adequately met, the infant is not meant to achieve self-satisfaction or exercise self-care, which, therefore, is forbidden, as is all wishing and fantasy-making about it. All comfort is reserved for the control of the object. However, if infantile trauma can be avoided, the separateness begins to develop comfortably and gradually, and the "transitional object is a symbol of this separateness in unity, unity in separateness. The transitional object is at the same time the infant (the omnipotently created extension of himself) and not the infant (an object he has discovered that is outside his omnipotent control)" (p. 132).

With brilliant insight, Ogden pointed out that this "discovery" of the transitional object permits the transition from an illusional unity to a "three-ness," involving the symbol, the symbolized, and the subject. With the idea of the premature interruption of the illusional unity, the infantile trauma, Ogden expressed the conditions before the trauma: "Within the context of the mother–infant unit, the person who an observer would see as the mother is invisible to the infant and exists only in the fulfillment of his need that he does not yet recognize as a need" (p. 133). But the illusional unity can be disrupted: "The mother-infant unity can be disrupted by the mother's substitution of something of herself for the infant's spontaneous gesture" (p. 133).

Ogden clearly understood the consequences for the child of the sudden premature disruption of his illusion of unity with the mother. A variety of paths can be taken from such a disaster area; for instance, the tentative distinction between reality and fantasy may collapse, with a repudiation of reality or a repudiation of fantasy. The first leads to psychosis; the second, to alexithymia. A lesser problem, but more common, is the relegation of fantasy to support denial and split-off (nonself) functions, as in fetishism. In this case, fantasy continues but is repressed. Otherwise, the withdrawal from the "external" experience may be so severe as to result in cessation of attribution of meaning to perceptions. In the extreme cases, when experiences are foreclosed, autistic development becomes apparent. In it, reality is denied and its registration excluded from consciousness (p. 133).

Ogden's elaboration of the consequences of these disturbances of early dialectic process provides a framework for which we have been searching. The use of reality as a defense against fantasy describes very well the dilemma of the "thing"- and "reality"-oriented person, as we have been repeatedly describing alexithymic behavior. Even some of the illustrations that Ogden uses reminds me of my alexithymic patients. I once had an alexithymic patient who, like Ogden's patients, prided himself on being a keen observer of reality and never missing the slightest change, of arrangements say, in my office. Many years later I had his wife in analysis, and she told me that he was so driven to watch the audience in a movie house (and so disinclined to follow a fantasy) that he missed the story of every movie, but he could report everything that happened in the darkened theater.

But the most fascinating part of Ogden's paper is the part on foreclosure of reality and fantasy, in which he explains those "blanks" and "manque caractéristique" disturbances that we have been encountering in the alexithymia patients. Ogden finds a perfect resonance to his thoughts in the writings of McDougall. He agrees that in a "state of experience" there is still perception, but it is registered as sensory data, that is, not attributed meaning. He explains that when meanings are not created, "foreclosure" takes place, and a "void" is later sensed clinically (p. 136). I can see that this kind of registration would be evoked in studies of "perceptive memory," which we discussed in the previous chapter. But Ogden feels that there would also be a void or "absence" analogus to a petit mal seizure (Meltzer, 1975), corresponding to "blank psychosis" (Green, 1975), or psychotic nonbeing (Grotstein, 1978), or even "death in life" (Laing, 1959, p. 136). It is the sense of discovery and relief that one obtains from finding an explanation to these phenomena, which we have been observing and describing as disparate, but which, once the key is supplied, can be seen to represent one and the same pattern.

Moreover, it is helpful to see how these patterns represent the sequelae of infantile psychic trauma. Ogden (1985) explains that he views

> the state of non-experience as a superordinate defense resorted to when all other defensive operations have proven insufficient to protect the infant against sustained overwhelming psychological pain. Under such circumstances the infant ceases to attribute meaning to his perception, thus failing to generate emotional significance (personal meaning) of any type [p. 136].

The posttraumatic sequelae described by Ogden seem to explain certain phenomena seen in some alexithymia patients: the severe disturbances of self- and object-representation, the severe blocking of imagination and vitality in cognitive aspects, that is, operative thinking. The other symptomatology— the affective regression and anhedonia—may be consequences of trauma of a later origin and therefore not as pervasively crippling. The inhibition of the capacity for self-caring signals a very wide spectrum of problems. On the other hand, there is the universally shared tendency to experience our lives and mental and affective function as beyond the purview of our authority; and hence, we all go around in a state analogus to a hysterical paralysis of our viscera. Among alexithymics are people with such severe distortions of their body image and so severely disabled in regard to any self-soothing or self-organization that the origin must be as early and as severe a trauma as Ogden suggests. Khantzian and Mack (1983) have focused on the most fundamental of the aspects of self-caring: self-preservation. They confirmed my reports that there was a continuum of self-caring functions. These authors found that the capacity to anticipate harm and prevent it was also dependent on a long and successful interaction and could be disrupted by chronic severe traumatic disturbances in nurturance.

The kind of trauma and the kind of developments Ogden (1985) described alert us also to the fact that now that just as neither one's affective responses nor the nature of self- and object-representation can be taken for granted, because they are subject to developmental vicissitudes, so also the *capacity for fantasy making must be examined from a developmental point of view.*

Ogden (1985) tells us that "the establishment of the distinction between the symbol and the symbolized is inseparable from the establishment of subjectivity: the two are facts of the same developmental event" (p. 137). Paraphrasing Winnicott (1956), one could say that "potential space lies between symbol and symbolized." Thus, the content of psychic reality must be seen as central to the understanding of these phemonena. As Ogden (1985) put it: "To distinguish symbol from symbolized is to distinguish one's thought from that which one is thinking about, one's feeling from that which one is responding to. For symbol to stand independently of the symbolized, there must be a subject engaged in the process of interpreting his perceptions" (p. 137). Ogden went on to explain the need to make this point, since, from the point of view of the observer, that reality was always observable—but, of course, from the point of view of the infant, the subject did not exist (was ideally not noticeable).

Ogden called attention to the crucial importance of the "discovery of subjectivity" as the central point of the discovery of the "I-ness" of experience and the discovery that the perception of the object is not the object. This, indeed, is the heart of the matter. It is the central point of all of Dorsey's writings and is the reason I have reviewed his work so extensively in this book. This view is the basis for much of our thinking in regard to the therapeutic approaches to the alexithymia patient.

14
Assessing Alexithymia

John H. Krystal, M.D.

Alexithymia has been difficult to operationalize reliably. Nevertheless, the clinical hallmarks of this phenomenon suggest methods of investigation. Early methods of alexithymia research focused on the global collection of alexithymia-associated deficits. The Beth Israel Psychosomatic Questionnaire (BIPQ) and the Schalling-Sifneos Scale (SSS) were early interviewer- and self-rated alexithymia measures exemplifying this approach. An alternative approach has been to find items from the MMPI that correlate with the BIPQ and SSS. Groups from Denver and Irvine developed MMPI Alexithymia Scales based on correlations with the BIPQ and SSS, respectively (Kleiger and Kinsman, 1980; Shipko and Noviello, 1984). Taylor and Doody (1985) took items from the SSS and other relevant self-report measures to develop the Toronto Alexithymia Scale (TAS). Transcript analysis methods have also been developed, both in monadic and dyadic settings, to quantify the verbal production of affect (von Rad and Lolas, 1982; Taylor and Doody, 1985). With the transcript analysis methods in mind, we modified a previously existing scale to produce a structured interview, the Alexithymia Provoked Response Questionnaire (APRQ) (J. Krystal, Giller, and Ciccheti, 1986). The APRQ utilizes questions to elicit differentiated affect, which is transcribed and rated blindly according to a simplified transcript analysis method. From another perspective, a group in Montreal focused on deficits in symbolic function rather than affective impairment. Based on anthropological theory, they produced a Scored Archetypal Test with Nine Elements (SAT9) (Cohen, Demers-Desrosiers, and Catchlove, 1983; Demers-Desrosiers et al., 1983).

In this review, I describe the principal methods for assessing alexithymia.

J. H. Krystal wishes to express his sincere appreciation to Laurence H. Price, M.D. for a critical reading and helpful comments on this chapter.

These include: self-rating measures, such as the TAS, SSS, and MMPI scales; interviewer-rated measures, such as the BIPQ; transcript analysis methods, such as the Giessen test, monadic and dyadic methods, and the APRQ; and measures of fantasy or symbolic function, such as the SAT9. In critically evaluating these measures, I hope to clarify their contribution to the alexithymia literature. Following this review, I will discuss methodological issues facing future alexithymia research.

SELF-RATED MEASURES OF ALEXITHYMIA

The Schalling-Sifneos Scale

The Schalling-Sifneos Scale (SSS) was the first self-rating scale for alexithymia. The scale consisted of 20 items that explicitly asked subjects to rate their own alexithymic characteristics, such as "I find the right words for my feelings" and "One may say I lack imagination," on a four-point scale. Two large studies conducted with college student populations suggested that SSS scores are normally distributed between 20 and 80, with a mean and median close to 60 and a normal distribution (Blanchard, Arena, and Pallmeyer, 1981; Martin, Pihl, and Dobkin, 1984). Based on Sifneos's criteria for alexithymia (a score less than 50), Blanchard and his associates found that 8.2% of male and 1.8% of female college students in their sample were alexithymic. Several studies found that the SSS is insensitive to differences between alexithymic and nonalexithymic groups distinguished by other rating scales (Fava, Baldaro, and Osti, 1980; Kleiger and Jones, 1980; Taylor, Doody, and Newman, 1981; J. Krystal et al., 1986). However, many of these studies reported mean scores suggesting that all or most of the patients studied met the Sifneos SSS alexithymia criteria.

The SSS has been criticized for producing unreliable results. Apfel and Sifneos (1979) noted: ". . . we have found in extensive use in our psychiatry clinic (150 forms completed) that the results are erratic, much more difficult to interpret than [a BethIsrael Psychosomatic Questionnaire prototype] and do not correlate with observer's assessment of some people. . . ." (p. 184). Subsequent studies demonstrated that the scale lacks internal consistency and scale items were irrelevant to its three primary factors derived by factor analysis (Shipko and Noviello, 1984; Bagby, Taylor, and Ryan, 1986).

We used the SSS, along with other measures of alexithymia, in inpatient populations of posttraumatic stress and affective disorder patients in a Veterans Administration Hospital (J. Krystal et al., 1986). Although Shipko and his associates (1983) had used the SSS to demonstrate alexithymia in posttraumatic stress patients, they did not assess its validity in their population. We found that our patients had such difficulty responding to the questionnaire items that the reliability of the items came into question. Unlike the BIPQ and the APRQ, the SSS did not differentiate the PTSD (n = 9) from the affective disorder (n = 14) patients. Nor did the SSS scores correlate significantly with the BIPQ, the APRQ, or the MMPI Alexithymia Questionnaire. Thus, in our population, the SSS failed to reliably assess alexithymia; that is, it lacked face validity, and it did not correlate with other alexithymia scales, suggesting that it lacked convergent validity according to the terminology employed by Sechrest (1984).

Possibly, in selected, highly educated populations, the SSS may show content validity. Studies that applied factor analytic techniques to large groups of college students found three factors that appeared to explain a little more than half of the variance: approximately 25% of the variance was explained by SSS questions assessing "difficulty expressing feelings"; approximately 15% was attributed to questions assessing daydreaming or fantasy; approximately 10–20% came from devaluing the importance of feelings, also labeled "apathy" (Blanchard et al., 1981; Martin et al., 1984). Yet, even in these settings, the sensitivity and clinical validity of the SSS has been questioned (Bagby et al., 1986).

One reason the SSS may lack clinical relevance is that many of its items assess alexithymic attitudes, rather than alexithymic behaviors. Careful review of our initial data (J. Krystal et al., 1986) and subsequent experience with the SSS suggested that some intelligent and verbally sophisticated subjects identified with nonalexithymic attitudes on the SSS such as "feelings are what make life worthwhile" despite their inability to express differentiated affect during a nonstructured interview or during administration of the APRQ. It is paradoxical to ask alexithymic persons with deficits in affective insight and fantasy to rate affective or symbolic experiences that they do not comprehend. This criticism applies to the MMPI scales as well (Cooper and Holmstrom, 1984), and to a lesser degree, the TAS.

In an attempt to improve the SSS, Martin et al., (1984) suggested decreasing the scale from twenty to nine items, which they selected after a factor analysis of the scale. Fava and his associates (1980) noted six items that seemed most important in distinguishing alexithymic patients. Alterations may improve the reliability of the scale, perhaps by making it easier to complete, but neither of these alterations addresses the impact of the alexithymic lack of insight on SSS scores or the difference between alexithymic attitudes and alexithymic behavior.

The SSS appears to correlate with the Speilberger Trait Anxiety Scale, the Briquet's Syndrome Questionnaire, the Psychosomatic Checklist, and the Maudsley Personality Inventory-Extroversion Scale (Fava et al., 1980; Blanchard et al., 1981). In the studies mentioned earlier, the SS did not correlate significantly with the Beck Depression Inventory, the Spielberger State Anxiety Scale, or the Rathus Assertiveness Scale. The correlation with the somatization questionnaires is not surprising, since the alexithymia concept grew out of work with psychosomatic patients. Trait anxiety scales have previously been implicated as useful in assessing the degree of affective repression exhibited by patients (Weinberger, Schwartz, and Davidson, 1979); thus, these correlations, too, are not surprising. However, the lack of correlation with the depression and anxiety scales does not imply that the SSS is a scale specifically assessing alexithymia, that is, has divergent validity. As noted earlier, the SSS also fails to correlate with most measures of alexithymia (Paulson, 1985; Taylor and Doody, 1985; Krystal et al., 1986). In summary, the SSS may assess alexithymic attitudes in high-functioning, nonclinical populations; when used in clinical populations, its validity and generalizability must be questioned. In both populations, however, the validity of the SSS alexithymia criterion score of 50 must be questioned. The derivation of this threshold has been incorporated into the literature despite a lack of empirical substantiation.

The MMPI Alexithymia Scales

The alexithymia scales derived from the MMPI constitute further efforts to produce a valid self-rating measure for alexithymia. Three alexithymia scales have been derived from the MMPI: two by a Denver group and a third (discussed later) by Shipko and his associates in Irvine, California. The MMPI-Denver Alexithymia Scale, referred to as the MMPI Alexithymia Scale unless otherwise specified, was developed by Kleiger and Kinsman (1980). It consists of 22 true–false items selected from the MMPI scale. These questions do not directly assess alexithymia. They were chosen by virtue of their association with high BIPQ scores (Kleiger and Kinsman, 1980). Kleiger and Kinsman found a high correlation ($r = 0.66$) and an 82% concordance rate between results from the BIPQ and MMPI alexithymia scales. Their data produced the regression equation: BIPQ score = MMPI score + 1.3675. Based on this equation, they suggested that an MMPI alexithymia score of 14 was equivalent to a BIPQ score of 6. A twenty-item MMPI Alexithymia scale with an alexithymia criteria of 12 has also been reported (Kleiger and Dirks, 1980). It shows a concordance rate of 94% with the longer form but does not present any clear advantages over the 22 item scale.

The MMPI Alexithymia Scale presents major problems to researchers hoping to find a self-rating scale for alexithymia. So far, no other study has been able to replicate a significant correlation between the MMPI Alexithymia scale and the BIPQ (Demers-Derosiers et al., 1983; Federman and Mohns, 1984; Paulson, 1985; J. Krystal et al., 1986). Also, the validity of the MMPI Alexithymia Scale is based entirely on correlation with BIPQ data collected by multiple observers. Yet, as will be discussed, interrater reliability for the BIPQ is an issue of significant debate. In addition, no other measure of alexithymia, including the SSS, BIPQ, APRQ, SAT9, Affect Word Transcript Analysis or

AVS, consistently correlates with data collected with the MMPI Alexithymia Scale (Demers—Desrosiers et al., 1983; Doody and Taylor, 1983; Paulson, 1985; Taylor and Doody, 1985; J. Krystal et al., 1986). Feiguine and Johnson (1985) suggested that the validity of the MMPI Alexithymia Scale is limited to chronic respiratory populations. However, the MMPI may lack validity in this population as well. We found that the BIPQ and APRQ, but not the MMPI Alexithymia Scale, could differentiate a "somatic illness" population that included asthmatics from an affective disorder population (J. Krystal et al., 1986).

Doody and Taylor (1983) noted significant correlations between the MMPI Alexithymia Scale and several MMPI subscales, including MMPI-F, MMPI-L, and MMPI-K subscales. The L, F, and K scales have been interpreted as indicators of social desirability, error or confusion, and affective defensiveness, respectively (Meehl and Hathaway, 1946; Colligan et al., 1984). Doody and Taylor suggested that the MMPI Alexithymia scale possessed limited content validity. They found that the MMPI scale did not assess expression of affect and fantasy but instead measured defensiveness, the absence of neurosis, and, inversely, abstract ability.

It was suggested in discussing the SSS that alexithymics might misreport somatic distress, thus distorting data from self-report measures. Cooper and Holstrom (1984) found that MMPI Alexithymia Scale scores correlated inversely ($r = 0.58$) with those from the MMPI-derived Repression-Sensitization (R-S) scale. These findings, as well as the previous suggestions by Millimet (1970) that the R-S scales and alexithymia responses are due to their relationship to the first factor of the MMPI, suggest that it lacks relevance for alexithymia in its present form.

Shipko and Noviello (1984) in Irvine, California, developed an MMPI Alexithymia Scale based on the Schallng-Sifneos Scale rather than the BIPQ (1984). The scale contains 20 items and bears the following relationship to SSS scores: SSS = 0.85 MMPI-Irvine × 36. As a result, a score of 17 on this scale is "equivalent" to an alexithymic score on the SSS based on Sifneos's criteria. Shipko and Noviello also suggested that one could calculate the SSS equivalent based on other MMPI scales with the relationship, SSS (estimated) = 0.49 (Scale 0) − 0.32 (Scale F) + 0.13 (Scale 3). In their sample, estimated and actual SSS scores correlated significantly ($r = 0.63$). This scale also showed a low but significant negative correlation with the scale developed by Kleiger and Kinsman ($r - 0.32$).

One must use caution in utilizing the new MMPI-Irvine Alexithymia Scale. As noted earlier, the SSS can be an erratic measure of alexithymia. One might consider it hazardous to develop a new scale on such an unsteady base. In addition, the sample used for this study is very small compared with other studies that attempted to provide normative data for the SSS (Blanchard et al., 1981; Martin et al., 1984). These studies found that fewer than 10% of their subjects met alexithymia criteria on the SSS. If their populations were comparable, fewer than five patients in the Irvine study probably met SSS alexithymia criteria.

Both the Irvine and the Denver scales are vulnerable to criticism of the exclusion criteria employed in their studies. Consistent with normative data (Kleiger and Kinsman, 1980; Colligan et al., 1984) exluded MMPI scores as invalid if: 1) the consistency was less than 75%, 2) FV > T score was greater than 100, and 3) the MMPT F-K scores were greater than a raw score of 11. In contrast, Shipko and Noviello (1984) included these patients in their study. However, F, K, and F-K scores may reflect affective defensiveness or a repressive affective style (Ullman, 1958). Thus, included or excluded, these selection criteria affected the validity of these scales. It is certainly premature to use the MMPI Alexithymia Scale alone to assess alexithymia.

The Toronto Alexithymia Scale

Taylor and his associates (1985) recently introduced a new self-rating measure: the Toronto Alexithymia Scale (TAS). After administering a 41-item scale, abstracted from self-rating measures that assessed aspects of alexithymia, to over 500 college students, they arrived at a 26-item scale that appeared to be internally consistent and reliable. Using factor analysis techniques, they found that the response variance could be largely accounted for by four factors: the ability to identify and describe feelings (11 items, 12.3% the variance), the ability to communicate feelings (7 items, 7.0% of the variance), the ability to daydream (5 items, 6.4% of the variance), and "externally oriented" thinking (6 items, 6.1% of the variance). Age and degree of education significantly correlated with the overall TAS score as well as with some of the subscales. However, these variables accounted for less than 5% of the variance of the test results, suggesting to the authors that the TAS is "not unduly" influenced by these variables (Taylor et al., 1985, p. 197). Like the SSS, which shares many of the test items, male subjects tended to score higher than females on the Toronto scale.

Taylor and his associates (1985) also explored the relationship between the TAS and other psychological measures. In their initial sample, they found a small negative correlation ($r < -.2$) between the Marlowe-Crowne Social Desirability Scale and a scale that has been interpreted as a measure of affective defensiveness, as well as the score on factors 1–3 (Taylor et al., 1985). In a sample of 81 college students (Bagby et al., in press), the TAS correlated inversely with verbal IQ ($r = 301 .27$), the "need for cognition scale ($r = -.42$), and a psychological mindedness scale ($r = -.33$). TAS scores correlated positively with the Beck Depression Inventory ($r = .60$) and the Spielberger State ($r = .56$) and Trait ($r = .59$) Anxiety Scales. The TAS also correlated with many of the subscales of the Basic Personality Inventory

(BPI). The BPI hypochondriasis ($r = .39$), depression ($r = .47$), social introversion ($r = .32$), persecutory ideation ($r = .31$) anxiety ($r = .26$), and impulse expression ($r = .23$) subscales showed the greatest correlation with the TAS. However, when depression and anxiety are controlled for, the magnitude of the BPI hypochrondriasis subscale-TAS and psychological mindedness-TAS partial correlations decreased significantly. Importantly, the BPI denial scale did not correlate with TAS scores.

The TAS is currently in the developmental stages. However, it is still the most promising self-rating scale available at this time. Revision of the scale is currently underway (Taylor, personal communication). However, it appears to be an internally consistent measure of traits related to the alexithymia hypothesis. Although as a self-report measure it is subject to many of the same criticisms as the SSS and the MMPI scale, a greater number of its items, unlike those of these scales, appear to describe behaviors or situations that an alexithymic person might be able to recall. Comparison with a transcript analysis technique such as the APRQ would be useful to address the possibility that the TAS, or some of its factors, are more relevant to the assessment of alexithymic attitudes than to the assessment of alexithymic behavior.

INTERVIEWER-RATED MEASURES OF ALEXITHYMIA: THE BETH ISRAEL PSYCHOSOMATIC QUESTIONNAIRE

The Beth Israel Psychosomatic Questionnaire (BIPQ) is the most widely used measure of alexithymia, a fact that probably reflects the youth of alexithymia research. The BIPQ consists of 17 questions that ask the interviewer to rate the subject's fantasy life and affective communication dichotomously; an additional six items describe the therapeutic relationship (Sifneos, 1973; Apfel and Sifneos, 1979). Of the 17 questions, Sifneos selected eight "key" alexithymic items. He noted in a personal communication that a score of 6 or more could be considered alexithymic (Kleiger and Kinsman, 1980). The incidence of alexithymia in the general population has not been assessed with the BIPQ. Under the alexithymia criteria previously noted, the incidence in selected "psychosomatic" populations appears to vary between 30% and 50% (Sifneos, 1973; Kleiger and Jones, 1980; Smith, 1983). These figures, however, do not apply to patients with a damaged corpus callosum, all of whom were preliminarily noted to demonstrate evidence of alexithymia using this scale (Hoppe and Bogen, 1977; Buchanan, Waterhouse, and West, 1980).

Although the BIPQ loosely directs the collection of data, it does not specify the format of the research interview. Thus, as noted by Schneider (1977), the setting of this interview, the skill of the interviewer, and other factors potentially influence the BIPQ scores. Taylor and his associates (1981) found that the BIPQ had unacceptable interrater reliability when different interviewers rated the same patients. Other studies also suggest that when interviewers of different skill or knowledge base administer the BIPQ, one may see significant differences in the resulting data (Sifneos, 1973; Lolas et al., 1980). In contrast, Apfel and Sifneos (1979) found 85% interrater reliability after one hour of training. The actual data, however, are not included in their report. Three groups found acceptable BIPQ interrater reliability. Using multiple ratings of recorded interviews, Kleiger and Jones (1980) and Federman and Mohns (1984) and Paulson (1985) noted Pearson product-moment coefficients between .76 and .94. Inasmuch as the BIPQ interview is so unstructured, it is not clear that the interrater reliability in these studies would be so high if different interviewers rated the same patient.

The influence of other factors on BIPQ data is also unclear. Although Kleiger and Jones (1980) found that alexithymia positively correlated with age, several other studies failed to find a significant influence of age on BIPQ scores (Pierloot and Vinck, 1977; Smith, 1983; J. Krystal et al., 1986). Gardos, Schniebolk, Mirin, Walk, and Rosenthal (1984) noted that three questions pertaining to dream frequency, history of psychosomatic illness, and impoverishment of fantasy life were associated with increased age and lower educational status. A number of studies suggest that alexithymic BIPQ scores correlate with lower intelligence and socioeconomic status (Pierloot and Vinck, 1977; Smith, 1983). Education was noted to have a significant impact on questions pertaining to fantasy life (Gardos et al., 1984). Sex was found to be a factor in some studies, with males more alexithymic than females (Sifneos, 1973; Smith, 1983). However, other studies did not find sex a significant variable in BIPQ scores (Pierloot and Vinck, 1977; Kleiger and Jones, 1980). The impact of these variables on BIPQ scores should become more clear when this scale is used in larger studies in healthy populations.

The Gardos study rated 178 "psychiatric patients" and found no correlation between DSM-III Axis I diagnosis and BIPQ results (Gardos et al., 1984). They did find a relationship with Axis II diagnoses: borderline, narcissistic, and compulsive personalities were more alexithymic, whereas dependent personalities scored lower on the BIPQ. In a comparison of the BIPQ with other ratings, poor expression of affect and impaired communication, which accounted for 64.2% of BIPQ variance, had low but significant correlations with the phobia, obsessive-compulsion, and somatization scores on the SCL-90 (Gardos et al., 1984). Pierloot and Vinck (1977) found that the BIPQ correlated with the Somatic Complaint Scale of the Psychiatric Status Schedule and their Somatic Worries Checklist but did not correlate significantly with the Hyponchrondriasis Scale of the MMPI.

Two approaches have been taken to improve BIPQ reliability: increasing the range of responses and standardizing training to produce interrater consistency. Bellak and Lombardo (1984) noted that increasing the range of scale responses, for example, from a dichotomous scale to an eight-point scale, increased the sensitivity of self-rating measures for anxiety. Although this technique potentially increases the variability of the scale, a number of authors have discussed or employed a multiple-point scale instead of the dichotomous distinctions for each of the BIPQ items (Lolas et al., 1981; Sjodin, 1983; Gardos et al., 1984).

The BIPQ owes its popularity to its apparent face validity, but the BIPQ interview is highly malleable. At best, it provides an accurate reflection of the patient's recollections of his fantasy life and his verbal expression of affect. At worst, BIPQ data may be biased by interviewer, patient, and setting variables that may be difficult to assess.

TRANSCRIPT ANALYSIS METHODS

The alexithymia concept developed, in part, out of psychotherapeutic work with psychosomatic populations. Attempts to operationalize alexithymia using transcript analysis (TA) methods have studied this dyadic setting. One of these methods, the Giessen test, analyzes dyadic transcripts for 12 variables pertaining to the temporal relationship of patient and therapist contributions (described in Overbeck, 1977). Both Overbeck and von Rad and associates (1977) suggested that in interview settings, alexithymic and psychosomatic patients exhibit decreased verbal productivity and longer pauses, and evoke more frequent therapist interventions.

Von Rad and his associates further noted that compared with neurotics, psychosomatic patients showed decreased use of the pronoun "I," a selective increase in the frequency of passive constructions, a smaller affect-laden vocabulary, and less frequent verbalization of affect-laden words, despite no differences in the therapist's use of affect-laden words. Knapp and his associates (Ross, Knapp, and Vachon, 1979; Knapp 1980), studying free association, also reported decreased verbal productivity, more frequent pauses, and more routine therapist interventions in psychosomatic patients.

Vocabulary analysis methods used to evaluate verbal expression of affect generally tally the total word production, an affect-word variable, adjectives, adverbs, and passive and active verbs. Affect-word variables include such categories as "affect-laden words," "affect words," and "affect vocabulary score." Von Rad and his associates (1977) defined their use of "affect-laden" words: "those nouns, adjectives or verbs in which an unambiguous manifest tone of feeling is evident. What is decisive is that the tone of feeling explicit in the word is comprehensible without long interpretations being used" (p. 91).

Despite the careful description, the particular criteria are still somewhat ambiguous. Although such verbs as "love" and "hate" suggest differentiated affect, it is not clear whether a verb like "kill" might be "affect-laden" while not qualifying as an "affect word." Taylor (personal communication, 1985) notes that in cases of conflict, the context of the word was taken into consideration. However, none of the transcript analysis studies indicated the reliability of classifying words into the "affect word" or "affect-laden" word categories. Our experience with the APRQ suggests that interrater reliability is high when affect words are evaluated in the context of a response (J. Krystal el al., 1986).

Taylor and Doody (1985) introduced another variable, the affect word vocabulary score, or AVS. This score indicates the number of different affect words employed in a sample. When an affect word is repeated in a sample, it does not increase the AVS. The significance of removing the impact of affect-word repetition is not clear. It may reflect such trait variables as education or verbal and abstract IQ to a greater extent than state-dependent variables. The authors suggest that AVS does not significantly correlate with BIPQ, SSS, MMPI Alexithymia Scale, and GG analysis data. Some of these measures, particularly the BIPQ and GG analysis, are highly state dependent (Gottschalk, Winget, and Gleser, 1969; Schneider, 1977; Taylor et al., 1981). However, the AVS correlates with total word production in response to TAT cards, the MMPI K scale, and the Rorschach M factor. The clinical significance of the AVS is unclear at this time.

The Heidelberg group found that in response to an assigned verbal task, psychosomatic patients used fewer total words, fewer adjectives or adverbs, more incomplete sentences, and fewer affect-laden words than did neurotic patients (von Rad et al., 1977). Although this trend remained for the responses to the TAT card 3BM, these differences were not significant. Taylor and his associates (1981) reported the reverse of this pattern. Using a broader range of TAT items, inflammatory bowel patients uttered fewer total and "affect" words than neurotics. However, their assigned verbal task elicited nonsignificant but similar trends for these variables. Consistent with these findings, total word production and the affect scale of the Rotter Sentence Completion Test correlated with alexithymia scores on the BIPQ (Lesser, Ford, and Friedmann, 1979). Taylor and Doody (1985) also noted a smaller AVS in psychosomatic patients in response to the TAT items. TenHouten and his colleagues (1985) found that commissurotomized patients, thought to be alexithymic on the basis of previous investigations, differed in their verbal response to a film depicting loss. The neurosurgery patients did not differ from control patients in total number of words emitted, but they did use fewer affect-laden words, more incomplete sentences, more passive auxilliary verbs, and fewer adjectives.

These data provide preliminary evidence that, compared with neurotics or "controls," neurosurgical and psychosomatic populations use fewer words indicative of affect, use a more "bland" style of communication characterized by fewer adjectives and more frequent passive constructions, and may use fewer total words in verbal responses. In addition, the differences in TAT and assigned verbal task data in the studies discussed earlier suggest that verbal expression, as measured by most vocabulary analysis techniques, is state and stimulus dependent. Both the TAT and verbal tasks produced data with similar trends suggesting no qualitative differences in response. However, they did produce quantitatively different data, suggesting that in order to distinguish alexithymic-psychosomatic from nonalexithymic-neurotic verbal behavior by TA methods, one must first evoke a significant degree of affect. In addition, altering the setting produced reversed TAT and verbal task response patterns, suggesting that these TA methods show stimulus and state dependence.

Gottschalk and Gleser (1969) developed a variety of scales for evaluating anxiety, hostility, and hope through analysis of a short verbal transcript. The Gottschalk-Gleser (GG) scales identify topics in the transcript relevant to a particular subscale—for example shame-anxiety—weighting this reference according to instructions and totaling the weighted references to produce a raw GG subscale score. This raw score is multiplied by 100, divided by the number of words per unit time, and the square root of this entire quantity is taken to produce the "affect magnitude" (Gottschalk et al., 1969). Although Gottschalk and his associates developed preliminary methods for computer analysis of transcripts, these methods have not yet attained the reliability of manual analysis (Gottschalk, Hausman, and Brown, 1975; Gottschalk and Bechtel, 1982).

The standard GG instructions require the subject to talk for five minutes about "any interesting or dramatic personal life experiences," but not to address the interviewer (Gottschalk et al., 1969, p. 5). In dyadic settings (discussed later), von Rad and his associates used the patient's first 1000 words for TA. Several studies utilizing GG methods suggest that psychosomatic patients verbally express less anxiety and hostility while exhibiting more denial than neurotic patients (von Rad et al., 1979; Lolas, Mergenthaler, and von Rad, 1982; von Rad and Lolas, 1982). The GG scales are primarily designed to assess state-dependent variables, although they may be modified to assess trait variables (Gottschalk et al., 1969).

The impact of setting and stimulus on verbal expression of affect was studied by von Rad, Lolas, and their associates using the GG scales Lolas et al., 1982; Lolas and von Rad, 1982; von Rad and Lolas, 1982). The Heidelberg group compared data elicited under standard GG conditions with data collected during a psychoanalytic interview (Lolas et al., 1982). In the standard GG setting, psychosomatic patients differed from neurotic patients by verbalizing less mutilation anxiety without showing any difference in a variety of other anxiety and hostility scales. This finding is consistent with data from Taylor and Doody (1985), who could not distinguish neurotic and inflammatory bowel patients by the anxiety subscales, total anxiety, hostility, or the hope GG scales. In comparison with psychosomatic patients, neurotics in the psychoanalytic intake interview expressed more guilt, shame, diffuse, and total anxiety as well as inward-directed and ambivalent hostility by GG analysis.

TenHouten and his associates (1985d) used mildly provocative films to produce GG data that differentiated commissurotomized from control subjects. Yet one must be careful in comparing the psychosomatic and commisurotomy patients. Unlike the psychosomatic patients, the commissurotomy patients exhibit alexithymic verbal deficits as part of a broad spectrum of cognitive deficits that may be relevant to alexithymia.

If there is a gold standard for evaluating the verbal expression of affect, it exists among the multitude of techniques for transcript analysis (TA). All the TA methods discussed earlier are, to varying degrees, means for assessing state-dependent expression of affect. Alexithymia has been hypothesized to be a relatively stable clinical variable, and in some cases, a result of genetic loading or structural lesion (Heiberg and Heiberg, 1977; TenHouten et al., 1985b). It is possible that verbal expression of affect has both state and trait components, perhaps analogous to the difference between AVS and affect-word or GG data.

Although psychosomatic and alexithymic populations have been loosely equated in the foregoing discussion, TA data suggest that the relationship between alexithymia and psychosomatic illness is complex and not clear at this time. Knapp and his associates (Knapp, 1980) found that asthmatics who displayed decreased verbal production manifested conflicted rather than impoverished fantasy lives, as would be suggested by the alexithymia concept. This is consistent with the observation by Overbeck (1977) that only one out of six groups of ulcer patients differentiated by Q-sort analysis were clinically alexithymic.

THE ALEXITHYMIA PROVOKED RESPONSE QUESTIONNAIRE (APRQ).

We became interested in this scale in our search for valid and time-efficient measures of alexithymia (J. Krystal et al., 1986; also see Appendix, this chapter). When the questionnaire is administered as a structured interview, one can minimize the response ambiguity that hampered use of this questionnaire as a self-report measure. Responses to the 17 items are scored 0 for an alexithymic response and 1 for a nonalexithymic response. APRQ scores range from zero to 17. Responses are scored as alexithymic if they: 1) described action but not affect, e.g., "I'd go," 2) contained detailed descriptions of situations, e.g., "It depends on how large the knife was; if it was small I might fight," 3) described physical sensations rather than affect, e.g., "I guess my head would ache," 4) were part of a series of responses in which a word indicating affect was used as a "buzz word" or automatic response rather than in a meaningful way. The APRQ produces data that can be rated by a researcher blind to the experimental conditions. Overall interrater reliability for rating APRQ data was 82.61%, with an excellent level of clinical significance based on total APRQ scores (interclass coefficient = .84).

We compared 10 inpatient posttraumatic stress patients (APRQ = 5.0 +/− 3.6), 14 inpatient affective disorder patients (APRQ = 11.0 +/− 4.8), 11 outpatient PTSD patients (APRQ = 8.7 +/− 5.5), and 11 inpatient somatic illness patients (APRQ = 7.3 +/− 4.2), comparable to "psychosomatic" groups in other studies. Using Tukey's Multiple Comparisons Test (Petrinovich and Hardyck, 1969), a conservative statistical method, we noted a trend approaching significance for the inpatient PTSD group ($p = 0.051$) and inpatient somatic group ($p = 0.053$) to be more alexithymic than the inpatient affective disorders group. The outpatient PTSD group did not differ significantly from the other groups on the APRQ or BIPQ. Similar discriminations were made in this population using the BIPQ, which correlated significantly with the APRQ($r = 0.72, p = 0.0001$). Neither the SSS nor the MMPI Alexithymia Scales differentiated the groups, nor did they correlate significantly with the APRQ (see Table 1).

The APRQ is essentially a TA method that utilizes a dyadic setting to stimulate verbal expression of affect. Unlike the detailed and somewhat cumbersome TA methods described earlier, the APRQ is relatively easy to use and time conserving. Although the binary analysis described earlier is somewhat crude, it appears to be sensitive to group differences. The scale also permits the researcher to sample a broad range of affect. The scale has significant face validity. Its clinical relevance is suggested by its sensitivity to group differences, correlation with the BIPQ, and our clinical sense that the APRQ elicits data indicative of the subject's verbal expression of affect. The degree to which the APRQ assesses fantasy and symbolic function is unclear. However, the scale requires patients to imagine themselves in a variety of situations and thus indirectly assesses capacity for fantasy. Comparison with the SAT9 would help to clarify this issue.

The APRQ highlights the "provoked response" format as a means of efficiently eliciting verbal expression of affect. So far, APRQ data has been analyzed only to distinguish alexithymic from nonalexithymic responses. Other recently introduced provoked-response scales highlight the flexibility of this format. Catchlove and Braha (1985) introduced a scale, similar in some respects to the APRQ, which assesses both the awareness and expression of

TABLE 1
Correlations Between Alexithymia Scales (a)

	BIPQ	MMPI-ALEX.	APRQ	Total Word TA	Affect Word TA	GG TOTAL	AVS
SS	N.S. (2,3)	N.S. (2)	N.S. (2)	N.S. (1)	N.S. (1)	varies inversely (8) (b)	N.S. (8)
	BIPQ	0.66** (4) N.S. (2,5,7)	0.72*** (2)	N.S. (8)	N.S. (8)	varies inversely (8)	N.S. (8)
MMPI		N.S. (2)	−0.33* (2)	N.S. (6)	varies (6,8)	N.S. inversely (8)	(8)
Total-Wd. TA							positive corr. (8)
SAT9	−0.47* (7)	N.S. (7)					

*: p < 0.05, **: p < 0.001, ***: p < 0.0001

a: correlations represent r values; b: varies inversely in regard to alexithymia Schalling-Sifneos Scale (positive correlations—inverse correlation to alexithymia). BIPQ = Beth Israel Psychosomatic Questionnaire. MMPI-ALEX. = MMPI Alexithymia Scale. APRQ = Alexithymia Provoked Response Questionnaire. Total-Ward TA = Transcript analysis based on total number of words produced. Affect-Word TA = Transcript analysis based on number of affect words produced. AVS = Affect Vocabulary Score from Taylor and Doody (1985). GGS-Total = Sum of scores on Gottschalk-Gleser Analysis: total anxiety + hostility outward + [hope].

(1) Taylor et al. (1981) Note: SS not sensitive to significant difference in TA; (2) Krystal et al., (1986); (3) Kleiger and Jones, (1980); (4) Kleiger and Kinsman (1980); (5) Federman and Mohns (1984); (6) Doody and Taylor (1983); (7) Demers-Desrosiers et al. (1983); (8) Taylor and Doody (1985).

anger. Using this scale in chronic pain patients, four groups were identified: patients without awareness or expression of affect, subjects without awareness but who expressed affect, those who were aware of affect but who did not express it, and a group without deficits in awareness or expression. In clinical settings, the three "deficit" groups are often lumped together under the alexithymic rubric. It may be helpful to maintain these distinctions in further research in subsequent studies.

Assessment of Symbolic Function.

None of the alexithymia scales discussed up to this point formally assess symbolic function or fantasy except by clinical impression. A number of investigations have reported striking deficits in the fantasy life of psychosomatic patients using the Rorschach test (Vogt et al., 1977; Safar et al., 1978; Taylor et al., 1981). Psychosomatic patients responded less frequently with reference to form and color and manifested a "restricted" response pattern (Vogt et al., 1977; Taylor et al., 1981). In sustained hypertensives, the deficits in fantasy were also associated with inability to express anxiety symbolically, as defined by the Rorschach test. Borderline hypertensives showed a nonsignificant trend in the same direction.

Demers-Desrosiers and her associates in Montreal adapted a test developed by Durand to assess symbolic function (Demers-Desrosiers, 1982; Demers-Desrosiers et al., 1983; Cohen et al., 1983, 1985). This test, the AT9, assesses the ability to link nine symbolic elements in a story that is also conveyed in a drawing. The AT9 was first developed as a projective test, the PAT9 (Demers-Derosiers, 1982). Using this test, 36 patients deemed alexthymic by virtue of their BIPQ scores were compared with 13 nonalexithymic patients. Although both groups of patients had somatic illness, the nonalexithymic patients demonstrated normal symbolic function, whereas alexithymic patients demonstrated a spectrum of abnormalities. Some of the most severely alexithymic patients were unable to produce a coherent story using the nine symbols, suggesting a marked impairment in symbolic function.

Further work with the PAT9 led to a standardized scoring system, the SAT9 (Cohen et al., 1983). In this study, normals scored greater than 65 on the SAT9, and this value has been preliminarily suggested as the cutoff for normal values. The SAT9 appears to have high interrater reliability (Cohen et al., 1983; Bourke, Taylor, and Crisp, 1985). Scores on the SAT9 correlate with the BIPQ but not with the MMPI alexithymia scale (Demers-Desrosiers et al., 1983). The majority of chronic pain patients (86.7%) and a lower percentage (45%) of anorexia nervosa patients showed impaired symbolic function using the SAT9 (Demers-Derosiers et al., 1983; Bourke et al., 1985). Both age and social status appeared to influence SAT9 results (Cohen et al., 1985).

The SAT9 represents a significant advance in assessing symbolic function in alexithymia. However, like the TA methods, the relationship between symbolic function and alexithymia has not been worked out. Symbolic function may be influenced by a variety of variables. Cohen and her associates (1985) suggested that the SAT9 overpredicted the impairment in symbolic function manifested by their acute medical group. It will be important to determine which impairments in fantasy and symbolic function assessed by the SAT9 are relevant to the alexithymia concept. In doing this, the relationship between this test and those assessing verbal expression of affect must be evaluated. In developing the alexithymia concept, analysts were impressed with the impairment in symbolic function and fantasy manifested by psychosomatic and posttraumatic stress syndrome patients (Marty and de M'Uzan, 1963; Sifneos, 1973; Krystal, 1977). The potential significance of the SAT9 as a research tool is suggested by its correlation with the BIPQ (Demers-Desrosiers et al., 1983). Further work is needed to clarify this potentially important area of research.

TenHouten and his associates (1985c) recently introduced another measure of symbolic function. They blindly rated transcripts of commissurotomized patients describing a film. The neurosurgery patients were distinguished from controls on three of six symbolization variables, a global assessment of symbolic function, and an "overall" measure derived from factor-analytic techniques.

OTHER SCALES POTENTIALLY RELEVANT TO THE ALEXITHYMIA CONCEPT

Scales derived from the MMPI have been used to define a "repressive" or "inhibiting" affective style. Byrne and his associates (Byrne, 1961; Byrne, Barry, and Nelson, 1963) selected items from the MMPI that distinguished patients who seemed to repress, minimize, or avoid affect from patients who magnified the cognitive components of affect. Although the "repression-sensitization" (R-S) scale has played an important role in psychosomatic research, its data appear to reflect a combination of state anxiety and repression (Weinberger et al., 1979; Asendorf and Scherer, 1983). Ullman (1958, 1962) derived a related scale that has 44 MMPI items, 20 of which are also included in the R-S scale. This scale correlates with the R-S scale and distinguishes "internalizers" who employ denial from "externalizers" who use projection extensively as a defensive style.

The Taylor Manifest Anxiety Scale (TMAS) and the Marlowe-Crowne Social Desirability Scale (SDS) have been the most important measures used to operationalize the concept of repressive affective style. The R-S scale correlates highly with the TMAS, a commonly used measure of trait anxiety (Millimet, 1970; Weinberger et al., 1979). The SDS, initially developed to evaluate susceptibility to external expectations, actually appears to measure a repressive-defensive affect style (Millimet, 1970; Weinberger et al., 1979). It has been demonstrated that repressors may be further broken down into two groups: "low anxious" subjects who score low on the TMAS and SDS, and "true repressors" who exhibit low manifest anxiety but high SDS scores (Weinberger et al., 1979). In response to a variety of stressors, repressors exhibited greater physiological arousal, a more global pattern of arousal, and cognitive disturbance as assessed by galvanic skin response, forehead EMG, heart rate change, and reaction time when compared to the low-anxious subjects (Hare, 1966; Weinberger et al., 1979; Asendorf and Scherer, 1983; Shaw, Cohen, Doyle, and Palesky, 1985). The repressors also experienced their anxiety as somatic rather than as a cognitive phenomenon, whereas low-anxious subjects did not dissociate their cognitive and somatic anxiety. In addition, the repressor group also recalled fewer negative childhood memories compared with both high-anxious and low-anxious subjects and fewer positive childhood memories compared with the low-anxiety subjects (Davis and Schwartz, 1987). Such deficits are consistent with the difficulties alexithymic patients encounter with insight-oriented psychotherapy. Repressors also differ from low-anxious subjects in functional aspects of cerebral lateralization (Wexler, Schwartz, Warrenburg, Servis, and Tarktyn, 1986). Using a fused dichotic stimulus presentation that selectively presents a positively or negatively charged work to one ear and thus may selectively stimulate the contralateral cortical hemisphere, one can assess the affective response to stimuli by measuring the corrugator muscle response (CMR). When the negatively charged stimulus is recalled in this paradigm, it is said to be conscious. If it can not be recalled, it is considered unconscious (Wexler et al., 1986). When negative affectively charged words are presented to the right ear, (and thus processed by the left cortical hemisphere), only repressors showed increased CMR when negatively charged words remained unconscious. In contrast, low-anxious subjects showed greater CMR responses when the word was consciously perceived. When negatively charged stimuli were presented to the right hemisphere, the groups did not differ (Wexler, 1987, personal communication). These findings suggest that alterations in lateralized cortical function may play important regulatory roles in cognitive, affective, linguistic, and autonomic aspects of the repressive affective style, and perhaps, alexithymia.

THE REPRESSIVE AFFECTIVE STYLE
AND ALEXITHYMIA

Unlike alexithymia, the repressive style is a primarily operationally defined clinical phenomenon. Its relationship to such clinical concepts as denial, repression, and alexithymia is unclear. The tendency of repressors to misread their anxiety level, to respond in an exaggerated or undifferentiated manner to unconsciously perceived stimuli, and to exhibit a functional disturbance in cerebral lateralization is consistent with alexithymia. Also consistent with this association, the transcript analysis techniques reviewed earlier suggest that alexithymics, internalizers, and repressors all respond to affectively provocative TAT cards with less verbal affect and fewer affect words than do neurotics, externalizers, and sensitizers (Ullman, 1958; Asendorf and Scherer, 1983;

Taylor, 1984b). Carroll (1972) also found that on an affect-word checklist repressors checked fewer "feeling words" in response to visual stimuli. However, Martin and Pihl (1985) suggest that repressors increase their verbal production of affect in response to stress while alexithymics increase their verbal affect expression. Although their formulation is consonant with the published studies on alexithymia, (Knapp, 1980; Lolas et al., 1981), the possibility that repressors exhibit increased affective production compared with alexithymics has not been explored. Taylor and his associates (Taylor, Ryan, and Bagby, 1985) also indirectly distinguished between repressors and alexithymic patients. They found that the TAS showed a small, but significant, negative correlation with the SDS.

Kleiger and Dirks (1980) described two alexithymia subtypes that, at least superficially, correspond to the high-anxious and repressor subtypes. Using the MMPI, they distinguished high and low "panic-fear" alexithymics. The high panic-fear subjects appeared to be overwhelmed by affect and as a result, had difficulty communicating affect. Low panic-fear subjects presented themselves as calm, stable, and self-controlled—the "pseudonormal" psychosomatic patient. The distinctions made by Kleiger and Dirks suggest that alexithymia occurs, and varies, independently of trait anxiety. These findings must be reassessed using a valid measure of alexithymia.

Safar and his associates (Safar, Kamieniecka, Levenson, Dimitriu, and Pauleau, 1978) provide evidence that the repressive affective style and alexithymia are related phenomena. They found that both borderline and sustained hypertensives exhibited significant deficits in symbolic function on Rorschach testing. Borderline hypertensives also exhibited increased autonomic reactivity, somatic distress, hostility, and aggression on the Rorschach. Sustained hypertensives manifested increased autonomic reactivity but experienced fewer somatic symptoms and exhibited more significant inhibition of symbolic expression of anxiety. The authors suggested that sustained hypertensives develop adaptive impairments in symbolic and affective functions that enable them to dampen their global hyperreactivity in the absence of other self-regulatory mechanisms. One might suggest that these impairments in symbolic and affective functions are consistent with alexithymia. In this formulation, a repressive style, as described by Martin and Pihl (1985), could represent a stage in the genesis of an alexithymic style. This formulation may help in the understanding of the association of alexithymia with chronic gastrointestional or respiratory illnesses, sustained hypertension, and the appearance of alexithymia among the long-term sequelae of traumatic disorders (Krystal, 1978a; J. Krystal et al., 1986). Safar and his associates (1978) also suggest that the deficits in symbolic function preceded development of the chronic hypertensive syndrome. This finding suggests that symbolic and affective deficits observed in chronic illness are related but develop independently.

CHECKLISTS

The Multiple Affect Adjective Checklist (MAACL) has been widely used to assess personality variables (Gough and Heibrun, 1965). Byrne (1961) found that the deviant subscale of the MAACL correlated with the R-S scale. However, Lesser and his associates (1981) found that the MAACL failed to correlate with the BIPQ. Heibrun and Pepe (1985) modified the MAACL to assess conscious and unconscious elements of repression and denial. In their study, unconscious repression was associated with excessive perceived stress, while conscious denial correlated with decreased reported stress. Evaluating conscious and unconscious defenses, perhaps analogous to the distinctions suggested by Catchlove and Braha (1985), may be useful in clarifying the relationships between repression, denial, and alexithymia.

We conducted preliminary tests with a 35-item affect checklist (J. Krystal, Giller, and Cicchetti, unpublished data; copies of this scale may be obtained from J. Krystal). The items were rated by subjects on a four-point scale. For the purposes of this discussion, the four-point scale was condensed to binary data. This did not significantly affect diagnostic sensitivity or correlations with other scales. These tests were carried out as part of a larger study described earlier (J. Krystal et al., 1986). We compared seven inpatients with affective disorder (Mean Checklist Score = $28.85 +/- 2.54$ SD) with ten inpatients with Posttraumatic Stress Disorder (Mean Checklist Score = $26.00 +/- 6.44$). In this preliminary sample, the checklist did not correlate significantly with the SSS, BIPQ, MMPI Alexithymia Scale, or APRQ. Similarly, the checklist failed to discriminate between populations distinguished by the BIPQ ($Z = 2.00, p = 0.042$) and APRQ ($Z = -1.95, p = .048$). The BIPQ and APRQ were the only scales to correlate significantly ($r = 0.69, p = .003$) in this sample.

ADDITIONAL SELF-REPORT MEASURES

A variety of other measures may also be relevant to the alexithymia concept. Garner and his associates (1983) developed an Eating Disorder Index, which contains an Interoceptive Awareness subscale. Although its application is limited to eating disorders, this subscale appears to assess affective perception, tolerance, and expression, making it potentially relevant to the alexithymia concept. Two scales used in chronic pain populations may also prove useful in alexithymia research. Factor 4 on the Illness Behavior Questionnaire reflects difficulty expressing feelings. Pilowsky and Spence (1975) found that in their sample, 27% of chronic pain patients showed evidence of impairment in this area. The McGill Pain Questionnaire, when used in conjunction with the global distress scale of the Brief Symptom Index, an SCL-90 subscale, distinguishes patterns of affective function in pain patients (Melzack, 1975; Atkinson, Kremer, and Ignelzi, 1982; Kremer and Atkinson, 1984). As suggested earlier for alexithymics, Atkinson and his associates (1982) found that affectively disturbed chronic pain patients use more diffuse language than do nondisturbed pain patients to describe pain of similar location and severity. The relevance of these scales for the alexithymia concept is only hypothetical at this point.

OVERVIEW AND RECOMMENDATIONS

Review of the Scales

The failure to develop reliable and valid measures has been a fundamental stumbling block to the development of the alexithymia concept. Ongoing work, summarized in Table 2, currently favors those scales which focus on one aspect of the alexithymia concept and measures this most precisely. TA methods such as the APRQ appear most promising for assessing verbal production of differentiated affect. The SAT9 scale, and the method introduced by TenHouten and his associates (1985c) are the most successful recent attempts to rigorously assess symbolic function. The TAS may prove to be the first valid self-rating measure of alexithymia. As it continues to be developed and tested its correlation with alexithymic behavior, rather than attitudes, will be a critical issue.

All of the widely used alexithymia measures, the SSS, MMPI, and the BIPQ have had their validity or reliability seriously questioned. The Schalling-Sifneos scale may not accurately or reliably assess alexithymia. In student populations, three factors derived from SSS data were consistent with the alexithymia concept. However, the clinical significance of these findings is placed in question by the failure of the SSS scale to correlate with other measures of alexithymia (see Table 1), to differentiate alexithymia from nonalexithymic patient populations, or to demonstrate sufficient internal consistency.

The MMPI-Denver Alexithymia Scale also fails to correlate with other measures of alexithymia (Table 1) despite the fact that its items were originally derived through correlation with the BIPQ. Its clinical utility is highly questionable.

The MMPI-Irvine scale was derived through correlation with the SSS, whose validity was questioned above. After the initial reports, this scale has not been seriously pursued. It is unlikely that it will prove to be a useful self-report measure.

The Beth Israel Psychosomatic Questionnaire appears to show face and content validity and correlates with virtually every measure of alexithymia (Table 2). However, its reliability has been questioned by a number of studies.

TABLE 2
Reliability and Validity of Alexithymia Scales

Scale	Face Validity	Content Validity	Convergent Validity	Divergent Validity	Inter-Rater Reliability
SSS	Questioned	Questioned	No	Suggested	N.A.
MMPI-Denver	No	No	No	Questioned	N.A.
TAS	Suggested	Suggested	Untested	Suggested	N.A.
BIPQ	Yes	Yes	Yes	Suggested	Questioned
Total-Wd TA	Suggested	Suggested	Suggested	Suggested	Yes
Affect-Wd. TA	Suggested	Suggested	Suggested	Suggested	Yes
AVS	Suggested	Suggested	Questioned	Suggested	Yes
APRQ	Yes	Suggested	Suggested	Untested	Yes
SAT9	Suggested	Suggested	Suggested	Untested	Yes

Face Validity: Does it appear to measure alexithymia?
Content Validity: Does it accurately measure the full range of alexithymic characteristics?
Convergent Validity: Does it correlate with other measures of alexithymia?
Divergent Validity: Does it measure alexithymia in distinction to other distinct phenomena?
Scale abbreviations are drawn from the test. Unless a convincing body of evidence points to a "yes" or "no" evaluation above, favorable or critical evaluations are indicated with "suggested" or "questioned".

Perhaps some of the BIPQ's apparently convergent validity is an artifact of the malleability of the BIPQ interview and poor interrater reliability. This scale is easy to use and reflects the clinical impression of the rater. Although limited as a research scale, the BIPQ may be useful clinically as a framework for identifying alexithymic behaviors.

Transcript analysis methods are cumbersome to employ. However, computer rating may make them more accessible. TA methods permit raters blind to experimental conditions to assess verbal expression of affect. However, interviewing technique, setting, and the type of affective provocation employed all influence verbal expression of affect. Total-word, affect-word, and "affect vocabulary" scores may prove the most sensitive measures of verbal expression of differentiated affect. The clinical significance of these approaches, though, may depensd on the stimulus chosen to elicit verbal production of affect. The clinical implications of each of these measures need further exploration.

The Alexithymia Provoked Response Questionnaire represents a simplified TA approach. Our experience with this scale suggests that it has content and face validity (Table 2). APRQ transcripts also show a high degree of interrater reliability. This scale correlated highly with the BIPQ and differentiated alexithymic from nonalexithymic patients. This scale shows a great deal of promise. However, researchers will need to further define its properties.

The AT9 test, designed to assess the capacity for fantasy, assesses the subject's ability to create a story utilizing nine symbols. It appears reliable and valid in assessing this variable. The clinical relevance of the SAT9 is suggested by its correlation with the BIPQ. Further research will be helpful in flishing out the clinical relevance of the SAT9 scale for alexithymia. An additional measure introduced by TenHouten and his associates (1985c) also appears promising.

DENIAL, REPRESSION, AND ALEXITHYMIA

The concepts of denial, repression, and alexithymia are blurred in the psychiatric literature, making the establishment of the divergent validity of alexithymia a complex, if not impossible, task. Hackett and Cassem (1974) in developing their widely used denial scale, initially defined denial as "the conscious or unconscious repudiation of part or all of the total available meaning of an event to allay fear, anxiety, or other unpleasant affects" (p. 94). Other definitions of denial are more circumscribed. Shaw and associates (1985) delineated the boundaries of the denial concept by distinguishing between defensive responses to an external threat (denial) and internal feeling (repression). A similar view is also stated in a more elaborate psychodynamic form earlier in this text. Nemiah (1975) also suggested that denial reflected a more focal deficit than alexithymia. Hackett and Cassem (1974) further blurred the boundaries of the denial concept by introducing the concept of "major denial" for patients "who stated unequivocally that they felt no fear at any time throughout their hospital stay or earlier in their lives" (p. 94). The major denier group did not express fear verbally, somaticized affects, was action oriented, showed deficits in dreaming, and other characteristics associated with alexithymia.

In order to provide operational clarity, it seems useful to preserve the boundaries of the clinical concept suggested earlier by Shaw and his associates. The processes of denial and repression should apply to context-dependent and stimulus-specific processes influencing affective response to external and internal stimuli respectively. In contrast, alexithymia refers to a more global process influencing affective and symbolic function across contexts and stimuli, making it a trait variable. Clearly, though, alexithymia is influenced by state-dependent characteristics such as denial and repression. It also appears to be influenced by such factors as disorders of cerebral lateralization and presumably other neurophysiological processes

(TenHouten et al., 1985a, b, c, d). Widely accepted operational definitions would facilitate further research and discussions on the relationship of these three concepts.

Attempts to operationalize the destinction between denial and alexithymia are mixed in their results. Utilizing Chabb scales, von Rad and his associates (1979) found a greater degree of denial in psychosomatic patients than in neurotic patients, suggesting an overlap between these concepts. However, another study failed to find a correlation between the BPI-denial scale and alexithymia assessed with the TAS (Bagby, Taylor, and Ryan, in press).

IMPLICATIONS FOR FURTHER RESEARCH

Some of the confusion surrounding the measures of alexithymia probably lies in the broad definitions of impairments in affective and symbolic function. For example, in regard to affective function, it is possible that patients who do not recognize differences in differentiated affect, patients who recognize these differences but who have a "repressive" response to them, and patients who do not express differentiated affect are independent but overlapping groups. Future work will require more rigorous definition of the impairment assessed in both affective and symbolic function.

Although alexithymia appears to be a continuous variable, much of the literature treats it dichotomously. There are currently no studies in the literature to suggest that the distinction between alexithymics and nonalexithymics is dichotomous. Data from all the scales suggest a broad and continuous distribution of subjects (Heiberg, 1980; Kleiger and Kinsman, 1980; Gardos et al, 1984; Martin et al., 1984).

Furthermore, there are no widely validated criteria for alexithymia on any of the current rating scales. Preliminary suggestions for alexithymia criteria, based on clinical experience and pilot work rather than systematic study, have been incorporated into the literature (Kleiger and Kinsman, 1980; Blanchard et al., 1981). Although these alexithymia criteria parse out a small percentage of the population, one has only a vague idea what qualities this subpopulation possesses. In addition, alexithymia criteria are pointless for invalid, erratic, or unreliable scales. At this time, it is probably not useful to report the percentage of alexithymic patients in a given sample or to compare groups based on such percentage. Instead, reports should base comparisons on the actual data, in the form of means, standard deviations, and the like.

The stability of alexithymia over time is an important variable also requiring further exploration. Alexithymia developed as a clinical construct. From the clinical perspective, rating scales may assist in diagnosis and measure change. As noted earlier, it is premature to dichotomize patients as alexithymic or nonalexithymic for research purposes. When these distinctions are necessary, one should realize that they are somewhat arbitrary. However, clinical work does not require this distinction. It is sufficient to identify those patients who are "at risk" in order to draw attention to potential modifications in psychotherapeutic style that may prove useful (H. Krystal, 1979; see also next chapter).

Alexithymia ratings may be useful for assessing changes in clinical status. However, the stability of alexithymia has yet to be thoroughly investigated. Therefore, it is difficult to know whether to attribute changes in scores to therapy or to background fluctuation due to state-dependent variables. Yet, despite the difficulties, research must rigorously address the impact of therapy on alexithymia.

As reviewed earlier, alexithymia is being integrated into the broader psychologic and psychiatric literatures. Hence, the relationship between alexithymia, denial, and repressive affective style must be clarified. In addition, alexithymia research must broaden its horizons to formally evaluate comprehension as well as expression of differentiated affect. Researchers studying alexithymia need to assess the degree to which current measures may be utilized in tandem with physiological and psychosocial research methods. If current measures do not suffice, new scales must be developed.

As noted, the alexithymia concept has faced significant methodological problems in its brief history. One might say that its current popularity oversteps the preliminary nature of most of the studies investigating it. Yet the alexithymic concept appears to have much to offer clinicians and researchers. Despite the confusion surrounding it, this concept appears to describe a dyadic variable that rings true to many clinicians. Moreover, this concept may help to clarify a roadblock to efficacious psychotherapy in some patient populations, and it may have important implications for understanding the cognitive regulation of somatic and affective states.

Alexithymia research has the potential to make methodological contributions to other areas of psychiatric research. There is evidence that alexithymia may interfere with psychiatric and medical diagnosis (B. A. Jones, 1984). In addition, other self-rating measures in psychiatry may be affected by alexithymic characteristics. For example, a repressive style appears to have a significant impact on self-reported anxiety (Weinberger et al., 1979; Kass, Klein, and Cohen, 1983). Before these contributions can have their full impact, however, the validity and reliability of measures of alexithymia must be established.

Formal alexithymia research is in its infancy. The material reviewed in this discussion reflects the scope and complexity of the alexithymia concept and its implications for clinical practice. It is probable that this concept will develop in accord with ongoing research. However, disturbances in affective and symbolic function may be reformulated in future dynamic, developmental, cognitive, or neuropsychological theories. Even in such cases, the clinical observations described here will retain their relevance to researchers and clinicians interested in affective function and its role in clinical states.

APPENDIX
The Alexithymia Provoked Response Questionnaire

INSTRUCTIONS: Please record (either by hand or tape recorder) the subject's response to the following questions. Please record the entire response. If you feel a response is ambiguous in regard to its affect content, use further questioning to decrease this ambiguity. Avoid introducing affect-words into the interview. You may repeat questions if necessary. The scale may be introduced as a measure of how people feel or act in a variety of situations. (as used in J. Krystal et al., 1986).

————— 1. When you are upset, do you like to take action or do you prefer to think or daydream?

————— 2. How would you feel if a policeman arrested you for a crime you did not commit?

————— 3. How would you feel if someone insulted you?

————— 4. How would you feel if you heard a suspicious noise while you were all alone in your house at night?

————— 5. How would you feel if you had an emergency and tried to make a telephone call but the line was continually busy?

————— 6. How would you feel if someone cut you off in heavy traffic?

————— 7. How would you feel if someone laughed at you?

————— 8. How would you feel if you saw a truck coming at you at 90 mph?

————— 9. How would you feel if someone called you a coward?

————— 10. How would you feel if someone called you a thief?

————— 11. How would you feel if someone complimented you?

————— 12. How would you feel if someone said that you are the best?

————— 13. How would you feel if someone you loved died suddenly?

————— 14. How would you feel if someone tried to attack you with a knife?

————— 15. How would you feel if someone pulled a gun on you?

————— 16. How do you feel when you are hungry?

————— 17. How do you feel when you are sick?

15
Therapeutic Considerations
in Alexithymia

The preceding chapter gives us considerable hope that in the foreseeable future we will have instruments available that will help us to estimate the nature and severity of alexithymic problems. Once we can establish tests for the affective function that can be used in conjunction with the currently described ones that check the cognitive disturbance, it may be possible to distinguish the cases of regression in affect from those representing an arrest in development. The use of such tests in considering a potential candidate for psychoanalytic psychotherapy should prevent a good deal of disappointment. In chapter 13 I referred to the work of two psychologists (Thompson, 1981, and Hering, 1987) who have been studying the level of maturity of affects with particular reference to the self-recognition of feelings. Lane and Schwartz (1987) have approached the question of emotional awareness from the point of view of the Piagetan levels of cognitive development. By combining this basic orientation with the observations of other investigators, they demonstrated that the levels of cognitive structural transformation determined the manner of experiencing and determining the experience of oneself and of our world. Lane and Schwartz organized a scheme of emotional development corresponding to six levels of cognitive development. They presented these levels of development in the following way: 1) On the first level of emotional awareness—during sensorimotor reflexive awareness—only body sensations are registered. 2) In the sensorimotor enactive stage, there is an awareness of the body in action, and affects are reflected in action tendencies based on global and all-consuming states of pleasure or distress. 3) In the preoperational level of cognitive development, there is an awareness of individual feelings. 4) In the concrete operational level of cognitive function, Lane and Schwartz found evidence of an awareness of blends of feelings. 5) In the formal operational cognitive level, they found a full expansion of awareness of a multitude of blends of feelings.

This is just a skeletal outline of a seminal contribution that will greatly advance our understanding of the information processing of the cognitive elements of affects. The authors correlated these developmental events with the differentiation of emotions, the ability to describe emotions, the level of complexity of the mental representation of self and objects, the utilization of emotion as information about inward or outward conditions, the degree of differentiation between self-representation and object-representations and the nature and extent of empathic capacity. By this complex and multifaceted approach they have created the criteria by which the clinical conditions can be studied in terms of the cognitive-affective component. I see this as one of the final prerequisite steps that will make possible the practical clinical evaluation of the integrated function of the cognitive and expressive aspect of affects.

In addition, Sashin (1985) has been able to devise a model of affect function by which he feels that he can measure the status of affect tolerance. Basically, Sashin set out to measure affect responses (A) to an affect-provoking stimulus (S). In his review of affective functions we find five characteristics of affect: 1) mutliple states—by which he means that a person may not respond to the stimulus with an affect (R) or may discharge the affect in a stormlike, impulsive manner with "an overload response," which may be observable as impulsive action, somatic disorganization (R_2); or one may respond with a subjectively recognized feeling. 2) He further observed that there may occur jumps between these states. 3) He also found that some affect responses (R_3) may not be observable in any manifest action and hence may be considered "inaccessible." 4) He noted that there may be poor correlation between intensity of stimulus, as judged by an observer, and the intensity of an individual's response. This phenomenon, called "divergence," refers to affect regulation. 5) Finally, there may be a delay in affect responses to a stimulus, which Sashin called "hysteresis." To be able to measure the affect tolerance, Sashin proposed the use of the catastrophe theory (Woodcock and Davis, 1978). The catastrophe theory is a graphic means to represent any natural phenomenon in which there is an abrupt change in the status of a system. Sashin uses the work of Zeeman (1977), who maintains that the catastrophe theory may be used to describe phenomena in which a gradually changing force produces sudden effects. "The use of models based on catastrophe theory is strongly suggested in any phenomenon having the properties of: the possibility of different states under similar circumstances (bimodality or trimodality; divergence), sudden change, the persistence of states and delays before these changes occur (hysteresis) and the inaccessibility of certain of those states" (Sashin, 1985, p. 180). Using this model, we end up with the formula: $A^5 = LA^3 + FA^3 + CA + S$, where A is the affect response, L is the degree of *impairment* of the ability to verbalize affects, F is the capacity to fantasize, C is the degree of *impairment* of the inner container (which Sashin defines as "the inner psychological structure based on self-representations and object-representations which enable [one] to experience, contain, modulate and bear his feelings" (p. 176), and S is the level of environmental affect-evoking stimulation (p. 194). The application of this equation to a three-dimensional graph produces a figure of a butterfly configuration, which is the cusp catastrophe surface. Using Thom's (1975, 1977) classification theorem, Sashin portrayed the function of affect expression and containment in terms of a graph using one dependent variable and two independent variables. The graph is designed to show the cusp catastrophic response, or butterfly-shaped line. What makes it especially helpful graphically is that it illustrates how affect in catastrophic situations would reach conspicuously "explosive" intensity in certain persons, but would "explode" and remain hidden in alexithymic people. The model and the conception permit the author to explore geometrically the interaction between the factors identified. After establishing these principles, Sashin moves on to the richer and more complex figure of the butterfly catastrophe models, in which he can employ and explore the relationship of all five variables. All of this produces very elegant and useful views. At this point, Shashin's contribution (which won the 1983 Felix and Helene Deutsch prize of the Boston Psychoanalytic Society and Institute) seems almost too good to be true.

There are, however, a number of assumptions in this model that will require testing of their validity. For one, Shashin used the following definition of affect tolerance: "the capacity to experience anxiety without having to discharge it" (p. 178), which he derived from the 1956 Menninger Foundation team efforts (Sargent, 1956), based on conceptions of the economic point of view. It further assumes that the capacity to fantasize and verbalize affect is *measurably* inversely correlated to affect responses. This idea in particular strikes me as too good to be true, but I am reassured by Shashin's statement that much testing of this formulation is underway. Whatever the studies show, we are sure to learn more about affect tolerance and various aspects of affect in general. It is hoped that some tests and insights will evolve to permit the evaluation of affective function in every candidate for psychotherapy.

None of the previously available theories or assumptions about traits related to psychosomatic diseases provides guides for therapy (Hinkle, 1961). Vaillant's (1978) explorations of the natural history of psychosomatic diseases produced no clues to causality. He did report a couple of fascinating observations of psychosomatic patients: 1) if their life history was available, one could observe that even as children their ability to *play* had been much below average and 2) people who had had a healthy childhood—without early physical illnesses—were less likely to have psychosomatic illnesses as adults. Vaillant's findings are also in harmony with the studies of the astronauts (Ruff and Korchin, 1967), referred to in chapter 6, that persons who had not been overwhelmed by challenges beyond their powers to master tended to grow up to have low physiological responses to anxiety and stress and became generally "unflappable."

When I first became aware of the problem that alexithymics have with their affects, it seemed natural to address myself to the two predominant obstacles: the nature of their transference and the affective disturbance (Krystal, 1979). In regard to the transference, I pointed out that although these patients were "stuck" in the patient-doctor attitude and were low in elaboration or evidence of emotional attachment, it seemed helpful to consider that this was a kind of transference that actualized the patient's infantile self-representation and the need to be cared for. In effect, I interpreted the transference just as McDougall (1978)—that the patient's behavior was a type of primitive communication, like the child's crying out in distress.

Instead of relieving the patients' distress, I would try to understand what they were reexperiencing and give them interpretations about the defensive nature of their regressive self- and object perception. I expected that eventually I would get to the conflicts and impulses behind them. But, since the patients were not responding adequately either with associations or with appropriate affects, I thought it might be necessary to address myself to the nature of their affective functions. It turned out that describing to the patients the nature of their emotions was helpful to them and was even appreciated by them. Many of the patients had noticed that they were different and that they reacted differently from other people. When they were helped to understand their pattern of physiological responses and their inability to identify a "feeling" and to use it as information, they were much relieved. Some commented that they were glad to find out that they were not crazy. They were particularly pleased to know that at those times when they were showing excessive "emotional expressiveness" without feeling proportionate excitement within, there was a reason and explanation for this "crazy intrusion" into their minds.

While they benefited in a number of ways from these interventions, there was no change in certain problem patterns. In the process of working with these, other issues emerged; for instance, the nature of their reaction to having the experience of affect. Working with affect tolerance, that is, investigating how the patients responded to *having* an affect, likewise turned out to be a very rewarding and eye-opening endeavor. Frequently it become clear that the patients had come to see me at the end of a chain of maladaptive responses to affects. Investigating how patients experienced and interpreted their emotions became a rich source of information. I would spend much time demonstrating to the patients how they promoted and magnified their distressful affective states. Even with depressive patients, who often prefer to spend most of their therapeutic time complaining about their symptoms, I'd be just as persistent in pointing out how they generated and perpetuated their depression out of a sense of guilt. Some of them would finally have enough of this confrontation and blurt out, "Well, what should I do when I am depressed?" At that point I would explain that depression is a form of pain, and I would invite them to review all the means they had at their disposal to attain relief from the particular pain from which they suffered.

But this conversation rarely takes place with alexithymic patients. Rather, as I start to point out the nature of the affective disturbance, the cognitive limitation of fantasy life and the problems with affect tolerance, I soon discover that the patients are also very poor at taking care of themselves. But, as already pointed out, they are not aware of this block and do not seem to be interested in correcting it. As far as they are concerned, it is not within their scope to assume self-regulation or self-caring functions. In fact, in their unconscious mind, this prohibition—that they must not try to usurp functions reserved to mother (God)—is the most important and powerful *commandment*. The result of this combination of forces is that the therapist can move into the only sphere in which he is given room to operate: he may address himself to interpreting and demonstrating the nature of the patients' behavior. In doing so, he can show that the patients tend to treat themselves, their love objects, and their therapist as machines.

In other words, the work has to start out with the demonstration that the patients lack empathy for every important object in their lives, including the therapist. Only *after* it has been demonstrated that, contrary to their opinions, the patients are not treating their love objects well, can they talk about self-care.

While demonstrating to the patients their lack of empathy with their love objects, one may find some surprising inconsistencies.

Case Illustration

One of my patients was famous for his generosity, which he dispensed with great flourish. It was all done with such excellent taste and involved such perfection in each such performance that his own championship in each class of largesse was clearly proven. It was not possible to question the generosity of the performance, for even its threatricality was suitable for the circumstances. It was just that he really didn't much care for the people, and if his attention was taken over by something else, he would forget them for that time. When he noticed them again, he was frequently surprised to find that they were angry with him. A very skilled lover of great endurance, he did not understand why there was something peculiar in his behavior when he devoted an entire night to making a streetwalker happy in every way possible, but then forgot about her. In general, his competitiveness, acrobatics in sex, taking unnecessary risks, and even flirting with criminality (which happened not to work out, but he could have become a major criminal) all could happen because he had no awareness of anxiety or other affective signals.

The early phases of treatment of the alexithymic patient contain a number of paradoxes. From the point of view of the patient, there seems to be no possible connection between the life of *reason* he is living—so filled with realistic pursuits—and the "illness." These patients feel that there is a totally alien obstacle to their plans, a psychosomatic disease or drug addiction, which periodically takes control of their lives like a demonic "possession." There may be an encapsulated story of trauma, sometimes hidden behind a number of traumatic screens, which emits a shower of physical symptoms just like the malaria fever.

For instance, this patient pointed out with considerable pride that since he was two years old both of his parents had worked and he took over his own care. Also since early childhood he had taken care of his brothers and even his parents. He explained that he had to take care of his family because his father was away for unpredictable periods of time and his mother was very childish and when the father left she would "collapse." Now this patient has to take care of everyone around him. He would point out that since he was very well able to do so, and since he would never permit himself to be dependent on anyone else, everything was fine. He had no recognition of drivenness and the self-defeating aspects of the periodic lapses in his "superman" structure.

As the therapist, I tried to "get into" the complex structure of the patient's problems by as many portals as I could find. I tried to deal with affect tolerance, affect verbalization, problems of self- and object-representation, and problems of empathy. Whenever he began to talk about emotions, he ran into an impenetrable wall. This is the walling off of the maternal object-representation, which contains extensive areas of the patient's mental representation of his body. (See chapter 10.)

Many patients have inhibitions regarding the exercising of self-caring functions, and they tend to attribute the ownership of their affective and vital functions to maternal transference objects. Their lives are dominated by ideas that are reflected in religious and legal thinking: that God, and not they, own their lives and that God takes their soul away for the night and then returns it, making possible their awakening. What to the naive therapist may appear as a simple task of helping the patients to recognize, verbalize, and regulate their emotions seems very different to the patients. The therapist seems to be asking them to do something inconceivable, something that for some reason fills them with unspeakable dread. Some patients react as if we had proposed to hypnotize them and then induce them to do something dangerous and forbidden, to stop their heart and then leave the matter of heartbeat regulation to their volitional efforts. The enormous potential of biofeedback training, which theoretically could eliminate the need for most medications, is defeated by the inhibitions, which are universal to some extent but are particularly severe in alexithymic patients. If such patients are consistently confronted with their opposition to consciously exercising the self-control or to recognizing the unity of their affective responses, it becomes clear that they are terrified of assuming these "forbidden" functions.[1] These "powers" are reserved for mother, doctor, God. When gradually and repeatedly confronted with this glaring and obvious pattern, the patients may recognize these themes as vaguely familiar, or at least capable of evoking some resonance in them with wishes to regain their self-regulatory and self-soothing powers.

At the same time, on another level, there may be a "living out" of oedipal transferences and resistances. One can, and often does, become preoccupied with them. Many alexithymics go through classical psychoanalysis, and, although they are considered boring and pedestrian analysands, they may finish their analyses by mutual consent. This sometimes leaves them with unresolved problems of psychosomatic diseases, addiction, or posttraumatic sequelae, as discussed herein. Experience shows that most alexithymics enter analytic treatment and produce enough material to stimulate the analyst to give them the kind of interpretation that Peterfreund (1983) calls "stereo-typic." The result is a proliferation of cliché responses that give the illusion of progress in the analytic endeavor. But, as we know, alexithymic patients really do not have the affective capacity to respond to interpretations with experiences of such intensity and conviction that a self-transmuting response can be expected. But this is rarely noticed by a psychoanalyst. If an analyst did try to address this problem, he would have to "fight" on two fronts at once: to work on the patients' affective and cognitive problems so that they can deal with the neurotic problems, which also are being worked on; and, at the same time, to avoid teaching the patients the analyst's idea of what they *should* be experiencing.

The paradox is that while the patients produce little of the interesting, exciting, and imaginative mentation characteristic of the "good hysteric," their lives may contain spectacular sexual and phallic exploits. However, their intrapsychic experiences bear the mark of alexithymic, not neurotic, conflicts. It may be that this is why European psychoanalysts, such as Stephanos (1975), hospitalize psychosomatic patients and promote a regression and infantile type of transference to an "ideal mother–father" object. They simply eliminate the stage for neurotic problems while promoting the acting out of early infantile states. With this strategy, they promote a regression that exposes the infantile nature of root conflicts. The alexithymic patients are used to acting out all kinds of "adult" roles, even though huge areas of their self-regulatory functions have been massively impaired since infancy.

---

1. Budzynski (1981) has found that chronically depressed patients cannot use biofeedback or cognitive therapy because they respond to every idea with "Oh no you're not." He proposed using "delta" twilight state (hypnogogic) learning to get around "hemispheric conflict" (p. 9).

From what we learned earlier about there being a dual coding of experiences, if we limit ourselves to dealing with the verbalized material we encounter only those memories and conflicts that are verbally encoded. Hence, we can deal only with memories that have been worked over and were registered at a high level of abstraction in adolescence. Furman (1978) reviewed Byrd's list of factors that make analyzability and transference possible. He commented that the list was missing "a most important component of the reality of the analytic situation, the most common one, which runs the least risk of interfering with the development of the transference, and which may most facilitate its emergence: verbalization of affects" (p. 210).

Oedipal conflicts can be found in memories that were translated into verbal and symbolic terms in adolescence from memory traces formed in childhood and latency. This phenomenon explains why child analysands do not recall their analyses when they are reinterviewed as adults. The technique of dealing with certain kinds of symbols that could be organized around libidinal developmental stages was responsible for the "discovery" of separation-individuation fifty years after the "anal" psychosexual developments of toddler age. Possibly it would have never been found if direct observations had not been used to augment analytic material. The analyst who intends to deal with residuals of *infantile* trauma has to be prepared to deal with memory traces that are exclusively affective and devoid of verbal or symbolic components. Such memories may be dominated by some global sensori-precept trace similar to the reported contents of stage IV nightmares (Fisher, 1956). To do such work however, one must take heed of Peterfreund's (1983) injunction to do heuristic rather than sterotypic psychoanalysis.

Since the analyst is constantly *selecting* the kind of material he highlights and the constellations he proposes as explanatory motifs, he has to keep in mind that double task I mentioned before: in dealing with alexithymic patients, one has to do interpretive work while simultaneously addressing oneself to those aspects of alexithymic problems that cannot be handled by interpretations alone.

If it were not for this predicament, the following outline, which I proposed in 1982–83, would be perfectly adequate. There I listed "a few simple principles of technical modifications":

1. The nature of the patient's affect and cognitive problems should be carefully explained to the patient, including the methods of covering up their deficiencies in their perceptions and object- and self-representations.
2. Affect tolerance must be improved. Before these patients can deal with the emotions themselves, one has to first attend to their "having" them. Handling one's emotions is a challenge in many situations in all affective disorders. However, for these patients, because of the relatively intense physiological responses, the emotions represent a special

burden. What affective responses are and how one uses them to one's advantage need to be taken up in great detail by the therapist and practiced by the patients. The acquisition and practicing of the skill of "managing" one's emotions is a necessary prerequisite to utilization of affects as signals.

3. Dealing with the inhibition in self-care is another early task. The idea of affects being signals to one's self to be used and regulated to one's best advantage is not at all self-evident for these patients. Many of them use their emotions to control their love-object and/or experience their emotions as emanating from their object-representations, and their regulation and utilization is reserved for the maternal object representation. Before some of the alexithymic individuals dare to extend their selfhood to include their emotions and proceed to activate their verbalization and utilization of their emotions, their inhibitions in this regard have to be interpreted.

4. Affect-naming and verbalization must be encouraged. Supplying to the alexithymic the words and names for emotions is a slow task, because verbalization represents just one half of the task. The other half consists in desomatization. That is why certain things must be repeated and re-experienced many times, and require time and practice. No statement of the patient's about how he or she felt can be taken for granted as one goes through a review of his or her reactions. Since the use of dreams and utilization of the transference is limited, it is necessary to start by pointing out the impairment in empathy and sensitivity that these patients show in their object relations. Because they do not have signal affects available to them, they also lack empathy. In particular, they have no feeling or conviction of loving anyone or of anyone loving them [p. 371].

If a broad view is taken, it may be found that the same affective and cognitive problems that interfere with these patients' performance in analysis also wreak havoc with their current object relations. Partly out of the necessity to help patients discern the nuances of their interaction of which they are oblivious (they do not even know what they are missing) and partly owing to the need to demonstrate to them the primitive forerunner of affective responses, one has to make observations, comments, elucidations, and confrontations regarding the patients' "outside" object experiences. Gradually, it may become possible to shift emphasis and begin to make direct transference interpretations. Even in these patients' current object relations, one must not presume that they are aware of even the most basic, common "human" feelings and perceptions. There is a great deal of variation in this respect with unpredictable lacunae coming into view.

These technical modifications do not represent such *radical* departures as would preclude later psychoanalytic psychotherapy by the same person. These methods may be most useful in mild to moderate alexithymia. Nevertheless, my previous writings on the subject have been somewhat misinterpreted, taken as advocacy of a primarily didactic attitude. As I see it, we must be very flexible in addressing ourselves to the complexity and fragility of these patients.

The problem in regard to the ideas of self-regulation and self-caring is that we run into a kind of transference that reveals a conflict more severe and horrifying than the oedipal one. If we were still using the idea of "complexes," I would have named this one the "Prometheus" complex. All the previous chapters of this book were intended to generate a "feel" for the magnitude and harshness of the nuclear conflict regarding assumption of conscious self-recognition and conscious self-responsibility.

But we cannot observe or understand these kinds of transferences if we wait for the patients to give us verbal or image clues. We can only sit back, listen on our accustomed wave length, and when there is nothing new on it, consider the patient to be boring (Taylor, 1984a).

As an example of this kind of sensitization, namely, "getting a feel" for alexithymia, I have struggled with the impairment of fantasy-making observed in these patients. We are accustomed to looking for some defensive blocking that could be removed by interpretation. However, like others who work with alexithymic patients (e.g., McDougall, 1974b), I long ago learned to look for the *absence* of fantasy. A similar situation was described by Tustin (1981) from her work with autistic children, and considering this gives us an additional view of infantile psychic trauma. Just as I had to postulate, Tustin also states, "All childhood psychoses in which psychogenic elements predominate seem to have their origin in situations in infancy in which a hyper-vulnerable child has been shocked into awareness too painfully or too soon" (p. 103). And the autistic objects "have no fantasy whatsoever associated with them, or they may be associated with extremely crude fantasies which are associated with bodily secretions" (p. 96). She points out that the world of the autistic child is globally apprehended, so that objects are not clearly distinguished from each other by clues other than *sensations*. The defect that we see in the alexithymics in regard to paucity of fantasy and impairment in clue processing is illustrated in the extreme in those children, who register only contour and outline but do not register the concepts of meaning or function. Consequently, when disturbances are found this early, the major question is not "What is male and what is female?"; these children flounder on the earlier mystery—the distinction between people and things, or "what is animate and what is inanimate?"

This orientation has, magnified as it were, the same characteristic as the alexithymics'—objects are the same to them as people if they arouse a desire. However Tustin (1981) makes the same point that we have discovered in the alexithymic—that autistics cannot consciously register desire, wish, or even need because they cannot tolerate the frustration in the failure to obtain instant gratification. This is the very defect that prevents the formation of such symbolic activities as fantasies and memories in the state of frustration. Thus Tustin shows in the psychotic child a magnification of the alexithymic's style of living in a bodily and concrete (operative, thing-related) way with a massive restriction of fantasy elaboration. In psychotic children this problem is some-times so severe that they appear to be mentally retarded.

And so it is also with alexithymic patients that they do not form fantasies, but can recognize their desires when fulfillment is immediately possible. "Otherwise," they rationalize, "what's the point of it?" They originally could not bear the tension, and now the tension is totally somatic and they do not recognize it consciously. Moreover, contrary to curently accepted analytic thinking, fantasies per se do not give pleasure, except through the evocation of an affective and hedonic response from them. Alexithymics generally do not receive such a response because of their affective disturbance and because of the frequent coincidence of anhedonia.

For the child to form the transition from the sensorimotor functioning to an illusion of self-gratification and through it to a world of fantasy, there has to be an attachment to the mother of such power and confidence that the infant can gradually extend the attachment from the nipple to her face, to her sounds, and to other sensory signals to words. Furman (1978) has described in detail how the mother encourages the development of emotions by responding to them. She helps the child to name and identify his emotions. If he is angry, she tries to understand the reason, explain it, and fix it. "If the child is sad, she comforts, if he is out of control, she supplies control, if he is happy, she shares." Particularly she shares in the beginnings of verbalization, lending it a magical aura, and "demonstrating that the verbalization of feelings leads to action or response and thus to mastery" (p. 204).

But what Furman describes is a later and successful stage of development. Earlier, the child is in danger of displaying a reaction more similar to what Tustin (1981) described, but not as severe and not leading to alexithymia. Kreisler (1983) has called it "affective atonia" and "empty behavior," which he feels is accompanied by repeated infections and retarded growth. In such situations the object relations are undifferentiated, without signs of individual attachment. Everything happens as if it were coming directly from the environment. These people behave as if they have been deprived of the phase of stranger distress, and there is no evidence of oral or transitional autoerotic activities. While their motor activity may be adequate, it "is dry of fantasy elaboration" (p. 466).

Kreisler felt that these disturbances were reversible in childhood. However, since the first autonomy developed has to do with respiration, the infant's psychosomatic functions are vulnerable very early particularly to asthma. Moreover, the response necessary at this age goes beyond speech; gestures and actions are more basic, as is the mother's face. The mother's face can be "like a reward, an encouragement"; but if the mothering parent cannot mobilize a loving response, "there is no beckoning encouragement . . . for now there is fear that envelops the child. It weighs him down and he cannot move forward. There is some wish to lead him to the goal but the wish is suddenly terrifying" (Riess, 1978, p. 403).

The aftereffects of such devastating experiences are the kind of "empty" responses we find in alexithymic patients' mental representations of self and objects. That is why there is such a struggle in McDougall's (1974b) ideas about the fate of the infantile fantasies and object-representations. At times, as we have seen, she felt that they are destroyed or given up without any compensation; at other times, she feels, they are buried deeply and not capable of verbal articulation or any symbolic representation. But she seems to find the solution (1980b) in Freud's (1911, 1918) term *Verwerfung*, which she translates as repudiation or foreclosure—to denote a defense mechanism more absolute and severe than repression. The impulses, object-representation, and even part of self-representation subjected to such repudiation are forever doomed to be denied access to consciousness or indirect expression via unconscious fantasies or dreams in any way. For all practical purposes, they are destroyed.

In trying to prepare for dealing with such patients, one looks back to portals of entry that have been found useful in other hard-to-reach situations. Little (1981), for example, working with regressed patients found that memories of early infantile experience have to be sought. In such patients one has to link bodily experiences in the analysis with early infantile somatic states. Otherwise, the separation between mind and body persists, and, with it, the state of infantile deprivation and rage. Pining for love persists and cannot heal. It is necessary to reconstruct the infantile experience as nearly as possible—and to provide "cover memories" with a meaning in the contents of current transference-related physical sensations. Little (1981) adds, "Any element of conjecture must be admitted" (p. 85).

What I have been emphasizing as the work related to helping the patients to verbalize their emotions pertains equally to early memory traces. We cannot hesitate to utilize "not only the nursery and onomatopeic words but [also] very primitive sounds and mouth movements, from where other movements and body happenings can be reached, so as to make contact between inner and outer reality and help change one from concrete and magical thinking to acceptance of substitutes and symbolization" (p. 86).

Inasmuch as transference interpretations are ineffective with psychotic children and with alexithymics, we have to search for other ways to reach them. Because these patients cannot furnish the same kind of material as neurotics do, the analyst has to reach for the manifestations of preverbal and bodily levels and relate these to the patient's current needs and yearnings. The analyst has to use his own fantasy of the patient's infantile perspective of the world to understand what the patient needs and why he or she dreads attending to it.

Little also described how in the process of her self-analysis, she did a kind of psychic "stretching" in order to reach a level of creative activity in a state that she described as "the opposite" of trance or catatonic state (p. 257). But the difference is only in the degree of integration, not in the subjective modification. The objective of this contemplative self-sight is to render some intrapsychic "barriers" more "porous." In fact, Little is describing the subjective experience that Hoppe (1979) called a "creative moment" (p. 24). It is also, as I mentioned in a previous chapter, that some alteration of receptivity, similar to what happens in some trances, may be necessary to reach these "walled off" areas and functions of the alexithymic patient. And, as Little well knew, the therapist has to mobilize *that kind of creativity* instead of being a bored spectator. This mobilization is necessary because there is a critical time in infancy when the capacity for symbolization may produce benign transitional objects and either blossom into preconscious symbolization or else turn into autistic objects and produce severe withdrawal, deadness, and disconnection (Tustin, 1980; Deri, 1984).

The step indicating that attachment, security, and maturation are permitting symbol formation is the transitional object "creation." Deri (1984) has made a point, which I also developed earlier in this volume, that early object-representations, which enter into the transitional object formation, may either become part of "good symbolization" or deteriorate into a fetish. This fateful development may depend on "the length of time the mother remains absent" (p. 257). Tustin (1980) is even more categorical. She defined the autistic object in the hand with which the child grips it as becoming a part of a *psychotic sensation-dominated body experience*. This is so because the psychotic child exists in a bodily way while the mental development is severely inhibited. She also believed that autistic objects are normal in early infancy. "It is a state in which sensations predominate but not in the addictive and rigid way that is characteristic of psychogenic psychosis" (p. 101). Thus, certain early objects that the baby handles become "sensation objects" and can be called autistic objects or selfobjects. Normal autistic objects attract all infants, and with certain children the mother has to be confident and resourceful in order "to muster sufficient firmness and resilience to attract her infant away from the illusory delights of his sensation-objects to the real enjoyment of her breast, which he gradually learns to use as separate from his body" (p. 31). Normally, says Tustin, children use their primary creativity to create the "illusion" of unity (and, as I pointed out earlier, also the illusion of self-caring). It is a very high challenge to intuitive responsiveness for the mother to rescue the child from the trance-producing autistic state. She does this by placing the breast precisely where the infant is ready "to create" it, and at the right moment.

When the child is safely and securely attached to this primary love object and has an image of her and her preparatory rituals indicating her readiness to gratify his need, then delays are desirable. They stimulate "creating anticipatory pictures and new responses to the mother" (p. 32) and, we may add, an increasing specialization and differentiation of affect vocalization.

Again, the work of Tustin contains a surprising statement about trances, namely, that if things go wrong in the nursing couple, "the infant is then driven to obtain almost instant trance-inducing ecstasy from his own body to distract his attention from the unutterable pain of the outside world" (p. 33). It is amazing that many authors, in dealing with infantile and adult catastrophic traumatic states, refer to trances as the particular modification of consciousness necessary for survival from unbearable stress and that the infants may thus become addicted to trances.

HOW TO ENTER THE ARENA OF INFANTILE CONFLICTS

It may be useful to remind ourselves at this point, as we are trying to reach the alexithymic patient therapeutically, of where the difficulties developed. There was no difficulty in talking with these patients about affect tolerance or in helping them to name affects. The problem was that they had an enormous block about self-regulatory and self-caring functions.

The history of the development of self-regulatory functions, including self-respect regulation, all self-soothing functions, and the operation of vital and affective organs, suggests a universal inhibition based on conflicts. If we include basic affective memories in our reportoire of considerations, then we can recognize transferences related to these conflicts. That does not mean, however, that we can interpret them as we do neuroses, nor can we expect these patients to respond as neurotics do.

Instead, we need to find some way to communicate *effectively* to patients that it is all right for them to claim their whole potential and, in particular, to bring their entire selves into the sphere of conscious self-recognition and use it consciously under their own aegis and authority. But to communicate this message in such a way that barriers can be lifted and self- and object-representations can be modified, we have to communicate differently than we ordinarily do.

We need to gain access to the part of the mind in which these controls and prohibitions, as well as functions, reside. Certainly, hypnosis is a proven way to do this. Every function that a person is able to exercise in a hypnotic trance is one that is otherwise blocked by an inhibition. All therapists use some hypnosis (suggestion) some of the time, knowingly or not (Paskewitz, 1977). The only problem with the use of hypnosis is that credit for the achievements is given to the hypnotist and not to the subject, and that attribution reinforces the patient's already distorted, diminished conscious self-recognition. It is amusing that the idea of using self-hypnosis for relaxation has gained a popular following, yet many people who talk about it do not catch on to the cognitive incongruity involved in the very term.

The many studies on transitional objects and transitional processes provide us with a most exciting opportunity for intervention. Horton and Sharp (1984) gave gone straight to the heart of the matter in regard to our previously noted aprosody and inhibition in self-care of the alexithymics: "Prosodic competence overlaps to some degree with solacing competence" (p. 167).

They explain the role of the transitional object in promoting comfortable and self-conscious self-care:

> Transitional objects (and "phenomena") acquire their power to relieve anxiety and to calm as a result of spillover from the first and most meaningful, psychologically internalized relationship with a loving presence. If the internalization is successful, each subsequent life experience with a transitional object is, in part, a solace dèjá-vu. If the essential comforting internalization does not occur, the person may continue to search and, to a limited degree, experience solace, but he or she will have no autonomy from the external source [p. 169].

The transitional object in infancy is a kind of auxiliary device by which the illusion of omnipotence is transformed into an acceptable view of the object—because it provides the illusion of magical control over the object. Adults must exercise caution because transitional objects have to be used with great delicacy and discretion so as not to diminish the subject's sense of integrity or mobilize the prohibition against self-soothing.

Self-solacing usually takes place under private circumstances, and in subtle and inconspicuous ways. It is important to acknowledge Horton and Sharp's (1984) observation that " . . . people, regardless of life stage, require solacing objects, activities . . . and . . . sounds to adapt to novel, stressful ever frightening circumstances" (p. 170). I believe that Horton and Sharp are absolutely correct in hypothesizing that an "important aspect of linguistic competence takes its origin in the transitional mode of functioning" (p. 173). This is certainly true of prosody and most likely also of the freedom to make metaphors and create fantasies. The authors point out that comforting vocalizations and other aspects of language emerge from the large variety of self-soothing sounds and motions.

However, I believe that the observations are from a later date than those of Kestenberg (1978), who considered tactile experiences, muscle tension, and stretching in regard to their influence on the formation of self-representation and self-regulation. She pointed out that various physical contacts between mother and baby, performed with love and in a state of trust, directly influence the baby's vital functions, for example, respiratory rate. This early influence is essential to helping the baby to establish his or her own homeostasis. Kestenberg takes her clues from certain German authors who feel that the desirable tension and relaxation with the optimal vital organ function (eutony) is characteristic of every infant and animal. In her view, the adult is able to achieve eutony through "transensus," that is, a sense of making contact with a caring person: "Transensus enables us to experience the center and the expanding boundaries of the body either seeking out or melting into an object" (p. 66). Kestenberg describes her experiences with physical therapy or massagelike approaches by Glaser in Germany in which she felt that she could "experience firsthand how the illusion of incorporating another person's hand, arm, or entire body produces an invigoration of breath and increases the elasticity of tissues" (p. 67). In other words, Kestenberg searched for that type of experience, for that moment in the mind, when there was receptivity to a greater self-acceptance based on the illusion of unity.

EXPERIMENTS IN TECHNICAL MODIFICATION

The search for these deep and profound levels has led European workers to make some radical departures from orthodoxy. Some European psychosomatists have recommended various relaxation techniques by means of which patients can be put into a receptive mood. There is a sense that the patients have to be removed from their usual environment, which is stressful and produces the patient's "frozen" posture and affect. Also, the use of medication to achieve relaxation and a return to infantile receptivity has been advocated (Bastiaans, 1977, p. 292). In addition to various relaxation techniques, such as meditation and hypnosis, there has been experimentation with the use of groups in which were "planted neurotic group members" who served as "affect translators" and with the use of videotape playbacks (Apfel-Savitz et al., 1977, p. 329).

Hospitalized alexithymic psychosomatic patients in the Heidelberg University Hospital were treated by group psychotherapy, "sensual awareness therapy" *(Konzentrative Bewegungstherapie)*, as well as "ergotherapy" *(Gestaltangstherapie)*, intended to give them an affective experience (Schellschopp-Rueppell, 1977). Braeutigam's (1977) comments on these experiments sum up the spirit of exploration of these efforts. In regard to the "sensual awareness therapy," he said, "We foster [body] awareness deliberately and encourage the patient to perceive and express bodily feelings in a differentiated manner" (p. 362). About "egotherapy" he explained, "We encourage patients to deal with emotionally charged material by way of creative expression, e.g. drawing pictures or modeling clay or other materials. Thus, anxieties, desires, memories, but also significant persons from the patient's life become accessible in an elementary fashion" (p. 362). Hence, nonverbal techniques are explored (Becker, 1977) as an adjunct to psychotherapy with alexithymic patients as well as a supplement to treatment with severely ill individuals. The early blocks are most difficult to reach in the usual way.

These studies may also have an implication for the problems of anhedonia. As psychotherapists, we are accustomed to removing inhibitions, whereupon patients' needs and ambitions are expected to rise up and motivate them to assume all previously blocked functions. In regard to anhedonia resulting from early or catastrophic traumatization, even after the removal of masochistic problems there seems to be an inability to experience pleasure, joy, or gratification. The question, then, is, How can we help these patients to *cultivate* these underdeveloped or severely suppressed capacities?

My impression is that it is possible to encourage and help anhedonic patients to cultivate their capacity for pleasure. In those cases, the therapist has to step out of the "neutral" role and declare himself in favor of the patient's efforts to attain some gratification in life. Admitting that we do not have the answers and offering to explore and look out for possibilities establishes a partnership of a type somewhat different from the usual psychoanalytic model.

Favorable results have been obtained with these approaches with some patients who were encouraged to keep doing certain things that they thought they might eventually enjoy. This technique was derived from working with depressive patients who had temporary anhedonia. If the patients resumed their recreational activities, the return of their capacity for pleasure seemed to be speeded. One cannot help speculating that soon drugs may be available to influence the hedonic state—for example, opioid endogenous peptides and cannabis, which, it has been suggested, directly stimulates the pleasure centers of the brain (Heath, 1973).

In fashioning "alexithymia" as a useful clinical concept, one has to be expecially aware of the mercurial quality of that state. It is a characteristic derived through a complex epigenetic process, one intimately related to early object-relations and involving the key elements of the self- and object-representation. It also involves such complex elements of cognition and reflective self-awareness that it becomes subject to fluctuations and regressions. The occurrence of alexithymia among psychoanalysts and other psychotherapists makes them particularly liable to missing these problems in their patients. There is another paradox: The degree of differentiation and verbalization (and desomatization) is strongly influenced by social and cultural elements (Leff, 1973), but also is subject to individual variation. Sharp contrasts have been found in attitudes and styles of upbringing in regard to the handling of emotions (Krystal, 1975a).

A new area for research is the fate of the children of alexithymic parents. Among the children of survivors of the Nazi Holocaust it has been found that the parents who have an exceedingly high rate of alexithymia are unable to assist their children in the process of affect maturation. One son of survivors observed, "The only word that was ever heard in my parent's home referring to emotions was 'upset.' " Yet, I have observed that the children of survivors do not have a rate of alexithymia higher than their schoolmates whose parents are not survivors. A tentative explanation of this observation is that the early responsiveness and attentiveness of the mothering parent is a more powerful factor in stimulating the process of affect vocalization and differentiation, and later verbalization, than is the countervailing effect of the parents' own alexithymia. Also, that the "second generation" resembled their peers more than their parents in the nature of their affective maturation, fantasy formation, and affect tolerance suggests that the social element and identification with peers during latency and adolescence may account for the demonstrated cultural variation in affect differentiation (Leff, 1973).

That there are fluctuations and variations in alexithymia should not be surprising. After all, so are other aspects that are correlated—psychosomatic and addictive disturbances are notably conditions characterized by relapses and remissions. We have not assumed a single causation of either of these conditions or of alexithymia. Naturally, hereditary, anatomic, physiological, and many other factors enter into this equation. Just as with memory, or any other highly complex function, when an impairment or regression is present, it is useful to identify some "tags" that lead to the recognition of the type of problem involved.

A basic question returns: Isn't alexithymia just a massive defense against anxiety? This author's experiences suggest that it is a defense in the teleogical sense only. We are dealing here with a regression or an arrest in affective and cognitive development, with severe distortions resulting from infantile or catastrophic adult trauma. We have to consider certain associated disturbances resulting from traumatization at *critical times* of epigenetic development, such as an inhibition of self-care, play, fantasy, and symbolization. Although all these are utilized in various defensive ways, they will not disappear with interpretation. Countless therapists have discovered the utter futility of saying to an alexithymic patient, "You do not permit yourself to experience anger (or love) toward me." They might as well have reproached a color-blind patient for not seeing them in technicolor.

If we now add Dorpat's (1985) formulation that denial is a primary defense that results in a cognitive arrest, we have only another confirmation and elaboration of the process of cognitive constriction we discovered in the traumatic process. We still have to assume that the original denial and cognitive constriction took place at the traumatic moment. However, once established, along with the intrapsychic splitting and the creation of traumatic screens, the denial and cognitive constriction continue and frequently are extended to involve related areas. Thus, symbolic representations of one's pretraumatic functions as states, or even words associatively linked with elements of the trauma, may become blocked. Weinstein and Kahn (1955) have noted that a kind of "paraphasia" may develop in brain-damaged veterans. Words referring to the hospital, operation work, or the military may permanently disappear from the veterans' vocabulary as a way of denying the loss.

In our efforts to approach the residues of infantile traumatic experiences and achieve a modification of early patterns, a number of useful ideas have surfaced. Taylor (1977) and McDougall (1982a) have addressed the problems of splitting and projective identification. They found that patients attribute their own "split off" (i.e., not consciously recognized as part of their self-representation) to their object-representations and subsequently try to control their attributes in their objects. McDougall (1982a) points out that projective identification includes reactions in the object, which has been chosen unconsciously to "represent a personage from the subject's inner theater. Thus one can observe the extent to which an individual's unconscious fantasies and mental conflicts may be used to bring psychological pressure and induce affects and actions in others" (p. 385).

The widespread repression (even repudiation) found in alexithymics suggests that they are prone to use projective identification. In fact, the many variations on this theme are characteristic of their lifestyle and become conspicuous in psychoanalytic work with them. The problem is when and how to interpret these phenomena. Doing so too early, before affective responses are felt subjectively, leads to cliché formation only.

Grostein's (1981) scholarly work on splitting and projective identification has especially elaborated the implications of the work of Bion (1950) and the "attacks on linking." This work reminds us of the point derived in other ways that patients experience the integration of their self- and object-representations as exceedingly dangerous, and coming anywhere close to such a possibility unleashes their defensiveness. The defense is particularly extensive since, as Grotstein put it, "projective identification aims to *disavow* identification and perhaps would be better called projective disidentification" (p. 131).

Kohut (1959) took a different view of these interactions. He felt that addicted patients in psychotherapy also became addicted to the therapist or the procedure. But he thought that the analyst became a substitute for a missing part of the patient. The patient needed the analyst to actively comfort him. In Kohut's opinion, the dependency cannot be analyzed and the patient cannot become able to exercise self-evaluating or self-soothing functions. The only thing to do is to help the patient to deny the need for it. This view, of course, is not one that I agree with, particularly because I feel that the patients have all the parts and functions they need but have walled them off by attributing them to the object. I feel that they are unable to take care of themselves and regulate their functions with conscious self-awareness. I do not agree with Kohut on the idea of the passive-receptive relationship. As I see it, even if the analyst or a mother comforts the baby, the baby is fully active, creating in his mind the representation of the helpers and proceeding to make the necessary modifications in himself. The analyst's soothing would be of no consequence if the patient had no "receiving set" with which to take in the help as a permission to become comfortable and carry it out.

We are dealing with patients' inhibitions, which are derived from early interactions, and that is why some of our observations are the same as those made of autistic children or even psychotics. However, the severe alexithymics often present either the same or opposite pictures dealing with identical issues. Moreover, as Lorenzer (1973) pointed out, psychosomatic disturbances and alexithymia sometimes cover disturbances in biological, neurological, and psychological substrates of dyadic and symbolic forms of interaction. The characteristic deficits in symbolic representation and fantasy-making seen in severe alexithymics are derived from disturbances of early relationships and early responses. Even the so-called separation or isolation call, which probably is the earliest and most basic mammalian vocalization, serves to maintain mother and infant together. MacLean (1985) demonstrated that the very nature of mammalian identity consisted of maternal responses, audio-vocal communication, and play. In the development of attachment and vocal contact, the infant is given the freedom to explore the world and his own nature. That is why the themes of verbalization of affect signals, symbolic representation, playing, and hedonic competence are intimately linked by a tie older than humankind.

The link between the love relationship and the security to explore the world has its dark side, which, in its elementary form, may be reduced to the "startle pattern." But the startle may take chronic forms and become elaborated into catatonoid, cataleptic, and severe unremitting tension (hypervigilant) states. That has been long known, as Landis and Hunt (1939) remind us: apparently Descartes and Malebranche understood the link between the essential "admiratio" and the terror and devastation of premature separation disasters.

We are looking at the foundations of the human soul, those developments which are as essential as the foundation of a house, and as invisible when all is well. Freud (1933) anticipated these findings when he pondered the later residues of the infantile psychological insatiability. He speculated that a *lack of love* must always be inferred and the pain of loss of the breast never assuaged. Now we know that Freud's anticipations come true in a most amazingly concrete manner. A number of studies, such as Hofer's (1978, 1980, 1984), prove that maternal ministrations regulate all the vital and self-regulatory functions in the young and that abnormalities and disturbances in these early regulations have lifelong implications. Since all influences affecting the newborn and infant act as if they were emanating from the mother, experimental evidence confirms that even perceptions of the environment modify the autonomic state (e.g., cold, noise, light, a scent), resulting in a slowing of the heart rate. A "restorative" tuning" by the protective contact with the mother "seems necessary for the full development of environmental awareness and since this autonomic state underlies the hedonic mode, the neurophysiological states provide evidence that, in the mode that liberates attention from confinement to social matters, an enhanced state of environmental awareness comes into being" (Chance, 1980, p. 94). We need to keep this in mind to understand how the transitional object promotes the acquisition of consciously self-recognized self-recognition. For, as Taylor (1987) pointed out, transitional objects are used at first for their physical, tactile, olfactory, and oral gustatory qualities to duplicate the effect that the mother has on the direct regulation of homeostatis. Only later can the transitional object be used for the same purpose but through the mediation of symbolic representation of the maternal object-representation that has been established in the meantime.

Any way we look at it, from any discipline we approach it, we find more clues that the disturbances in the cognitive, perceptive, affective, and hedonic style that we find in alexithymia stem from very early interactions; and we must find ways to influence those fundamental patterns. This is an awesome task; and we can't blame the people who are not even interested in trying. But certain talented therapists, such as McDougall (1980a) and Edgcumbe (1983), are able to give their patients the kind of support that finally enables them to zero in on these early mental structures and patterns.

How can it be done? All we really need to do is demonstrate to the patients who have alexithymic, "disaffected" patterns that *love is real and that it works*. They do not believe that love does work because they want it to instantly fulfill all their wishes. They demand concrete gratification of infantile, sexual, and aggressive needs—instantly, magically, and simultaneously. What they need, in our view, is to learn, slowly and patiently, the most difficult lessons about the *power and limitations of love*. In our attempt to resolve the stalemate, we must start out from the insights derived from the chapter on the model affect. Love is the life-power, and *all the other affects are moieties of it, modifications of it to be recognized even in the "psychosomatic attack."* Psychosomatic illness is an attempt to heal a lesion resulting from the hyperactivity of the so-called expressive (physiological) component of an affect, which was of the infantile variety, undifferentiated and mostly somatic. At its essence, though, at its historical root and future potential, was love. It is a modified love response—love outraged, love deprived. Here we find the insatiability of the infant and the pain of the loss of the breast, which is never assuaged and which Freud was sure had to surface somewhere.

Getting patients to accept such a view of themselves is asking them to exercise their imagination mightily. In fact, it may be the most daring thing we invite patients to do—to participate with the analyst in exercising their imagination. A specific instance of this is the employment of the imaging function (Horowitz, 1983). A whole field of psychology is burgeoning with techniques of applying imaging therapeutically. There is no doubt that significant advances and therapeutic modalities will evolve from these advances. (See, for example, Brachfeld and Stokvis, 1963; Leuner, 1969; Grinder and Bandler; 1981; Horowitz and Zilberg, 1983.)

Kestenberg and Weinstein (1978) demonstrated that an atmosphere of love and trust are essential for the child to develop autoerotic capacities. From these activities evolve many other functions based on the freedom to lend oneself solace and create helpful images and ideas. The authors point out that the infant's creation of a transitional object aids in the integration and reintegration of body parts into the totality of the child's body image as separate from that of the mother (p. 79). Horton's work (1973, 1974, 1981) on solace and transitional states seems directly applicable to alexithymic patients. He described patients who were able to use transitional processes to achieve a special therapeutic experience. Through the use of the wide variety of transitional objects and contents even the illusion of oceanic union or mystical experiences can be attained. The therapist's understanding of transitional states enables him to reproduce in therapy the situation that duplicates the infantile act of creation. By it, the infant, using imagination, "invents" a way to gain comfort. This special state is what I referred to in an earlier chapter as trancelike. We must strive to create the situation, insight, and relationship in which some belated integrational, that is, inhibition-removing, steps may be taken by the patient.

These techniques are not relevant exclusively to alexithymic patients. In fact, Horton's patients were adolescents in suicidal crisis, "borderline," and others. Nevertheless, when we want to address problems with early traumatic roots, where the memories may be purely affective and nonsymbolic, we can neither understand them nor communicate them to the patient verbally. If we simply accept Horton's (1981) view that transitional relatedness is a lifelong developmental process that is especially useful to lending oneself solace, then it becomes self-evident that we need to keep perfecting its uses in helping alexithymic patients to cultivate their capacity for self-caring.

As I have mentioned before, a mistaken notion was conveyed by our classical psychoanalytic terminology. We gave the impression that we could help patients to "express" their emotions, thus playing into the desire of many people to rid themselves of undesirable parts. I frequently have occasion to point out to patients that they are proposing a surgical solution (to "cut out" some behavior or part of themselves), whereas I am engaged in a psychoanalytic endeavor, dedicated to accepting, lovingly, as a consciously recognized part of oneself, every part of oneself.

The work on accepting what needs to be accepted requires effective grieving. In the last analysis, the idea of accepting one's autonomy involves giving up the demand for an "instant mother." Many patients are angered by the very idea of self-caring. They refuse to consider any renunciation of their wishes, and they demand that someone else love them and make them feel perfectly well. Woollcott (1981) has pointed out, from his work with addictive patients, that the analytic therapist is really requesting a kind of regeneration, following the renunciation of what he called the "fusion-individuation conflict." In other words, he is prepared to go through the process of separation and individuation with his patients so that they can finally assume a self-sufficient lifestyle. Veterans of struggles with addictive-alexithymic patients will appreciate Woollcott's pithy summation: "The *drugged state will be found to represent an affect-dominated nucleus of primitive pleasurable experiences of merger or bliss"* (p. 199). Drug-intoxication states have much in common with trances and traumatic states. These kinds of regressive phemonena and consequences are even described in near-death experiences (Noyes, 1980).

Many posttraumatic characteristics described here make their appearance in a variety of patients. It is very helpful to be able to recognize alexithymic characteristics and to dare to reconstruct and imagine their genesis. Residuals of early traumata are not bound by the rules of verbal logic and may be purely affective. In this respect we must be prepared to face some of the inconvenience described by Searles (1984) in being confronted with "limitlessly unusual" transferences in patients who at the core of their problems do not differentiate human from nonhuman surrounding environments: *"[These are linked with affect memory clusters of an extremely fearful and pathological kind, specific to a particular patient.]* Usually paranoid fears and suspicion disrupt the more pleasurable experiences in the transference and make the development of therapeutic alliance problematic" (p. 199). If we think of alexithymic patients as posttraumatic, we start looking out for the multiple sequelae of overwhelming situations in their past.

But, in the aftermath of massive *personal* disasters, patients do not volunteer any such clues because they are struggling with enormous shame and much guilt. Survivors of infantile psychic trauma have no idea or suspicion of the disaster that almost killed them. We have to look for the clues and signs as outlined in this book. Sometimes disturbed time sense *alone* may be a clue to the traumatic origin of other problems (Spiegel, 1981; Terr, 1984).

So what do alexithymic patients need in order to be able to keep their emotions within manageable limits and provide maximum information so that they can begin to maximize their loving relations and enjoyment of life?

They need just a little less than a miracle. Though they are most distrustful and long ago gave up hope that anyone would penetrate their shell and love them, they need to receive just that message. Also, since they have built up high walls, intrapsychically separating all the split-off, denied, disavowed parts of themselves, they desperately need someone to help them to put themselves in a trancelike state in which these intrapsychic barriers can be lifted and repression through externalization can be lovingly renounced. But it must be absolutely clear that they are doing it to and for themselves, that they can exercise all their self-regulating and self-caring functions. They have to be able to receive the message that it is all right for them to exercise all of their human powers—particularly their physical solacing powers. Hardly anyone could receive such a theophanic message without being tempted to further diminish one's self-view and attribute all these miraculous powers to the healer. So here is the challenge: we have to do the same thing, only we have to do it slowly, subtly, gradually, sometimes even in such slow motion that the patient will not notice that it is happening.

At certain stages in the therapy of some alexithymic patients (especially alcoholics), I have found that they have such an exquisite sensitivity to shame that I had to be exceedingly careful about the timing and phrasing of any comment. In my mind, I compared this situation to the Hungarian equestrian rules in which the rider has such delicately balanced control of his horse that no motion can be seen in the hand that holds the reins.

From my own experiences, and from what I glean from the reports of the many talented therapists who have dared to try to work with alexithymics, I am getting the impression that for a change in the basic inhibitions of those patients to take place, a special event has to take place. The transference must reach a point where patients find themselves repeatedly in a state analogous to trance. More precisely, the state is analogous to the enthrallment in love. In this stage, patients may be able to receive a message by which they grant themselves permission to lovingly integrate themselves and claim their right to grant themselves all the solace and self-control necessary. To put it differently, we have to get the patient in a state similar to the infantile creativity—when one has the power and the freedom to create the transitional object. Like Ogden (1985), we want to work with the patient in that potential (nonexisting) space between mother and infant, where fantasy was active and love could be experienced without guilt or shame. But now, with the help of Taylor (1987), we can understand in simple clinical terms the nature of that creative "potential space" between the mother's and the child's psychic reality. It is related to the fact that the young infant can be viewed as an "open system," that is, his physiological functions, such as heartbeat, breathing, movement, and even growth and development, are directly controlled by the mother's actions and what she provides. The baby, in turn, by his responses, influences the behavior of the mother.

But the use of the transitional object in the mother's absence is at first a means of maintaining the mother's influence by using the substitute object to produce the same tactile, olfactory, and gustatory sensation to obtain an illusion of the mother's presence and thus the physiological aspect of self-regulation can be achieved with imitation of the mother's presence. The use of the transitional object is at first presymbolic, and it is primarily used in homeostatic regulation. Gradually, in this potential, nonexisting space of creativity, the transitional object is endowed with psychological meaning and *represents* the mother in a *symbolic way*.

Eventually, the benign mental representations become so secure that the direct use of a security blanket can be given up. Dreams, fantasies, and play can be used to activate the image of the mother so that self-caring can be carried out. But with this creative solution, the illusion is built up that the mother continues (for the life of the child) to control all vital and affective homeostatic functions. The mothering parent or maternal-transference objects (God, doctors) have to be mobilized—in person or symbolically—to dispense the enabling in order for the infant to maintain homeostasis, self-soothing, self-caring, and self-regulation. Most people have a multitude of transitional objects and operations available and can obtain the desired effect easily and without paying any attention to the fact that they are activating infantile mechanisms derived from those ancient, scarcely noticeable mother–child interactions.

However, some people develop enormous blocks about accessing these inner resources and inner structures—the products of their own imagination. Some people can access these inner resources, their own functions, only in states of modified consciousness, in dissociative states, in special states of "falling in love" or high inspiration—in a trance.

This special, trancelike state in which the patient is capable of receiving a message that repairs and liberates his love forces has been also described with great clarity by Kinston and Cohen (1986). These authors have called it a "primary relatedness" and "positive therapeutic reaction" (p. 343) in which trauma can be healed and the voids resulting from primal repression can be recreated.

Obviously much work has to be done interpreting the layers upon layers of defensive fantasy and superstition. A burden of defensively designed magic controls has to be renounced and many precious, painful, gratifying, and addicting behaviors have to be renounced lovingly through effective grieving. Forgiving has to be practiced a great deal. One has to forgive oneself. One has to forgive the love objects of one's past. Forgiving early objects that exist nowhere but in one's mind and forgiving the present, imperfect therapist has to take place slowly and gradually. In the meantime, we analysts keep busy working on the countertransference in the manner of a mother who keeps busy with providing food, shelter, and the like while also providing a safe psychological holding environment in which her children can grow and try out all of their capacities and functions. The children even go through the illusion of acquiring their own self-grown functions from the parents. We have much work to do operating on a dual track: conducting analytic work and at the same time attending to our patients' impaired capacity for empathy with themselves and their significant objects. We are also reviewing with them how they experience emotions and how they manage them, that is, reacting to having them. We are mindful of the balance between the verbal (cognitive) and somatic aspects of the affect. We are prepared to look for the somatic manifestations of tensions and needs and physical needs. By supplying names, words, and explanations, we nourish affect differentiation, verbalization, and desomatization. At the same time, we promote the lifting of repression and integration of self- and object-representations.

We are particularly attentive to the patient's ability to take good care of themselves and are continuously involved in explanation, elucidation, and, finally, interpretation of the blocks in self-regulating, self-preserving, and self-solacing functions. In doing this, we have to create plausible reconstructions of the infantile traumatic experiences which were interpreted by the child as conveying the prohibition against assuming full autonomy.

And, again when the material comes, it is not going to be in the form of fantasy, a dream, or an elaborately verbalized product, but as a physical sensation or an action. The therapist may have to have in mind an entire differential theory of emotions (Plutchik, 1962; Tompkins, 1962–63; Ekman and Friesen, 1975; Izard, 1977; Schwartz, Weinberger and Singer, 1981; Singer, 1985) before daring to duplicate McDougall's (1984) feat: "I limited myself to the remark that sadness and joy were valuable psychic possessions" (p. 402).

This simple statement, which had a great impact on her patient, required years of preparation, during which McDougall discovered that these patients had gone through years of analysis in which many neurotic problems had been overcome; but now there was before her and her patient "a strong but undifferentiated dissatisfaction with life, of which the analysands had hitherto been unaware . . ." (p. 392). Moreover, the analyst realized at about the same time that this kind of affect problem "*may have passed unnoticed*" in her own analytic work for many years (p. 392).

Work with alexithymia is so difficult and painful because we are addressing conflicts and transferences that are a matter of life and death. And, because the patient does not know it and cannot tell us, much communication is nonverbal—gestural, postural, reflected in the color and heat of the face, and mimical. For this reason, the patient has to look at the analyst and the analyst has to look at the patient. For these patients lying down on the couch does not lead to regression into fantasyland, but rather to experiencing an abandonment into oblivion. Therefore, these patients must *see* the analyst face to face during their treatment sessions.

Even though, for reasons of resistance, they request to be put back on the couch as they were in their previous analyses, the granting of this request provides for them another asylum from communication and from resuming the face-to-face staring at each other on which mother and babies, as well as lovers, spend so much time. It may be that there is a need for such direct preoccupation with the face and the eyes to stimulate imaging, which is possibly the portal for the reentry into an active and powerful fantasy life (Mowrer, 1977; Reyher, 1977; Gawain, 1978).

There is no ground for therapeutic zeal here, just a ray of hope for making contact with people who, to borrow a phrase from Winnicott (1954), have their "true self" so carefully tucked inside that they don't have the slightest suspicion that it is there. But in trying to reach that true self, one runs into many obstacles. In the effort to help the patients develop their emotions to the point that effective grieving is possible, one encounters problems of inhibitions of self-care that have to be dealt with.

The application of these observations goes beyond alexithymic-psychosomatic, drug-dependent, or posttraumatic patients. Alexithymic characteristics have a wide distribution and are observable in temporary regressions in the wake of overwhelming experiences. Their presence constitutes a serious handicap to the patients' benefiting from psychoanalytic psychotherapy. With the present state of the art, only patients with mild or reactive types of alexithymia can be prepared for utilizing "uncovering" or "insight" psychotherapy. With some, it is necessary to have a preliminary phase of psychotherapy in which their alexithymic problems are given special attention. However, whether or not there is a specially designated preliminary phase, the therapist, having identified alexithymic traits, will undoubtedly raise these issues with many patients who enter treatment for primary neurotic or characterological problems. Most of all, because of the lack of empathy evidenced by these patients, because they do not have affects available as signals, one cannot assume the ideal psychoanalytic stance of limiting one's intervention to transference interpretation. First, one has to attend to the quasi-didactic task of helping patients discover the bizarreness of their mechanistic, "inhuman" relationships with their objects. Similarly, these patients assume that their treatment of themselves as robots or machines is the norm. They have to be disabused of this attitude. Thus, the concept of alexithymia opens up a number of psychodynamic and psychotherapeutic challenges.

In my view, the *keystone* to the whole group of characteristics and problems of alexithymia is the severe prohibition against exercising self-caring and self-regulating functions. Unless it is recognized, accepted, and lovingly renounced, all efforts to improve affect tolerance, affect verbalization and desomatization, affect differentiation, and anhedonia have the same low degree of effectiveness as biofeedback training with psychosomatic-alexithymic patients. Hoppe's (1977) model of a functional commissurotomy is the best metaphor for the picture. However, the inhibitions of self-caring functions are based on a different type of transference than we are accustomed to find: the identification with a caretaking mother. Surprisingly, this transference turns out to be severely *conflictual*. The alexithymic tends to experience vital and affective functions as reserved for mother, and all one's viscera, even one's life, as belonging to her and her surrogates (doctor, the State, God). However, unlike neurotic inhibitions, these cannot be overcome by interpretation alone. They are mostly preverbal; and the memories are, for the most part, affective and frequently devoid of verbal or even symbolic components. Consequently, some new way has to be found to provide a situation in which these patients can reclaim their soul and try to exercise their physical and emotional potential for self-care.

The work of a number of people who took their clues from Winnicott has opened for therapeutic access the world of transitional phenomena. Operative thinking probably has its origin in the failure of transitional phenomena to evolve into symbols that are at the self-directed disposal of these patients for adaptation and self-gratification. What the patients need is an *enabling* sign of an inspirational nature. However, because of their tendency to idolatry, it is difficult for them to receive such help without reinforcing idealizing transferences at the expense of their already impoverished resources. Hence, great caution and circumspection is indicated. However, as Horton (1981) pointed out, the need for solace is universal, and transitional phenomena come in a wide range of experiences. Far more experimentation is going on in this respect than can be imagined. It is hoped that psychoanalytic discipline will be applied to these approaches and that the work of the experimentation on the use of imaging will be subjected to psychoanalytic discourse.

There are, however, certain limitations to dealing with patients whose traumatic experiences and disturbances were so early that when we examine them as adults we find that their affects cannot be verbalized and the affective states defy description and mastery. In the last analysis, we have to acknowledge that the necessity to verbalize poses limitations on the contents (Shands, 1971). If we recall the extension of the definition of repression that became necessary in the chapter on psychic reality, we have to acknowledge that, for the most part, language serves to maintain repression (Dorsey, 1971b). In addition, to the extent that the major conflict of these patients relates to their exercising self-care with fully conscious recognition of the fact, that goal can not be materialized while they are in analysis or in any therapeutic relationship. There are theoretical limitations to what can be achieved in a dyadic therapeutic relationship using ordinary verbal communication. Language itself modifies the kind of reality that can be perceived. Similarly with our visual orientation, the use of lenses and similar devices interferes with our ability to imagine a holographic operation of the brain (Pribram, 1971). Consequently, the ultimate "interpretations" have to be achieved by analysands in their own "idiolect"—a self process that goes beyond verbalization into affective self-acceptance. But particularly with patients whose major problem is their tendency to idolatry and externalization, we have to accept the limitations of treatment. Such an analysis has to become a consciously recognized self-analysis at the point the patient can take it on. A salutary purpose is served by working toward the goal of declaring the therapeutic relationship to be the start of a lifelong process of self-analysis and conscious cultivation of the patient's self-regulating and self-caring capacities. In the treatment, the analyst can hope to be of help in providing patients with a benevolent influence by which to heal themselves and take major strides in recognizing their self-imposed blocks and externalizations. Like a parent who gives help temporarily and minimally, the analyst needs to point in the direction of self-recognition of the patient's own capacities. The analyst has to pay attention to his countertransferences, which we have defined as including all the instances when self-sight is lost from one's own mental material. This is the orientation that is most conducive to the patients' discovering that they have always owned their personal capacities for self-care and self-regulation. In some areas of posttraumatic problems, such an anhedonia, it will be primarily the patients' own task to cultivate their capacity for pleasure for the rest of their lives.

The most important outcome of this review of the problems of alexithymic patients may be that these patients, by their nature, remind us that we are confined to dealing with our own mental representations exclusively. Surprisingly, the avoidance of the healthier-than-thou attitude will be the finest mental health principle in this therapeutic undertaking.

References

Abraham, K. (1908). The psychological relation between sexuality and alcoholism. *Internat. J. Psycho-Anal.* 7:2, 1926.

———— (1911). Notes on the psycho-analytical investigation and treatment of manic-depressive insanity and allied conditions. In *Selected Papers of Karl Abraham.* New York: Basic Books, 1954, pp. 137–156.

———— (1924). The influence of oral erotism on character formation. In *Selected Papers of Karl Abraham.* New York: Basic books, 1954, pp. 393–406.

Achterberg, J., Simonton, C. O., & Mathews-Simonton, S. (1976). *Stress, Psychological Factors and Cancer.* Fort Worth, TX: New Med. Press.

Aeschylus (1953). Prometheus bound. In *The Complete Greek Tragedies,* eds. D. Green & R. Latimore. Chicago: University of Chicago Press, pp. 304–351.

Ainsworth, M. D. S, Blehar, M. C., Walters, E. & Wall, S. (1978). *Patterns of Attachment: A Psychological Study of the Strange Situation.* Hillsdale, NJ: Lawrence Erlbaum Associates.

Alexander, F. (1943). Fundamental concepts of psychosomatic research. *Psychosom. Med.* 5:205–210.

———— (1950). *Psychosomatic Medicine.* New York: Norton.

———— French, F. (1948). *Studies in Psychosomatic Medicine.* New York: Ronald Press.

Allerton, C. W. (1964). Mass casualty care and human behavior. *Medical Annual of the District of Columbia* 33:206–206.

Allport, F. (1955). *Theories of Perception and the Concept of Structure.* New York: Wiley..

Altman, B., & Johnson, D. A. (1976). Aircraft passenger safety: Passenger education and survival. *Flightlog,* 14:14–15.

Ambrose, A. (1961). The development of the smiling response in early infancy. In *Determinants of Infant Behavior,* ed. B. M. Fess. New York: Wiley, pp. 179–201.

American Psychiatric Association (1980). *Diagnostic and Statistical Manual of Mental Disorders (3rd edition).* Washington, DC: American Psychiatric Association.

American Psychoanalytic Association (1985). *Standards for Training in Psychoanalysis.* New York: American Psychoanalytic Association.

Angel, K. (1973). The role of internal objects and external objects in object relationships, separation anxiety, object constancy and symbiosis. *Internat. J. Psycho-Anal.* 13:541–546.

Apfel, R. J., & Sifneos, P. E. (1979). Alexithymia: Concept and measurement. *Psychother. Psychosom.* 32:180–190.

Apfel-Savitz, R., Silverman, D., & Bennett, J. J. (1977). Group psychotherapy of patients with somatic illnesses and alexithymia. *Psychother. Psychosom.* 28:323–329.

Appelbaum, S. A. (1977). The refusal to take one's medicine. *Bull. Menn. Clin.* 41:511–521.

Archibald, H. C., & Tuddenham, K. D. (1965). Persistent stress reaction after combat. *Arch. Gen. Psychiat.* 12:425–481.

Arieti, S. (1955). *Interpretation of Schizophrenia.* New York: Brunner.

341

Arlow, J., & Brenner, C. (1964). *Psychoanalytic Concepts and the Structural Theory*. New York: International Universities Press.

Arnold, M. D. (1950). An excitatory theory of emotions. In *Feelings and Emotions*, ed. M. L. Reynert. New York: Hafner, pp. 11–34.

Arvanitakis, K. (1985). The third soter who ordaineth all. *Internat. Rev. Psycho-Anal.* 12:431–440.

Asendorf, J. B., & Scherer, K. (1983). The discrepant repressor: Differentiation between low anxiety, high anxiety, and repression of anxiety by autonomic-facial-verbal patterns of behavior. *J. Personal. & Soc. Psychol.* 45:1334–1346.

Atkin, S. (1973). Discussion of Krystal's paper: Therapeutic modification in impairment of affect tolerance. Fall meeting, American Psychoanalytic Association, New York.

Atkinson, J. H., Kremer, E. F., & Ignelzi, R. J. (1982). diffusion of pain language with affective disturbance confounds differential diagnosis. *Pain*, 12:375–384.

Ayers, S. Jr. (1964). The fine art of scratching. *J. Amer. Med. Assn.* 189:1003–1006.

Bagby, R. M., Taylor, G. J., & Ryan, D. P. (1986). The measurement of alexithymia: Psychometric properties of the Schalling-Sifneos Personality Scale. *Comprehen. Psychiat.* 27:287–294.

———— Taylor, G. J., & Ryan, D. P. (in press) The Toronto Alexithymia Scale: Relationship with personality and psychopathology measures. *Psychother. Psychosomat.*

Bahnson, C. B. (1975). Psychologic and emotional issues in cancer: The psychotherapeutic care of the cancer patient. *Sem. in Oncol.* 2:293–307.

———— (1980). Stress and cancer: The state of the art, Part I. *Psychother. Psychosomat.* 21:975–981.

Balint, M. (1964). *The Doctor, His Patient and the Illness*. New York: International Universities Press.

———— (1968). *The Basic Fault*. London: Tavistock.

Barber, T. S. (1970). Physiological effects of hypnosis and suggestion. In *Biofeedback and Self Control*, ed. T. S. Barber et al. Chicago: Aldine Atherton, pp. 188–256.

Barrett, B. B. (1984). *Psychic Reality and Psychoanalytic Knowing*. Hillsdale, NJ: The Analytic Press.

Bartemeier, L. H., Kubie, L. S., Menninger, K. A., Romano, J., & Whitehorn, J. E. (1946). Combat exhaustion. *J. Nerv. Ment. Dis.* 104:358–389.

Basch, M. F. (1974). Interference with perceptual transformation in the service of defense. *Annual of Psychoanalysis* 2:87–97. New York: International Universities Press.

———— (1976). Developmental psychology and explanatory theory in psychoanalysis. *Annual of Psychoanalysis* 4:229–263. New York: International Universities Press.

———— (1981). Psychoanalytic interpretation and cognitive transformation. *Internat. J. Psycho-Anal.* 4:229–263.

Bastiaans, J. (1957). *Psychosomatische Gevolgen von onderdrukking en verzet*. Amsterdam; Noordhollandische Vitgeres Maetschappii.

Becker, H. (1977). A non-verbal therapeutic approach to psychosomatic disorders. *Psychother. Psychosom.* 28:330–336.

Beecher, H. (1956). The subjective response to sensation. *Amer. J. Med.* 20:101–103.

———— (1961). Surgery as placebo. *J. Amer. Med. Assn.* 176:1102–1107.

Bellack, A. S., & Lombardo, T. W. (1984). Measurement of anxiety. In *Behavioral Theories and Treatment of Anxiety*, ed. S. M. Turner. New York: Plenum Press, pp. 51–89.

Benedek, T. (1956). Toward the biology of the depressive constellation. *J. Amer. Psychoanal. Assn.*, 4:389–427.

Benjamin, J. D. (1965). Developmental biology and psychoanalysis. In *Psychoanalysis and Current Biological Thought*, ed. N. S. Greenfield & W. C. Lewis. Madison: University of Wisconsin Press, pp. 57–80.

Benner, P., Roskier, S., & Lazarus, R. S. (1980). Stress and coping under extreme conditions.

In *Survivors, Victims and Perpetrators,* ed. J. Dimsdale. Washington, DC: Hemisphere, pp. 219–258.

Bensheim, H. (1960). Die K. Z. Neurose rassish Verfolger. *Nervenarzt,* 31:462–471.

Beres, D., & Joseph, E. D. (1970). The concept of mental representation in analysis. *Internat. J. Psycho-Anal.* 51:1–11.

Bergmann, M. V. (1982). Thoughts on superego pathology of survivors and their children. In *Generations of the Holocaust,* ed. M. S. Bergmann & M. E. Jucovy. New York: Basic Books, pp. 287–310.

Bettelheim, B. (1943). Individual and mass behavior in extreme situations. *J. Abn. Psychol.,* 38:417–452.

Bibring, E. (1953). The mechanism of depression. In *Affective Disorders,* ed. P. Greenacre. New York: International Universities Press, pp. 13–48.

Bion, W. R. (1959). Attachks on linking. *Internat. J. Psycho-Anal.* 40:308–315.

Blanchard, E. G., Arena, J. G., & Pallmeyer, T. P. (1981). Psychometric properties of a scale to measure alexithymia. *Psychother. Psychosom.* 35:64–71.

Bogen, J. E., & Bogen, G. M. (1969). The other side of the brain: The corpus callosum and creativity. *Bull. Los Angeles Neurol. Soc.* 34:191–220.

Bonaparte, M., Freud, A., & Kris, E., ed. (1954). *The Origins of Psycho-Analysis: Letters to Wilhelm Fliess, Drafts and Notes: 1887–1902,* trans. E. Mosbacher & J. Strachey. New York: Basic Books.

Borens, R., Grosse-Schulte, E., & Kortemme, H. H. (1977). Is "alexithymia" but a social phenomenon? An empirical investigation in psychosomatic patients. *Psychother. Psychosom.* 28:193–198.

Bourke, M., Taylor, G., & Crisp, A. (1985). Symbolic functioning in anorexia nervosa. *J. Psychiat. Res.* 19:273–278.

Bowers, G. H. (1981). Mood and memory. *Amer. Psychol.* 2:129–140.

Bowlby, J. (1961). Processes of mourning. *Internat. J. Psycho-Anal.* 42:317–340.

————— (1969). *Attachment and Loss.* Vol 1, New York: Basic Books.

————— (1977). The making and breaking of affectional bonds. *Brit. J. Psychiat.* 130:201–210.

————— (1980). Information processing approach to defense. In *Attachment and Loss,* Vol. 2. New York: Basic Books, pp. 44–74.

Boyer, L. B. (1977). Working with a borderline patient. *Psychoanal. Quart.* 46:386–424.

Brachfeld, O., & Stovis, B. (1963). Aus der Praxis der gelenkter Tag Traeme. *Zeitschrift fuer Psychotherapie und medicinische Psychologie,* 13:73–81.

Braeutigam, W. (1977). Panel-and plenum-discussion: Psychotherapeutic problems with psychosomatic patients. In *Toward a Theory of Psychosomatic Disorders,* ed. W. Braeutigam & M. Von Rad. New York: S. Karger, pp. 361–375.

Brenner, C. (1953). An addendum to Freud's theory of anxiety. *Internat. J. Psycho-Anal.* 34:18–24.

Brett, E. A., & Ostroff, R. (1985). Imagery and posttraumatic stress disorder: An overview. *Amer. J. Psychiat.* 142:417–424.

Breuer, J., & Freud, S. (1893–1895). Studies on hysteria. *Standard Edition* 2, London: Hogarth Press, 1955.

Bridges, K. M. B. (1930). A genetic theory of emotions. *J. Gen. Psychol.* 37:517–527.

Brierley, M. (1937). Affects in theory and practice. *Internat. J. Psycho-Anal.* 18:256–268.

————— (1945). Metapsychology and personalology. In *Trends in Psychoanalysis.* London: Hogarth Press, pp. 124–179.

Brill, N. W., & Beebe, G. W. (1955). *A follow-up study of war neuroses.* Washington, DC: Veterans Administration Medical Monograph.

Brinich, D. M. (1982). Rituals and meanings. *The Psychoanalytic Study of the Child* 36:71–103, New Haven: Yale University Press.

Broucek, F. (1979). Efficacy in infancy. *Internat. J. Psycho-Anal.* 60:311–316.

Bruner, J. S. (1973). *Beyond the Information Given,* New York: Norton.

Bucci, W. (1985). Dual coding: A cognitive model for psychoanalytic research. *J. Amer. Psychoanal. Assn., 33*:571–608.

Buchanan, F., Waterhouse, G. J., & West, S. C., Jr. (1980). A proposed neuphysiological basis of alexithymia. *Psychother. Psychosom.* 34:248–255.

Budzynski, T. (1981). Brain lateralization and rescripting. *Somatics,* spring/summer:3–9.

Burrell, R. J. W. (1963). The possible bearing of curse death and other factors in Bantu culture on the etiology of Myocardial infarction. In *The Etiology of Myocardial Infarction,* ed. T. W. James & J. W. Keys. Boston: Little, Brown, pp. 95–101.

Bush, F. (1974). Discussion of a paper on: The nature of the primary transitional object. Michigan Psychoanalytic Society, February 14, 1974.

Byrne, D. (1961). The repression-sensitization scale. Rationale, reliability, validity. *J. Personal.* 29:334–349.

—— Barry, J., & Nelson, D. (1963). Relation of the revised repression-sensitization scale to measures of self-description. *Psychol. Rep.* 13:323–334.

Cannon, W. B. (1915). *Bodily Changes in Pain, Hunger, Fear, and Rage.* New York: Appleton.

—— (1942). "Voodoo" deaths. *Amer. Anthropol.* 44:169–181.

Caplan, G. (1981). Mastery of stress: Psychosocial aspects. *Amer. J. Psychiat.* 138:413–420.

Carlson, V. R. (1957). Individual differences in recall of word association test words. *J. Personal.* 23:77–87.

Carroll, B. J., Feinberg, M., Greden, J. F., Tarika, J. Albala, A. A., Haskett, R. F., James N., Kronfal, Z., Lohr, N., Steiner, M., de Vigne, J. P., & Young, E. (1981). A specific laboratory test for the diagnosis of melancholia. *Arch. Gen. Psychiat.* 38:15–22.

Carroll, D. (1972). Repression-sensitization and the verbal elaboration of experience. *J. Consul. Clin. Psychol., 38*:147.

Catchlove, R. F. H., & Braha, R. E. D. (1985). A test to measure the awareness and expression of anger. *Psychother. Psychosom.* 39:77–88.

Catell, R. B. (1935). Perseveration and personality: Some experiments and a hypothesis. *J. Ment. Sci.* 81:115–167.

Chance, M. R. A. (1980). Ethological assessment of emotions. In *Emotions: Theory, Research and Experience,* ed. R. Plutchik & H. Kellerman. New York: Academic Press, pp. 81–102.

Chessick, R. D. (1960). The pharmacogenic orgasm. *Arch. Gen. Psychiat.* 3:117–128.

Chethik, M. (1977). The borderline child. In *Basic Handbook of Child Psychiatry,* Vol 2, ed. J. D. Noshpitz. New York: Basic Books, pp. 304–321.

Chodoff, P. (1980). Psychotherapy with the survivor. In *Survivors, Victims and Perpetrators,* ed. J. Dimsdale. Washington, DC: Hemisphere, pp. 205–218.

Chodorkoff, B., & Chodorkoff, J. (1958). Perceptual defense: An integration with other research findings. *J. Gen. Psychol.* 58:75–80.

Chomsky, N. (1975). *The Logical Structure of Linguistic Theory.* Chicago: University of Chicago Press.

Coelho, G. V., Hamburg, D. A., & Adams, J. E., eds. (1974). *Coping and Adaptation.* New York: Basic Books.

Cohen, J. (1954). *A Follow-up Study of World War II Prisoners of War.* Washington DC: U. S. Government Printing Office.

—— (1985). Trauma and repression. *Psychoanal. Inq.* 5:163–189.

Cohen, K. R., Auld, F., Demers, L., & Catchlove, R. (1985). The development of a valid and reliable projective measure (the objectively scored archetypal-9 test). *J. Nerv. Ment. Dis.* 173:621–627.

—— Demers-Desrosiers, L. A., & Catchlove, R. F. H. (1983). The SAT9: A quantitative scoring system for the AT9 test as a measure of symbolic function central to alexithymic presentation. *Psychother. Psychosom.* 39: 77–88.

Colligan, R. C., Osborne, D., Swenson, W. M., & Offord, K. P. (1984). The aging MMPI: Development of contemporary norms. *Mayo Clin. Proc.* 59:377–390.

Conrad, J. (1900). *Lord Jim.* New York: Dell, (1961).

Coolidge, J. C. (1969). Unexpected death in a patient who wished to die. *J. Amer. Psychoanal. Assn.*, 17:413–420.

Cooper, D. E., & Holmstrom, R. W. (1984). Relationship between alexithymia and somatic complaints in a normal sample. *Psychother. Psychosom.* 41:20–24.

Danieli, Y. (1981a). Differing adaptational styles in families of survivors of the Nazi Holocaust: Some implications for treatment. *Children Today,* 10:34–35.

——— (1981b) Families of survivors of the Nazi Holocaust: Some short- and long-term effects. In *Stress and Anxiety.* Vol. 8, ed. C. D. Spielberger, I. G. Sarason, & N. Milgram. New York: McGraw Hill, pp. 405–421.

Darrow, C. W., & Heath, L. L. (1932). Reaction tendencies related to personality. In *Studies in the Dynamics of Behavior,* ed. K. Lashley. Chicago: University of Chicago Press, pp. 59–261.

Darwin, C. (1872). *The Expression of Emotion in Man and Animals.* London: University of Chicago Press, 1965.

Dashiel, J. F. (1928). Are there any native emotions? *Psychol. Rev., 35:319–327.*

Davis, P. J., & Schwartz, G. E. (1987). Repression and the inaccessibility of affective memories. *J. Personal. Soc. Psychol.* 52:155–162.

Deikman, A. J. (1963). Experimental meditations. *J. Nerv. Ment. Dis.* 136:329–343.

Defourny, M., Hubin, P., & Luminet, D. (1976/1977). Alexithymia "pensée opératoire" and predisposition to coronopathy: Pattern "A" of Friedman and Rosenman. *Psychother. Psychosom.* 27:106–114.

Delgado, J. M. R., Roberts, W. W., & Miller, N. E. (1954). Learning motivated by electrical stimulation of the brain. *Amer. J. Physiol.* 179:587–593.

Demers-Desrosiers, L. A. (1982). Influence of alexithymia on symbolic function. *Psychother. Psychosom.* 38:103–120.

——— Cohen, K. R., Catchlove, R. F. H., & Ramsay, R. A. (1983). The measure of symbolic function in alexithymia pain patients. *Psychother. Psychosom.* 39:65–76.

Demos, E. V. (1974). Children's understanding and use of affect terms. Unpublished doctoral dissertation, Harvard University.

de M'Uzan, M. (1974a) Analytical process and the notion of the past. *Internat. Rev. Psycho-Anal.* 1:461–480.

——— (1974b) Psychodynamic mechanisms in psychosomatic symptom formation. *Psychother. Psychosom.* 23:103–110.

Dennett, D. C. (1983). Intentional systems in cognitive ethology: The Panglossian paradigm defended. *Beh & Brain Sci.* 6: 343–390.

Deri, S. K. (1984). *Symbolization and Creativity.* New York: International Universities Press.

Des Pres, T. (1976). *The Survivor.* New York: Oxford University Press.

Deutsch, F. (1926). Der gesunde und der knauke Koerper in psychoanalytischer Betrachtung. *Internat. Zeitschrift fuer Psychoanalyse,* 19:130–146.

——— (1959). *On the Mysterious Leap from Mind to Body.* New York: International Universities Press.

DiCara, L. (1972). Learning mechanisms. In *Biofeedback and Self Control* ed. D. Shapiro et al. Chicago: Aldine Atherton.

Dill, D. B. (1954). *Human Reactions in Disaster Situations.* DN–18–108–CML–2275. National Opinion Research Center, Chicago: University of Chicago Press.

Dimsdale, J. (1980) (ed) *Survivors, Victims, and Perpetrators.* Washington, DC: Hemisphere.

Dixon, N. F. (1971). *Subliminal Perception. The Nature of a Controversy.* London: McGraw-Hill.

Dobroszycki, L., ed. (1984) *The Chronicle of the Lodz Ghetto 1941–1944.* New Haven: Yale University Press.

Doody, K., & Taylor, G. (1983). Construct validation of the MMPI alexithymia scale. In *Psychosomatic Medicine: Theoretical, Clinical, and Transcultural Aspects,* ed. A. J. Krakowski & C. P. Kimball. New York: Plenum Press, pp. 17–24.

Dorpat, T. L. (1977). Depressive affect. *The Psychoanalytic Study of the Child* 32:3–27, New Haven: Yale University Press.

——— (1985). *Denial and Defense in the therapeutic Situation.* Northvale, NJ: Aronson.

Dorsey, J. M. (1943). Some considerations of psychic reality. *Internat. J. Psycho-Anal.,* 24:147–151.

——— (1954). The science of sanity. *Samiksa,* 8:47–124.

——— (1965). *Allness or Illness.* Detroit, MI: Wayne State University Press.

——— (1971a). *Psychology of Emotion: Self Discipline by Conscious Emotional Continence.* Detroit, MI: Wayne State University Press.

——— (1971b). *Psychology of Language: A Local Habitation and a Name.* Detroit, MI: Wayne State University Press.

——— (1976). The science of the senescent process. In *Selected Essays.* Detroit, MI: Wayne State University Press, pp. 450–486.

——— & Seegers, W. H. (1959). *Living Consciously: The Science of Self.* Detroit, MI: Wayne State University Press.

Duffy, E. (1934). An example of the need for reorientation in psychology. *Psychol. Rev.* 41:184–198.

——— (1941). The conceptual categories of psychology: A suggestion for revision. *Psychol. Rev.* 48:177–203.

——— (1949). A systematic framework for the description of personality. *J. Abn. Soc. Psychol.* 44:175–190.

——— (1951). The concept of energy mobilization. *Psychol. Rev.* 58:30–40.

——— (1957). The psychological significance of the concept of "arousal" or "activation." *Psychol. Rev.* 64:265–275.

——— (1972). Activation. In *Handbook of Psychophysiology,* ed. M. S. Greenfield & R. A. Steinback. New York: Holt, Reinhart & Winston, pp. 577–622.

Dunbar, F. (1946). *Emotions and Bodily Changes,* 3rd ed. New York: Columbia University Press.

Edel, L. (1975). The madness of art. *Amer. J. Psychiat.* 132:1005–1012.

Edgcumbe, R. (1981). Toward a development for the acquisition of language. *The Psychoanalytic Study of the Child,* 36:71–103. New Haven: Yale University Press.

——— (1983). On learning to talk to oneself. *Bull. Brit. Psychoanal. Soc.* 5:1–13.

Editorial (1974). Panic. *Flightlog,* 12:4–5.

——— (1975). Inaction. *Flightlog,* 13:7–8.

Eissler, K. R. (1953). Emotionality of a schizophrenic patient. *The Psychoanalytic Study of the Child,* 8:199–256. New York: International Universities Press.

——— (1955). *The Psychiatrist and the Dying Patient.* New York: International Universities Press.

——— (1966). A note on trauma, dream, anxiety and schizophrenia. *The Psychoanalytic Study of the Child,* 21:17–50. New York: International Universities Press.

Eitinger, L. (1980). The concentration camp syndrome and its late sequelae. In *Survivors, Victims and Perpetrators,* ed. J. Dimsdale. New York: Hemisphere, pp. 127–162.

——— & Strøm, A. (1973). *Mortality and Morbidity of Excessive Stress.* New York: Humanities Press.

Ekman, P., & Friesen, H. V. (1975). *Unmasking the Face.* Englewood Cliffs, NJ: Prentice-Hall.

Emde, R. N. (1981). Paper on affective-signal communications between infants and mothers presented to Interdisciplinary Colloquium on Infant Research, American Psychoanalytic Association, New York, December.

———— (1983). The prerepresentational self and its affective core. *The Psychoanalytic Study of the Child*, 38:165–192. New Haven: Yale University Press.

———— Gaensbauer, T. J., & Harmon, R. J. (1976). Emotional expression in infancy. *Psychological Issues*, Monogr. 37. New York: International Universities Press.

Engel, G. L. (1962a). Anxiety and depression-withdrawal: The primary affects of unpleasure. *Internat. J. Psycho-Anal.* 43:89–98.

———— (1962b). *Psychological Development in Health and Disease.* Philadelphia: Saunders.

———— (1963). Toward a classifiction of affects. In *Expression of Emotion in Man.* ed. P. H. Knapp. New York: International Universities Press, pp. 262–293.

———— (1968). A life setting conducive to illness. *Annals of Internal Medicine*, 69:293–300.

———— (1971). Sudden and rapid death during psychological stress. *Annals of Internal Medicine* 74:771-782.

Ephron, H. S., & Carrington, P. (1967). Ego functioning in rapid eye movement sleep: Implication for dream theory. In *Science and Psychoanalysis, XI, The Ego*, ed. J. Masserman. New York: Grune & Stratton, pp. 75–99.

Erdelyi, M. T. (1974). A new look at the "new look." Perceptual influence and vigilance. *Psychol. Rev.* 81:1–25.

Ericksen, C. W. (1951a). Perceptual defense as a function of unacceptable needs. *J. Abn. Soc. Psychol.* 46:283–288.

———— (1951b). Some implications for TAT interpretation arising from need and perception experiments. *J. Personal.* 19:283–288.

Erickson, M. H., & Rossi, E. L. (1981). *Experiencing Hypnosis: Therapeutic Approaches to Altered States.* New York: Irvington Press.

Erikson, E. H. (1956). The problem of ego identity. *J. Amer. Psychoanal. Assn.*, 4:56–72.

———— (1959). Ego development and historical change. In *Identity and the Life Cycle (Psychological Issues I.)* New York: International Universities Press, pp. 18–49.

———— (1963). *Childhood and Society*, 2nd ed. New York: Norton.

———— (1968a). *Youth and Crisis.* New York: Norton.

———— (1968b). *The Human Life Cycle International Encyclopedia of Social Sciences.* New York: Macmillan.

Erikson, K. T. (1976). *Everything in Its Path—Destruction of Community in the Buffalo Creek Flood.* New York: Simon & Schuster.

Ettigi, P., & Brown, G. M. (1977). Psychoendicrinology of affective disorders: An overview. *Amer. J. Psychiat.* 134:493–501.

Fain, M. (1971). Prelude a la vie fantasmatique. *Rev. Franç. Psychanal.* 35:291–364.

———— & David, C. (1963). Aspects fonctionels de la vie onirique. *Rev. Franç. Psychanal.*, 27:241–243.

———— Kreisler, L. (1970). Discussion sur la genese des fontions representives. *Rev. Franç. Psychanal.* 34:285–300.

Fava, G. A., Baldaro, B., & Osti, R. M. A. (1980). Towards a self-rating scale for alexithymia: A report on 150 medical patients. *Psychother. Psychosom.* 34:34–39.

Fawcett, J., Clerk, D. C., Scheftner, W. A., & Hedeker, D. (1983). Differences between anhedonia and normal hedonic depressive states. *Arch. Gen. Psychiat.* 40:1027–1030.

Federman, R., & Mohns, E. (1984). A validity study of the MMPI alexithymia subscale conducted on migraine headache outpatients. *Psychother. Psychosom.* 41:29–32.

Feiguine, R. J., & Johnson, F. A. (1985). Alexithymia and chronic respiratory disease: A review of current research. *Psychother. Psychosom.* 43:77–89.

Fenichel, O. (1939). The counter-phobic attitude. *Internat. J. Psycho-Anal.* 20:263–274.

——— (1941). The ego and the affects. In *Collected Papers, Second Series.* New York: Norton, 1954, pp. 215–228.

——— (1945). *The Psychoanalytic Theory of the Neuroses.* New York: Norton.

Fingarette, H. (1969). *Self Deception.* New York: Routledge & Kegan Paul.

Finkelstein, L. (1975). Awe and premature ejaculation: A case study. *Psychoanal. Quart.* 44:232–252.

Fish-Murray, C. C., Koby, E., & van der Kolk, B. (1985). Cognitive impairment in abused children. Mimeographed.

Fisher, C. (1956). Dreams, images, and perception. *J. Amer. Psychoanal. Assn.*, 4:5–60.

——— (1960). Preconscious stimulation in dreams, associations, and images. *Psychological Issues*, Monogr. 7. New York: International Universities Press, pp. 1–40.

Fischer, R. (1971). A cartography of the ecstatic and meditative states. *Science*, 187:897–904.

Flach, F. F. (1980). Psychobiologic resilience, psychotherapy and the creative process. *Comprehen. Psychiat.* 21:510–518.

Flannery, J. G. (1978). Alexithymia: The association with unexplained physical distress. *Psychother. Psychosom.* 3:193–197.

Flavel, J. H. (1956). Abstract thinking and social behavior in schizophrenia. *J. Abn. Soc. Psychol.* 52:208–211.

——— (1963). *The Developmental Psychology of Jean Piaget.* New York: Van Nostrand.

——— Draguns, J. (1957). A microgenetic approach to perception and thought. *Psychol. Bull.* 54:197–217.

Foulks, E. F. (1979). Interpretations of human affect. *J. Oper. Psychiat.* 10:20–27.

Frankel, F. H. (1978). Hypnosis and related clinical behavior. *Amer. J. Psychiat.*, 135:664–6.

——— Apfel-Savitz, R., Nemiah, J. C., & Sifneos, P. E. (1977). The Relationship between hypnotizability and alexithymia. *Psychother. Psychosom.*, 20:172–178.

Frankenhauser, M. (1967). Some aspects of research in psysiological psychology. In *Emotional Stress*, ed. L. Lennard. New York: Elsevier, pp. 209–234.

Frankenthal, K. (1969). Autohypnosis and other aids for survival in situations of extreme stress. *Internat. J. Clin. Exper. Hyp.* 17:153–159.

Freeman, G. L. (1933). The postural substrate. *Psychol. Rev.* 45:324–334.

——— (1948). *The Energetics of Behavior.* Ithaca, NY: Cornell University Press.

Freud, A. (1952). The role of bodily illness in the mental life of children. *The Writings of Anna Freud, 4.* New York: International Universities Press.

——— (1967). Comment on Trauma. In *Psychic Trauma*, ed. S. S. Furst. New York: Basic Books, pp. 235-245.

——— Dann, S. (1951) An experiment in group upbringing. *The Psychoanalytic Study of the Child*, 6:127–168. New Haven: Yale University Press.

Freud, S. (1886). Report on my studies in Paris and Berlin. *Standard Edition*, 1:5–15. London: Hogarth Press, 1966.

——— (1893a). Sketches for the "Preliminary Communication." *Standard Edition*, 1:147–156.. London: Hogarth Press, 1966.

——— (1893b). On the psychical mechanisms of hysterical phenomena. *Standard Edition*, 3:25–39. London: Hogarth Press, 1962.

——— (1893–1895). Studies on hysteria. *Standard Edition, 2. London: Hogarth Press, 1955.*

——— (1895). Project for a scientific psychology. *Standard Edition*, 1:281–387. London: Hogarth Press, 1966.

——— (1898). Sexuality in the etiology of the neuroses. *Standard Edition*, 3:263–235. London: Hogarth Press, 1962.

——— (1900). The interpretation of dreams. *Standard Edition*, 4 & 5. London: Hogarth Press, 1953.

——— (1906). Jensen's "Gradiva." *Standard Edition*, 9:3–95. London: Hogarth Press, 1959.

—— (1907). Obsessive actions and religious practices. *Standard Edition*, 9:115–128. London: Hogarth Press, 1959.

—— (1911). Psychoanalytic notes on an autographical account of a case of paranoia (dementia paranoides). *Standard Edition*, 12:9–82. London: Hogarth Press, 1958.

—— (1912). A note on the unconscious in psycho-analysis. *Standard Edition*, 12: London: Hogarth Press, 1958.

—— (1913). Totem and taboo. *Standard Edition*, 13:1–161. London: Hogarth Press, 1955.

—— (1914). On the history of the psycho-analytic movement. *Standard Edition*, 14:7–66. London: Hogarth Press, 1957.

—— (1915). The unconscious. *Standard Edition*, 14:166–204. London: Hogarth Press, 1957.

—— (1917). Mourning and melancholia. *Standard Edition*, 14:237–258. London: Hogarth Press, 1957.

—— (1918). From the history of an infantile neurosis. *Standard Edition*, 17:3–124. London: Hogarth Press, 1955.

—— (1919). Introduction to psycho-analysis and the war neuroses. *Standard Edition*, 17:205–210. London: Hogarth Press, 1955.

—— (1923). The ego and the id. *Standard Edition*, 19:3–66. London: Hogarth Press, 1961.

—— (1925). A note upon the "mystic writing pad." *Standard Edition*, 19:227–233. London: Hogarth Press, 1961.

—— (1926. Inhibitions, symptoms and anxiety. *Standard Edition*, 20:77–175. London: Hogarth Press, 1959.

—— (1930). Civilization and its discontents. *Standard Edition*, 21:57–145. London: Hogarth Press, 1961.

—— (1933). New introductory lectures on psycho-analysis. *Standard Edition*, 22:5–182, 1964. London: Hogarth Press, 1964.

—— (1937). Analysis terminable and intermable. *Standard Edition*, 23:209–253. London: Hogarth Press, 1964.

—— (1938). Findings, ideas, problems. *Standard Edition*, 23:300. London: Hogarth Press, 1964.

—— (1939). Moses and monotheism. *Standard Edition*, 23:3–137. London: Hogarth Press, 1964.

—— Breuer, J. (1893). On the psychical mechanism of hysterical phenomena: Preliminary communication. *Standard Edition*, 2:1–18. London: Hogarth Press, 1955.

Freyberger, H. (1977). Supportive psychotherapeutic techniques in primary and secondary alexithymia. In *Toward a Theory of Psychosomatic Disorders*, ed. W. Brautigam & M. von Rad. Basel: Karger, pp. 337–346. Also published in *Psychother. Psychosom.* 28:337–342.

Furman, R. A. (1978). Some developmental aspects of the verbalization of affects. *The Psychoanalytic Study of the Child*, 33:187–212. New Haven: Yale University Press.

Furst, S. S., ed. (1967). *Psychic Trauma*, New York: Basic Books.

—— (1978). The stimulus barrier and the pathogenicity of trauma. *Internat. J. Psycho-Anal.* 59:345–352.

Gaensbauer, T. J. (1982). The differentiation of discrete affects: A case report. *The Psychoanalytic Study of the Child*, 17:29–66. New York: International Universities Press.

Gardner, R., Holzman, P. S. Klein, G. S., Linton, H., & Spence, D. P. (1959). Cognitive control, *Psychological Issues*, Monogr. 4. New York: International Universities Press.

Gardos, G., Schniebolk, S., Mirin, S. M., Walk, P. C., & Rosenthal, K. L. (1984). Alexithymia: Towards validation and measurement. *Comprehen. Psychiat.* 25:278–282.

Garner, D. M., Olmstead, M. P., & Polivy, J. (1983). Development and validation of a multidimensional eating disorder inventory for anorexia nervosa and bulimia. *Internat. J. Eat. Dis.* 2:15–34.

Gawain, S. (1978). *Creative Visualization*. Mill Valley, CA: Whatever.

Gediman, H. K. (1971). The concept of the stimulus barrier: Its review and reformation as an adaptive ego function. *Internat. J. Psycho-Anal.* 52:243–255.

Gedo, J. E. (1979). *Beyond Interpretation: Toward a Revised Theory of Psychoanalysis.* New York: International Universities Press.

—— Goldberg, A. (1973). *Models of the Mind: A Psychoanalytic Theory.* Chicago: University of Chicago Press.

Gessell, A. L., & Thompson, H. (1934) *Infant Behavior: Its Genesis and Growth.* New York: McGraw Hill.

Giora, Z. (1981). Dream styles and the psychology of dreaming. *Psychoanal. Contemp. Thought,* 4:291–381.

Giovacchini, P. L., & Muslin, H. (1965). Ego equilibrim and cancer of the breast. *Psychosom. Med.* 27:524–532.

Glover, E. (1931). The prevention and treatment of drug addiction. *Brit. J. Inebriety,* 29:13–18.

—— (1935). A developmental study of the obsessional neuroses. In *On the Early Development of Mind.* ed. E. Glover. New York: International Universities Press. 1956, pp. 267–282.

Glucksman, M. L. (1981). Physiological measures and feedback during psychotherapy. *Psychother. Psychosom.* 36:185–199.

—— (1983). Physiological responses and clinical phenomena during the psychotherapeutic process. *J. Amer. Acad. Psychoanal.* 11:475–491.

Goethe, J. W. (1815). Sprichwortlich. In *Gott, Gemueht und Welt,* vol. 2 of *Complete Works.* Munich: Deutscher Taschenbuch Verlag, 1961.

Goldstein, A. (1976). Opioid peptides (endorphins) in pituitary and brain. *Science,* 193:1081–1086.

Goldstein, D., Fink, D., & Meeter, K. K. (1972). Cognition of arousal and actual arousal as determinants of emotion. *J. Personal. Soc. Psychol.* 21:41.

Gottschalk, L. A. (1971). Discussion. *Amer. J. Psychiat.* 127:1496–1497.

Gottschalk, L. A., & Bechtel, R. J. (1982). The measurement of anxiety through the computer analysis of verbal samples. *Comprehens. Psychiat.* 23:364–369.

—— Glesser, G. C. (1969). *The Measurement of Psychological States Through the Content Analysis of Verbal Behavior.* Berkeley: University of California Press.

—— Hausman, C., & Brown, J. S. (1975). A computerized scoring system for use with content analysis scales. *Comprehen. Psychiat.* 16:77–90.

—— Winget, C. N., & Gleser, G. C. (1969). *Manual of Instructions for Using the Gottschalk-Gleser Content Analysis Scales: Anxiety, Hostility, and Social Alienation-Personal Disorganization.* Berkeley: University of California Press.

Gough, H. G., & Heibrun, A. B., Jr. (1965). *The Adjective Check List Manual.* Palo Alto, CA: Consulting Psychologists Press.

Gouin-Decarie, T. (1965). *Intelligence and Affectivity in Early Childhood.* New York: International Universities Press.

Gracey, D. R., & De Remee, R. A. (1981). The University of Vienna Medical School. *Mayo Clin. Proc.* 56:634–638.

Graves, R. (1959). *The Greek Myths* Vol. I. New York: George Brazilier.

Greden, J. F., & Carroll, B. J. (1981). Psychomotor function in affective disorders: An overview of new monitoring techniques. *Amer. J. Psychiat.* 138:1441–1448.

Green, A. (1975). The analysts, symbolization and absence in the analytic setting. (On changes in analytic practice and analytic experience). *Internat. J. Psycho-Anal.* 56:1–22.

Green, E. E., Green, A. M., & Walters, E. D. (1970). Voluntary control of internal states. In *Biofeedback and Self Control,* ed. T. S. Barber et al. Chicago: Aldine Atherton, pp. 3–28.

Greenacre, P. (1952). The puberty trauma in girls. In *Trauma, Growth and Personality.* New York: International Universities Press, pp. 204–223.

—— (1958). Towards an understanding of the physical nucleus of some defense reactions. In *Emotional Growth.* New York: International Universities Press, 1971, pp. 128–144.

Greenblatt, M. (1963). Discussion. In *Expression of the Emotions in Man,* ed. P. H. Knapp. New York: International Universities press, pp. 199–205.

Greenspan, S. I. (1981). *Psychopathology and Adaptation in Infancy and Early Childhood.* New York: International Universities Press.

———— Lieberman, A. F. (1980). Infant, Mothers and their interaction: A quantitative clinical approach to developmental assessment. In *The Course of Life: Psychoanalytic Contributions Toward Understanding Personality Development,* Vol 7. ed. S. I. Greenspan & G. H. Pollack. Washington, DC: National Institutes of Mental Health, pp. 271–312.

Grinder, J., & Bandler, R. (1981). *Trance-formations.* Moab, UT: Real People Press.

Grotstein, J. S. (1981). *Splitting and Projective Identification.* New York: Aronson.

Guillemin, R. (1977). Endorphins, brain peptides that act like opiates. *New Eng. J. Med.* 296:226–228.

Gunderson, E. K., & Rahe, E. (1974). *Stress and Illness.* Springfield, IL: Chas. C. Thomas.

Hackett, T. P., & Cassem, N. H. (1974). Development of a quantitative rating scale to assess denial. *J. Psychosom. Res.* 18:93–100.

Hadley, J. (1983). The representational system: A bridging concept for psychoanalysis and trauma physiology. *Internat. Rev. Psycho-Anal.* 10:13–30.

———— (1985). Attention, affect, and attachment. *Psychoanal. contemp. Thought,* 8:529–550.

Haggard, E. A. (1967). Discussion of "adaptive stress behavior" by G. E. Ruff & S. J. Korchin. In *Psychological Stress: Issues in Research,* ed. M. H. Appley & R. Trumbull. New York: Appleton-Century-Crofts, pp. 330–334.

Hamilton, V. (1975). Socialization, anxiety and information processing: A capacity model of anxiety-induced performance deficits. In *Stress and Anxiety,* Vol 2, ed. I. G. Saranson & C. O. Spielberger. New York: Wiley, pp. 45–68

Handler, M. (1977). Oral report of a survey of the American Psychoanalytic Association, Affiliate Institutes to the Curriculum Committee. Southfield, MI: Michigan Psychoanalytic Institute.

Hare, R. D. (1966). Denial of threat and emotional response to impeding painful stimulation. *J. Consult. Psychol.* 30:359–361.

Harlow, H. F. (1958). The nature of love. *Amer. J. Psychol.* 13:673–685.

Hartmann, H. (1955). Notes on a theory of sublimation. *The Psychoanalytic Study of the Child,* 10:9–29. New York: International Universities Press.

Heath, R. G. (1973). Marijuana effect on deep and surface EGG on rhesus monkey. *Neuropharm.* 12:1–4.

———— (1974). Application of Sandor Rado's adaptational psychodynamics formulations to brain physiology. *J. Amer. Acad. Psychoanal.* 2:19–25.

———— (1977). Modulation of emotion with a brain pacemaker. *J. Nerv. Men. Dis.* 165:300–317.

Heiberg, A., & Heiberg, A. (1977). Alexithymia: An inherited trait? A study of twins. *Psychother. Psychosom.* 28:221–225.

Heiberg, A. N. (1980). Alexithymic characteristics and somatic illness. *Psychother. Psychosom.* 34:261–266.

Heibrun, A. B., Jr., & Pepe V. (1985). Awareness of cognitive defences and stress management. *Brit. J. Med. Psychol.,* 58:9–17.

Helson, H. (1967). Perception. In *Contemporary Approaches to Psychology,* ed. H. Helson & W. Bevan. Princeton, NJ: Van Nostrand.

Hering, A. M. (1987). Alexithymia: A developmental view using a differentiation model of affect maturity. Unpublished doctoral dissertation, University of Michigan.

Hilgard, E. R. (1970). *Personality and Hypnosis: A Study of Imaginative Involvement.* Chicago: University of Chicago Press.

———— (1974). Divided consciousness in hypnosis: The implications of the hidden observer. In *Hypnosis: Developments in Research and New Perspectives,* 2nd ed., ed. E. Fromm & R. E. Shor. New York: Aldine Press, pp. 45–80.

Hinkle, L. E. (1961). Ecological observations of the relation of physical illness, mental illness and the social enviroment. *Psychosom. Med.* 23:289–296.

Hirschfeld, R. M. A., Klerman, G. L., Clayton, P. J., Keller, M., McDonald-Scott, P., & Larkin, B. H. (1983). Effects of depressive states on trait measurement. *Amer. J. Psychiat.* 140:695–699.

Hofer, M. A. (1978). Hidden regulatory processes in early social relationship. In *Perspectives in Ethology*, Vol 3., ed. P. G. Bateson & P. H. Klopfer. New York: Plenum Press.

——— (1980). *The Roots of Human Behavior.* San Francisco: Freeman.

——— (1984). Relationships as regulators: A psychobiologic perspective on bereavement. *Psychosom. Med.* 42:15–25.

Holden, C. (1978). Cancer and the mind: How are they connected? *Science*, 200:1363–1369.

Holmes, T. H. & Rahe, R. H. (1967). The social readjustment rating scale. *J. Psychosom. Res.* 11:213–218.

Holt, R. R. (1976). Drive or wish? A reconsideration of the psychoanalytic theory of motivation. *Psychological Issues*, Monogr. 9. New York: International Universities Press.

Hoppe, K. D. (1962). Persecution, depression and aggression. *Bull. Menn. Clin.* 26:195–203.

——— (1968). Psychotherapy with concentration camp survivors. In *Massive Psychic Trauma*, ed. H. Krystal. New York: International Universities Press, pp. 204–219.

——— (1969). Reactions of psychiatrists to examination of survivors of Nazi persecution. *Psychoanal. Forum*, 3:182–211.

——— (1971). The aftermath of Nazi persecutions reflected in recent psychiatric literature. In *Psychic Traumatization*, ed. H. Krystal & W. G. Niederland. Boston: Little Brown, pp. 169–204.

——— (1977). Split brain and psychoanalysis. *Psychoanal. Quart.* 46:220–244.

——— (1979). Affects and Neuropsychology. Paper presented at American Academy of Psychoanalysis, December 1, New York.

——— (1984). Brain function, symbolization and alexithymia. Mimeographed.

——— Bogen, J. E. (1977). Alexithymia in twelve commisurotomized patients. *Psychother. Psychosom.* 28:148–155.

——— Molnar, J., & Newell, J. E. (1965). Love and hate addiction in delinquent male adolescents. *Psychother. Psychosom.* 13:271–277.

Horowitz, M. J. (1976). *Stress Response Syndromes.* New York: Aronson.

——— Zilberg, H. (1983). Regressive alterations of the self concept. *Amer. J. Psychiat.* 140:284–289.

Horton, P. L. (1973). The mystical experience as a suicide preventive. *Amer. J. Psychiat.* 130:294–296.

——— (1974). The mystical experience: Substance of illusion. *J. Amer. Psychoanal. Ass.* 22:363–380.

——— (1981). *Solace. The Missing Dimension in Psychiatry.* Chicago: University of Chicago Press.

——— Sharp, S. L. (1984). Language, solace, and transitional relatedness. *The Psychoanalytic Study of the Child*, 39:167–194. New Haven: Yale University Press.

Howarth, E. (1954). Postscript to a new theory of hypnosis. *Internat. J. Clin. Exper. Hyp.* 2:91–92.

Huizinga, J. (1950). *Homo Ludens: A Study of the Play Element in Culture.* Boston: Beacon Press.

Hyland, J. (1978). Death by giving up. *Bull. Menn. Clin.* 42:339–350.

Ianzito, B. M, Carodet, R. J., & Pugh, D. D. (1974). Thought disorders in depression. *Amer. J. Psychiat.* 131:703–709.

Ionescu-Tongyonk, J. (1978). The depressive equivalents of orientals and occidentals. *Transcult. Psychiat. Res. Rev.* 15:77–78.

Izard, C. E. (1971). *The Face of Emotions.* New York: Basic Books.

———— (1977). *Human Emotions.* New York: Plenum Press.

———— (1978). Emotions and emotion-cognition relationship. In *The Development of Affect,* ed. M. Lewis & L. A. Rosenblum. New York: Plenum Press.

———— (1979). *The Maximally Discriminative Facial Movement Coding Systems.* Newark: Instructional Coding Center, University of Delaware.

———— Beuchler, S. (1979). Emotion expressions and personality integration in infancy. In *Emotions in Personality and Psychopathology,* ed. C. E. Izard. New York: Plenum Press.

———— Beuchler, S. (1980). Aspects of consciousness and personality in terms of differential emotions theory. In *Emotion, Theory, Research and Experience,* ed. R. Plutchick & H. Kellerman. New York: Academic Press, pp. 165–188.

Jacobson, E. (1953). The affects and their pleasure-unpleasure qualities in relation to psychic discharge processes. In *Drives, Affect, Behavior,* ed. R. M. Loewenstein. New York: International Universities press, pp. 38–66.

———— (1957). Normal and pathological moods: Their nature and their function. *The Psychoanalytic Study of the Child,* 12:73–113. New York: International Universities Press.

Janis, I. L. (1951) *Air War and Emotional Stress.* New York: McGraw Hill.

———— (1971). *Stress and Frustration.* New York: Harcourt

———— (1982). Decision making under stress. In *Handbook of Stress,* ed. L. Goldberger & S. Breznitz. New York: Free Press, pp. 69–87.

———— Leventhal, H. (1968). Human reaction to stress. In *Handbook of personality Theory and Research,* ed. E. Borgetta and W. Lambert. Chicago: Rand McNally.

Jaspers, K. (1923). *General Psychopathology.* Berlin: Springer Verlag; Translation, Chicago: University of Chicago Press, 1963.

Joffe, W. G. (1969). A critical review of the status of the ego concept. *Internat. J. Psycho-Anal.* 50:533–547.

Johnson, D. A. (1970). An experimental evaluation of behavioral inaction under stress. IRAD Technical Report #D23-70-215, McDonnell Douglas Corp. Rep. #MDCi1008.

———— (1971). Behavior of aircraft passengers following survivable aircraft accidents; Behavior classification. McDonnel Douglas Aircraft Corp. Rpt. #MDC 70874.

———— (1972). Behavioral inaction under stress conditions similar to the survivable aircraft accident. *SAFE Journal,* 1st quarter: 42–47.

Jones, B. A. (1984). Panic attacks with panic masked by alexithymia. *Psychosom.* 25:858–859.

Jones, E. (1929). Fear, guilt and hate. In *Papers on Psychoanalysis.* London: Bailliere, Tindall & Cox, 1950, pp. 304–319.

———— (1953). *The Life and Work of Sigmund Freud,* Vol. 1. New York: Basic Books, pp. 265–267.

Jones, H. E. (1967). The study of patterns of emotional expression. In *Feelings and Emotions,* ed. M. R. Reynert. New York: Hafner, pp. 161–168.

Jones, J. M. (1981). Affects—A nonsymbolic information processing system. Presented to the American Psychoanalytic Association as a "pre-circulated" paper, December, 1982.

———— (1983). the somatic substrate of the stranger anxiety syndrome. Unpublished manuscript.

———— (1984). Affect as a process. Unpublished manuscript.

Juliusberger, O. (1913). Psychology of alcoholism, Z. fur Psychoanalyse 3:1 Abstract in *Psychoanal. Rev.,* 1:469 (1913–1914).

Kagan, J. (1984). *the Nature of the Child.* New York: Basic Books.

Kaplan, E. H., & Wieder, H. (1969). Drug use in adolescents: Psychodynamic meaning and pharmacogenic effect. *The Psychoanalytic Study of the Child,* 24:399–431. New York: International Universities Press.

———— & Spiegel, H. (1947). *War Stress and Neurotic Illness.* New York: Hoeber.

Kardiner, A. (1941). *The Traumatic Neuroses of War.* New York: Hoeber.

Kass, F., Charles, E., Klein, D. F., & Cohen, P. (1983). Discordance between the SCL-90 and therapists psychopathology ratings: Implications for assessment. *Arch. Gen. Psychiat.* 40:389–393.

Katan, A. (1951). The role of "displacement" in agoraphobia. *Internat. J. Psycho-Anal.* 32(1):41–50.

——— (1961). Some thoughts about the role of verbalization in early childhood. *The Psychoanalytic Study of the Child*, 16:184–188. New York: International Universities Press.

Keiser, S. (1967). Freud's concept of trauma and a specific ego function. *J. Amer. Psychoanal. Ass.*, 15:781–794.

Kernberg, O. F. (1975). *Borderline Conditions and Pathological Narcissism.* New York: Aronson.

——— (1976). Structural derivatives of object relations. In *Object Relations Theory and Clinical Psychoanalysis.* New York: Aronson.

——— (1982a) Discussion panel: New directions in affect theory. reporter, E. P. Lester *J. Amer. Psychoanal. Ass.*, 30:197–212.

——— (1982b). Self, ego, affects and drives. *J. Amer. Psychoanal. Assn.*, 30:893–918.

Kestenberg, J. S. (1978) Transensus-outgoingness and Winnicott's intermediate zone. In *Between Reality and Fantasy: Transitional Objects and phenomena*, ed. S. A. Grolick, L. Barkin, & W. Muensterberger. New York: Aronson.

——— Weinstein, J. (1978) Transitional object and body image formation. In *Between Reality and Fantasy*, ed. S. A. Grolnick, L. Barkin, & W. Muensterberger. New York: Aronson. pp. 75–96.

Khan, M. M. R. (1963). The concept of cumulative trauma. *The Pychoanalytic Study of the Child*, 18:286–306. New York: International Universities Press.

Khantzian, E. (1978). The ego, the self and opiate addiction. *Internat. Rev. Psycho-Anal.* 5:189–198.

——— Mack, J. E. (1983). Self-preservation and the case of the self. *The Psychoanalytic Study of the Child*, 38:209–232. New Haven: Yale University Press.

Kimble, G. H., & Perlmuter, L. C. (1970). The problem of volition. In *Biofeedback and Self Control* ed. T. S. Barber et al., Chicago: Aldine Atherton, pp. 508–531.

Kinston, W. & Cohen, J. (1986). Primal repression: Clinical and theoretical aspect. *Internat. J. Psycho-Anal.* 67:337–356.

Kleiger, J. H., & Dirks, J. F. (1980). Psychomaintenance aspects of alexithymia: Relationship to medical outcome variables in a chronic respiratory illness population. *Psychother. Psychosom.* 34:25–33.

——— Jones, N. F. (1980). Characteristics of alexithymic patients in a chronic respiratory illness population. *J. Nerv. Ment. Dis.* 168:465–470.

——— Kinsman, R. A. (1980). the development of an MMPI alexithymia scale. *Psychother. Psychosom.* 34:17–24.

Klein, D. (1974). Endogenomorphic depression: A conceptual and terminological revision. *Arch. Gen. Psychiat.* 31:447–454.

——— (1987). Depression and anhedonia. In *Anhedonia and Affect Deficit States*, ed. D. Clark & C. D. Fawcett, Jr. Great Neck, NY: PMA Publishing, pp. 1–14.

Klein, G. S. (1970). *Perception, Motives and Personality.* New York: Knopf.

——— (1976). *Psychoanalytic Theory: An Exploration of Essentials.* New York: International Universities Press.

Klein, M. (1946). Notes on some schizoid mechanisms. *Internat. J. Psycho-Anal.* 27:99–110.

Knapp, P. H. (1967). Some riddles or riddance: Relationship between eliminative processes and emotion. *Arch. Gen. Psychiat.* 16:586–602.

——— (1980). Free association as a biopsychosocial probe. *Psychosom. Med.* 42 (Suppl. 2):197–219.

——— (1981). Core Processes in the organization of emotions. *J. Amer. Acad. Psychoanal.* 9:415–434.

—— Mushatt, C., & Nemetz, S. H. (1966). Asthma, melancholia and death. *Psychosom. Med.* 28:114–133.

Knox, J. V., Morgan, A. H., & Hilgard, E. R. (1974). Pain and suffering in ischemia. *Arch. Gen. Psychiat.* 30:840–847.

Kohut, H. (1959). Introspection, empathy and psychoanalysis. *J. Amer. Psychoanal. Assn.*, 7:459–483.

—— (1971). *The Analysis of the Self.* New York: International Universities Press.

Kolb, L. C, Burris, C. D., & Griffits, S. (1984). Propanalol and clonidine: A treatment of the chronic posttraumatic stress disorder of war. In *Post-Traumatic Stress Disorder: Psychological and Biological Sequelae*, ed. B. A. van derKolk. Washington, DC: American Psychiatric Association, pp. 97–107.

Koranyi, E. R. (1977). Psychobiological correlates of battlefield psychiatry. *Psychiat. Jrnl.* (University of Ottawa), 2:3–19.

Korchin, S. J., & Ruff, H. G. (1964). Personality characteristics of the Mercury astronauts. In *The Threat of Impending Disaster: Contributions to the Psychology of Stress*, ed. G. H. Grosser, H. Wechsler, & M. Greenblatt. Cambridge, MA: MIT Press, pp. 197–207.

Kosinski, J. (1965). *The Painted Bird.* Boston: Houghton Mifflin.

Kragh, U. (1955). *The Actual-Genetic Model of Perception-Personality.* Lund, Sweden: Gleerup.

Kreisler, L. (1983). The bases of clinical psychosomatics in childhood. In *Psychosomatic Medicine*, ed. A. J. Krakowski & C. P. Kimball. New York: Plenum Press, pp. 461–468.

Kremer, R., & Atkinson, J. H. (1984). Pain language: Affect. *J. Psychosom. Res.* 28:125–132.

Kris, E. (1956). The recovery of childhood memories in psychoanalysis. *The Psychoanalytic Study of the Child*, 11:54–88. New York: International Universities Press.

Krupnick, J. L., & Horowitz, M. J. (1981). Stress response syndromes: Recurrent themes. *Arch. Gen. Psychiat.* 38:428–435.

Krystal, H. (1959). The physiological basis of the treatment of delirium tremens. *Amer. J. Psychiat.* 116:137–147.

—— (1962). The opiate withdrawal syndrome as a state of stress. *Psychiat. Quart.*, Sup. 36:53–65.

—— (1964). Therapeutic assistants in psychotherapy with regressed patients. In *Current Psychiatric Therapies*, ed. J. Masserman. New York: Grune & Stratton, pp. 23–232.

—— (1966a). Withdrawal from drugs. *Psychosom.* 7:199–302.

—— (1966b). Giorgio de Chirico. Ego states and artistic production. *Amer. Imago* 23:210–226.

—— (1968a). Study of juvenile survivors of concentration camps. Reported to discussion group of "Children of Disaster." Meeting of American Psychoanalytic Association, New York.

—— (1968b). Psychotherapy with survivors of Nazi persecution. In *Massive Psychic Trauma*, ed. H. Krystal. New York: International Universities Press, pp. 256–276.

—— (1968c). Studies of concentration camp survivors. In *Massive Psychic Trauma*, ed. H. Krystal. New York: International Universities Press, pp. 23–30.

—— (1970). Trauma and the stimulus barrier. Paper presented to meeting of American Psychoanalytic Association, New York.

—— (1971). Trauma: Consideration of its intensity and chronicity. In *Psychic Traumatization*, ed. H. Krystal & W. G. Niederland. Boston: Little, Brown, pp. 11–28.

—— (1974). The genetic development of affects and affect regression. *The Annual of Psychoanalysis*, 2:98–126. New York: International Universities Press.

—— (1975). Affect tolerance. *The Annual of Psychoanalysis*, 3:179–219. New York: International Universities Press.

—— (1977). Aspects of affect theory. *Bull. Menn. Clin.* 41:1–26.

—— (1978a). Trauma and affect. *The Psychoanalytic Study of the Child*, 33:81–116. New York: International Universities Press.

—— (1978b). Self-representation and the capacity for self-care. *The Annual of Psychoanalysis*, 6:209–247. New York: International Universities Press.

—— (1978c). Catastrophic psychic trauma and psychogenic death. In *Psychiatric Problems in Medical Practice*, ed. G. U. Balis, L. Wurmser, E. McDaniel, & R. G. Grenell. Boston: Butterworth, pp. 79–97.

—— (1979). Alexithymia and psychotherapy. *Amer. J. Psychother.*, 33:17–28.

—— (1981a). The hedonic element in affectivity. *The Annual of Psychoanalysis*, 9:93–115. New York: International Universities Press.

—— (1981b). Integration and self-healing in posttraumatic states. *J. Gen. Psychiat.* 14:165–189.

—— (1982–1983). Alexithymia and the effectiveness of psychoanalytic treatment. *Internat. J. Psychoanal. Psychother.* 9:353–388.

—— Moore, R. A., & Dorsey, J. M. (1967). Alcoholism and the force of education. *Personnel Guid. J.* Oct:134–139.

—— Niederland, W. G. (1968). Clinical Observations of the survivor syndrome. In *Massive Psychic Trauma*, ed. H. Krystal. New York: International Universities Press, pp. 327–348.

—— Niederland, W. G., ed. (1971). *Psychic Traumatization. International Psychiatry Clinics.* Boston: Little, Brown.

—— Petty, T. A. (1961). The psychological aspects of normal convalescence. *Psychosom.*, 2:1–7.

—— Raskin, H. (1963). Addiction and pain. Mimeographed.

—— —— (1970). *Drug Dependence: Aspects of Ego Function.* Detroit, MI: Wayne State University Press.

Krystal, J. H. (1984). Animal models of stress and depression: Mechanisms of illness and recovery. Mimeographed.

—— Giller, E. L., Jr., & Cicchetti, D. V. (1986). Assessment of alexithymia in post-traumatic stress disorder and somatic illness: Introduction of a reliable measure. *Psychosom. Med.* 48:84–94.

Lacey, J. I. (1967). Somatic response patterning and stress: Some revisions of activation theory. In *Psychological Stress: Issues in Research*, ed. M. H. Appley & R. Trumbull. New York: Appleton-Century-Crofts, pp. 14–42.

—— Kogan, J., Lacey, G. D., & Moss, H. H. (1963). The visceral level: Situational determinants and behavioral correlates of automatic response patterns. In *Expression of the Emotions in Men*, ed. P. H. Knapp. New York: International Universities Press, pp. 161–196.

Lachmann, F. M., & Stolorow, R. D. (1980). The developmental significance of affective states: Implications for psychoanalytic treatment. *The Annual of Psychoanalysis*, 8:215–229. New York: International Universities Press.

Laforgue, R. (1930). On eroticization of anxiety. *Internat. J. Psycho-Anal.* 11:312–321.

Laing, R. D. (1959). *The Divided Self.* Baltimore: Pelican.

Landis, C., & Hunt, W. (1939). *The Startle Pattern.* New York: Foner & Rinehart.

Lane, R. D., & Schwartz, G. E. (1987). Levels of emotional awareness: A cognitive-developmental theory and its application to psychopathology. *J. Amer. Psychiat. Assn.* 144:133–143.

Langs, R. (1978–1979). Some communicative properties of the bipersonal field. *Internat. J. Psychoanal. Psychother.* 7:87–135.

Lanzmann, C. (1985). *Shoah: An Oral History of the Holocaust.* New York: Pantheon.

Laufer, R. S., Brett, E. A., & Gallops, M. (1984). Post-traumatic stress disorder reconsidered; PTSD among Vietnam veterans. In *PTSD: Psychological and Biological Sequelae*, ed. B. van der Kolk. Washington, DC: American Psychiatric Association, pp. 59–80.

Lazarus, R. S., Averill, J. R., & Orton, E. M. Jr. (1970). Towards a cognitive theory of emotion. In *Feelings and Emotions: The Loyola Symposium*, ed. M. B. Arnold. New York: Academic Press, pp. 207–232.

Leeper, R. W. (1970). The motivational and perceptual properties of emotions as indicating their fundamental character and role. In *Feelings and Emotions*, ed. M. Arnold. New York: Academic Press.

Leff, J. P. (1973). Culture and the differentiation of emotional states. *Brit. J. Psychol.*, 23:299–306.

Lehman, D. S. (1961). Hormonal regulation of parental behavior. In *Sex and Internal Secretions*, ed. W. C. Young. Baltimore: Williams & Wilkins.

Leites, N. (1953). Trends in affectlessness. In *Personality in Nature, Society and Culture*, ed. C. Kluckhohn, H. A. Murphy, & D. M. Schneider New York: Knopf, pp. 618–632.

Le Shan, L. (1959). Personality factors in the development of malignant disease: A critical review. *J. Nat. Cancer Inst.* 22:1–18.

—— (1966). An emotional life-history pattern associated with neoplastic disease. *Annals New York Academy of Science*, 125:780–793.

Lesser, I. M. (1981). A review of the alexithymia concept. *Psychosom. Med.*, 43:531–543.

—— Ford, C. V., & Friedmann, C. T. H. (1979). Alexithymia in somatizing patients. *Gen. Hosp. Psychiat.*, 1:256–261.

Leuner, H. (1969). Guided affect imagery. *Amer. J. Psychother.*, 23:4–22.

Levin, S. (1964). Mastery of fear in psychoanalysis. *Psychoanal. Quart.*, 33:375–388.

Lewin, K. (1938). The conceptual representation and measurement of psychological forces. In *Contributions to Psychological Theory* Vol. 1, Durham, NC: Duke University Press.

Lewis, W. C., Wolman, R. N., & King, M. (1971). The development of the language of emotions. *Amer. J. Psychiat.*, 127:1491–1496.

—— Michalson, L. (1983). *Children's Emotions and Moods: Developmental Theory and Management*. New York: Plenum Press.

Lichtenberg, J. D. (1983). *Psychoanalysis and Infant Research*. Hillsdale, NJ: The Analytic Press.

Liddel, H. S. (1967). Animal origins of anxiety. In *Feelings and Emotions*, ed. M. A. Arnold. New York: Academic Press.

Lieberman, M. A. (1977). Adaptive processes in later life. In *Lifespan Developmental Psychology*, ed. N. Datan & H. W. Reese. New York: Academic Press, pp. 135–159.

Lifton, R. J. (1963). Psychological effects of the atomic bomb in Hiroshima—The theme of death. *Daedalus*, 92:462–497.

—— (1967). *Death in Life: Survivors of Hiroshima*. New York: Random House.

—— (1968). Observations on Hiroshima survivors. In *Massive Psychic Trauma*, ed. H. Krystal. New York: International Universities Press.

—— (1976). *The Life of the Self*. New York: Simon & Schuster.

—— (1979). *The Broken Connection*. New York: Simon & Schuster.

—— Olson, E. (1976). The human meaning of total disaster: The Buffalo Creek experience. *Psychiat.*, 39:1–18.

Lindemann, E. (1944). Symptomatology and management of acute grief. *Amer. J. Psychiat.*, 101:141–148.

Lindsey, D. B. (1951). Emotion. In *Handbook of Experimental Psychology*, ed. S. S. Stevens. New York: Wiley, pp. 473–516.

Linn, L. (1953). The role of perception in the mechanism of denial. *J. Amer. Psychoanal. Assn.*, 1:690–705.

Little, M. I. (1981). *Transference Neurosis and Transference Psychosis*. New York: Aronson.

Lolas, F., de la Parra, G., Aronsohn, S., & Collin, C. (1980). On the measurement of alexithymic behavior. *Psychother. Psychosom.* 33:139–146.

—— Mergenthaler, E. & von Rad, M. (1982) Content analysis of verbal behaviour in psychotherapy research: A comparison between two methods. *Brit. J. Med. Psychol.* 55:327–333.

—— von Rad, M. (1982). Psychosomatic disease and neurosis: A study of dyadic verbal behavior. *Comprehen. Psychiat.*, 23:19–24.

——— ——— Scheibler, D. (1981). Situational influences on verbal affective expression of psychosomatic and psychoneurotic patients. *J. Nerv. Mental Dis.* 169:619–623.

Lorenzer, A. (1973). *Sprach stoerung und Rekonstruction.* Frankfurt/Main:Suhrkamp.

Ludwig, A. (1966). Altered states of consciousness. *Arch. Gen. Psychiat.* 15:225–234.

——— Levine, J. (1965a). Alterations in consciousness produced by hypnosis. *J. Nerv. Ment. Dis.,* 140:146–153.

——— ——— (1965b). Alterations in consciousness produced by combinations of LSD, hypnosis and psychotherapy. *Psychopharmacol.* 7:123–137.

MacLean, P. D. (1949). Psychosomatic disease and the "visceral brain." *Psychosom. Med.,* 11:338–353.

——— (1985). Brain evolution relating to family, play and the separation call. *Arch. Gen. Psychiat.,* 42:405–417.

Mahler, M. S. (1966). Notes on the development of basic moods: The depressive affect. In *Psychoanalysis—A General Psychology: Essays in Honor of Heinz Hartmann,* ed. R. M. Loewenstein et al. New York: International Universities Press, pp. 152–168.

Main, M. (1977). Analysis of a peculiar form of reunion behavior seen in some day-care children: Its history and sequelae in children who are home reared. In *Social Development in Childhood: Daycare Programs and Research,* ed. R. Webb, Baltimore, MD: Johns Hopkins University Press.

——— Weston, D. R. (1982). Avoidance of the attachment figure in infancy: Descriptions and interpretations. In *The Place of Attachment in Human Behavior,* ed. C. M. Parkes & J. Stevenson-Hinde. New York: Basic Books, pp. 31–59.

Malamud, W., & Lindner, F. E. (1931). Dreams and their relationship to recent impressions. *Arch. Neurol. Psychiat.,* 25:1081–1099.

Malcolm, J. (1980). African wild dogs play every game by their own rules. *Smithson. Mag.,* 2:62–71.

Malmo, R. B. (1959). Activation: A neuropsychological dimension. *Psychol. Rev.* 66:367–386.

Mandler, G. (1975). *Mind and Emotions.* New York: Wiley.

——— (1980). The generation of emotion. In *Emotion theory, Research and Experience,* ed. R. Plutchik & H. Kellerman. New York: Academic Press, pp. 219–244.

Margolis, M., Krystal, H., & Siegel, H. (1964). Psychotherapy with sexual offenders. *Quart. J. Alcohol.,* 25:85–89.

Marris, P. (1982). Attachment and society. In *The Place of Attachment in Human Behavior,* ed. C.M. Parkes & J. Stevenson-Hinde. New York: Basic Books.

Marshall, J. R. (1972). The expression of feelings. *Arch. Gen. Psychiat.,* 27:786–790.

Martin, J. B., & Pihl, R. O. (1985). The stress-alexithymia hypothesis: Theoretical and empirical considerations. *Psychother. Psychosom.,* 43:169–176.

——— ——— Dobkin, P. (1984). Schalling Sifneos Personality Scale: Findings and recommendations. *Psychother. Psychosom.* 41:145–152.

Marty, P., & de M'Uzan, M. (1963). La pensée opératoire. *Rev. Franç. Psychanal.,* 27: suppl. pp. 345–356.

——— ——— David, C. (1963). *L'investigation Psychosomatique.* Paris: Presses Universitaires.

Maslach, C., Marshall, G., & Zimbardo, P. D. (1972). Hypnotic control of periferal skin temperature. *Psychophysiol.* 9:600–605.

Mathis, J. L. (1964). A sophisticated version of voodoo death. *Psychosom. Med.* 26:104–107.

McCleary, R. A., & Lazarus, R. S. (1949). *Perception and Personality,* ed. J. Buchner & O. Kurch. Durham, NC: Duke University Press.

McClure, C. M. (1959). Cardiac arrest through volition. *Calif. Med.,* 90:440–441. Reprinted in *Biofeedback and Self Control,* ed. D. Shapiro, N.E. Miller, T.X. Barger, L.V. DiCara, J. Kamiya, & J. Stoyva. Chicago: Aldine Atherton, 1972, pp. 49–50.

McDougall, J. (1974a). Primitive Communication and the use of the Countertransference: Reflections on early psychic trauma and its transference effects. In *Plea for a Measure of Abnormality.* New York: International Universities Press, 1980, pp. 247–298.

—— (1974b). The psychosoma and psychoanalytic process. *Internat. Rev. Psycho-Anal.*, 1:437–454.

—— (1978). Primitive communications and the use of countertransference. *Contemp. Psychoanal.*, 14:173–209.

—— (1980a). A child is being beaten. *Contemp. Psychoanal.*, 16:417–459.

—— (1980b). The antianalysand in analysis. In *Psychoanalysis in France*. New York: International Universities Press. pp. 333–354.

—— (1982a). Alexithymia, psychotomatosis and psychosis. *Internat. J. Psychoanal. Psychother.*, 9:377–388.

—— (1982b). Alexithymia: A psychoanalytic viewpoint. *Psychother. Psychosom.*, 38:81–90.

—— (1984). The "dis-affected" patient: Reflections on affect pathology. *Psychoanal. Quart.* 53:386–409.

McKinnon, J. (1979). The semantic form. Neuropsychological and psychoanalytic descriptions. *Psychoanal. Contemp. Thought*, 2:25–76.

Meehl, P. E. (1975). Hedonic capacity; Some conjectures. *Bull. Menn. Clin.* 30:295–307.

—— Hathaway, S. R. (1946). The K factor as a suppressor variable in the Minnesota Multiphasic Personality Inventory. *J. App. Psychol.* 30:525–564.

—— Likken, D., Schafield, W., & Pellegen, L. (1971). Recaptured item technique (RIT): A method for reducing somewhat the subjective element in factor naming. *J. Exp. Res. Personal.* 5:171–190.

Meerloo, J. A. M. (1948). *Patterns of Panic*. New York: International Universities Press.

—— (1959). Shock, catalepsy and psychogenic death. *Internat. Rec. Med.* 172:384–393.

Mellor, C. S. (1981). Speech pause time may be promising test in depression. *Clin. Psychiat. News*, 9:42.

Meltzer, D. (1975). The psychology of autistic states and postautistic mentality in explorations. In *Autism*. London: Clinic Press, pp. 6–29.

Melzack, R. (1969). Role of the early experience in emotional arousal. *New York Acad. Sci. Annals*, 159:721–730.

—— (1975). The McGill pain questionnaire: major properties and scoring methods. *Pain*, 1:277–299.

Mienninger von Lerchenthal, E. (1936). Death from psychic causes. *Bull. Menn. Clin.* 12:31–36, 1948.

Michels, R (1985). Introduction to anel: Perspectives on the nature of psychic reality. *J. Amer. Psychoanal. Ass.*, 33;515–520.

Milechnin, A. (1962). The Pavlovian syndrome: A trance state developed in starvation victim. *Amer. J. Clin. Hyp.* 4:162–168.

Miller, A. (1981). *Prisoners of Childhood*, tr. R. Ward. New York: Basic Books.

—— (1983). *For Your Own Good. Hidden Cruelty in Child Rearing and the Root of Violence*, tr. H. Hurter. New York: Hannum.

—— (1984). *Thou Shalt Not Be Aware*. New York: Faner-Strauss-Giroux.

Miller, N. E. (1951). Learnable drives and rewards. In *Handbook of Experimental Psychology*, ed. S. S. Stevens. London; Wiley, pp. 351–359.

—— DiCara, L. V., Soloman, H., Weiss, J. M., & Dworking, B. (1970). Learned modification of automatic functions: A review and some new data. In *Biofeedback and Self Control*, ed. T. S. Barber et al. Chicago: Aldine Atherton, pp. 351–359.

Miller, S. M., & Seligman, M. E. P. (1982). The reformulated model of helplessness and depression: Evidence and theory, In *Psychological Stress and Psychopathology*, ed. R. W. J. Neufeld. New York: McGraw Hill, pp. 149–178.

Millimet, C. R. (1970). Manifest anxiety-defensiveness scale: First factor of the MMPI revisited. *Psychol. Rep.* 27:603–616.

Minkowski, E. (1946). L'anesthesie affective. *Ann. Medicopsychol.* 104:8–13.

Mittelman, B., & Wolff, H. G. (1943). Emotions and skin temperature observations on patients during psychotherapeutic (psychoanalytic) interviews. *Psychosom. Med.* 5:211–231.

Mood, J. J. L. (1975). *Rilke on Love and Other Difficulties.* New York: Norton.

Moore, U. A., & Amstey, M. S. (1960). Animal hypnosis. *Anat. Rec.* 38:371.

——— (1962). Tonic immobility: Differences in susceptibility of experimental and normal sheep and goats. *Science* 135:729–730.

——— (1963). Tonic immobility II: Effect of mother-neonate separation. *J. Neuropsychiat.* 4:338–344.

Mowrer, O. H. (1977). Mental imagery: An indispensable psychological concept. *J. Ment. Imag.* 1:313–326.

Murphy, W. F. (1958). Character trauma and sensory perception. *Internat. J. Psycho-Anal.* 40:94–104.

——— (1961). A note on trauma and loss. *J. Amer. Psychoanal. Assn.,* 9:519–532.

Murray, H. A. (1937). Visceral manifestations of personality. *J. Abn. Soc. Psychol.* 32:161–184.

——— (1938). *Explorations in Personality.* New York: Oxford University Press.

——— (1967). Dead to the world. In *Essays in Self-Destruction,* ed. E. S. Shneidman. New York: Science House, pp. 7–29.

Nash, J. L. and Cavenar, Jr., J. O. (1978). The self-soothing function: Its appearance in dreams. *Bull. Menn. Clin.,* 42:119–132.

Nemiah, J. C. (1972). The psychosomatic nature of anorexia nervosa. *Adv. Psychosom. Med.,* 7:316–321.

——— (1975). Denial revisited: Reflections on psychosomatic theory. *Psychother. Psychosom.* 26:140–147.

——— (1978). Alexithymia and psychosomatic illness. *J. Cont. Ed. Psychiat.,* Oct:25–37.

——— Freyberger, H., & Sifneos, P. E. (1976). Alexithymia: A view of the psychosomatic process. In *Modern Trends in Medicine,* Vol. 3, ed. O. W. Hill. London: Butterworth, pp. 430–439.

——— Sifneos, P. E. (1970a). Affect and fantasy in psychosomatic disorders. In *Modern Trends in Psychosomatic Medicine,* Vol. 2, ed. O. W. Hill. London: Butterworth, pp. 26–34.

——— ——— (1970b). Psychosomatic illness: A problem of communication. *Psychother. Psychosom.,* 18:154–160.

Niederland, W. G. (1961). The problem of the survivor. *J. Hillside Hosp.* 10:233–247.

——— (1965), An analytic inquiry into the life and work of Heinrich Schlieman. In *Drives, Affects, Behavior,* ed. M. Schur. New York: International Universities Press, pp. 369–396.

——— (1968). Clinical observations of the "survivor syndrome." *Internat. J. Psycho-Anal.* 49:313–315.

——— (1981). Survivor syndrome: Further observations and dimensions. *J. Amer. Psychoanal. Assn.,* 29:413–426.

Nietzke, A. (1972). The American obsession with fun. *Sat. Rev.,* 55:33–35.

Norman, D. A. (1976). *Memory and Attention.* New York: Wiley.

Novey, S. (1958). The meaning of the concept of mental representation of objects. *Psychoanal. Quart.* 27:57–80.

——— (1959). Clinical view of affect theory in psychoanalysis. *Internat. J. Psycho-Anal.* 40:94–104.

——— (1961). Further considerations on affect theory in psychoanalysis. *Internat. J. Psycho-Anal.* 42:21–32.

——— (1963). Discussion of Engel's paper. In *Expression of Emotion in Man,* ed. P. H. Knapp. New York: International Universities Press, pp. 294–299.

Noyes, R. J. (1980). Attitude change following near-death experiences. *Psychiat.* 43:234–242.

Ogden, E., & Shock, N. W. (1939). Voluntary hypercirculation. *Amer. J. Med. Sci.* 198:329–342. Reprinted in *Biofeedback and Self Control 1972,* ed. D. Shapiro et al. Chicago: Aldine Atherton, pp. 34–48.

Ogden, T. H. (1985). On potential space. *Internat. J. Psycho-Anal.* 66:129–141.

Okun, D., Grinker, R., & Sabshin, M. (1962). Relation of physiological response of affect expression including studies of autonomic response specificity. *Arch. Gen. Psychiat.* 6:336–351.

Olds, J. & Milner, P. (1954). Positive reinforcement produced by electric stimulation of septal area and other regions of rat brain. *J. Comp. Physiol. Psychol.* 47:419–427.

——— Olds, M. E. (1963). Approach avoidance analysis of rat diencephalon. *J. Comp. Neurol.* 120:259–295.

Ornstein, A. (1985). Survival and recovery. *Psychoanal. Inq.* 5:99–123.

Oswald, I., Taylor, A. M., & Trierman, M. (1960). Discriminative responses to stimulation during human sleep. *Brain,* 83:440–453.

Overbeck, G. (1977). How to operationalize alexithymic phenomena: Some findings from speech analysis and the Giesen test (GT) *Psychother. Psychosom.* 28:106–117.

Panel (1968). Psychoanalytic theory of affect. L. B. Lofgren, reporter. *J. Amer. Psychoanal. Ass.,* 16:638–650.

Papousek, H., & Papousek, M. (1975). *Parent–Infant Interaction.* New York: Associated Science.

Parkes, C. M. & Stevenson-Hinde, J, ed. (1982). *The Place of Attachment in Human Behavior.* New York: Basic Books.

Paskewitz, D. A. (1977). EEP alpha activity and its relationship to altered states of consciousness. *Annals New York Academy of Sciences,* 296:154–161.

Paulson, J. R. (1985). State of the art of alexithymia measurement. *Psychother. Psychosom.* 44:57–64.

Peterfreund, E. (1971). Information, Systems, and Psychoanalysis. *Psychological issues,* Monograph 25/26. New York: International Universities Press.

——— (1983). *The Process of Psychoanalytic Therapy.* Hillsdale, NJ: The Analytic Press.

Peto, A. (1967). Dedifferentiations and fragmentations during analysis. *J. Amer. Psychoanal. Assn.,* 15:534–551.

Petrie, A. (1967). *Individuality in Pain and Suffering.* Chicago: University of Chicago Press.

Petrinovich, L. F. & Hardyck, C. D. (1969). Error rates for multiple comparison methods: Some evidence concerning frequency of erroneous conclusions. *Psychol. Bull.* 71:43–54.

Petty, T. A., Krystal, H., Lipson, C. T., Raskin, H. A., & Warren, M. (1974). The emergency and the psychoanalyst. Presented at meeting of American Psychoanalytic Association.

Pierloot, R., & Vinck, J. (1977). A pragmatic approach to the concept of alexithymia. *Psychother. Psychosom.* 28:156–166.

Pilowsky, I., & Spence, N. D. (1975). Patterns of illness behavior in patients with intractable pain. *J. Psychosom. Res.* 19:279–287.

Pine, F. (1979). On the expansion of the affect array. *Bull. Menn. Clin.* 43:79–95.

Plaut, E. A. (1979). Play and adaptation. *The Psychoanalytic Study of the Child,* 34:217–234. New Haven: Yale University Press.

Plutchik, R. (1962). *The Emotions: Facts, Theories and a New Model.* New York: Random House.

Pollock, G. H. (1977). The psychosomatic specificity concept: Its evaluation and reevaluation. *The Annual of Psychoanalysis,* 5:141–168. New York: International Universities Press.

Pribram, K. H. (1968). The new neurology and the biology of emotions: A structural approach. *Amer. Psychol.* 22:830–838.

——— (1970). Feelings as emotions. In *Feelings and Emotions,* ed. M. Arnold. New York: Academic Press, pp. 41–54.

——— (1971). *Languages of the Brain.* Englewood Cliffs, NJ: Prentice-Hall.

——— (1980). The biology of emotions and other feelings. In *Emotions: Theory, Research and Experience,* ed. R. Plutchik & H. Kellerman. New York: Academic Press, pp. 245–270.

——— McGuinness, D. (1975). Arousal, activation, and effort in the control of attention. *Psychol. Rev.* 32:116–140.

Pulver, S. E. (1971). Can affects be unconscious? *Internat. J. Psycho-Anal.* 42(4):347–354.

Rado, S. (1926). The psychic effect of intoxicants: An attempt to evolve a psychoanalytic theory of morbid craving. *Internat. J. Psychoanal.* 7:396–413. Also in *Psychoanalysis of Behavior.* New York: Grune & Stratton, 1956.

——— (1933). The psychoanalysis of pharmacothymia. *Psychoanal. Quart.* 11:1–3. Also in *Psychoanalysis of Behavior.* New York: Grune & Stratton, 1956.

——— (1964). Hedonic self-regulation of the organism. In *The Role of Pleasure in Behavior,* ed. R. Heath, New York: Harper & Row, pp. 257–264.

——— (1969). The emotions. In *Adaptational Psychodynamics: Motivation and Control,* ed. H. Klein, New York: Science House. pp. 21–30.

Rahe, R. E., Meyer, M., Smith, M., Kiaerg, G., & Holmes, T. H. (1964). Social stress and illness onset. *J. Psychosom. Res.* 8:35–44.

Ramzy, I., & Wallerstein, R. S. (1958). Pain, fear, and anxiety. *The Psychoanalytic Study of the Child,* 13:147–190. New York: International Universities Press.

Rapaport, D. (1951a). States of consciousness: a psychopathological and psychodynamic view. In *The Collected Papers of David Rapaport,* ed. M. M. Gill. New York: Basic Books, pp. 385–404.

——— (1951b). Toward a theory of thinking. In *Organization and Pathology of Thought,* ed. D. Rapaport. New York: Columbia University Press, pp. 689–729.

——— (1953). On the theory of affect. *Internat. J. Psycho-Anal.* 34:117–198.

Ratner, S. C. (1967). Comparative aspects of hypnosis. In *Handbook of Clinical and Experimental Hypnosis,* ed. J. Gordon. New York: Macmillan, pp. 550–587.

Rees, W. D. & Lutkins, S. G. (1967). Mortality of bereavement. *Brit. Med. J.* 4:13–16.

Reiser, M. P. (1978). Psychoanalysis in patients with psychosomatic disorders. In *Psychotherapeutics in Medicine,* ed. T. B. Karasu & P. I. Steinmuller. New York: Grune & Stratton, pp. 63–74.

Reyher, J. (1977). Spontaneous visual imagery: Implications for psychoanalysis, Psychopathology and Psychotherapy. *J. Ment. Imag.* 1:253–277.

Richter, C. P. (1957). On the phenomenon of sudden death in animals and men. *Psychosom. Med.* 19:191–198.

——— (1959). The phenomenon of unexplained sudden death in animal and man. in *The Meaning of Death,* ed. H. Feifel. New York: McGraw Hill, pp. 302–313.

Rickles, W. H. (1972). Central nervous system substrates of some psychophysiological variables. In *Handbook of Psychophysiology,* ed. N. S. Greenfield & R. A. Steinbach. New York: Holt, Reinhart & Winston, pp. 93–121.

——— (1976). Some aspects of the psychodynamics of successful biofeedback treatment. Presented at Seventh Annual Meeting of the Biofeedback Research Society.

——— (1981). Biofeedback therapy and transitional phenomena. *Psychiat. Ann.,* 11:86–93.

Riess, A. (1978). The mother's eye. *The Psychoanalytic Study of the Child,* 33:187–212. New Haven: Yale University Press.

Riviere, J. (1936). The genesis of psychical conflict in early infancy. *Internat. J. Psycho-Anal.,* 17:398–422.

Roessler, R. (1973). Presidential address 1972: Personality, psychophysiology and performance. *Psychophysiol.* 10:315–327.

Ross, R. N., Knapp, P. H., & Vachon, L. (1979). Speech and stress in mild asthmatics. *Psychosom. Med.* 41:77.

Roueche, B. (1960). Placebo. Annals of Medicine. *New Yorker,* October 15, pp. 85–103.

Rouget, G. (1985). *Music and Trance.* Chicago: University of Chicago Press.

Routtenberg, A. (1978). The reward system of the brain. *Scient. Amer.* 239:154–165.

Rudin, A. J. (1974). Crisis at the Bronfman Center: "The man in the glass booth" controversy. *Midstream,* 29:4–5.

——— (1975). Letter to the editor. *Midstream,* 29:4–5.

Ruesch, J. (1948). The infantile personality. The case problem of psychosomatic medicine. *Psychosom. Med.* 10:134–142.

Ruff, G. E., & Korchin, S. J. (1967). Adaptive stress behavior. In *Psychological Stress: Issues in Research*, ed. M. H. Appley & R. Trumbull. New York: Appleton-Century-Crofts, pp. 297–323.

Ruwet, J. C. (1972). *Introduction to Ethology: The Biology of Behavior*, tr. J. Diamanti. New York: International Universities Press.

Safar, M. E., Kamieniecka, H. A., Levenson, J. A., Dimitriu, V. N., & Pauleau, N. F. (1978). Hemodynamic factors and Rorschach testing in borderline and sustained hypertension. *Psychosom. Med.* 40:620–630.

Sandler, J. (1967). Trauma, Strain, and development. In *Psychic Trauma*, ed. S.S. Furst, New York: Basic Books, pp. 154–174.

———— Rosenblatt, B. (1962). The concept of the representational world. *The Psychoanalytic Study of the Child*, 17:128–145. New York: International Universities Press.

Santostefano, S. (1977). New views on motivation and cognition in psychoanalytic theory: The horse (id) and rider (ego) revisited. *McLean Hosp. J.* 11:48–63.

Sargent, H. D. (1956). Psychotherapy research project of the Menninger Foundation. Part II: Rationale. *Bull. Menn. Clin.* 20:226–258.

Sarnoff, C. A. (1978). The shifting symbolic forms of latency and early adolescence—Their relation to the observing object in the mind's eye. Unpublished manuscript.

Sashin, J. T. (1985). Affect tolerance: A model of affect-response using catastrophe theory. *J. Soc. Biol. Struct.* 8:175–202.

Saul, L. J. (1966). Sudden death at impasse. *Psychoanal. Forum*, 1:88–93.

Savitt, R. A. (1963). Psychoanalytic studies on addiction: Ego structure in narcotic addicts. *Psychoanal. Quart.* 32:43–57.

Schachter, S. (1967). Cognitive effects on bodily functioning: Studies of obesity and overeating. In *Neurophysiology and Emotion (Biology and behavior, Vol 1)*, ed. D. C. Glass. New York: Rockefeller University Press/Russell Sage Foundation, pp. 117–44.

Schafer, R. (1964). The clinical analysis of affect. *J. Amer. Psychoanal. Assn.*, 12:275–300.

———— (1972). Internalization: Process or fantasy? *The Psychoanalytic Study of the Child*, 27:411–438. New Haven: Yale University Press.

———— (1973). Concepts of self and identity and the experience of separation-individuation in adolescence. *Psychoanal. Quart.*, 42:42–59.

Schellschopp-Rueppell, A. (1977). Behavioral characteristics in inpatient group psychotherapy with psychosomatic patients. *Psychother. Psychosom.* 28:316–322.

Schlesinger, H. J. (1954). Cognitive attitudes in relation to susceptibility to interference. *J. Personal.* 22:354–374.

Schmale, A. H., Jr. (1964). A genetic view of affects: With special reference to the genesis of helplessness and hopelessness. *The Psychoanalytic Study of the Child*, 19:287–310. New York: International Universities Press.

Schneider, P. B. (1977). The observer, the psychosomatic phenomenon and the setting of observation. *Psychother. Psychosom.* 28:36–46.

Schnurmann, A. (1949). Observation of a phobia. *The Psychoanalytic Study of the Child*, 3/4:253–270. New York: International Universities Press.

Schur, M. (1955). Comments on the metapsychology of somatization *The Psychoanalytic Study of the Child*, 10:119–164. New York: International Universities Press.

———— (1969). Affect and cognition. *Internat. J. Psycho-Anal.* 50:647–653.

Schwartz, F., & Rouse, P. O. (1961). The activation and recovery of associations. *Psychological Issues*, Monogr. 9. New York: International Universities Press.

Schwartz, G. E. (1973). Biofeedback as therapy: Some theoretical and practical issues. *Amer. Psychol.* August:666–673.

———— Weinberger, D., & Singer, J. A. (1981). Cardiovascular differentiation of happiness, sadness, anger and fear following imagery and exercise. *Psychosom. Med.* 43:343–364.

Searles, H. F. (1984) Transference-responses in borderline patients. *Psychiat.* 47:37–49.

Sechehaye, M. A. (1951). *Symbolic Realization*. New York: International Universities Press.
Sechrest, L. (1984). Reliability and validity. In *Research Methods in Clinical Psychology*, ed. A. S. Bellack & M. Hersen. New York: Pergamon, pp. 24–54.
Seligman, M. E. P. (1975). *Helplessness: On Depression, Development and Death*. San Francisco: Freeman.
Seton, P. H. (1965). Uses of affects observed in a histrionic patient. *Internat. J. Psycho-Anal.* 46:226–236.
Shands, H. C. (1948). The infantile personality. The case problem of psychosomatic medicine. *Psychosom. Med.* 10:134–142.
—— (1971). *The War with Words: Structure and Transcendence*. The Hague: Mouton.
—— (1976). Suitability for psychotherapy I: Transference and formal operations. Paper presented at 10th Congress of the International College for Psychosomatic Medicine, Paris.
—— (1977). Suitability for psychotherapy II: Unsuitability and psychosomatic diseases. *Psychother. Psychosom.* 28:28–35.
Shapiro, A. T. (1960) Contribution the A history of the placebo affect. *Beh. Sci.* 5: 109–135.
Shatan, C. F. (1972). The post-Vietnam syndrome. *New York Times*, May 6.
—— (1973). The grief of soldiers: Vietnam combat veterans' self-help movement. *Amer. J. Orthopsychiat.* 43:640–653.
Shaw, R. (1967). *The Man in the Glass Booth*. London: Chatto & Winders.
Shaw, R., Cohen, F., Doyle, B., & Palesky, J. (1985). The impact of denial and repressive style on information gain and rehabilitation outcomes in myocardial infarction patients. *Psychosom. Med.*, 47:262–273.
Shelley, P. B. (1925). Prometheus unbound. In *The Poetical Works of Shelley (Percy Bysshe Shelley)*, ed. N. F. Ford. Boston: Houghton Mifflin, 1975, pp. 160–205.
Sherrington, C. (1906). *The Integrative Function of the Nervous System*. New York: Cambridge University Press, 1947.
Shevrin, H. (1976). Rapaport's contribution to research: A look into the future. *Bull. Menn. Clin.* 40:211–228.
—— Luborsky, L. (1958). The measurement of perceptions in dreams and images: An investigation of the Potzl phenomenon. *J. Abn. Psychol.*, 56:285–294.
Shipko, S., Alvarez, W. A., & Noviello, N. (1983). Toward a teleological model of alexithymia: Alexithymia and post-traumatic stress disorder. *Psychother. Psychosom.* 39:122–126.
—— Noviello, N. (1984). Psychometric properties of self-report scales of alexithymia. *Psychother. Psychosom.* 41:85–90.
Shneidman, E. S. (1976a) A psychologic theory of suicide. *Psychiatric Annals*, 6:51–89.
—— (1976b). Suicide notes reconsidered. *Psychiatric Annals*, 6:90–91.
Shor, R. E. (1960). The frequency of naturally occurring hypnoidlike experiences in normal college population. *Internat. J. Clin. Exper. Hyp.* 8:151–163.
—— (1962). Physiological effects of painful stimulation during hypnotic analgesia under conditions designed to minimize anxiety. *Internat. J. Clin. Exper. Hyp.* 10:183–192.
Siegman, A. J. (1954). Emotionality: A hysterical character defense. *Psychoanal. Quart.* 23:339–354.
Sifneos, P. (1967). Clinical observations on some patients suffering from a variety of psychosomatic diseases. *Acta Medica Psychosomatica*, Proceedings of the 7th European Conference on Psychosomatic Research, Rome, Sept. 11–16, pp. 452–458.
—— (1972–1973). Is dynamic psychotherapy contraindicated for a large number of patients with psychosomatic disease? *Psychother. Psychosom.* 21:133–136.
—— (1973). The prevalence of "alexithymic" characteristics in psychosomatic patients. *Psychother. Psychosom.* 22:255–262.
—— (1974). A reconsideration of psychodynamic mechanisms in psychosomatic symptom formation in view of recent clinical observations. *Psychother. Psychosom.* 24:151–155.
—— (1975). Problems of psychotherapy of patients with alexithymic characteristics and physical disease. *Psychother. Psychosom.* 26:65–70.

Sigall, H., & Helmreich, R. (1969). Opinion change as a function of stress and communicator credibility. *J. Exper. Soc. Psychol.* 5:70–78.

Silverman, E. K., Weingarten, H., & Post, R. M. (1983). Thinking disorder in depression. *Arch. Gen. Psychiat.* 40:775–780.

Silverman, J. (1968). A paradigm for the study of altered states of consciousness. *Brit. J. Psychol.* 114:1201–1218.

Simmel, E. (1930). Morbid habits and cravings. *Psychoanal. Rev.* 17:48–54.

—— (1948). Alcoholism and Addiction. *Psychoanal. Quart.* 17:6–31.

Simpson, M. A. (1976). Self-mutilation and suicide. In *Suicidology,* ed. E. S. Shneidman. New York: Grune & Stratton, pp. 231–316.

Singer, J. L. (1985). Transference and the human condition: A cognitive-affective perspective. *Psychoanal. Psychol.* 2:189–220.

Sjodin, I. (1983). Psychotherapy in peptic ulcer disease: A controlled outcome study. *Acta Psychiatrica Scandinavia,* Suppl. 307(6):1–90.

Sklar, L., & Anisman, H. (1979). Stress and coping factors influence tumor growth. *Science* 205: 513–515.

Smith G. J. W., & Hendricksson, M. (1956). The effect on an established percept of a perceptual process beyond awareness. *Acta Psychologica.* 11:346–355.

Smith G. R., Jr. (1983). Alexithymia in medical patients referred to a consultation/liaison service. *Amer. J. Psychiat.* 140:99–101.

Snyder, S. E. (1980). Brain peptides as neurotransmitters. *Science,* 209:175–181.

Snygg, D., & Combs, A. W. (1949). *Individual Behavior.* New York: Harper & Row.

Solnit, A. J., & Kris, M. (1967). Trauma and infantile experiences. In *Psychic Trauma,* ed. S. S. Furst, New York: Basic Books, pp. 175–220.

Spence, D. P., & Paul, I. H. (1959). Importation above and below awareness. *Amer. Psychol.* 14:359.

Spiegel, D., (1981). Man as timekeeper. *Amer. J. Psychoanal.,* 41:5–14.

Spiegel, H., & Spiegel, D. (1978). *Trance and Treatment—Clinical Uses of Hypnosis.* New York: Basic Books, pp. 45–68.

Spitz, R. A. (1946). anaclitic depression. *The Psychoanalytic Study of the Child,* 2:313–342. New York: International Universities Press.

—— (1959). *A Genetic Field Theory of Ego Formation.* New York: International Universities Press.

—— (1963). Ontogenesis: The proleptic fucntion of emotion. In *Expression of the Emotion in Man,* ed. P. H. Knapp. New York: International Universities Press, pp. 36–60.

Stechler, G., & Carpenter, G. (1967). A viewpoint on early affective development in exceptional infants. In *The Normal Infant,* Vol. I, ed. J. Hellmuth. New York: Brunner/Mazel, pp. 165–189.

—— Kaplan, S. (1980). The development of the self: A psychoanalytic perspective. *The Psychoanalytic Study of the Child,* 35:85–106. New Haven: Yale University Press.

Stephanos, S. (1975). A concept of analytical treatment for patients with psychosomatic disorders. *Psychother. Psychosom.* 26:178–187.

Sterba, E. (1949). Emotional problems in displaced children. *J. Casework,* 30:175–181.

—— (1968). The effect of persecutions on adolescents. In *Massive Psychic Trauma,* ed. H. Krystal. New York: International Universities Press. pp. 51–59, 259–263.

Stezba, R., (1960). Therapeutic goal a present day reality. *J. Hillside Hosp.* 9:195–217.

—— (1969). The psychoanalyst in a world of change. *Psychoanal. Quart.* 38:432–454.

Stern, D. N. (1983). Implications of infancy research for psychoanalytic theory and practice. In *Psychiatry Update II,* ed. L. Grinspoon. Washington: American Psychiatric Association, pp. 8–12.

—— (1985). *The Interpersonal World of the Infant.* New York: Basic Books.

Stern, M. M. (1951a). Pavor nocturnus. *Internat. J. Psycho-Anal.* 32:302–309.

—— (1951b.) Anxiety, trauma, and shock. *Psychoanal. Quart.* 20:179–203.

———— (1953). Trauma and sympton formation. *Internat. J. Psycho-Anal.* 34:202-218.

———— (1968a). Fear of death and neurosis. *J. Amer. Psychoanal. Assn.*, 16:3–31.

———— (1968b). Fear of death and trauma. *Internat. J. Psycho-Anal.,* 49:458–461.

Stevens, J. (1973), An anatomy of schizophrenia. *Arch. Gen. Psychiat.,* 29: 177–186.

Stoyva, J. (1970). The public (scientific) study of private events. In *Biofeedback and Self-Control 1970,* ed. T. S. Barber et al. Chicago: Aldine Atherton, pp. 29–42.

———— Budzynski, T. H. (1974). cultivated low arousal an anti stress response? In *Limbic and Autonomic Nervous Systems Research,* ed. L. V. Di Cara. New York: Plenum Press, pp. 369–384.

Strachey. J. (1961). Editor's note to "the ego and the id". *Standard Edition,* 3:19:57. London: Hogarth Press.

Stratton, G. M. (1928). Excitement: An undifferentiated emotion. In *The Wittenberg Symposium on Feelings and Emotions,* ed. C. Murchison & M. L. Reynert. Worcester, MA: Clark University Press.

Stuttman, R. K., & Bliss, E. L. (1985). Posttraumatic stress disorder, hypnotizability, and imagery. *Amer. J. Psychiat.* 142:741–743.

Szasz, T. S. (1958), The counterphobic mechanism in addiction. *J. Amer. Psychoanal. Assn.* 6:309–325.

Takeo-Doi, L. (1962). Amae: A key concept for the understanding of Japanese personality structure. In *Japanese Culture, Its Development and Characteristics,* ed. R. J. Smith & R. K. Beardsley. Chicago: Alpine.

Taylor, G. J. (1977). Alexithymia and the countertransference. *Psychother. Psychosom.* 28:141–147.

———— (1984a). The boring patient. *Can. J. Psychiat.* 29:217–222.

———— (1984b). Alexithymia: Concept, measurement, and implications for treatment. *Amer. J. Psychiat.,* 141:725–732.

———— (1987). The psychodynamics of panic disorder. *Psychosomatic Medicine and Contemporary Psychoanalysis.* New York: International Universities Press.

———— Doody, K. (1985). Verbal measures of alexithymia: What do they measure? *Psychother. Psychosom.* 43:32–37.

———— ———— Newman, A. (1981). Alexithymic characteristics in patients with inflammatory bowel disease. *Can. J. Psychiat.* 26:470–474.

———— Ryan, D., & Bagby, R. (1985). Toward the development of a new self-report alexithymia scale. *Psychother. Psychosom.* 44:191–199.

TenHouten, W. D., Hoppe, K. D., Bogen, J. E., & Walter, D. O. (1985a). Alexithymia and the split brain: II. Sentential-level content analysis. *Psychother. Psychosom.* 44:1–5.

———— ———— ———— ———— (1985b.) Alexithymia and the split brain: III. Global level content analysis of fantasy and symbolization. *Psychother. Psychosom.* 44:89–94.

———— ———— ———— ———— (1985c). Alexithymia and the split brain: IV. Gottschalk-Gleser content analysis, an overview. *Psychother. Psychosom.* 44:113–121.

Terr, L. C. (1979). Children of Chowchilla. *The Psychoanalytic Study of the Child,* 34:552–623. New Haven: Yale University Press.

———— (1981a) Psychic trauma in children. *Amer. J. Psychiat.* 20:741–760.

———— (1981b). "Forbidden Games". *J. Amer. Acad. Child Psychiat.* 20:741–760.

———— (1984). Time and trauma. *The Psychoanalytic Study of the Child,* 39:633–665. New Haven: Yale Univeresity Press.

Thom, R. (1975). *Structural Stability and Morphogenesis.* Reading, PA: Benjamin.

———— (1977). SIAM. *Revas,* 19:189–201.

Thomas, A., & Chess, S. (1984). Genesis and evolution of behavioral disorders: From infancy to early adult life. *Amer. J. Psychiat.* 141:1–9.

Thompson, A. E. (1981). A theory of affect development and maturity. Applications to the Thematic Apperception Test. Unpublished doctoral dissertation. University of Michigan, Ann Arbor, MI.

Tolpin, M (1971). On the beginning of the cohesive self: An application of the concept of transmuting internalization to the study of the transitional object and signal anxiety. *The Psychoanalytic Study of the Child*, 26:316–354. New Haven: Yale University Press.

Tompkins, S. S. (1962). *Affect, Imagery, Consciousness*. New York: Springer.

——— (1965). The psychology of being right—and left. *Trans-act.* 3(1):23–27.

——— (1980). Affect as amplification. In *Emotion: Theory Research and Experience*, ed. R. Plutchik & H. Kellerman. New York: Academic Press, pp. 141–164.

Tursky, B., & Sternbach, R. A. (1967). Further psychological correlates of ethnic differences in responses to shock. *Psychophysiol.* 4:67–74.

Tustin, F. (1980). Autistic objects. *Internat. Rev. Psycho-Anal.*, 7:30–38.

——— (1981). *Autistic States in Children*. London: Routledge & Kegan Paul.

Tyhurst, J. S. (1951). Individual reactions to community disaster. *Amer. J. Psychiat.* 107:764–769.

Ullman, L. P. (1958). Clinical correlates of facilitation and inhibition of response to emotional stimuli. *J. Proj. Tech.* 22:341–347.

——— (1962). An empirically derived MMPI scale which measures facilitation-inhibition of recognition of threatening stimuli. *J. Clin. Psychol.* 18:127–132.

Vaillant, G. E. (1973). The dangers of transference in the treatment of alcoholism. Paper presented to Symposium on Alcoholism, Boston University, November 14.

——— (1978). Natural history of male psychological health IV. What kind of men do not get psychosomatic illness? *Psychosom. Med.* 40:420–431.

——— (1979). Health consequences of adaptation to life. *Amer. J. Med.* 67:732–734.

Valenstein, A. F. (1962). the psychoanalytic situation: Affects, emotional reliving, and insight in the psycho-analytic process. *Internat. J. Psycho-Anal.* 43(4/5):315–324.

——— (1973). On attachment to painful feelings and the negative therapeutic reaction. *The Psychoanalytic Study of the Child*, 28:365–392. New Haven: Yale University Press.

van der Kolk, B. A., Boyd, C., Krystal, J. H., & Greenberg, M. (1984). Posttraumatic stress disorder: Psychological and biological sequence. In *Posttraumatic Disorders, Clinical Insight Series*, ed. B. A. van der Kolk. Washington: American Psychiatric Association, pp. 123–134.

Van Lawick-Goodall, J. (1973). The behavior of chimpanzees in their natural habitat. *Amer. J. Psychiat.* 130:1–13.

Venzlaff, U. (1963). Erlebnisgrund und dynamik seelicher verfolgrupschaden. In *Psychische Spaetscheden nach politischer verfolgung*. Basel: Karger. pp. 111–124.

Vogt, R., Brueckstummer, G., Ernst, L., Meyer, K., & von Rad, M. (1977). Differences in phantasy life of psychosomatic and psychoneurotic patients. *Psychother. Psychosom.* 28:98–105.

——— ——— ——— ——— (1983). Alexithymia and Phantasie—Eine experimentelle rorschack-Untersuchung Zur "pensée opératoir." In *Alexithymie*, ed. M. von Rad. Berlin: Springer Verlag.

von Rad, M., ed. (1983) *Alexithymie*. Berlin: Springer Verlag,

——— (1984). Alexithymia and symptom formation. *Psychother. Psychosom.* 42:80–89.

——— Drucke, M., Knauss, W., & Lolas, F. (1979). Alexithymia: Anxiety and hostility in psychosomatic and psychoneurotic patients. *Psychother. Psychosom.* 31:223–234.

——— Lalucat, L., & Lolas, F. (1977). Differences of verbal behavior in psychosomatic and psychoneurotic patients. *Psychother. Psychosom.* 28:83–97.

——— Lolas, F. (1982). empirical evidence of alexithymia. *Psychother. Psychosom.* 38:91–102.

Wallach, H. (1976). *On Perception*. New York: Quandrangle/New York Times.

Wallach, M. B., & Wallach. S. S. (1964). Involuntary eye movements in certain schizophrenics. *Arch. Gen. Psychiat.* 11:71–73.

Wallant, E. L. (1962). *The Pawnbroker*. New York: Macfadden.

Warnes, H. (1983). Alexithymia and the grieving process. *Psychiat. J. Univ. Ottawa*, 10:41–44.

Watson, J. B. (1919). *Psychology from the Standpoint of a Behaviorist.* Philadelphia: Lippincott, pp. ix, 429.

Weinberger, D. A., Schwartz, G. E., & Davidson, R. J. (1979). Low-anxious, high-anxious, and repressive coping styles: Psychometric patterns and behavioral and physiological responses to stress. *J. Abn. Psychol.* 88:369–380.

Weinstein, E. A., & Kahn, R. L. (1955). *Denial of Illness.* Springfield, IL: Chas. C. Thomas.

Weiss, J. M. Glazier, H. I. Pohorecky, L. A., Brick, J., & Miller, N. E. (1975). Effect of chronic exposure to stressors on avoidance-escape behavior and on brain norpinephrine. *Psychosom. Med.* 37:522–534.

Wenger, M. A. (1947). Preliminary study of significant measures of autonomic balance. *Psychosom. Med.* 9:301–309.

Werner, H. (1956). Microgenesis and aphasia. *J. Abn. Soc. Psychol.* 52:347–353.

Westerlundh, B., and Smith, G. (1983). Perceptgenesis and the psychodynamics of perception. *Psychoanal. Contemp. Thought,* 6:597–640.

Wetmore, R. I. (1963). The role of grief in psychoanalysis. *Internat. J. Psycho-Anal.* 44:97–103.

Wexler, B. E., Schwartz, G. Warrenburg, S., Servis, M., & Tarktyn, I. (1986). Effect of emotions on perceptual assymetry: Interactions with personality. *Neuropsychologia,* 24:699–710.

Wilder, E. (1957). The Law of initial value in neurology and psychiatry: Facts and problems. *J. Nerv. Ment. Dis.* 125:73–86.

Winnicott, D. W. (1958). *Through Pediatrics to Psychoanalysis (1956): Primary Maternal Preoccupation.* London: Hogarth Press, pp. 300–305.

——— (1965). *The Motivational Process and the Facilitating environment.* London: Hogarth Press.

——— (1971). *Playing and Reality.* New York: Basic.

Wolf, S. (1970). Emotions and the autonomic nervous system. *Arch. Intern. Med.* 126(6):1124–1130.

——— Pinsky, R. H. (1942). Effect of placebo administration and occurance of toxic reactions. *J. Amer. Med. Assn.* 135:339–341.

Wolfenstein, M. (1966). How is mourning possible? *The Psychoanalytic Study of the Child,* 21:92–126. New York: International Universities Press.

——— (1977). *Disaster: A Psychological Essay.* New York: Arno Press.

Wolff, H. H. (1977a). The concept of alexithymia and the future of psychosomatic research. In *Toward a Theory of Psychosomatic Disorders,* ed. W. Brautigamm & M. von Rad. Basel: S. Karger, pp. 376–387.

——— (1977b). The contribution of the interview situation to the restriction in fantasy and emotional experience in psychosomatic patients. *Psychother. Psychsom.* 28:58–67.

Woodcock, A., & Davis, M. (1978). *Catastrophe Theory.* New York: Dutton.

Woollcott, P. Jr. (1981). Addiction: Clinical and theoretical considerations. *The Annual of Psychoanalysis,* 9:189–204. New York: International Universities Press

Wulff, M. (1951). The problem of neurotic manifestations in children of preoedipal age. *The Psychoanalytic Study of the Child,* 6:169–179. New York: International Universities Press.

Wundt, W. (1920). *Grundriss der psychologie,* 2nd ed. Stuttgart: Engelmann.

Wurmser, L. (1978). *The Hidden Dimension.* New York: Aronson.

——— (1981). *The Mask of Shame.* Baltimore: Johns Hopkins University Press.

Zajonc. R. B. (1980). Feeling and thinking. *Amer. Psychol.* 35:151–175.

Zeeman, E. C. (1977). *Catastrophe Theory: Selected Papers.* Reading, PA: Benjamin.

Zetzel, E. R. (1949). Anxiety and the capacity to bear it. *Internat. J. Psycho-Anal.* 30:1–12.

——— (1965). Depression and the incapacity to bear it. In *Drives, Affects, Behavior,* ed. M. Schur. New York: International Universities Press, pp. 243–274.

——— (1970). *The Capacity for Emotional Growth.* New York: International Universities Press, pp. 82–114.

Zinberg, N. E. (1975). Addiction and ego function. *The Psychoanalytic Study of the Child,* 30:567–588. New Haven: Yale University Press.

Author Index

Subject Index

INTEGRATION AND SELF-HEALING